SUNDAY
MISSAL

2018-2019

Living with Christ
1 Montauk Avenue, Suite 200
New London, CT 06320
1-800-321-0411
www.livingwithchrist.us

 A DIVISION OF
BAYARD, INC.

Design and Layout: Jessica Llewellyn

Illustrations and photo credits: page 8, Michael Connors

ISBN 978-1-62785-363-7

Printed in Canada

To order more copies:
Tel: 1-800-321-0411
Website: www.livingwithchrist.us

CONTENTS

How to Use
This Missal

YOUR COMPANION FOR PRAYING AND LIVING THE EUCHARIST

Over the years, the use of personal missals has changed. Before Vatican Council II (1962-65), when the Mass was said in Latin, most people needed a missal during the Mass to understand the priest's words.

Vatican II made important changes in the Mass because it recognized that the celebration of Mass was lacking several important things. First, it needed to be in language the people could understand. Second, the people were to be truly involved as "full, conscious, and active" participants in the many prayers, songs, and ritual actions of the celebration.

The Mass is not to be something that just the priest does, but something that the whole community or assembly does together—singing, listening to God's word, praying for the needs of the Church and world, thanking God, sharing the consecrated bread and wine, and finally being sent back to their homes, schools, and workplaces to live what they celebrated: God present with us to change our lives and gather us into God's own community of justice, love, and peace.

As a result, after Vatican II many parishes encouraged more participation and discouraged using missals during Mass, except perhaps by those who could not hear the readings. The focus was on listening when the Scriptures were proclaimed aloud—a reminder that God was present and speaking to us in that word.

USING THE MISSAL TO PREPARE FOR SUNDAY

So, if we are not encouraged to use our missal at Mass, is there still a use for a Sunday missal? The answer is yes. But we should now use our missal at home to help us prepare to celebrate the Sunday Eucharist more fully.

The Mass celebrates God's presence with us in word and sacrament. Through Scripture we learn how God has been present with us and what we must do to live rightly in relation to God and others. But making Scripture's message our own is not always easy. In order to get more out of our Sunday listening, we should preview the readings at home during the week.

This Sunday Missal offers resources for you, your family, and your friends to prepare for a richer celebration each Sunday. Different from other Sunday missals, this missal includes not only all the prayers and Scripture readings for the Sunday Masses, but also a variety of other helps to use at home so you can participate at Mass more "fully, consciously, actively, and as befits a community," as Vatican II desired.

WEEKLY RESOURCES FOR PREPARING FOR SUNDAY

This Sunday Missal helps you to pray and live the Eucharist by preparing each week for a richer celebration of Mass. For each Sunday throughout the year, you will find:

- **A brief reflection** inspired by the readings to consider how God's message might resonate with everyday life
- **The complete text of all of the Mass prayers and Scripture readings** chosen by the Church. Also included are these other major feast days: Mary's Immaculate Conception (December 8), Ash Wednesday (March 6), the sacred three days of Holy Week, i.e., the Triduum—Holy Thursday, Good Friday, and Holy Saturday (April 18-20)—Mary's Assumption into Heaven (August 15), and All Saints (November 1)
- At the end of each Sunday, there are helps for deepening your appreciation of both the Scripture readings and the Mass prayers from the Roman Missal:

- **Responding to the word**: questions that help you pray about and discuss the meaning and application of the Scripture readings
- **Taking a closer look**: information and reflections on biblical words and themes from the Scripture texts (indicated in bold and followed by a ✝ in the text)

GENERAL HELPS FOR PRAYING AND LIVING THE EUCHARIST

In addition to the weekly helps, this missal contains several features that you will find helpful for deepening both your understanding of the Church's liturgical year and your prayer, including:

- **Seasonal backgrounds** at the start of each liturgical season, together with suggestions for praying and living each liturgical season (e.g., pages 65-66)
- **Basic questions for exploring Scripture** (see page 583) that you can use to discover the meaning and application to your life of any Scripture reading
- **Explanations of the Church's liturgical year,** including the Church's liturgical calendar (see page 586) and the lectionary (see page 588)
- **A brief overview of Luke's gospel** (see page 590), the primary gospel proclaimed on Sundays this year
- **The differences between liturgical and devotional prayer** (see page 594), both of which help us grow in our life as disciples
- **A treasury of prayers** (see page 597) taken from Scripture, the saints, and the Christian tradition; and also a simple ritual for receiving Communion outside of Mass
- **A pronunciation guide for biblical words** (see page 616) for words indicated by an asterisk (*) in the Scripture readings

Our Eucharistic

Liturgy *The Order of Mass*

WE ARE A EUCHARISTIC PEOPLE

The celebration of the Eucharist or Mass is the central action that defines us as Catholics and directs our efforts to realize God's kingdom community today.

Our celebration is a ritual action that is repeated over and over so that by participating in it we can bring to consciousness, through word and sacrament, the deepest meaning of our lives.

Our celebration is *eucharist*, Greek for "thanksgiving," to remind us that our basic human relationship to God is a response to God's gifts. Everything that we have is God's gift. In our ritual, we celebrate the gift of God's own presence in the assembly that gathers, in God's word that we hear, in the consecrated bread and wine that are Christ's body and blood, and in the person of the priest who presides during the celebration.

Our celebration is also Mass, from the final Latin words of sending, *Ite missa est*, meaning "Go, you are sent." As we finish our prayer, we are reminded that we are sent to discover and proclaim God's presence in all the situations of our daily lives.

As Christians, we not only *pray* the Eucharist, but we are also called upon to *live* "eucharistic" lives. Just as Jesus took the bread, his body, and blessed and broke it to share with others, so we ask God to *take* us, *bless* us, *break* us, and *share* us with others so that "through him, and with him, and in him" we may also become sources of God's new life for the world.

INTRODUCTORY RITES

ENTRANCE ANTIPHON (Turn to the appropriate day)

GREETING

In the name of the Father, and of the Son,
   and of the Holy Spirit. *Amen.*

❶ The grace of our Lord Jesus Christ,
   and the love of God,
   and the communion of the Holy Spirit
   be with you all.
   And with your spirit.

❷ Grace to you and peace from God our Father
   and the Lord Jesus Christ.
   And with your spirit.

❸ The Lord be with you.
   And with your spirit.

PENITENTIAL ACT

Brethren (brothers and sisters), let us acknowledge our sins,
and so prepare ourselves to celebrate the sacred mysteries.

After a brief pause for silence, one of the following forms is used:

❶ *I confess to almighty God*
   and to you, my brothers and sisters,
   that I have greatly sinned,
   in my thoughts and in my words,
   in what I have done and in what I have failed to do,
      (And, striking their breast, they say:)

through my fault, through my fault,
through my most grievous fault;
therefore I ask blessed Mary ever-Virgin,
all the Angels and Saints,
and you, my brothers and sisters,
to pray for me to the Lord our God.

May almighty God have mercy on us,
forgive us our sins,
and bring us to everlasting life.
Amen.

2 Have mercy on us, O Lord.
For we have sinned against you.

Show us, O Lord, your mercy.
And grant us your salvation.

May almighty God have mercy on us,
forgive us our sins,
and bring us to everlasting life.
Amen.

3 The celebrant makes the following or other invocations:

You were sent to heal the contrite of heart:
Lord, have mercy. Or Kyrie, eleison.
Lord, have mercy. Or *Kyrie, eleison.*

You came to call sinners:
Christ, have mercy. Or Christe, eleison.
Christ, have mercy. Or *Christe, eleison.*

You are seated at the right hand of the Father
to intercede for us:

Lord, have mercy. Or Kyrie, eleison.
Lord, have mercy. Or *Kyrie, eleison.*

May almighty God have mercy on us,
forgive us our sins,
and bring us to everlasting life.
Amen.

The following invocations in either English or the ancient Greek are said, unless they have just occurred in a formula of the Penitential Act:

Lord, have mercy.   Or   Kyrie, eleison.
  Lord, have mercy.   *Kyrie, eleison.*
Christ, have mercy.   Christe, eleison.
  Christ, have mercy.   *Christe, eleison.*
Lord, have mercy.   Kyrie, eleison.
  Lord, have mercy.   *Kyrie, eleison.*

GLORY TO GOD
**Glory to God in the highest,
and on earth peace to people of good will.**

**We praise you,
we bless you,
we adore you,
we glorify you,
we give you thanks for your great glory,
Lord God, heavenly King,
O God, almighty Father.**

Lord Jesus Christ, Only Begotten Son,
Lord God, Lamb of God, Son of the Father,
you take away the sins of the world,
    have mercy on us;
you take away the sins of the world,
    receive our prayer;
you are seated at the right hand of the Father:
    have mercy on us.

For you alone are the Holy One,
you alone are the Lord,
you alone are the Most High,
Jesus Christ,
with the Holy Spirit,
in the glory of God the Father. Amen.

COLLECT (Turn to the appropriate day)

LITURGY OF THE WORD

READINGS (Turn to the appropriate day)

HOMILY

PROFESSION OF FAITH: NICENE CREED
I believe in one God,
the Father almighty,
maker of heaven and earth,
of all things visible and invisible.
I believe in one Lord Jesus Christ,

the Only Begotten Son of God,
born of the Father before all ages.
God from God, Light from Light,
true God from true God,
begotten, not made, consubstantial with the Father;
through him all things were made.
For us men and for our salvation
he came down from heaven,

> (At the words that follow, up to and including
> and became man, all bow.)

and by the Holy Spirit was incarnate of the Virgin Mary,
and became man.

For our sake he was crucified under Pontius Pilate,
he suffered death and was buried,
and rose again on the third day
in accordance with the Scriptures.
He ascended into heaven
and is seated at the right hand of the Father.
He will come again in glory
to judge the living and the dead
and his kingdom will have no end.

I believe in the Holy Spirit, the Lord, the giver of life,
who proceeds from the Father and the Son,
who with the Father and the Son is adored and glorified,
who has spoken through the prophets.

I believe in one, holy, catholic and apostolic Church.
I confess one Baptism for the forgiveness of sins
and I look forward to the resurrection of the dead
and the life of the world to come. Amen.

OR

APOSTLES' CREED

The baptismal Symbol of the Roman Church, known as the
Apostles' Creed, may be used instead of the Nicene Creed,
especially during Lent and Easter Time:

I believe in God,
the Father almighty,
Creator of heaven and earth,
and in Jesus Christ, his only Son, our Lord,
   (At the words that follow, up to and including
    the Virgin Mary, all bow.)
who was conceived by the Holy Spirit,
born of the Virgin Mary,
suffered under Pontius Pilate,
was crucified, died and was buried;
he descended into hell;
on the third day he rose again from the dead;
he ascended into heaven,
and is seated at the right hand of God the Father almighty;
from there he will come to judge the living and the dead.

I believe in the Holy Spirit,
the holy catholic Church,
the communion of saints,
the forgiveness of sins,
the resurrection of the body,
and life everlasting. Amen.

PRAYER OF THE FAITHFUL

LITURGY OF THE EUCHARIST

PREPARATION OF GIFTS

Blessed are you, Lord God of all creation,
for through your goodness we have received
the bread we offer you:
fruit of the earth and work of human hands,
it will become for us the bread of life.
Blessed be God for ever.

By the mystery of this water and wine
may we come to share in the divinity of Christ
who humbled himself to share in our humanity.

Blessed are you, Lord God of all creation,
for through your goodness we have received
the wine we offer you:
fruit of the vine and work of human hands,
it will become our spiritual drink.
Blessed be God for ever.

With humble spirit and contrite heart
may we be accepted by you, O Lord,
and may our sacrifice in your sight this day
be pleasing to you, Lord God.

Wash me, O Lord, from my iniquity
and cleanse me from my sin.

Pray, brethren (brothers and sisters),
that my sacrifice and yours
may be acceptable to God,
the almighty Father.

May the Lord accept the sacrifice at your hands
for the praise and glory of his name,
for our good
and the good of all his holy Church.

PRAYER OVER THE OFFERINGS (Turn to the appropriate day)

EUCHARISTIC PRAYER
The Lord be with you.
And with your spirit.
Lift up your hearts.
We lift them up to the Lord.
Let us give thanks to the Lord our God.
It is right and just.

PREFACE
The celebrant chooses from among the possible prefaces corresponding to liturgical seasons and feasts. These prefaces are for use with Eucharistic Prayers 1-3. Eucharistic Prayer 4 has its own fixed preface.

PREFACE 1 OF ADVENT
It is truly right and just, our duty and our salvation,
always and everywhere to give you thanks,
Lord, holy Father, almighty and eternal God,
through Christ our Lord.

For he assumed at his first coming
the lowliness of human flesh,
and so fulfilled the design you formed long ago,
and opened for us the way to eternal salvation,
that, when he comes again in glory and majesty
and all is at last made manifest,
we who watch for that day

may inherit the great promise
in which now we dare to hope.

And so, with Angels and Archangels,
with Thrones and Dominions,
and with all the hosts and Powers of heaven,
we sing the hymn of your glory,
as without end we acclaim:
Holy, Holy, Holy Lord God of hosts... (page 35)

PREFACE 2 OF ADVENT

It is truly right and just, our duty and our salvation,
always and everywhere to give you thanks,
Lord, holy Father, almighty and eternal God,
through Christ our Lord.

For all the oracles of the prophets foretold him,
the Virgin Mother longed for him
with love beyond all telling,
John the Baptist sang of his coming
and proclaimed his presence when he came.

It is by his gift that already we rejoice
at the mystery of his Nativity,
so that he may find us watchful in prayer
and exultant in his praise.

And so, with Angels and Archangels,
with Thrones and Dominions,
and with all the hosts and Powers of heaven,
we sing the hymn of your glory,
as without end we acclaim:
Holy, Holy, Holy Lord God of hosts... (page 35)

PREFACE 1 OF THE NATIVITY OF THE LORD

It is truly right and just, our duty and our salvation,
always and everywhere to give you thanks,
Lord, holy Father, almighty and eternal God.

For in the mystery of the Word made flesh
a new light of your glory has shone upon the eyes of our mind,
so that, as we recognize in him God made visible,
we may be caught up through him in love of things invisible.

And so, with Angels and Archangels,
with Thrones and Dominions,
and with all the hosts and Powers of heaven,
we sing the hymn of your glory,
as without end we acclaim:

Holy, Holy, Holy Lord God of hosts... *(page 35)*

PREFACE 2 OF THE NATIVITY OF THE LORD

It is truly right and just, our duty and our salvation,
always and everywhere to give you thanks,
Lord, holy Father, almighty and eternal God,
through Christ our Lord.

For on the feast of this awe-filled mystery,
though invisible in his own divine nature,
he has appeared visibly in ours;
and begotten before all ages,
he has begun to exist in time;
so that, raising up in himself all that was cast down,
he might restore unity to all creation
and call straying humanity back to the heavenly Kingdom.

And so, with all the Angels, we praise you,
as in joyful celebration we acclaim:
Holy, Holy, Holy Lord God of hosts... *(page 35)*

PREFACE 3 OF THE NATIVITY OF THE LORD

It is truly right and just, our duty and our salvation,
always and everywhere to give you thanks,
Lord, holy Father, almighty and eternal God,
through Christ our Lord.

For through him the holy exchange that restores our life
has shone forth today in splendor:
when our frailty is assumed by your Word
not only does human mortality receive unending honor
but by this wondrous union we, too, are made eternal.

And so, in company with the choirs of Angels,
we praise you, and with joy we proclaim:
Holy, Holy, Holy Lord God of hosts... *(page 35)*

PREFACE OF THE EPIPHANY OF THE LORD

It is truly right and just, our duty and our salvation,
always and everywhere to give you thanks,
Lord, holy Father, almighty and eternal God.

For today you have revealed the mystery
of our salvation in Christ
as a light for the nations,
and, when he appeared in our mortal nature,
you made us new by the glory of his immortal nature.

And so, with Angels and Archangels,
with Thrones and Dominions,

and with all the hosts and Powers of heaven,
we sing the hymn of your glory,
as without end we acclaim:
Holy, Holy, Holy Lord God of hosts... *(page 35)*

PREFACE 1 OF LENT

It is truly right and just, our duty and our salvation,
always and everywhere to give you thanks,
Lord, holy Father, almighty and eternal God,
through Christ our Lord.

For by your gracious gift each year
your faithful await the sacred paschal feasts
with the joy of minds made pure,
so that, more eagerly intent on prayer
and on the works of charity,
and participating in the mysteries
by which they have been reborn,
they may be led to the fullness of grace
that you bestow on your sons and daughters.

And so, with Angels and Archangels,
with Thrones and Dominions,
and with all the hosts and Powers of heaven,
we sing the hymn of your glory,
as without end we acclaim:
Holy, Holy, Holy Lord God of hosts... *(page 35)*

PREFACE 2 OF LENT

It is truly right and just, our duty and our salvation,
always and everywhere to give you thanks,
Lord, holy Father, almighty and eternal God.

For you have given your children a sacred time
for the renewing and purifying of their hearts,
that, freed from disordered affections,
they may so deal with the things of this passing world
as to hold rather to the things that eternally endure.

And so, with all the Angels and Saints,
we praise you, as without end we acclaim:
Holy, Holy, Holy Lord God of hosts... *(page 35)*

PREFACE 3 OF LENT

It is truly right and just, our duty and our salvation,
always and everywhere to give you thanks,
Lord, holy Father, almighty and eternal God.

For you will that our self-denial should give you thanks,
humble our sinful pride,
contribute to the feeding of the poor,
and so help us imitate you in your kindness.

And so we glorify you with countless Angels,
as with one voice of praise we acclaim:
Holy, Holy, Holy Lord God of hosts... *(page 35)*

PREFACE 4 OF LENT

It is truly right and just, our duty and our salvation,
always and everywhere to give you thanks,
Lord, holy Father, almighty and eternal God.

For through bodily fasting you restrain our faults,
raise up our minds,
and bestow both virtue and its rewards,
through Christ our Lord.

Through him the Angels praise your majesty,
Dominions adore and Powers tremble before you.
Heaven and the Virtues of heaven and the blessed Seraphim
worship together with exultation.
May our voices, we pray, join with theirs
in humble praise, as we acclaim:
Holy, Holy, Holy Lord God of hosts... *(page 35)*

PREFACE 1 OF THE PASSION OF THE LORD

It is truly right and just, our duty and our salvation,
always and everywhere to give you thanks,
Lord, holy Father, almighty and eternal God.

For through the saving Passion of your Son
the whole world has received a heart
to confess the infinite power of your majesty,
since by the wondrous power of the Cross
your judgment on the world is now revealed
and the authority of Christ crucified.

And so, Lord, with all the Angels and Saints,
we, too, give you thanks, as in exultation we acclaim:
Holy, Holy, Holy Lord God of hosts... *(page 35)*

PREFACE 2 OF THE PASSION OF THE LORD

It is truly right and just, our duty and our salvation,
always and everywhere to give you thanks,
Lord, holy Father, almighty and eternal God,
through Christ our Lord.

For the days of his saving Passion
and glorious Resurrection are approaching,

by which the pride of the ancient foe is vanquished
and the mystery of our redemption in Christ is celebrated.

Through him the host of Angels adores your majesty
and rejoices in your presence for ever.
May our voices, we pray, join with theirs
in one chorus of exultant praise, as we acclaim:
Holy, Holy, Holy Lord God of hosts... *(page 35)*

PREFACE 1 OF EASTER

It is truly right and just, our duty and our salvation,
at all times to acclaim you, O Lord,
but (on this night / on this day / in this time) above all
to laud you yet more gloriously,
when Christ our Passover has been sacrificed.

For he is the true Lamb
who has taken away the sins of the world;
by dying he has destroyed our death,
and by rising, restored our life.

Therefore, overcome with paschal joy,
every land, every people exults in your praise
and even the heavenly Powers, with the angelic hosts,
sing together the unending hymn of your glory,
as they acclaim: *Holy, Holy, Holy Lord God of hosts...* *(page 35)*

PREFACE 2 OF EASTER

It is truly right and just, our duty and our salvation,
at all times to acclaim you, O Lord,
but in this time above all to laud you yet more gloriously,
when Christ our Passover has been sacrificed.

Through him the children of light rise to eternal life
and the halls of the heavenly Kingdom
are thrown open to the faithful;
for his Death is our ransom from death,
and in his rising the life of all has risen.

Therefore, overcome with paschal joy,
every land, every people exults in your praise
and even the heavenly Powers, with the angelic hosts,
sing together the unending hymn of your glory,
as they acclaim: *Holy, Holy, Holy Lord God of hosts...* (page 35)

PREFACE 3 OF EASTER

It is truly right and just, our duty and our salvation,
at all times to acclaim you, O Lord,
but in this time above all to laud you yet more gloriously,
when Christ our Passover has been sacrificed.

He never ceases to offer himself for us
but defends us and ever pleads our cause before you:
he is the sacrificial Victim who dies no more,
the Lamb, once slain, who lives for ever.

Therefore, overcome with paschal joy,
every land, every people exults in your praise
and even the heavenly Powers, with the angelic hosts,
sing together the unending hymn of your glory,
as they acclaim: *Holy, Holy, Holy Lord God of hosts...* (page 35)

PREFACE 4 OF EASTER

It is truly right and just, our duty and our salvation,
at all times to acclaim you, O Lord,

but in this time above all to laud you yet more gloriously,
when Christ our Passover has been sacrificed.

For, with the old order destroyed,
a universe cast down is renewed,
and integrity of life is restored to us in Christ.

Therefore, overcome with paschal joy,
every land, every people exults in your praise
and even the heavenly Powers, with the angelic hosts,
sing together the unending hymn of your glory,
as they acclaim: *Holy, Holy, Holy Lord God of hosts...* (page 35)

PREFACE 5 OF EASTER

It is truly right and just, our duty and our salvation,
at all times to acclaim you, O Lord,
but in this time above all to laud you yet more gloriously,
when Christ our Passover has been sacrificed.

By the oblation of his Body,
he brought the sacrifices of old to fulfillment
in the reality of the Cross
and, by commending himself to you for our salvation,
showed himself the Priest, the Altar, and the Lamb of sacrifice.

Therefore, overcome with paschal joy,
every land, every people exults in your praise
and even the heavenly Powers, with the angelic hosts,
sing together the unending hymn of your glory,
as they acclaim: *Holy, Holy, Holy Lord God of hosts...* (page 35)

PREFACE 1 OF THE ASCENSION OF THE LORD

It is truly right and just, our duty and our salvation,
always and everywhere to give you thanks,
Lord, holy Father, almighty and eternal God.

For the Lord Jesus, the King of glory,
conqueror of sin and death,
ascended (today) to the highest heavens,
as the Angels gazed in wonder.

Mediator between God and man,
judge of the world and Lord of hosts,
he ascended, not to distance himself from our lowly state
but that we, his members, might be confident of following
where he, our Head and Founder, has gone before.

Therefore, overcome with paschal joy,
every land, every people exults in your praise
and even the heavenly Powers, with the angelic hosts,
sing together the unending hymn of your glory,
as they acclaim: *Holy, Holy, Holy Lord God of hosts...* *(page 35)*

PREFACE 2 OF THE ASCENSION OF THE LORD

It is truly right and just, our duty and our salvation,
always and everywhere to give you thanks,
Lord, holy Father, almighty and eternal God,
through Christ our Lord.

For after his Resurrection
he plainly appeared to all his disciples
and was taken up to heaven in their sight,
that he might make us sharers in his divinity.

Therefore, overcome with paschal joy,
every land, every people exults in your praise
and even the heavenly Powers, with the angelic hosts,
sing together the unending hymn of your glory,
as they acclaim: *Holy, Holy, Holy Lord God of hosts...* *(page 35)*

PREFACE 1 OF THE SUNDAYS IN ORDINARY TIME

It is truly right and just, our duty and our salvation,
always and everywhere to give you thanks,
Lord, holy Father, almighty and eternal God,
through Christ our Lord.

For through his Paschal Mystery,
he accomplished the marvelous deed,
by which he has freed us from the yoke of sin and death,
summoning us to the glory of being now called
a chosen race, a royal priesthood,
a holy nation, a people for your own possession,
to proclaim everywhere your mighty works,
for you have called us out of darkness
into your own wonderful light.

And so, with Angels and Archangels,
with Thrones and Dominions,
and with all the hosts and Powers of heaven,
we sing the hymn of your glory,
as without end we acclaim:
Holy, Holy, Holy Lord God of hosts... *(page 35)*

PREFACE 2 OF THE SUNDAYS IN ORDINARY TIME

It is truly right and just, our duty and our salvation,
always and everywhere to give you thanks,

Lord, holy Father, almighty and eternal God,
through Christ our Lord.

For out of compassion for the waywardness that is ours,
he humbled himself and was born of the Virgin;
by the passion of the Cross he freed us from unending death,
and by rising from the dead he gave us life eternal.

And so, with Angels and Archangels,
with Thrones and Dominions,
and with all the hosts and Powers of heaven,
we sing the hymn of your glory,
as without end we acclaim:
Holy, Holy, Holy Lord God of hosts... (page 35)

PREFACE 3 OF THE SUNDAYS IN ORDINARY TIME

It is truly right and just, our duty and our salvation,
always and everywhere to give you thanks,
Lord, holy Father, almighty and eternal God.

For we know it belongs to your boundless glory,
that you came to the aid of mortal beings with your divinity
and even fashioned for us a remedy out of mortality itself,
that the cause of our downfall
might become the means of our salvation,
through Christ our Lord.

Through him the host of Angels adores your majesty
and rejoices in your presence for ever.
May our voices, we pray, join with theirs
in one chorus of exultant praise, as we acclaim:
Holy, Holy, Holy Lord God of hosts... (page 35)

PREFACE 4 OF THE SUNDAYS IN ORDINARY TIME
It is truly right and just, our duty and our salvation,
always and everywhere to give you thanks,
Lord, holy Father, almighty and eternal God,
through Christ our Lord.

For by his birth he brought renewal
to humanity's fallen state,
and by his suffering, canceled out our sins;
by his rising from the dead
he has opened the way to eternal life,
and by ascending to you, O Father,
he has unlocked the gates of heaven.

And so, with the company of Angels and Saints,
we sing the hymn of your praise,
as without end we acclaim:
Holy, Holy, Holy Lord God of hosts... *(page 35)*

PREFACE 5 OF THE SUNDAYS IN ORDINARY TIME
It is truly right and just, our duty and our salvation,
always and everywhere to give you thanks,
Lord, holy Father, almighty and eternal God.

For you laid the foundations of the world
and have arranged the changing of times and seasons;
you formed man in your own image
and set humanity over the whole world in all its wonder,
to rule in your name over all you have made
and for ever praise you in your mighty works,
through Christ our Lord.

And so, with all the Angels, we praise you,
as in joyful celebration we acclaim:
Holy, Holy, Holy Lord God of hosts... *(page 35)*

PREFACE 6 OF THE SUNDAYS IN ORDINARY TIME

It is truly right and just, our duty and our salvation,
always and everywhere to give you thanks,
Lord, holy Father, almighty and eternal God.

For in you we live and move and have our being,
and while in this body
we not only experience the daily effects of your care,
but even now possess the pledge of life eternal.

For, having received the first fruits of the Spirit,
through whom you raised up Jesus from the dead,
we hope for an everlasting share in the Paschal Mystery.

And so, with all the Angels, we praise you,
as in joyful celebration we acclaim:
Holy, Holy, Holy Lord God of hosts... *(page 35)*

PREFACE 7 OF THE SUNDAYS IN ORDINARY TIME

It is truly right and just, our duty and our salvation,
always and everywhere to give you thanks,
Lord, holy Father, almighty and eternal God.

For you so loved the world
that in your mercy you sent us the Redeemer,
to live like us in all things but sin,
so that you might love in us what you loved in your Son,
by whose obedience we have been restored to those gifts of yours
that, by sinning, we had lost in disobedience.

And so, Lord, with all the Angels and Saints,
we, too, give you thanks, as in exultation we acclaim:
Holy, Holy, Holy Lord God of hosts... *(page 35)*

PREFACE 8 OF THE SUNDAYS IN ORDINARY TIME

It is truly right and just, our duty and our salvation,
always and everywhere to give you thanks,
Lord, holy Father, almighty and eternal God.

For, when your children were scattered afar by sin,
through the Blood of your Son and the power of the Spirit,
you gathered them again to yourself,
that a people, formed as one by the unity of the Trinity,
made the body of Christ and the temple of the Holy Spirit,
might, to the praise of your manifold wisdom,
be manifest as the Church.

And so, in company with the choirs of Angels,
we praise you, and with joy we proclaim:
Holy, Holy, Holy Lord God of hosts... *(page 35)*

PREFACE 1 OF THE MOST HOLY EUCHARIST

It is truly right and just, our duty and our salvation,
always and everywhere to give you thanks,
Lord, holy Father, almighty and eternal God,
through Christ our Lord.

For he is the true and eternal Priest,
who instituted the pattern of an everlasting sacrifice
and was the first to offer himself as the saving Victim,
commanding us to make this offering as his memorial.
As we eat his flesh that was sacrificed for us,

we are made strong,
and, as we drink his Blood that was poured out for us,
we are washed clean.

And so, with Angels and Archangels,
with Thrones and Dominions,
and with all the hosts and Powers of heaven,
we sing the hymn of your glory,
as without end we acclaim:
Holy, Holy, Holy Lord God of hosts... *(page 35)*

PREFACE 2 OF THE MOST HOLY EUCHARIST

It is truly right and just, our duty and our salvation,
always and everywhere to give you thanks,
Lord, holy Father, almighty and eternal God,
through Christ our Lord.

For at the Last Supper with his Apostles,
establishing for the ages to come the saving memorial of the Cross,
he offered himself to you as the unblemished Lamb,
the acceptable gift of perfect praise.

Nourishing your faithful by this sacred mystery,
you make them holy, so that the human race,
bounded by one world,
may be enlightened by one faith
and united by one bond of charity.

And so, we approach the table of this wondrous Sacrament,
so that, bathed in the sweetness of your grace,
we may pass over to the heavenly realities here foreshadowed.

Therefore, all creatures of heaven and earth
sing a new song in adoration,
and we, with all the host of Angels,
cry out, and without end we acclaim:
Holy, Holy, Holy Lord God of hosts... (page 35)

PREFACE 1 OF THE BLESSED VIRGIN MARY

It is truly right and just, our duty and our salvation,
always and everywhere to give you thanks,
Lord, holy Father, almighty and eternal God,
and to praise, bless, and glorify your name
(on the Solemnity of the Motherhood /
on the feast day / on the Nativity / in veneration)
of the Blessed ever-Virgin Mary.

For by the overshadowing of the Holy Spirit
she conceived your Only Begotten Son,
and without losing the glory of virginity,
brought forth into the world the eternal Light,
Jesus Christ our Lord.

Through him the Angels praise your majesty,
Dominions adore and Powers tremble before you.
Heaven and the Virtues of heaven and the blessed Seraphim
worship together with exultation.
May our voices, we pray, join with theirs
in humble praise, as we acclaim:
Holy, Holy, Holy Lord God of hosts... (page 35)

HOLY, HOLY, HOLY

Holy, Holy, Holy Lord God of hosts.
Heaven and earth are full of your glory.
Hosanna in the highest.
Blessed is he who comes in the name of the Lord.
Hosanna in the highest.

EUCHARISTIC PRAYER 1

To you, therefore, most merciful Father,
we make humble prayer and petition
through Jesus Christ, your Son, our Lord:
that you accept
and bless these gifts, these offerings,
these holy and unblemished sacrifices,
which we offer you firstly
for your holy catholic Church.
Be pleased to grant her peace,
to guard, unite and govern her
throughout the whole world,
together with your servant N. our Pope
and N. our Bishop,
and all those who, holding to the truth,
hand on the catholic and apostolic faith.

Remember, Lord, your servants N. and N.
and all gathered here,

whose faith and devotion are known to you.
For them, we offer you this sacrifice of praise
or they offer it for themselves
and all who are dear to them:
for the redemption of their souls,
in hope of health and well-being,
and paying their homage to you,
the eternal God, living and true.

On the Nativity of the Lord and throughout the Octave add:
Celebrating the most sacred night (day)
on which blessed Mary the immaculate Virgin
brought forth the Savior for this world,
and

On the Epiphany of the Lord add:
Celebrating the most sacred day
on which your Only Begotten Son,
eternal with you in your glory,
appeared in a human body, truly sharing our flesh,
and

On Holy Thursday add:
Celebrating the most sacred day
on which our Lord Jesus Christ
was handed over for our sake,
and

**From the Mass of the Easter Vigil until the Second Sunday
of Easter add:**
Celebrating the most sacred night (day)

of the Resurrection of our Lord Jesus Christ in the flesh,
and

On the Ascension of the Lord add:
Celebrating the most sacred day
on which your Only Begotten Son, our Lord,
placed at the right hand of your glory
our weak human nature,
which he had united to himself,
and

On Pentecost Sunday add:
Celebrating the most sacred day of Pentecost,
on which the Holy Spirit
appeared to the Apostles in tongues of fire,
and

In communion with those whose memory we venerate,
especially the glorious ever-Virgin Mary,
Mother of our God and Lord, Jesus Christ,
and blessed Joseph, her Spouse,
your blessed Apostles and Martyrs,
Peter and Paul, Andrew,
(James, John,
Thomas, James, Philip,
Bartholomew, Matthew,
Simon and Jude;
Linus, Cletus, Clement, Sixtus,
Cornelius, Cyprian,
Lawrence, Chrysogonus,
John and Paul,
Cosmas and Damian)

and all your Saints;
we ask that through their merits and prayers,
in all things we may be defended
by your protecting help.
(Through Christ our Lord. Amen.)

Therefore, Lord, we pray:
graciously accept this oblation of our service,
that of your whole family;

> **On Holy Thursday add:**
> which we make to you
> as we observe the day
> on which our Lord Jesus Christ
> handed on the mysteries of his Body and Blood
> for his disciples to celebrate;

> **From the Mass of the Easter Vigil until the Second Sunday
> of Easter add:**
> which we make to you
> also for those to whom you have been pleased to give
> the new birth of water and the Holy Spirit,
> granting them forgiveness of all their sins;

order our days in your peace,
and command that we be delivered from eternal damnation
and counted among the flock of those you have chosen.
(Through Christ our Lord. Amen.)

Be pleased, O God, we pray,
to bless, acknowledge,
and approve this offering in every respect;
make it spiritual and acceptable,

so that it may become for us
the Body and Blood of your most beloved Son,
our Lord Jesus Christ.

On the day before he was to suffer,

> On Holy Thursday add:
> for our salvation and the salvation of all,
> that is today,

he took bread in his holy and venerable hands,
and with eyes raised to heaven
to you, O God, his almighty Father,
giving you thanks, he said the blessing,
broke the bread
and gave it to his disciples, saying:

TAKE THIS, ALL OF YOU, AND EAT OF IT,
FOR THIS IS MY BODY,
WHICH WILL BE GIVEN UP FOR YOU.

In a similar way, when supper was ended,
he took this precious chalice
in his holy and venerable hands,
and once more giving you thanks, he said the blessing
and gave the chalice to his disciples, saying:

TAKE THIS, ALL OF YOU, AND DRINK FROM IT,
FOR THIS IS THE CHALICE OF MY BLOOD,
THE BLOOD OF THE NEW AND ETERNAL COVENANT,
WHICH WILL BE POURED OUT FOR YOU AND FOR MANY
FOR THE FORGIVENESS OF SINS.

DO THIS IN MEMORY OF ME.

The mystery of faith.

1. *We proclaim your Death, O Lord,*
   and profess your Resurrection
   until you come again.

2. *When we eat this Bread and drink this Cup,*
   we proclaim your Death, O Lord,
   until you come again.

3. *Save us, Savior of the world,*
   for by your Cross and Resurrection
   you have set us free.

Therefore, O Lord,
as we celebrate the memorial of the blessed Passion,
the Resurrection from the dead,
and the glorious Ascension into heaven
of Christ, your Son, our Lord,
we, your servants and your holy people,
offer to your glorious majesty
from the gifts that you have given us,
this pure victim,
this holy victim,
this spotless victim,
the holy Bread of eternal life
and the Chalice of everlasting salvation.

Be pleased to look upon these offerings
with a serene and kindly countenance,
and to accept them,
as once you were pleased to accept
the gifts of your servant Abel the just,

the sacrifice of Abraham, our father in faith,
and the offering of your high priest Melchizedek,
a holy sacrifice, a spotless victim.

In humble prayer we ask you, almighty God:
command that these gifts be borne
by the hands of your holy Angel
to your altar on high
in the sight of your divine majesty,
so that all of us, who through this participation at the altar
receive the most holy Body and Blood of your Son,
may be filled with every grace and heavenly blessing.
(Through Christ our Lord. Amen.)

Remember also, Lord, your servants N. and N.,
who have gone before us with the sign of faith
and rest in the sleep of peace.
   (Pause)
Grant them, O Lord, we pray,
and all who sleep in Christ,
a place of refreshment, light and peace.
(Through Christ our Lord. Amen.)

To us, also, your servants, who, though sinners,
hope in your abundant mercies,
graciously grant some share
and fellowship with your holy Apostles and Martyrs:
with John the Baptist, Stephen,
Matthias, Barnabas,
(Ignatius, Alexander,
Marcellinus, Peter,
Felicity, Perpetua,

Agatha, Lucy,
Agnes, Cecilia, Anastasia)
and all your Saints;
admit us, we beseech you,
into their company,
not weighing our merits,
but granting us your pardon,
through Christ our Lord.

Through whom
you continue to make all these good things, O Lord;
you sanctify them, fill them with life,
bless them, and bestow them upon us.

Through him, and with him, and in him,
O God, almighty Father,
in the unity of the Holy Spirit,
all glory and honor is yours,
for ever and ever. *Amen.*

(Turn to the Lord's Prayer, page 53)

EUCHARISTIC PRAYER 2

PREFACE

It is truly right and just, our duty and our salvation,
always and everywhere to give you thanks, Father most holy,
through your beloved Son, Jesus Christ,
your Word through whom you made all things,
whom you sent as our Savior and Redeemer,
incarnate by the Holy Spirit and born of the Virgin.

Fulfilling your will and gaining for you a holy people,
he stretched out his hands as he endured his Passion,
so as to break the bonds of death and manifest the resurrection.

And so, with the Angels and all the Saints
we declare your glory,
as with one voice we acclaim:
Holy, Holy, Holy Lord God of hosts... *(page 35)*

You are indeed Holy, O Lord,
the fount of all holiness.

Make holy, therefore, these gifts, we pray,
by sending down your Spirit upon them like the dewfall,
so that they may become for us
the Body and Blood of our Lord Jesus Christ.

At the time he was betrayed
and entered willingly into his Passion,
he took bread and, giving thanks, broke it,
and gave it to his disciples, saying:

TAKE THIS, ALL OF YOU, AND EAT OF IT,
FOR THIS IS MY BODY,
WHICH WILL BE GIVEN UP FOR YOU.

In a similar way, when supper was ended,
he took the chalice
and, once more giving thanks,
he gave it to his disciples, saying:

TAKE THIS, ALL OF YOU, AND DRINK FROM IT,
FOR THIS IS THE CHALICE OF MY BLOOD,
THE BLOOD OF THE NEW AND ETERNAL COVENANT,

WHICH WILL BE POURED OUT FOR YOU AND FOR MANY
FOR THE FORGIVENESS OF SINS.

DO THIS IN MEMORY OF ME.

The mystery of faith.

We proclaim your Death, O Lord,
and profess your Resurrection
until you come again.

(For other acclamations, see page 40)

Therefore, as we celebrate
the memorial of his Death and Resurrection,
we offer you, Lord,
the Bread of life and the Chalice of salvation,
giving thanks that you have held us worthy
to be in your presence and minister to you.

Humbly we pray
that, partaking of the Body and Blood of Christ,
we may be gathered into one by the Holy Spirit.

Remember, Lord, your Church,
spread throughout the world,
and bring her to the fullness of charity,
together with N. our Pope and N. our Bishop
and all the clergy.

Remember also our brothers and sisters
who have fallen asleep in the hope of the resurrection,
and all who have died in your mercy:
welcome them into the light of your face.

Have mercy on us all, we pray,
that with the Blessed Virgin Mary, Mother of God,
with blessed Joseph, her Spouse,
with the blessed Apostles,
and all the Saints who have pleased you throughout the ages,
we may merit to be coheirs to eternal life,
and may praise and glorify you
through your Son, Jesus Christ.

Through him, and with him, and in him,
O God, almighty Father,
in the unity of the Holy Spirit,
all glory and honor is yours,
for ever and ever. *Amen.*

(Turn to the Lord's Prayer, page 53)

EUCHARISTIC PRAYER 3
You are indeed Holy, O Lord,
and all you have created
rightly gives you praise,
for through your Son our Lord Jesus Christ,
by the power and working of the Holy Spirit,
you give life to all things and make them holy,
and you never cease to gather a people to yourself,
so that from the rising of the sun to its setting
a pure sacrifice may be offered to your name.

Therefore, O Lord, we humbly implore you:
by the same Spirit graciously make holy
these gifts we have brought to you for consecration,

that they may become the Body and Blood
of your Son our Lord Jesus Christ,
at whose command we celebrate these mysteries.

For on the night he was betrayed
he himself took bread,
and, giving you thanks, he said the blessing,
broke the bread and gave it to his disciples, saying:

TAKE THIS, ALL OF YOU, AND EAT OF IT,
FOR THIS IS MY BODY,
WHICH WILL BE GIVEN UP FOR YOU.

In a similar way, when supper was ended,
he took the chalice,
and, giving you thanks, he said the blessing,
and gave the chalice to his disciples, saying:

TAKE THIS, ALL OF YOU, AND DRINK FROM IT,
FOR THIS IS THE CHALICE OF MY BLOOD,
THE BLOOD OF THE NEW AND ETERNAL COVENANT,
WHICH WILL BE POURED OUT FOR YOU AND FOR MANY
FOR THE FORGIVENESS OF SINS.

DO THIS IN MEMORY OF ME.

The mystery of faith.

When we eat this Bread and drink this Cup,
we proclaim your Death, O Lord,
until you come again.

(For other acclamations, see page 40)

Therefore, O Lord, as we celebrate the memorial
of the saving Passion of your Son,
his wondrous Resurrection
and Ascension into heaven,
and as we look forward to his second coming,
we offer you in thanksgiving
this holy and living sacrifice.

Look, we pray, upon the oblation of your Church
and, recognizing the sacrificial Victim by whose death
you willed to reconcile us to yourself,
grant that we, who are nourished
by the Body and Blood of your Son
and filled with his Holy Spirit,
may become one body, one spirit in Christ.

May he make of us
an eternal offering to you,
so that we may obtain an inheritance with your elect,
especially with the most Blessed Virgin Mary, Mother of God,
with blessed Joseph, her Spouse,
with your blessed Apostles and glorious Martyrs
(with Saint N.)
and with all the Saints,
on whose constant intercession in your presence
we rely for unfailing help.

May this Sacrifice of our reconciliation,
we pray, O Lord,
advance the peace and salvation of all the world.
Be pleased to confirm in faith and charity
your pilgrim Church on earth,

with your servant N. our Pope and N. our Bishop,
the Order of Bishops, all the clergy,
and the entire people you have gained for your own.

Listen graciously to the prayers of this family,
whom you have summoned before you:
in your compassion, O merciful Father,
gather to yourself all your children
scattered throughout the world.

To our departed brothers and sisters
and to all who were pleasing to you
at their passing from this life,
give kind admittance to your kingdom.
There we hope to enjoy for ever the fullness of your glory
through Christ our Lord,
through whom you bestow on the world all that is good.

Through him, and with him, and in him,
O God, almighty Father,
in the unity of the Holy Spirit,
all glory and honor is yours,
for ever and ever. *Amen.*

(Turn to the Lord's Prayer, page 53)

EUCHARISTIC PRAYER 4

PREFACE
It is truly right to give you thanks,
truly just to give you glory, Father most holy,
for you are the one God living and true,
existing before all ages and abiding for all eternity,

dwelling in unapproachable light;
yet you, who alone are good, the source of life,
have made all that is,
so that you might fill your creatures with blessings
and bring joy to many of them by the glory of your light.

And so, in your presence are countless hosts of Angels,
who serve you day and night
and, gazing upon the glory of your face,
glorify you without ceasing.

With them we, too, confess your name in exultation,
giving voice to every creature under heaven,
as we acclaim:
Holy, Holy, Holy Lord God of hosts... *(page 35)*

We give you praise, Father most holy,
for you are great
and you have fashioned all your works
in wisdom and in love.
You formed man in your own image
and entrusted the whole world to his care,
so that in serving you alone, the Creator,
he might have dominion over all creatures.

And when through disobedience he had lost your friendship,
you did not abandon him to the domain of death.
For you came in mercy to the aid of all,
so that those who seek might find you.
Time and again you offered them covenants
and through the prophets
taught them to look forward to salvation.

And you so loved the world, Father most holy,
that in the fullness of time
you sent your Only Begotten Son to be our Savior.
Made incarnate by the Holy Spirit
and born of the Virgin Mary,
he shared our human nature
in all things but sin.
To the poor he proclaimed the good news of salvation,
to prisoners, freedom,
and to the sorrowful of heart, joy.
To accomplish your plan,
he gave himself up to death,
and, rising from the dead,
he destroyed death and restored life.

And that we might live no longer for ourselves
but for him who died and rose again for us,
he sent the Holy Spirit from you, Father,
as the first fruits for those who believe,
so that, bringing to perfection his work in the world,
he might sanctify creation to the full.

Therefore, O Lord, we pray:
may this same Holy Spirit
graciously sanctify these offerings,
that they may become
the Body and Blood of our Lord Jesus Christ
for the celebration of this great mystery,
which he himself left us
as an eternal covenant.

For when the hour had come
for him to be glorified by you, Father most holy,
having loved his own who were in the world,
he loved them to the end:
and while they were at supper,
he took bread, blessed and broke it,
and gave it to his disciples, saying:

TAKE THIS, ALL OF YOU, AND EAT OF IT,
FOR THIS IS MY BODY,
WHICH WILL BE GIVEN UP FOR YOU.

In a similar way,
taking the chalice filled with the fruit of the vine,
he gave thanks,
and gave the chalice to his disciples, saying:

TAKE THIS, ALL OF YOU, AND DRINK FROM IT,
FOR THIS IS THE CHALICE OF MY BLOOD,
THE BLOOD OF THE NEW AND ETERNAL COVENANT,
WHICH WILL BE POURED OUT FOR YOU AND FOR MANY
FOR THE FORGIVENESS OF SINS.

DO THIS IN MEMORY OF ME.

The mystery of faith.

Save us, Savior of the world,
for by your Cross and Resurrection
you have set us free.

(For other acclamations, see page 40)

Therefore, O Lord,
as we now celebrate the memorial of our redemption,
we remember Christ's Death
and his descent to the realm of the dead,
we proclaim his Resurrection
and his Ascension to your right hand,
and, as we await his coming in glory,
we offer you his Body and Blood,
the sacrifice acceptable to you
which brings salvation to the whole world.

Look, O Lord, upon the Sacrifice
which you yourself have provided for your Church,
and grant in your loving kindness
to all who partake of this one Bread and one Chalice
that, gathered into one body by the Holy Spirit,
they may truly become a living sacrifice in Christ
to the praise of your glory.

Therefore, Lord, remember now
all for whom we offer this sacrifice:
especially your servant N. our Pope,
N. our Bishop, and the whole Order of Bishops,
all the clergy,
those who take part in this offering,
those gathered here before you,
your entire people,
and all who seek you with a sincere heart.

Remember also
those who have died in the peace of your Christ
and all the dead,

whose faith you alone have known.

To all of us, your children,
grant, O merciful Father,
that we may enter into a heavenly inheritance
with the Blessed Virgin Mary, Mother of God,
with blessed Joseph, her Spouse,
and with your Apostles and Saints in your kingdom.
There, with the whole of creation,
freed from the corruption of sin and death,
may we glorify you through Christ our Lord,
through whom you bestow on the world all that is good.

Through him, and with him, and in him,
O God, almighty Father,
in the unity of the Holy Spirit,
all glory and honor is yours,
for ever and ever. *Amen.*

COMMUNION RITE

LORD'S PRAYER

At the Savior's command
and formed by divine teaching,
we dare to say:

Our Father, who art in heaven,
hallowed be thy name;
thy kingdom come,
thy will be done

on earth as it is in heaven.
Give us this day our daily bread,
and forgive us our trespasses,
as we forgive those who trespass against us;
and lead us not into temptation,
but deliver us from evil.

Deliver us, Lord, we pray, from every evil,
graciously grant peace in our days,
that, by the help of your mercy,
we may be always free from sin
and safe from all distress,
as we await the blessed hope
and the coming of our Savior, Jesus Christ.

For the kingdom,
the power and the glory are yours
now and for ever.

SIGN OF PEACE
Lord Jesus Christ,
who said to your Apostles:
Peace I leave you, my peace I give you,
look not on our sins,
but on the faith of your Church,
and graciously grant her peace and unity
in accordance with your will.
Who live and reign for ever and ever. *Amen.*

The peace of the Lord be with you always.
And with your spirit.
Let us offer each other the sign of peace.

FRACTION OF THE BREAD

May this mingling of the Body and Blood
of our Lord Jesus Christ
bring eternal life to us who receive it.

Lamb of God, you take away the sins of the world,
  have mercy on us.
Lamb of God, you take away the sins of the world,
  have mercy on us.
Lamb of God, you take away the sins of the world,
  grant us peace.

Lord Jesus Christ, Son of the living God,
who, by the will of the Father
and the work of the Holy Spirit,
through your Death gave life to the world,
free me by this, your most holy Body and Blood,
from all my sins and from every evil;
keep me always faithful to your commandments,
and never let me be parted from you.

Or

May the receiving of your Body and Blood,
Lord Jesus Christ,
not bring me to judgment and condemnation,
but through your loving mercy
be for me protection in mind and body
and a healing remedy.

COMMUNION

Behold the Lamb of God,
behold him who takes away the sins of the world.
Blessed are those called to the supper of the Lamb.

Lord, I am not worthy
that you should enter under my roof,
but only say the word
and my soul shall be healed.

May the Body (Blood) of Christ
keep me safe for eternal life.

COMMUNION ANTIPHON (Turn to the appropriate day)

PRAYER AFTER COMMUNION (Turn to the appropriate day)

CONCLUDING RITES

BLESSING

On certain days or occasions, this blessing is preceded by a solemn formula of blessing (see page 57) or prayer over the people.

The Lord be with you.
And with your spirit.

May almighty God bless you,
the Father, and the Son, and the Holy Spirit.
Amen.

DISMISSAL

① Go forth, the Mass is ended.
Thanks be to God.

② Go and announce the Gospel of the Lord.
Thanks be to God.

③ Go in peace, glorifying the Lord by your life.
Thanks be to God.

④ Go in peace.
Thanks be to God.

During the Easter Octave and on Pentecost Sunday, the double alleluia is added:

① Go forth, the Mass is ended, alleluia, alleluia.
Thanks be to God, alleluia, alleluia.

② Go in peace, alleluia, alleluia.
Thanks be to God, alleluia, alleluia.

OPTIONAL SOLEMN BLESSINGS

ADVENT

May the almighty and merciful God,
by whose grace you have placed your faith
in the First Coming of his Only Begotten Son
and yearn for his coming again,
sanctify you by the radiance of Christ's Advent
and enrich you with his blessing. *Amen.*

As you run the race of this present life,
may he make you firm in faith,
joyful in hope and active in charity. *Amen.*

So that, rejoicing now with devotion
at the Redeemer's coming in the flesh,
you may be endowed with the rich reward of eternal life
when he comes again in majesty. *Amen.*

And may the blessing of almighty God,
the Father, and the Son, and the Holy Spirit,
come down on you and remain with you for ever. *Amen.*

THE NATIVITY OF THE LORD

May the God of infinite goodness,
who by the Incarnation of his Son
    has driven darkness from the world
and by that glorious Birth has illumined
    this most holy night (day),
drive far from you the darkness of vice
and illumine your hearts with the light of virtue. *Amen.*

May God, who willed that the great joy
of his Son's saving Birth
be announced to shepherds by the Angel,
fill your minds with the gladness he gives
and make you heralds of his Gospel. *Amen.*

And may God, who by the Incarnation
brought together the earthly and heavenly realm,
fill you with the gift of his peace and favor
and make you sharers with the Church in heaven. *Amen.*

And may the blessing of almighty God,
the Father, and the Son, and the Holy Spirit,
come down on you and remain with you for ever. *Amen.*

THE BEGINNING OF THE YEAR

May God, the source and origin of all blessing,
grant you grace,
pour out his blessing in abundance,
and keep you safe from harm throughout the year. *Amen.*

May he give you integrity in the faith,
endurance in hope,
and perseverance in charity
with holy patience to the end. *Amen.*

May he order your days and your deeds in his peace,
grant your prayers in this and in every place,
and lead you happily to eternal life. *Amen.*

And may the blessing of almighty God,
the Father, and the Son, and the Holy Spirit,
come down on you and remain with you for ever. *Amen.*

THE EPIPHANY OF THE LORD

May God, who has called you
out of darkness into his wonderful light,
pour out in kindness his blessing upon you
and make your hearts firm
in faith, hope and charity. *Amen.*

And since in all confidence you follow Christ,
who today appeared in the world
as a light shining in darkness,
may God make you, too,
a light for your brothers and sisters. *Amen.*

And so when your pilgrimage is ended,
may you come to him
whom the Magi sought as they followed the star
and whom they found with great joy, the Light from Light,
who is Christ the Lord. *Amen.*

And may the blessing of almighty God,
the Father, and the Son, and the Holy Spirit,
come down on you and remain with you for ever. *Amen.*

THE PASSION OF THE LORD

May God, the Father of mercies,
who has given you an example of love
in the Passion of his Only Begotten Son,
grant that, by serving God and your neighbor,
you may lay hold of the wondrous gift of his blessing. *Amen.*

So that you may receive the reward of everlasting life from him,
through whose earthly Death
you believe that you escape eternal death. *Amen.*

And by following the example of his self-abasement,
may you possess a share in his Resurrection. *Amen.*

And may the blessing of almighty God,
the Father, and the Son, and the Holy Spirit,
come down on you and remain with you for ever. *Amen.*

EASTER TIME

May God, who by the Resurrection of his Only Begotten Son
was pleased to confer on you
the gift of redemption and of adoption,

give you gladness by his blessing. *Amen*.

May he, by whose redeeming work
you have received the gift of everlasting freedom,
make you heirs to an eternal inheritance. *Amen*.

And may you, who have already risen with Christ
in Baptism through faith,
by living in a right manner on this earth,
be united with him in the homeland of heaven. *Amen*.

And may the blessing of almighty God,
the Father, and the Son, and the Holy Spirit,
come down on you and remain with you for ever. *Amen*.

THE ASCENSION OF THE LORD
May almighty God bless you,
for on this very day his Only Begotten Son
pierced the heights of heaven
and unlocked for you the way
to ascend to where he is. *Amen*.

May he grant that,
as Christ after his Resurrection
was seen plainly by his disciples,
so when he comes as Judge
he may show himself merciful to you for all eternity. *Amen*.

And may you, who believe he is seated
with the Father in his majesty,
know with joy the fulfillment of his promise
to stay with you until the end of time. *Amen*.

And may the blessing of almighty God,
the Father, and the Son, and the Holy Spirit,
come down on you and remain with you for ever. *Amen.*

THE HOLY SPIRIT

May God, the Father of lights,
who was pleased to enlighten the disciples' minds
by the outpouring of the Spirit, the Paraclete,
grant you gladness by his blessing
and make you always abound with the gifts
    of the same Spirit. *Amen.*

May the wondrous flame that appeared above the disciples,
powerfully cleanse your hearts from every evil
and pervade them with its purifying light. *Amen.*

And may God, who has been pleased to unite many tongues
in the profession of one faith,
give you perseverance in that same faith
and, by believing, may you journey from hope
    to clear vision. *Amen.*

And may the blessing of almighty God,
the Father, and the Son, and the Holy Spirit,
come down on you and remain with you for ever. *Amen.*

THE BLESSED VIRGIN MARY

May God, who through the childbearing
    of the Blessed Virgin Mary
willed in his great kindness to redeem the human race,
be pleased to enrich you with his blessing. *Amen.*

May you know always and everywhere the protection of her,
through whom you have been found worthy
 to receive the author of life. *Amen.*

May you, who have devoutly gathered on this day,
carry away with you the gifts of spiritual joys
 and heavenly rewards. *Amen.*

And may the blessing of almighty God,
the Father, and the Son, and the Holy Spirit,
come down on you and remain with you for ever. *Amen.*

ALL SAINTS

May God, the glory and joy of the Saints,
who has caused you to be strengthened
by means of their outstanding prayers,
bless you with unending blessings. *Amen.*

Freed through their intercession from present ills
and formed by the example of their holy way of life,
may you be ever devoted
to serving God and your neighbor. *Amen.*

So that, together with all,
you may possess the joys of the homeland,
where Holy Church rejoices
that her children are admitted in perpetual peace
to the company of the citizens of heaven. *Amen.*

And may the blessing of almighty God,
the Father, and the Son, and the Holy Spirit,
come down on you and remain with you for ever. *Amen.*

Sunday Readings & Prayers

Christ lights our darkness

Advent (literally, "at the coming") prepares for the annual celebration of Jesus' birth at Christmas and his revelation to the nations at Epiphany. The Church year moves in a cycle of promise–fulfillment–proclamation, often using the images of darkness and light to accentuate the movement.

With Advent we enter the first part of the cycle—promise—as the dark period of the solar year begins. God's goodness gives us light, the light of the Messiah that dawns in the birth of Christ at Bethlehem and that will shine in its fullness at his coming again as King and Judge.

So in this Advent season as we begin a new Church year, we focus our attention on the demands of responding to the light of Jesus' presence. We desire to let his vision and values enlighten us and transform the darkness of our lives so that we may become a light that will lead others to God.

As we live through the seasons of the Church year, we will learn that the way of Christian discipleship always leads through the darkness of suffering to the experience of new life in Christ. Preparing the way is the first step to which our Advent experience is directed.

Praying and living the Advent season

An Advent wreath can help you and your household focus on waiting for Christ. Create a wreath from evergreen boughs and four candles (three purple and one rose or white for the joyful third week). Use the following format each week.

INVITATION TO PRAYER *As you light the candles (one for each week of Advent), invite all to share in the response.*

Leader: We look for light, and lo, darkness;
for brightness, but we walk in gloom! *(Isaiah 59:9)*

All: You, Lord, give light to my lamp;
you brighten the darkness about me. *(Psalm 18:28)*

SCRIPTURE READING *When the candles are lit, read aloud one of the Scripture readings from the day or Sunday. Either reflect quietly or invite each household member to respond to these questions:*

- How do I want Jesus to be my light this Advent (tonight)?
- How do the words of this reading help me to wait for Jesus to come?

CLOSING PRAYER *(adapted from Ephesians 5:1-2, 8-14)*
O God of light, help us be imitators of you and live in love.
For we were once darkness, but now we are light in the Lord.
Help us live as children of light,
for light produces every kind of goodness and truth.
Help us learn what is pleasing to the Lord.
We want to take no part in the works of darkness
but rather to expose them.
Christ will give us light! Amen.

December 2

DEC 2

Look beyond, see the light!

Today we begin the new liturgical year. We will spend the year, like every liturgical year, following the life of Jesus from the time of John the Baptist's preaching to the great salvific events of Jesus' passion, death, resurrection, ascension, and giving of the Holy Spirit. Each liturgical season helps us meditate upon and pray over the life of Jesus, whom we strive to imitate as disciples.

Today's gospel paints a frightening picture of huge natural calamities heralding the end. We pray not to have to live through such events. Similarly, as Advent progresses we will hear the call of John the Baptist to repent and amend our ways. Being honest with our sinfulness in the face of such preaching can be depressing.

But do not stop at the frightening side of these modes of preparing ourselves. Realize that we are being called to look beyond them to see the light, the beauty of God's promise. "When these signs begin to happen, stand erect and raise your heads because your redemption is at hand."

Our Redeemer is coming; indeed, he is in our midst. Regardless of what we must go through, whether it be disaster or the slavery of sin, our merciful and loving God is waiting to wrap warm and tender arms around us.

▓ **Fr. Mark Miller, CSsR**

ENTRANCE ANTIPHON *(Cf. Psalm 25 [24]:1-3)*
To you, I lift up my soul, O my God. In you, I have trusted; let me not be put to shame. Nor let my enemies exult over me; and let none who hope in you be put to shame.

INTRODUCTORY RITES *(page 10)*

COLLECT
Grant your faithful, we pray, almighty God,
the resolve to run forth to meet your Christ
with righteous deeds at his coming,
so that, gathered at his right hand,
they may be worthy to possess the heavenly Kingdom.
Through our Lord Jesus Christ, your Son,
who lives and reigns with you in the unity of the Holy Spirit,
one God, for ever and ever. *Amen.*

FIRST READING *(Jeremiah 33:14-16)*
The days are coming, says the LORD, when I will fulfill the promise I made to the house of Israel and Judah. In those days, in that time, I will raise up for David a just shoot; he shall do what is right and just in the land. In those days Judah shall be safe and Jerusalem shall dwell secure; this is what they shall call her: "The LORD our justice."

The word of the Lord. *Thanks be to God.*

RESPONSORIAL PSALM *(Psalm 25:4-5, 8-9, 10, 14)*
℟ To you, O Lord, I lift my soul.

Your ways, O LORD, make known to me;
    teach me your paths,
guide me in your truth and teach me,
    for you are God my savior,

and for you I wait all the day. ℟
Good and upright is the LORD;
   thus he shows sinners the way.
He guides the humble to justice,
   and teaches the humble his way. ℟
All the paths of the LORD are kindness and constancy
   toward those who keep his covenant and his decrees.
The friendship of the LORD is with those who fear him,
   and his covenant, for their instruction. ℟

SECOND READING *(1 Thessalonians 3:12–4:2)*

Brothers and sisters: May the Lord make you increase and abound in love for one another and for all, just as we have for you, so as to strengthen your hearts, to be blameless in holiness before our God and Father at the coming of our Lord Jesus with all his holy ones. Amen.

Finally, brothers and sisters, we earnestly ask and exhort you in the Lord Jesus that, as you received from us how you should conduct yourselves to please God—and as you are conducting yourselves—you do so even more. For you know what instructions we gave you through the Lord Jesus.

The word of the Lord. *Thanks be to God.*

ALLELUIA *(Psalm 85:8)*
Alleluia, alleluia. Show us, Lord, your love; and grant us your salvation. *Alleluia, alleluia.*

GOSPEL *(Luke 21:25-28, 34-36)*
A reading from the holy Gospel according to Luke.
Glory to you, O Lord.

Jesus said to his disciples: "There will be signs in the sun, the moon, and the stars, and on earth nations will be in dismay, perplexed by the roaring of the sea and the waves. People will die of fright in anticipation of what is coming upon the world, for the powers of the heavens will be shaken. And then they will see the **Son of Man**✢ coming in a cloud with power and great glory. But when these signs begin to happen, stand erect and raise your heads because your redemption is at hand.

"Beware that your hearts do not become drowsy from carousing and drunkenness and the anxieties of daily life, and that day catch you by surprise like a trap. For that day will assault everyone who lives on the face of the earth. Be vigilant at all times and pray that you have the strength to escape the tribulations that are imminent and to stand before the Son of Man."

The Gospel of the Lord. *Praise to you, Lord Jesus Christ*

PROFESSION OF FAITH *(page 13)*

PRAYER OF THE FAITHFUL

PREPARATION OF GIFTS *(page 16)*

PRAYER OVER THE OFFERINGS
Accept, we pray, O Lord, these offerings we make,

• Taking a Closer Look •

✢ **Son of Man** In Semitic languages, when connected to a collective noun, "son of" designates the individual member belonging to a group. Thus a "son of man" means a human being, especially in contrast to God. This title takes on an important meaning for Christians because the prophet Daniel (7:13) describes God's final agent, a "son of man," to whom all power is given to accomplish God's rule in the world. Jesus adds further meaning by connecting the Son of Man with the suffering of his messianic task and with the forgiveness of sins that only God could do.

gathered from among your gifts to us,
and may what you grant us to celebrate devoutly here below
gain for us the prize of eternal redemption.
Through Christ our Lord. *Amen.*

PREFACE *(Advent 1, page 17)*

COMMUNION ANTIPHON *(Psalm 85 [84]:13)*
The Lord will bestow his bounty, and our earth shall yield its
increase.

PRAYER AFTER COMMUNION
May these mysteries, O Lord,
in which we have participated,
profit us, we pray,
for even now, as we walk amid passing things,
you teach us by them to love the things of heaven
and hold fast to what endures.
Through Christ our Lord. *Amen.*

SOLEMN BLESSING: ADVENT *(Optional, page 57)*

BLESSING & DISMISSAL *(page 56)* ❖

❖ RESPONDING TO THE WORD ❖

God declares that now is the time for fulfilling promises.

▶ What promises do I most desire to be fulfilled?

Paul encourages us to grow in love as we await Jesus' coming.

▶ What act of loving kindness can I do today to show my eagerness for Jesus' coming?

Jesus urges us to watch for him so as not to be completely surprised.

▶ What daily anxieties make it hard to watch for Christ?

December 8

It must have been this way

Many of the Marian doctrines and feasts—so troublesome to those who hold that Scripture is the sole source of what can be known about Jesus and Mary—have roots in the earliest centuries of the Christian faith. These Christians seem to have had a certain *intuition* about Mary that had its roots in their reading of Scripture and their trust in God's constancy throughout the ages. For example, since the first woman was created sinless in a pristine garden, surely must Mary, the "new Eve," have been immaculately conceived in her mother's pristine womb.

This *intuition* about the purity of Mary first appeared in an eighth-century hymn, in which she was called "alone holy without stain." By the Middle Ages there was a grassroots faith that the Mother of God would have been kept free from all exposure to sin. Through the centuries this doctrine of her immaculate conception—not to be confused with the virginal conception of Jesus in her womb—gradually won such wide acceptance that Pius IX proclaimed it a dogma on December 8, 1854.

Note the care with which the Church assigned these dates. Since Mary's birth had long been celebrated on September 8, her conception must have been a perfect nine months previous, December 8. Again, it was an *intuition* that, where Mary was concerned, even the enigmatic timing of childbirth would be perfectly in tune with a perfect Creator.

■ **KATHY MCGOVERN**

ENTRANCE ANTIPHON *(Isaiah 61:10)*

I rejoice heartily in the Lord, in my God is the joy
of my soul; for he has clothed me with a robe of
salvation, and wrapped me in a mantle of justice,
like a bride adorned with her jewels.

INTRODUCTORY RITES *(page 10)*

COLLECT

O God, who by the Immaculate Conception of the Blessed Virgin
prepared a worthy dwelling for your Son,
grant, we pray,
that, as you preserved her from every stain
by virtue of the Death of your Son, which you foresaw,
so, through her intercession,
we, too, may be cleansed and admitted to your presence.
Through our Lord Jesus Christ, your Son,
who lives and reigns with you in the unity of the Holy Spirit,
one God, for ever and ever. ***Amen.***

FIRST READING *(Genesis 3:9-15, 20)*

After the man, Adam, had eaten of the tree, the LORD God
called to the man and asked him, "Where are you?" He
answered, "I heard you in the garden; but I was afraid, because I
was naked, so I hid myself." Then he asked, "Who told you that you
were naked? You have eaten, then, from the tree of which I had forbidden you to eat!" The man replied, "The woman whom you put
here with me—she gave me fruit from the tree, and so I ate it." The
LORD God then asked the woman, "Why did you do such a thing?"
The woman answered, "The serpent tricked me into it, so I ate it."

Then the LORD God said to the serpent:
  "Because you have done this, you shall be banned
    from all the animals
    and from all the wild creatures;
  on your belly shall you crawl,
    and dirt shall you eat
    all the days of your life.
  I will put enmity between you and the woman,
    and between your offspring and hers;
  he will strike at your head,
    while you strike at his heel."
The man called his wife Eve, because she became the mother
of all the living.

The word of the Lord. *Thanks be to God.*

RESPONSORIAL PSALM *(Psalm 98:1, 2-3ab, 3cd-4)*
℟ Sing to the Lord a new song, for he has done marvelous deeds.

Sing to the LORD a new song,
  for he has done wondrous deeds;
His right hand has won victory for him,
  his holy arm. ℟
The LORD has made his salvation known:
  in the sight of the nations he has revealed his justice.
He has remembered his kindness and his faithfulness
  toward the house of Israel. ℟
All the ends of the earth have seen
  the salvation by our God.
Sing joyfully to the LORD, all you lands;
  break into song; sing praise. ℟

SECOND READING (*Ephesians 1:3–6, 11–12*)

Brothers and sisters: Blessed be the God and Father of our Lord Jesus Christ, who has blessed us in Christ with every spiritual blessing in the heavens, as he chose us in him, before the foundation of the world, to be holy and without blemish before him. In love he destined us for adoption to himself through Jesus Christ, in accord with the favor of his will, for the praise of the glory of his grace that he granted us in the beloved.

In him we were also chosen, destined in accord with the purpose of the One who accomplishes all things according to the intention of his will, so that we might exist for the praise of his glory, we who first hoped in Christ.

The word of the Lord. *Thanks be to God.*

ALLELUIA (*See Luke 1:28*)
Alleluia, alleluia. Hail, Mary, full of grace, the Lord is with you; blessed are you among women. *Alleluia, alleluia.*

GOSPEL (*Luke 1:26–38*)
A reading from the holy Gospel according to Luke.
Glory to you, O Lord.

The angel Gabriel was sent from God to a town of Galilee called Nazareth, to a virgin betrothed to a man named Joseph, of the house of David, and the virgin's name was Mary. And coming to her, he said, "**Hail, full of grace!**✝ The Lord is with you." But she was greatly troubled at what was said and pondered what sort of greeting this might be. Then the angel said to her, "Do not be afraid, Mary, for you have found favor with God. Behold, you will conceive in your womb and bear a son, and you shall name him Jesus. He will be great and will be called Son of the Most High, and the Lord God will give him the throne of David his father, and he will rule over the house of Jacob forever, and of his Kingdom there will be no end." But Mary said to the angel, "How can this be, since I have no relations with a man?" And the angel said to her in reply, "The Holy Spirit will come upon you, and the power of the Most High will overshadow you. Therefore the child to be born will be called holy, the Son of God. And behold, Elizabeth, your relative, has also conceived a son in her old age, and this is the sixth month for her who was called barren; for nothing will be impossible for God." Mary said, "Behold, I am the handmaid of the Lord. May it be done to me according to your word." Then the angel departed from her.

The Gospel of the Lord. *Praise to you, Lord Jesus Christ.*

PROFESSION OF FAITH *(page 13)*

PRAYER OF THE FAITHFUL

PREPARATION OF GIFTS *(page 16)*

PRAYER OVER THE OFFERINGS
Graciously accept the saving sacrifice
which we offer you, O Lord,
on the Solemnity of the Immaculate Conception
of the Blessed Virgin Mary,
and grant that, as we profess her,
on account of your prevenient grace,
to be untouched by any stain of sin,
so, through her intercession,
we may be delivered from all our faults.
Through Christ our Lord. *Amen.*

PREFACE: THE MYSTERY OF MARY AND THE CHURCH

It is truly right and just, our duty and our salvation,
always and everywhere to give you thanks,
Lord, holy Father, almighty and eternal God.

For you preserved the most Blessed Virgin Mary
from all stain of original sin,
so that in her, endowed with the rich fullness of your grace,
you might prepare a worthy Mother for your Son
and signify the beginning of the Church,
his beautiful Bride without spot or wrinkle.

She, the most pure Virgin, was to bring forth a Son,
the innocent Lamb who would wipe away our offenses;
you placed her above all others
to be for your people an advocate of grace
and a model of holiness.

● TAKING A CLOSER LOOK ●

✛ **Hail, full of grace!** Although we tend to hear these words as overflowing with theological meaning, note that they are a greeting that Mary finds perplexing. The sense is given by Gabriel, the messenger angel: "You have found favor with God." The basic meaning of the word grace (Greek, *charis*; Latin, *gratia*) describes a free gift that is bestowed not out of merit (then it would be owed rather than a true gift) but because the giver has found some reason to single out or favor the recipient. The choice of one recipient (a favorite) from many possible ones for the gift led to the common connection of grace and honor. As the text indicates, Mary's gift is that God is with her (as God also is with us!), which is indeed both a great favor and an honor.

And so, in company with the choirs of Angels,
we praise you, and with joy we proclaim:
Holy, Holy, Holy Lord God of hosts... *(page 35)*

COMMUNION ANTIPHON

Glorious things are spoken of you, O Mary, for from you arose
the sun of justice, Christ our God.

PRAYER AFTER COMMUNION

May the Sacrament we have received,
O Lord our God,
heal in us the wounds of that fault
from which in a singular way
you preserved Blessed Mary in her Immaculate Conception.
Through Christ our Lord. *Amen.*

SOLEMN BLESSING: THE BLESSED VIRGIN MARY *(Optional, page 62)*

BLESSING & DISMISSAL *(page 56)* ✣

• RESPONDING TO THE WORD •

Adam was afraid because he had sinned. ➡ *What sins keep me hidden from God in fear?*	God desires us to be holy and without blemish. ➡ *What can I do today to live as God wants me to?*	Mary was asked to give birth to Jesus. ➡ *How can I give birth to Jesus in myself or the world today?*

December 9

Making the crooked straight

Lately I've been feeling that a lot of things are off track in the world. Despite our having enough food to feed the planet, millions are starving. Even in our country, a land of plenty, countless families rely on food banks. We know we need to care for the Earth, our common home, but we buy too much stuff and fill our world with garbage and pollution. Despite seeing the damage conflict causes, we think peace is out of our reach.

Baruch and John the Baptist speak of the Lord making the crooked straight and the rough ways smooth; this gives me hope that we can find some balance. John the Baptist invites the people of his day, and us, to turn back to God and prepare the way of the Lord— not only during Advent, but all year long.

As followers of Christ, we are meant to live in ways that make the crooked straight. Of course, it's not always easy. It means doing things differently. We may even need to spend some time in the wilderness— disconnected from social media, the Internet, malls, and TV—to adjust our attitudes and rediscover what's important. But when we do, we will truly understand that, as today's psalm tells us, "The Lord has done great things for us," and we will be "filled with joy."

■ **ANNE LOUISE MAHONEY**

ENTRANCE ANTIPHON *(Cf. Isaiah 30:19, 30)*
O people of Sion, behold, the Lord will come to save the nations,
and the Lord will make the glory of his voice heard in the joy of
your heart.

INTRODUCTORY RITES *(page 10)*

COLLECT
Almighty and merciful God,
may no earthly undertaking hinder those
who set out in haste to meet your Son,
but may our learning of heavenly wisdom
gain us admittance to his company.
Who lives and reigns with you in the unity of the Holy Spirit,
one God, for ever and ever. ***Amen.***

FIRST READING *(Baruch 5:1-9)*
Jerusalem, take off your robe of mourning and misery;
  put on the splendor of glory from God forever:
wrapped in the cloak of justice from God,
    bear on your head the mitre*
    that displays the glory of the eternal name.
For God will show all the earth your splendor:
    you will be named by God forever
    the peace of justice, the glory of God's worship.

Up, Jerusalem! stand upon the heights;
    look to the east and see your children
gathered from the east and the west
    at the word of the Holy One,
    rejoicing that they are remembered by God.
Led away on foot by their enemies they left you:

but God will bring them back to you
    borne aloft in glory as on royal thrones.
For God has commanded
    that every lofty mountain be made low,
and that the age-old depths and gorges
    be filled to level ground,
    that Israel may advance secure in the glory of God.
The forests and every fragrant kind of tree
    have overshadowed Israel at God's command;
for God is leading Israel in joy
    by the light of his glory,
    with his mercy and justice for company.

The word of the Lord. *Thanks be to God.*

RESPONSORIAL PSALM *(Psalm 126:1-2, 2-3, 4-5, 6)*
℞ **The Lord has done great things for us; we are filled with joy.**

When the LORD brought back the captives of Zion,*
    we were like men dreaming.
Then our mouth was filled with laughter,
    and our tongue with rejoicing. ℞

Then they said among the nations,
    "The LORD has done great things for them."
The LORD has done great things for us;
    we are glad indeed. ℞

Restore our fortunes, O LORD,
    like the torrents in the southern desert.
Those who sow in tears
    shall reap rejoicing. ℞

Although they go forth weeping,

carrying the seed to be sown,
they shall come back rejoicing,
carrying their sheaves.
℟. **The Lord has done great things for us; we are filled with joy.**

SECOND READING *(Philippians 1:4-6, 8-11)*

Brothers and sisters: I pray always with joy in my every prayer for all of you, because of your partnership for the gospel from the first day until now. I am confident of this, that the one who began a good work in you will continue to complete it until the day of Christ Jesus. God is my witness, how I long for all of you with the affection of Christ Jesus. And this is my prayer: that your love may increase ever more and more in knowledge and every kind of perception, to discern what is of value, so that you may be pure and blameless for the day of Christ, filled with the fruit of righteousness that comes through Jesus Christ for the glory and praise of God.

The word of the Lord. ***Thanks be to God.***

ALLELUIA *(Luke 3:4, 6)*

Alleluia, alleluia. Prepare the way of the Lord, make straight his paths: all flesh shall see the salvation of God. ***Alleluia, alleluia.***

GOSPEL *(Luke 3:1-6)*

A reading from the holy Gospel according to Luke.
Glory to you, O Lord.

In the fifteenth year of the reign of Tiberius Caesar,* when Pontius Pilate was governor of Judea, and Herod was tetrarch* of Galilee, and his brother Philip tetrarch of the region of Ituraea* and Trachonitis,* and Lysanias* was tetrarch of Abilene, during the high priesthood of Annas and Caiaphas,* the word of God came to John the son of Zechariah* in the desert. John went throughout the whole region of the Jordan, proclaiming a baptism of **repentance**✢ for the forgiveness of sins, as it is written in the book of the words of the prophet Isaiah:

A voice of one crying out in the desert:
"Prepare the way of the Lord,
* make straight his paths.*
Every valley shall be filled
* and every mountain and hill shall be made low.*
The winding roads shall be made straight,
* and the rough ways made smooth,*
* and all flesh shall see the salvation of God."*

The Gospel of the Lord. ***Praise to you, Lord Jesus Christ.***

PROFESSION OF FAITH *(page 13)*

PRAYER OF THE FAITHFUL

PREPARATION OF GIFTS *(page 16)*

● TAKING A CLOSER LOOK ●

✢ **Repentance** Because we tend to limit the meaning of repentance to being sorry for something, repentance is a somewhat inadequate translation of the Greek word *metanoia*, which describes the more basic change of mind, heart, and attitude demanded by personal conversion. It demands a reforming of our self and our life by turning toward God and away from the evil forces that pervade our world. It is a life-long challenge to order ourselves and our world according to the vision and values of Jesus and live out the obligations of belonging to his community of disciples.

PRAYER OVER THE OFFERINGS

Be pleased, O Lord, with our humble prayers and offerings,
and, since we have no merits to plead our cause,
come, we pray, to our rescue
with the protection of your mercy.
Through Christ our Lord. *Amen.*

PREFACE *(Advent 1, page 17)*

COMMUNION ANTIPHON *(Baruch 5:5; 4:36)*

Jerusalem, arise and stand upon the heights, and behold the joy
which comes to you from God.

PRAYER AFTER COMMUNION

Replenished by the food of spiritual nourishment,
we humbly beseech you, O Lord,
that, through our partaking in this mystery,
you may teach us to judge wisely the things of earth
and hold firm to the things of heaven.
Through Christ our Lord. *Amen.*

SOLEMN BLESSING: ADVENT *(Optional, page 57)*

BLESSING & DISMISSAL *(page 56)* :::

• RESPONDING TO THE WORD •

God levels the road so we can draw near to God more easily.	Paul prays in gratitude for his partners in the gospel.	John prepares a way so that God can come to us.
➡ *How has God made my way easier than I thought it would be?*	➡ *For which of my partners in the gospel would I like to pray today?*	➡ *What obstacles need to be removed this Advent so that God can come to me?*

December 16

**DEC
16**

Prepare for Christ's coming

Rejoice! It is the word that best embodies the Third Sunday of Advent. It's like a beautifully wrapped gift that we can't wait to open. We know we are getting close to Christmas and close to receiving a most wondrous gift: the birth of Christ.

This expectation and the need to prepare ourselves for this wondrous event mark Advent. We are eager to celebrate an event that changed everything and gave all people new hope.

What is more joyous than a newborn—and yet what is more vulnerable? It is in such poverty and vulnerability that Jesus comes.

Advent is about preparing for Christ's coming. We must renew our commitment as Christians to reach out to others, especially the most vulnerable, and our "kindness should be known to all."

In the gospel, when people ask John the Baptist what they should do, he says whoever has two coats must share with someone who has none. If they have food to eat, they must ensure the hungry are fed.

As we prepare for Christ's coming, bear in mind that Jesus comes not as a great ruler in flowing robes of gold and silk. He comes as a vulnerable child who requires our concern, nurturing, and care.

■ **JACK PANOZZO**

ENTRANCE ANTIPHON *(Philippians 4:4-5)*

Rejoice in the Lord always; again I say, rejoice. Indeed, the Lord is near.

INTRODUCTORY RITES *(page 10)*

COLLECT

O God, who see how your people
faithfully await the feast of the Lord's Nativity,
enable us, we pray,
to attain the joys of so great a salvation
and to celebrate them always
with solemn worship and glad rejoicing.
Through our Lord Jesus Christ, your Son,
who lives and reigns with you in the unity of the Holy Spirit,
one God, for ever and ever. *Amen.*

FIRST READING *(Zephaniah 3:14–18a)*

Shout for joy, O daughter Zion!*
Sing joyfully, O Israel!
Be glad and exult with all your heart,
O daughter Jerusalem!
The LORD has removed the judgment against you
he has turned away your enemies;
the King of Israel, the LORD, is in your midst,
you have no further misfortune to fear.
On that day, it shall be said to Jerusalem:
Fear not, O Zion, be not discouraged!
The LORD, your God, is in your midst,
a mighty **savior**;✝
he will rejoice over you with gladness,
and renew you in his love,

> he will sing joyfully because of you,
>> as one sings at festivals.

The word of the Lord. *Thanks be to God.*

RESPONSORIAL PSALM *(Isaiah 12:2-3, 4, 5-6)*

℟ **Cry out with joy and gladness: for among you is the great and Holy One of Israel.**

God indeed is my savior;
  I am confident and unafraid.
My strength and my courage is the LORD,
  and he has been my **savior.**✝
With joy you will draw water
  at the fountain of salvation. ℟

Give thanks to the LORD, acclaim his name;
  among the nations make known his deeds,
  proclaim how exalted is his name. ℟

Sing praise to the LORD for his glorious achievement;
  let this be known throughout all the earth.
Shout with exultation, O city of Zion,*
  for great in your midst
  is the Holy One of Israel! ℟

SECOND READING *(Philippians 4:4-7)*

Brothers and sisters: Rejoice in the Lord always. I shall say it again: rejoice! Your kindness should be known to all. The Lord is near. Have no anxiety at all, but in everything, by prayer and petition, with thanksgiving, make your requests known to God. Then the peace of God that surpasses all understanding will guard your hearts and minds in Christ Jesus.

The word of the Lord. *Thanks be to God.*

ALLELUIA *(Isaiah 61:1; Luke 4:18)*
Alleluia, alleluia. The Spirit of the Lord is upon me, because he has anointed me to bring glad tidings to the poor. *Alleluia, alleluia.*

GOSPEL *(Luke 3:10–18)*
A reading from the holy Gospel according to Luke.
Glory to you, O Lord.

The crowds asked John the Baptist, "What should we do?" He said to them in reply, "Whoever has two cloaks should share with the person who has none. And whoever has food should do likewise." Even tax collectors came to be baptized and they said to him, "Teacher, what should we do?" He answered them, "Stop collecting more than what is prescribed." Soldiers also asked him, "And what is it that we should do?" He told them, "Do not practice extortion, do not falsely accuse anyone, and be satisfied with your wages."

Now the people were filled with expectation, and all were asking in their hearts whether John might be the Christ. John answered them all, saying, "I am baptizing you with water, but one mightier than I is coming. I am not worthy to loosen the thongs of his sandals. He will baptize you with the Holy Spirit and fire. His winnowing fan is in his hand to clear his threshing floor and to gather the wheat into his barn, but the chaff he will burn with unquenchable fire." Exhorting them in many other ways, he preached good news to the people.

The Gospel of the Lord. *Praise to you, Lord Jesus Christ.*

PROFESSION OF FAITH *(page 13)*

PRAYER OF THE FAITHFUL

PREPARATION OF GIFTS *(page 16)*

PRAYER OVER THE OFFERINGS

May the sacrifice of our worship, Lord, we pray,
be offered to you unceasingly,
to complete what was begun in sacred mystery
and powerfully accomplish for us your saving work.
Through Christ our Lord. *Amen.*

PREFACE *(Advent 1, page 17)*

COMMUNION ANTIPHON *(Cf. Isaiah 35:4)*

Say to the faint of heart: Be strong and do not fear. Behold, our
God will come, and he will save us.

• TAKING A CLOSER LOOK •

✛ **Savior** Before it became a theological term, "savior" simply
meant one who rescued someone from a difficult situation. Thus
it was commonly attributed to the king, emperor, or general who
saved the nation by winning a war. For the Jews, God was their
primary Savior because God rescued them from their oppression
in Egypt. For Christians, Jesus is the Savior because he rescued us
from our broken relationship with God and offered us a new relationship under God's rule.

PRAYER AFTER COMMUNION

We implore your mercy, Lord,
that this divine sustenance may cleanse us of our faults
and prepare us for the coming feasts.
Through Christ our Lord. *Amen.*

SOLEMN BLESSING: ADVENT *(Optional, page 57)*

BLESSING & DISMISSAL *(page 56)* ✜

• RESPONDING TO THE WORD •

Zephaniah tells us to be glad and rejoice.	Paul reminds us that God is near.	The crowds ask John what to do to change their lives.
➡ *What makes me glad and joyful today?*	➡ *When have I felt God near me this past week?*	➡ *What should I do this week to change my life to be more like what Jesus wants?*

December 23

**DEC
23**

Be ready!

As a mother, I remember well those first fleeting taps that signaled the kicks of my growing baby and knowing that one day, soon, the baby would arrive. After all the preparation and waiting, we would welcome an everyday miracle into a home that would perhaps never be truly ready enough.

This Advent, we hear once more how Elizabeth greeted Mary, and we feel the Christ child move, already within us through the grace of baptism. Christ quickens within us in anticipation as we clean, shop, bake, write cards or emails, practice for the pageant, and wrap gifts. But sometimes we feel like the child is not leaping with joy but rather lagging a little. We miss loved ones and are burdened by imperfect relationships. We can feel that no matter how hard we work, something is lacking. And it is so easy to become caught up in the material aspects of the season. We forget that all we need to do is be ready.

This Sunday, we are so close to the fulfillment of the promise contained in today's readings. What does fulfillment mean for us? For Elizabeth, it meant she was assured of God's blessing. This Christmas, let us, with Elizabeth, lay claim to that promise and may we all find some small moments to leap for joy.

■ **MAUREEN WICKEN**

ENTRANCE ANTIPHON *(Cf. Isaiah 45:8)*

Drop down dew from above, you heavens, and let the clouds rain down the Just One; let the earth be opened and bring forth a Savior.

INTRODUCTORY RITES *(page 10)*

COLLECT

Pour forth, we beseech you, O Lord,
your grace into our hearts,
that we, to whom the Incarnation of Christ your Son
was made known by the message of an Angel,
may by his Passion and Cross
be brought to the glory of his Resurrection.
Who lives and reigns with you in the unity of the Holy Spirit,
one God, for ever and ever. *Amen.*

FIRST READING *(Micah 5:1–4a)*

Thus says the LORD:
   You, Bethlehem-Ephrathah*
      too small to be among the clans of Judah,
from you shall come forth for me
      one who is to be ruler in Israel;
whose origin is from of old,
      from ancient times.
Therefore the Lord will give them up, until the time
      when she who is to give birth has borne,
and the rest of his kindred shall return
      to the children of Israel.
He shall stand firm and shepherd his flock
      by the strength of the LORD,
      in the majestic name of the LORD, his God;

and they shall remain, for now his greatness
shall reach to the ends of the earth;
he shall be peace.

The word of the Lord. *Thanks be to God.*

RESPONSORIAL PSALM *(Psalm 80:2-3, 15-16, 18-19)*

R̶ **Lord, make us turn to you; let us see your face and we shall
be saved.**

O shepherd of Israel, hearken,
from your throne upon the cherubim,* shine forth.
Rouse your power,
and come to save us. R̶
Once again, O LORD of hosts,
look down from heaven, and see;
take care of this vine,
and protect what your right hand has planted,
the son of man whom you yourself made strong. R̶
May your help be with the man of your right hand,
with the son of man whom you yourself made strong.
Then we will no more withdraw from you;
give us new life, and we will call upon your name. R̶

SECOND READING *(Hebrews 10:5-10)*

Brothers and sisters: When Christ came into the world,
he said:
"Sacrifice and offering you did not desire,
but a body you prepared for me;
in **holocausts and sin offerings**✝ you took no delight.
Then I said, 'As is written of me in the scroll,
behold, I come to do your will, O God.'"

First he says, "Sacrifices and offerings, holocausts and sin offerings, you neither desired nor delighted in." These are offered according to the law. Then he says, "Behold, I come to do your will." He takes away the first to establish the second. By this "will," we have been consecrated through the offering of the body of Jesus Christ once for all.

The word of the Lord. *Thanks be to God.*

ALLELUIA *(Luke 1:38)*
Alleluia, alleluia. Behold, I am the handmaid of the Lord. May it be done to me according to your word. *Alleluia, alleluia.*

GOSPEL *(Luke 1:39–45)*
A reading from the holy Gospel according to Luke.
Glory to you, O Lord.

Mary set out and traveled to the hill country in haste to a town of Judah, where she entered the house of Zechariah* and greeted Elizabeth. When Elizabeth heard Mary's greeting, the infant leaped in her womb, and Elizabeth, filled with the Holy Spirit, cried out in a loud voice and said, "Blessed are you among women, and blessed is the fruit of your womb. And how does this happen to me, that the mother of my Lord should come to me? For at the moment the sound of your greeting reached my ears, the infant in my womb leaped for joy. Blessed are you who believed that what was spoken to you by the Lord would be fulfilled."

The Gospel of the Lord. *Praise to you, Lord Jesus Christ.*

PROFESSION OF FAITH *(page 13)*

PRAYER OF THE FAITHFUL

PREPARATION OF GIFTS *(page 16)*

PRAYER OVER THE OFFERINGS

May the Holy Spirit, O Lord,
sanctify these gifts laid upon your altar,
just as he filled with his power the womb of the
    Blessed Virgin Mary.
Through Christ our Lord. *Amen.*

PREFACE *(Advent 2, page 18)*

COMMUNION ANTIPHON *(Isaiah 7:14)*

Behold, a Virgin shall conceive and bear a son; and his name will
be called Emmanuel.

• TAKING A CLOSER LOOK •

✛ **Holocausts and sin offerings** Sacrifice in the biblical
world was a way of expressing one's relationship with God by setting apart something for God (thus making it "holy") and offering
it as a gift to God. To show the complete character of the gift, it
would be burned so that the giver could not take the gift back. This
whole burnt offering is a *holocaust* (from the Greek words meaning
a complete burning). A sin-offering was a gift offered to God that
would help to restore the relationship when it was threatened by
unintentional rather than deliberate sins.

PRAYER AFTER COMMUNION

Having received this pledge of eternal redemption,
we pray, almighty God,
that, as the feast day of our salvation draws ever nearer,
so we may press forward all the more eagerly
to the worthy celebration of the mystery of your Son's Nativity.
Who lives and reigns for ever and ever. *Amen.*

SOLEMN BLESSING: ADVENT *(Optional, page 57)*

BLESSING & DISMISSAL *(page 56)* ✣

✦ RESPONDING TO THE WORD ✦

God will bring forth a ruler for Israel from a small and insignificant clan.

➡ *How has God worked wonders today through persons who were not rich and famous?*

Jesus always does what God wants.

➡ *What lures me away from doing what God wants?*

Mary is blessed because she believed that what God promised would be fulfilled.

➡ *Which of God's promises most inspires me with confidence?*

Christ's light shines in the darkness

Christmas celebrates God's becoming incarnate in time and history. The God who promised to be among us has come and continues to be with us, now and always, through Jesus and the Holy Spirit.

As the shortest days of the year end and the light of a new year begins, we celebrate Christ's presence with us to transform our world. The darkness of sin and the reign of evil now must confront the light of the nations and the reign of God. Where Christ's light is allowed to shine, the dark shadows of sin will be illumined, allowing us to live in the light. So each day, as the light intensifies, we proclaim that "Christ's light shines in the darkness, and the darkness has not overcome it" (John 1:5).

Like John the Baptist, we too are called "to testify to the light, so that all might believe through him" (John 1:7). Our testimony to Christ's light will be evident in our words and in our actions. As we are more and more enlightened by Christ, we become beacons of hope for others in a world still steeped in darkness.

Our lives are Christmas in miniature. We are invited to let God enlighten us so that we become "divinized" persons, full of the gift of the divine life and its power to change us completely. In us, God makes an appeal to all humanity to enter into this new life and live in God's light.

Praying and living the Christmas season

The twelve days between Christmas and Epiphany are a special time to celebrate Jesus as God's great gift to us and share gifts with one another. This reminds us that Eucharist (Greek for "thanksgiving") sums up our Christian lives. Let us focus our attention on God's everyday gifts to us and the gifts that we in turn receive and give. As we become more and more attentive to these gifts, we will also grow in our attitude of gratitude and be more aware of how much we have to be thankful for when we celebrate Eucharist.

Whenever your household gathers for a meal or your faith-sharing group meets, take time to thank God for being present in your daily lives. You may wish to do this as part of your grace (another word for "gift"!) before the meal.

INVITATION TO PRAYER

Leader: Jesus said, "I am the light of the world. Whoever follows me will not walk in darkness, but will have the light of life." *(John 8:12)*

All: Thanks be to God for this indescribable gift!

AROUND THE TABLE *Invite each member of the household or group to respond to these questions:*

- What gifts did I receive today from others? from God?
- How did I express my gratitude?
- What gifts did I give today to others? to God?

THINGS TO DO *Each day find one way to give a small gift of time, attention, or care for someone in your household, at work, or at school.*

December 25

Behold, the Lamb of God!

It was to the shepherds that the message of the Savior's birth was first delivered. An angel invited them to seek out an infant wrapped in swaddling clothes and lying in a manger. The shepherds' role in the Christmas story suggests that they were in an excellent position to understand the angel's message and discern the ultimate destiny of the infant Jesus.

The shepherds who tended their flocks, almost in the shadow of Jerusalem, may have been associated with the temple priesthood. In the course of the birthing process, they would take the lambs from their mothers, wash them, and wrap them in protective coverings. Before returning the newborn lambs to their nursing mothers, the shepherds carefully examined them: lambs without blemish would be destined for eventual sacrifice in the temple.

It is from this perspective that the angel's message resonates with the shepherds' experience. The newborn infant wrapped in swaddling clothes and lying in a manger was the Lamb of God already being prepared for sacrifice. His ultimate destiny would unfold when, after his sacrifice had been accomplished, he would once again be wrapped and laid to rest, awaiting rebirth into Easter glory. As participants in the Christmas Eucharist, we enter into this amazing drama in ways beyond anything the shepherds could ever have imagined.

■ **REV. CORBIN EDDY**

MASS DURING THE NIGHT

ENTRANCE ANTIPHON *(Psalm 2:7)*
The Lord said to me: You are my Son. It is I who have begotten you this day.

Or

Let us all rejoice in the Lord, for our Savior has been born in the world. Today true peace has come down to us from heaven.

INTRODUCTORY RITES *(page 10)*

COLLECT
O God, who have made this most sacred night
radiant with the splendor of the true light,
grant, we pray, that we, who have known the mysteries of his
   light on earth,
may also delight in his gladness in heaven.
Who lives and reigns with you in the unity of the Holy Spirit,
one God, for ever and ever. *Amen.*

FIRST READING *(Isaiah 9:1-6)*
The people who walked in darkness
   have seen a great light;
upon those who dwelt in the land of gloom
   a light has shone.
You have brought them abundant joy
   and great rejoicing,
as they rejoice before you as at the harvest,
   as people make merry when dividing spoils.
For the yoke that burdened them,
   the pole on their shoulder,

and the rod of their taskmaster
　　you have smashed, as on the day of Midian.*
For every boot that tramped in battle,
　　every cloak rolled in blood,
　　will be burned as fuel for flames.
For a child is born to us, a son is given us;
　　upon his shoulder dominion rests.
They name him Wonder-Counselor, God-Hero,
　　Father-Forever, Prince of Peace.
His dominion is vast
　　and forever peaceful,
from David's throne, and over his kingdom,
　　which he confirms and sustains
by judgment and justice,
　　both now and forever.
The zeal of the LORD of hosts will do this!

The word of the Lord. *Thanks be to God.*

RESPONSORIAL PSALM *(Psalm 96:1-2, 2-3, 11-12, 13)*
R. **Today is born our Savior, Christ the Lord.**

Sing to the LORD a new song;
　　sing to the LORD, all you lands.
Sing to the LORD; bless his name. R.
Announce his salvation, day after day.
　　Tell his glory among the nations;
　　among all peoples, his wondrous deeds. R.
Let the heavens be glad and the earth rejoice;
　　let the sea and what fills it resound;
　　let the plains be joyful and all that is in them!
Then shall all the trees of the forest exult. R.

They shall exult before the LORD, for he comes;
  for he comes to rule the earth.
He shall rule the world with justice
  and the peoples with his constancy.
R̷ **Today is born our Savior, Christ the Lord.**

SECOND READING *(Titus 2:11-14)*

Beloved: The grace of God has appeared, saving all and training us to reject godless ways and worldly desires and to live temperately, justly, and devoutly in this age, as we await the blessed hope, the appearance of the glory of our great God and savior Jesus Christ, who gave himself for us to deliver us from all lawlessness and to cleanse for himself a people as his own, eager to do what is good.

The word of the Lord. *Thanks be to God.*

ALLELUIA *(Luke 2:10-11)*

Alleluia, alleluia. I proclaim to you good news of great joy: today a Savior is born for us, Christ the Lord. *Alleluia, alleluia.*

GOSPEL *(Luke 2:1-14)*

A reading from the holy Gospel according to Luke.
Glory to you, O Lord.

In those days a decree went out from Caesar* Augustus that the whole world should be enrolled. This was the first enrollment, when Quirinius* was governor of Syria. So all went to be enrolled, each to his own town. And Joseph too went up from Galilee from the town of Nazareth to Judea, to the city of David that is called Bethlehem, because he was of the house and family of David, to be enrolled with Mary, his betrothed, who was with child. While they were there, the time came for her to have her child, and she gave birth to her firstborn son. She wrapped him in swaddling clothes and laid him in a manger, because there was no room for them in the inn.

Now there were shepherds in that region living in the fields and keeping the night watch over their flock. The angel of the Lord appeared to them and the glory of the Lord shone around them, and they were struck with great fear. The angel said to them, "Do not be afraid; for behold, I proclaim to you good news of great joy that will be for all the people. For today in the city of David a savior has been born for you who is **Christ and Lord**.✦ And this will be a sign for you: you will find an infant wrapped in swaddling clothes and lying in a manger." And suddenly there was a multitude of the heavenly host with the angel, praising God and saying:

> "Glory to God in the highest
> and on earth peace to those on whom his favor rests."

The Gospel of the Lord. Praise to you, Lord Jesus Christ.

PROFESSION OF FAITH *(page 13)*

PRAYER OF THE FAITHFUL

PREPARATION OF GIFTS *(page 16)*

● TAKING A CLOSER LOOK ●

✦ **Christ and Lord** These two terms summarize Luke's understanding of who Jesus really is as human and divine. Christ (Greek for "anointed"; in Hebrew, *messiah*) identifies him as the agent of salvation (savior) whom God would send to bring God's covenant people into the right relationship with God. Lord (Greek, *kyrios*) is the usual Greek title for a god and the circumlocution used by Jews to avoid speaking the sacred name of God, YHWH. This name is now given to Jesus, and the honor due to God is now due him.

PRAYER OVER THE OFFERINGS

May the oblation of this day's feast
be pleasing to you, O Lord, we pray,
that through this most holy exchange
we may be found in the likeness of Christ,
in whom our nature is united to you.
Who lives and reigns for ever and ever. *Amen.*

PREFACE *(Nativity of the Lord, pages 19–20)*

COMMUNION ANTIPHON *(John 1:14)*

The Word became flesh, and we have seen his glory.

PRAYER AFTER COMMUNION

Grant us, we pray, O Lord our God,
that we, who are gladdened by participation
in the feast of our Redeemer's Nativity,
may through an honorable way of life become worthy of union
    with him.
Who lives and reigns for ever and ever. *Amen.*

SOLEMN BLESSING: THE NATIVITY OF THE LORD *(Optional, page 58)*

BLESSING & DISMISSAL *(page 56)* ✢

● RESPONDING TO THE WORD ●

Isaiah envisions a time of great joy when the Promised One comes.	Paul knows that Jesus' presence changes our lives.	Finding Jesus is a sign of good news for the shepherds.
◼ *What joy have I experienced as I prepared for Christmas?*	◼ *How has my attention to God changed my behavior recently?*	◼ *What good news does this sign point to for me?*

MASS AT DAWN

ENTRANCE ANTIPHON *(Cf. Isaiah 9:1, 5; Luke 1:33)*
Today a light will shine upon us, for the Lord is born for us;
and he will be called Wondrous God, Prince of peace, Father of
future ages: and his reign will be without end.

INTRODUCTORY RITES *(page 10)*

COLLECT
Grant, we pray, almighty God,
that, as we are bathed in the new radiance of your incarnate Word,
the light of faith, which illumines our minds,
may also shine through in our deeds.
Through our Lord Jesus Christ, your Son,
who lives and reigns with you in the unity of the Holy Spirit,
one God, for ever and ever. *Amen.*

FIRST READING *(Isaiah 62:11–12)*

See, the LORD proclaims
to the ends of the earth:
say to daughter Zion,*
    your savior comes!
Here is his reward with him,
    his recompense before him.
They shall be called the holy people,
    the redeemed of the LORD,
and you shall be called "Frequented,"
    a city that is not forsaken.

The word of the Lord. *Thanks be to God.*

RESPONSORIAL PSALM *(Psalm 97:1, 6, 11-12)*

℞ **A light will shine on us this day: the Lord is born for us.**

The LORD is king; let the earth rejoice;
  let the many isles be glad.
The heavens proclaim his justice,
  and all peoples see his glory. ℞
Light dawns for the just;
  and gladness, for the upright of heart.
Be glad in the LORD, you just,
  and give thanks to his holy name. ℞

SECOND READING *(Titus 3:4-7)*

Beloved:
  When the kindness and generous love
  of God our savior appeared,
not because of any righteous deeds we had done
  but because of his mercy,
he saved us through the bath of rebirth
  and renewal by the Holy Spirit,
whom he richly poured out on us
  through Jesus Christ our savior,
so that we might be justified by his grace
  and become heirs in hope of eternal life.

The word of the Lord. *Thanks be to God.*

ALLELUIA *(Luke 2:14)*

Alleluia, alleluia. Glory to God in the highest, and on earth
peace to those on whom his favor rests. *Alleluia, alleluia.*

GOSPEL *(Luke 2:15-20)*

A reading from the holy Gospel according to Luke.
Glory to you, O Lord.

When the angels went away from them to heaven, the shepherds said to one another, "Let us go, then, to Bethlehem to see this thing that has taken place, which the Lord has made known to us." So they went in haste and found Mary and Joseph, and the infant lying in the manger. When they saw this, they made known the message that had been told them about this child. All who heard it were amazed by what had been told them by the shepherds. And Mary kept all these things, reflecting on them in her **heart.** ✚ Then the shepherds returned, glorifying and praising God for all they had heard and seen, just as it had been told to them.

The Gospel of the Lord. *Praise to you, Lord Jesus Christ.*

PROFESSION OF FAITH *(page 13)*

PRAYER OF THE FAITHFUL

PREPARATION OF GIFTS *(page 16)*

• TAKING A CLOSER LOOK •

✚ **Heart** For biblical people, the heart does not just identify the physical organ but rather the psychological activity associated with it. Since the heart was associated with emotional changes (speeding up when we are excited) and physical life (ceasing to beat when we die), "heart" becomes a general word to identify the location of the distinctively human activities of feeling, thinking, and deciding. Today we might describe this as the "self." So Mary reflects deeply within her "self" about these wondrous experiences arising from her mysterious relationship with Jesus.

PRAYER OVER THE OFFERINGS

May our offerings be worthy, we pray, O Lord,
of the mysteries of the Nativity this day,
that, just as Christ was born a man and also shone forth as God,
so these earthly gifts may confer on us what is divine.
Through Christ our Lord. *Amen.*

PREFACE *(Nativity of the Lord, pages 19–20)*

COMMUNION ANTIPHON *(Cf. Zechariah 9:9)*

Rejoice, O Daughter Sion; lift up praise, Daughter Jerusalem:
Behold, your King will come, the Holy One and Savior of the
world.

PRAYER AFTER COMMUNION

Grant us, Lord, as we honor with joyful devotion
the Nativity of your Son,
that we may come to know with fullness of faith
the hidden depths of this mystery
and to love them ever more and more.
Through Christ our Lord. *Amen.*

SOLEMN BLESSING: THE NATIVITY OF THE LORD *(Optional, page 58)*

BLESSING & DISMISSAL *(page 56)* ✦

• RESPONDING TO THE WORD •

The Savior's presence makes us a holy people.

➔ *How have I been drawn closer to God this Advent?*

Paul knows that God's presence in Christ is a great gift.

➔ *What thanks can I give for this gift today?*

The shepherds shared their Christmas joy with others.

➔ *With whom shall I share my joy today?*

MASS DURING THE DAY

ENTRANCE ANTIPHON *(Cf. Isaiah 9:5)*

A child is born for us, and a son is given to us; his scepter of power rests upon his shoulder, and his name will be called Messenger of great counsel.

INTRODUCTORY RITES *(page 10)*

COLLECT

O God, who wonderfully created the dignity of human nature and still more wonderfully restored it,
grant, we pray,
that we may share in the divinity of Christ,
who humbled himself to share in our humanity.
Who lives and reigns with you in the unity of the Holy Spirit,
one God, for ever and ever. *Amen.*

FIRST READING *(Isaiah 52:7-10)*

How beautiful upon the mountains
    are the feet of him who brings glad tidings,
announcing peace, bearing good news,
    announcing salvation, and saying to Zion,*
    "Your God is King!"

Hark! Your sentinels raise a cry,
    together they shout for joy,
for they see directly, before their eyes,
    the LORD restoring Zion.
Break out together in song,
    O ruins of Jerusalem!
For the LORD comforts his people,

he redeems Jerusalem.
The LORD has bared his holy arm
 in the sight of all the nations;
all the ends of the earth will behold
 the salvation of our God.

The word of the Lord. *Thanks be to God.*

RESPONSORIAL PSALM *(Psalm 98:1, 2–3, 3–4, 5–6)*

℟ **All the ends of the earth have seen the saving power of God.**

Sing to the LORD a new song,
 for he has done wondrous deeds;
his right hand has won victory for him,
 his holy arm. ℟
The LORD has made his salvation known:
 in the sight of the nations he has revealed his justice.
He has remembered his kindness and his faithfulness
 toward the house of Israel. ℟
All the ends of the earth have seen
 the salvation by our God.
Sing joyfully to the LORD, all you lands;
 break into song; sing praise. ℟
Sing praise to the LORD with the harp,
 with the harp and melodious song.
With trumpets and the sound of the horn
 sing joyfully before the King, the LORD. ℟

SECOND READING *(Hebrews 1:1–6)*

Brothers and sisters: In times past, God spoke in partial and
various ways to our ancestors through the prophets; in these
last days, he has spoken to us through the Son, whom he made heir

of all things and through whom he created the universe,
> who is the refulgence of his glory, the very imprint of his being,
> and who sustains all things by his mighty word.
> When he had accomplished purification from sins,
> he took his seat at the right hand of the Majesty on high,
> as far superior to the angels
> as the name he has inherited is more excellent than theirs.

For to which of the angels did God ever say:
> *You are my son; this day I have begotten you?*

Or again:
> *I will be a father to him, and he shall be a son to me?*

And again, when he leads the firstborn into the world, he says:
> *Let all the angels of God worship him.*

The word of the Lord. ***Thanks be to God.***

ALLELUIA

Alleluia, alleluia. A holy day has dawned upon us. Come, you nations, and adore the Lord. For today a great light has come upon the earth. *Alleluia, alleluia.*

GOSPEL *(John 1:1-18)*
For the shorter reading, omit the indented parts in brackets.

A reading from the holy Gospel according to John.
Glory to you, O Lord.

In the beginning was the Word,
and the Word was with God,
and the Word was God.
He was in the beginning with God.
All things came to be through him,
> and without him nothing came to be.

What came to be through him was life,
  and this life was the light of the human race;
the light shines in the darkness,
  and the darkness has not overcome it.
[A man named John was sent from God. He came for testimony, to testify to the light, so that all might believe through him. He was not the light, but came to testify to the light.]
The true light, which enlightens everyone, was coming into the world.

He was in the world,
  and the world came to be through him,
  but the world did not know him.
He came to what was his own,
  but his own people did not accept him.
But to those who did accept him he gave power to become children of God, to those who believe in his name, who were born not by natural generation nor by human choice nor by a man's decision but of God.

And the Word became **flesh**✝
  and made his dwelling among us,
  and we saw his glory,
  the glory as of the Father's only Son,
  full of grace and truth.
[John testified to him and cried out, saying, "This was he of whom I said, 'The one who is coming after me ranks ahead of me because he existed before me.'" From his fullness we have all received, grace in place of grace, because while the law was given through Moses, grace and truth came through Jesus

Christ. No one has ever seen God. The only Son, God, who is at the Father's side, has revealed him.]

The Gospel of the Lord. *Praise to you, Lord Jesus Christ.*

PROFESSION OF FAITH *(page 13)*

PRAYER OF THE FAITHFUL

PREPARATION OF GIFTS *(page 16)*

PRAYER OVER THE OFFERINGS
Make acceptable, O Lord, our oblation on this solemn day,
when you manifested the reconciliation
that makes us wholly pleasing in your sight
and inaugurated for us the fullness of divine worship.
Through Christ our Lord. *Amen.*

PREFACE *(Nativity of the Lord, pages 19-20)*

• TAKING A CLOSER LOOK •

✢ **Flesh** The word "flesh" does not just refer to the skin but is often a shorthand summary for the living human body (hence "flesh and blood" to describe a whole living person). But flesh also describes what is corruptible (for we all die) and prone to sin (for we are not perfect). Because "flesh" describes the reality of human existence, it is appropriate to highlight Jesus' becoming human. But because "flesh" points to that which moves us toward sin and alienation from God, it is startling to apply this to Jesus. Normally, God and flesh would not go together, but in the divine-human reality of Jesus they must.

COMMUNION ANTIPHON *(Cf. Psalm 98 [97]:3)*
All the ends of the earth have seen the salvation of our God.

PRAYER AFTER COMMUNION
Grant, O merciful God,
that, just as the Savior of the world, born this day,
is the author of divine generation for us,
so he may be the giver even of immortality.
Who lives and reigns for ever and ever. *Amen.*

SOLEMN BLESSING: THE NATIVITY OF THE LORD *(Optional, page 58)*

BLESSING & DISMISSAL *(page 56)* ❖

❖ RESPONDING TO THE WORD ❖

God's presence brings peace for the people.

➔ *What peace might I bring to others today?*

Jesus is the finest revelation of who God is and what God wants for us.

➔ *How can I pay closer attention to Jesus' example for my life?*

Jesus desires to be with us and share our human experience.

➔ *How has Jesus revealed his presence in my life today?*

DEC
30

December 30

Be patient, listen, and reflect

The journey to Jerusalem for the Passover is difficult, often taking days of walking. The city is crowded, filled to the edges with people from all over the region and beyond. The air is thick with smoke and the smell of burnt offering and blood. And of course, Roman soldiers keep a watchful eye.

Imagine losing your child in this city, searching frantically for three days, and the joyful relief at finding him safe! Jesus' cheeky response on being found always takes me by surprise. Even at twelve, he is aware of his origin. But Mary, his mother, the life-giver, the courageous woman who said yes, knows there is more to her son's destiny. She collects these moments and ponders as she did when the shepherds visited Bethlehem at Jesus' birth. She and Joseph, after all, are the first people to know Jesus' true nature and have the greatest hand in shaping him.

Their approach of patience, listening, and thoughtful meditation as they raise Jesus is a key touchstone that can guide us during our most difficult times. Like Mary, we too can benefit from this reflection on our own lives, listening to the messages from God to help us navigate our destinies.

▩ **SASKIA SIVANANTHAN**

ENTRANCE ANTIPHON *(Luke 2:16)*

The shepherds went in haste, and found Mary and Joseph and the Infant lying in a manger.

INTRODUCTORY RITES *(page 10)*

COLLECT

O God, who were pleased to give us
the shining example of the Holy Family,
graciously grant that we may imitate them
in practicing the virtues of family life and in the bonds of charity,
and so, in the joy of your house,
delight one day in eternal rewards.
Through our Lord Jesus Christ, your Son,
who lives and reigns with you in the unity of the Holy Spirit,
one God, for ever and ever. *Amen.*

These are the readings for Year C. The first reading, responsorial psalm, and second reading from Year A (Sirach 3:2-6, 12-14; Psalm 128:1-2, 3, 4-5; Colossians 3:12-21 or 3:12-17) may also be used.

FIRST READING *(1 Samuel 1:20-22, 24-28)*

In those days Hannah conceived, and at the end of her term bore a son whom she called Samuel, since she had asked the LORD for him. The next time her husband Elkanah was going up with the rest of his household to offer the customary sacrifice to the LORD and to fulfill his vows, Hannah did not go, explaining to her husband, "Once the child is weaned, I will take him to appear before the LORD and to remain there forever; I will offer him as a perpetual **nazirite**."✝

Once Samuel was weaned, Hannah brought him up with her,

along with a three-year-old bull, an ephah* of flour, and a skin of wine, and presented him at the temple of the LORD in Shiloh. After the boy's father had sacrificed the young bull, Hannah, his mother, approached Eli and said: "Pardon, my lord! As you live, my lord, I am the woman who stood near you here, praying to the LORD. I prayed for this child, and the LORD granted my request. Now I, in turn, give him to the LORD; as long as he lives, he shall be dedicated to the LORD." Hannah left Samuel there.

The word of the Lord. *Thanks be to God.*

RESPONSORIAL PSALM *(Psalm 84:2-3, 5-6, 9-10)*

℟ **Blessed are they who dwell in your house, O Lord.**

How lovely is your dwelling place, O LORD of hosts!
  My soul yearns and pines for the courts of the Lord.
My heart and my flesh cry out for the living God. ℟

Happy they who dwell in your house!
  Continually they praise you.
Happy the men whose strength you are!
  Their hearts are set upon the pilgrimage. ℟

O LORD of hosts, hear our prayer;
  hearken, O God of Jacob!
O God, behold our shield,
  and look upon the face of your anointed. ℟

SECOND READING *(1 John 3:1-2, 21-24)*

Beloved: See what love the Father has bestowed on us that we may be called the children of God. And so we are. The reason the world does not know us is that it did not know him. Beloved, we are God's children now; what we shall be has not yet been revealed. We do know that when it is revealed we shall be like him, for we shall see him as he is.

Beloved, if our hearts do not condemn us, we have confidence in God and receive from him whatever we ask, because we keep his commandments and do what pleases him. And his commandment is this: we should believe in the name of his Son, Jesus Christ, and love one another just as he commanded us. Those who keep his commandments remain in him, and he in them, and the way we know that he remains in us is from the Spirit he gave us.

The word of the Lord. *Thanks be to God.*

ALLELUIA *(See Acts 16:14b)*
Alleluia, alleluia. Open our hearts, O Lord, to listen to the words of your Son. *Alleluia, alleluia.*

GOSPEL *(Luke 2:41-52)*
A reading from the holy Gospel according to Luke.
Glory to you, O Lord.

Each year Jesus' parents went to Jerusalem for the feast of Passover, and when he was twelve years old, they went up according to festival custom. After they had completed its days, as they were returning, the boy Jesus remained behind in Jerusalem, but his parents did not know it. Thinking that he was in the caravan, they journeyed for a day and looked for him among their relatives and acquaintances, but not finding him, they returned to Jerusalem to look for him. After three days they found him in the temple, sitting in the midst of the teachers, listening to them and asking them questions, and all who heard him were astounded at his understanding and his answers. When his parents saw him, they were astonished, and his mother said to him, "Son, why have you done this to us? Your father and I have been looking for you with great anxiety." And he said to them, "Why were you looking for me? Did you not know that I must be in my Father's house?"

But they did not understand what he said to them. He went down with them and came to Nazareth, and was obedient to them; and his mother kept all these things in her heart. And Jesus advanced in wisdom and age and favor before God and man.

The Gospel of the Lord. *Praise to you, Lord Jesus Christ.*

PROFESSION OF FAITH *(page 13)*

PRAYER OF THE FAITHFUL

PREPARATION OF GIFTS *(page 16)*

PRAYER OVER THE OFFERINGS
We offer you, Lord, the sacrifice of conciliation,
humbly asking that,
through the intercession of the Virgin Mother of God
    and Saint Joseph,
you may establish our families firmly in your grace and your peace.
Through Christ our Lord. *Amen.*

• TAKING A CLOSER LOOK •

✝ **Nazirite** A *nazirite* (Hebrew, "one set apart as sacred") is one who is dedicated to God by a temporary or permanent promise or vow. If temporary, when the obligation was fulfilled, the person cut his hair and submitted to purification rites. Nazirites were to abstain from alcoholic beverages, not cut their hair, and have no contact with a corpse. (See the Book of Numbers, chapter 6, for fuller details.) Lifelong nazirites included Samson (Judges 13:5, 7, 16:17), Samuel (1 Samuel 1:11), and John the Baptist (Luke 1:15). It was probably a nazirite vow that Paul took (Acts 18:18), after which he had his hair cut to signify the ending of obligation.

PREFACE *(Nativity of the Lord, pages 19–20)*

COMMUNION ANTIPHON *(Baruch 3:38)*
Our God has appeared on the earth, and lived among us.

PRAYER AFTER COMMUNION
Bring those you refresh with this heavenly Sacrament,
most merciful Father,
to imitate constantly the example of the Holy Family,
so that, after the trials of this world,
we may share their company for ever.
Through Christ our Lord. *Amen.*

BLESSING & DISMISSAL *(page 56)* ✣

• RESPONDING TO THE WORD •

As God's children, we are to be dedicated to God's ways.	We are called to be more like Jesus in our actions.	Jesus' parents were perplexed by his behavior.
➔ *How might I offer myself in God's service today?*	➔ *How have I acted as Jesus would this week?*	➔ *How can I be more understanding of the behavior of others, especially of young people?*

January 1

Celebrate God's presence

Mothers do ponder! Pregnancy itself begs consideration of new life within—even without angelic visits. For generations, Aaron's blessing had been spoken daily into the families of Mary and Joseph. Our Holy Mother was accustomed to considering the *blessing* and the *keeping*, the *shining* and the *peace* of God being woven into her life.

Then shepherds burst into the scene of the Nativity, blurting out the angels' message of the night. God's *blessing* of humanity was so clear. It is no wonder Luke reported that Mary kept all these things and pondered them in her heart.

Truly the Lord was blessing Mary's family, and indeed all of creation, with the presence of God's only-begotten Son. Through God's *keeping*, God orchestrated the safe delivery of Jesus despite Roman oppression. In spite of the shadows, God's face was *shining* on Mary's family—in her infant son's face, in Joseph's eyes, and in the other-worldly joy of the shepherds. And *peace*? "Peace on Earth" was the song of the angels. What Joy! What Peace! What Hope!

Let us with our Holy Mother ponder and celebrate the *blessing*, the *keeping*, the *shining*, and the *peace* of our Lord's presence among us and within us, today and throughout this coming year.

■ BEVERLY ILLAUQ

ENTRANCE ANTIPHON

Hail, Holy Mother, who gave birth to the King who rules heaven and earth for ever.

Or *(Cf. Isaiah 9:1, 5; Luke 1:33)*

Today a light will shine upon us, for the Lord is born for us; and he will be called Wondrous God, Prince of peace, Father of future ages: and his reign will be without end.

INTRODUCTORY RITES *(page 10)*

COLLECT

O God, who through the fruitful virginity of Blessed Mary
bestowed on the human race
the grace of eternal salvation,
grant, we pray,
that we may experience the intercession of her,
through whom we were found worthy
to receive the author of life,
our Lord Jesus Christ, your Son.
Who lives and reigns with you in the unity of the Holy Spirit,
one God, for ever and ever. *Amen.*

FIRST READING *(Numbers 6:22-27)*

The LORD said to Moses: "Speak to Aaron and his sons and tell them: This is how you shall bless the Israelites. Say to them:

The LORD bless you and keep you!
The LORD let his face shine upon you,
    and be gracious to you!
The LORD look upon you kindly and give you peace!

So shall they invoke my name upon the Israelites, and I will bless them."

The word of the Lord. *Thanks be to God.*

RESPONSORIAL PSALM *(Psalm 67:2-3, 5, 6, 8)*
℟ **May God bless us in his mercy.**

May God have pity on us and bless us;
    may he let his face shine upon us.
So may your way be known upon earth;
    among all nations, your salvation. ℟
May the nations be glad and exult
    because you rule the peoples in equity;
    the nations on the earth you guide. ℟
May the peoples praise you, O God;
    may all the peoples praise you!
May God bless us,
    and may all the ends of the earth fear him! ℟

SECOND READING *(Galatians 4:4-7)*

Brothers and sisters: When the fullness of time had come, God sent his Son, born of a woman, born under the law, to ransom those under the law, so that we might receive adoption as sons. As proof that you are sons, God sent the Spirit of his Son into our hearts, crying out, "**Abba, Father!**"✢ So you are no longer a slave but a son, and if a son then also an heir, through God.

The word of the Lord. *Thanks be to God.*

ALLELUIA *(Hebrews 1:1-2)*
Alleluia, alleluia. In the past God spoke to our ancestors through the prophets; in these last days, he has spoken to us through the Son. *Alleluia, alleluia.*

GOSPEL *(Luke 2:16-21)*
A reading from the holy Gospel according to Luke.
Glory to you, O Lord.

The shepherds went in haste to Bethlehem and found Mary and Joseph, and the infant lying in the manger. When they saw this, they made known the message that had been told them about this child. All who heard it were amazed by what had been told them by the shepherds. And Mary kept all these things, reflecting on them in her heart. Then the shepherds returned, glorifying and praising God for all they had heard and seen, just as it had been told to them.

When eight days were completed for his circumcision, he was named Jesus, the name given him by the angel before he was conceived in the womb.

The Gospel of the Lord. *Praise to you, Lord Jesus Christ.*

PROFESSION OF FAITH *(page 13)*

PRAYER OF THE FAITHFUL

PREPARATION OF GIFTS *(page 16)*

PRAYER OVER THE OFFERINGS

O God, who in your kindness begin all good things
and bring them to fulfillment,
grant to us, who find joy in the Solemnity
    of the holy Mother of God,
that, just as we glory in the beginnings of your grace,
so one day we may rejoice in its completion.
Through Christ our Lord. *Amen.*

PREFACE *(Blessed Virgin Mary 1, page 34)*

• Taking a Closer Look •

✠ **Abba, Father!** *Abba* is the Aramaic (the spoken language of Jews in the Holy Land in Jesus' time) word for "father." It is a more familiar form than the common but slightly more formal *pater*, the Greek word for "father," and thus represents the more intimate and close relationship that Jesus has with God. Paul does not expect the Galatians to know its meaning so he connects the Aramaic term with its Greek translation: "Abba, Father."

COMMUNION ANTIPHON *(Hebrews 13:8)*
Jesus Christ is the same yesterday, today, and for ever.

PRAYER AFTER COMMUNION
We have received this heavenly Sacrament with joy, O Lord:
grant, we pray,
that it may lead us to eternal life,
for we rejoice to proclaim the blessed ever-Virgin Mary
Mother of your Son and Mother of the Church.
Through Christ our Lord. *Amen.*

SOLEMN BLESSING: THE BEGINNING OF THE YEAR *(Optional, page 59)*
   OR THE BLESSED VIRGIN MARY *(Optional, page 62)*

BLESSING & DISMISSAL *(page 56)* ❊

❊ RESPONDING TO THE WORD ❊

Mary is the model of our prayer, reflecting in her heart upon the meaning of Jesus presence among us.

➡ *How can I deepen my experience of Jesus' presence during the coming year?*

Moses learns a blessing for God's people.

➡ *Whom would I like to bless like this today?*

Paul teaches us to pray to God as our loving parent.

➡ *What would I like to ask God for today?*

JAN
6

January 6

Christ has come among us

"They set out. And behold, the star that they had seen at its rising preceded them"—leading them toward the the child who had been born king of the Jews. When the star stopped, the wise men were overjoyed. They entered the house and saw "the child with Mary his mother. They prostrated themselves and did him homage."

We have heard this story many times. This would be the time, when our children were young, that we would bring out the tiny camels and the wise men and place them in our nativity crèche. It would be the last act of our Christmas story. In a few days the small figures and other decorations still up from this joyous season would be carefully put away for another year.

Astronomers debate whether the star marked the arrival of a comet, a super nova, or possibly a rare celestial conjunction of Jupiter and Saturn. Theologians note that only Matthew records the story, and some suggest it is a pious fiction designed to integrate older writings into the birth narrative of Jesus.

Questions abound but the essential messages remain. For Paul, it is the mystery now made known to humankind. Isaiah urges rejoicing: "Rise up in splendor, Jerusalem! Your light has come!" The Epiphany reveals that Christ had come among us all.

■ MICHAEL DOUGHERTY

MASS DURING THE DAY

ENTRANCE ANTIPHON *(Cf. Malachi 3:1; 1 Chronicles 29:12)*
Behold, the Lord, the Mighty One, has come; and kingship is in his grasp, and power and dominion.

INTRODUCTORY RITES *(page 10)*

COLLECT
O God, who on this day
revealed your Only Begotten Son to the nations
by the guidance of a star,
grant in your mercy
that we, who know you already by faith,
may be brought to behold the beauty of your sublime glory.
Through our Lord Jesus Christ, your Son,
who lives and reigns with you in the unity of the Holy Spirit,
one God, for ever and ever. *Amen.*

FIRST READING *(Isaiah 60:1-6)*

Rise up in splendor, Jerusalem! Your light has come,
the **glory of the LORD** ✝ shines upon you.
See, darkness covers the earth,
    and thick clouds cover the peoples;
but upon you the LORD shines,
    and over you appears his glory.
Nations shall walk by your light,
    and kings by your shining radiance.
Raise your eyes and look about;
    they all gather and come to you:
your sons come from afar,
    and your daughters in the arms of their nurses.

Then you shall be radiant at what you see,
  your heart shall throb and overflow,
for the riches of the sea shall be emptied out before you,
  the wealth of nations shall be brought to you.
Caravans of camels shall fill you,
  dromedaries from Midian* and Ephah;*
all from Sheba* shall come
  bearing gold and frankincense,
  and proclaiming the praises of the LORD.

The word of the Lord. *Thanks be to God.*

RESPONSORIAL PSALM *(Psalm 72:1-2, 7-8, 10-11, 12-13)*
R⧸ **Lord, every nation on earth will adore you.**

O God, with your judgment endow the king,
  and with your justice, the king's son;
he shall govern your people with justice
  and your afflicted ones with judgment. R⧸
Justice shall flower in his days,
  and profound peace, till the moon be no more.
May he rule from sea to sea,
  and from the River to the ends of the earth. R⧸
The kings of Tarshish* and the Isles shall offer gifts;
  the kings of Arabia and Seba* shall bring tribute.
All kings shall pay him homage,
  all nations shall serve him. R⧸
For he shall rescue the poor when he cries out,
  and the afflicted when he has no one to help him.
He shall have pity for the lowly and the poor;
  the lives of the poor he shall save. R⧸

SECOND READING *(Ephesians 3:2-3a, 5-6)*

Brothers and sisters: You have heard of the stewardship of God's grace that was given to me for your benefit, namely, that the mystery was made known to me by revelation. It was not made known to people in other generations as it has now been revealed to his holy apostles and prophets by the Spirit: that the Gentiles are coheirs, members of the same body, and copartners in the promise in Christ Jesus through the gospel.

The word of the Lord. *Thanks be to God.*

ALLELUIA *(Matthew 2:2)*

Alleluia, alleluia. We saw his star at its rising and have come to do him homage. *Alleluia, alleluia.*

GOSPEL *(Matthew 2:1-12)*

A reading from the holy Gospel according to Matthew.
Glory to you, O Lord.

When Jesus was born in Bethlehem of Judea, in the days of King Herod, behold, magi from the east arrived in Jerusalem, saying, "Where is the newborn king of the Jews? We saw his star at its rising and have come to do him homage." When King Herod heard this, he was greatly troubled, and all Jerusalem with him. Assembling all the chief priests and the scribes of the people, he inquired of them where the Christ was to be born. They said to him, "In Bethlehem of Judea, for thus it has been written through the prophet:

And you, Bethlehem, land of Judah,
are by no means least among the rulers of Judah;
since from you shall come a ruler,
who is to shepherd my people Israel."

Then Herod called the magi secretly and ascertained from them the time of the star's appearance. He sent them to Bethlehem and said, "Go and search diligently for the child. When you have found him, bring me word, that I too may go and do him homage." After their audience with the king they set out. And behold, the star that they had seen at its rising preceded them, until it came and stopped over the place where the child was. They were overjoyed at seeing the star, and on entering the house they saw the child with Mary his mother. They prostrated themselves and did him homage. Then they opened their treasures and offered him gifts of gold, frankincense, and myrrh.* And having been warned in a dream not to return to Herod, they departed for their country by another way.

The Gospel of the Lord. ***Praise to you, Lord Jesus Christ.***

PROFESSION OF FAITH *(page 13)*

PRAYER OF THE FAITHFUL

PREPARATION OF GIFTS *(page 16)*

PRAYER OVER THE OFFERINGS
Look with favor, Lord, we pray,
on these gifts of your Church,

• TAKING A CLOSER LOOK •

✛ **The glory of the Lord** In Hebrew, the word "glory" is related to weight or heaviness and describes someone's inner worth or importance. When applied to humans, it can be associated with what gives a person dignity and commands respect, such as honor, wealth, or wisdom. When glory is associated with God, the meaning becomes more complex. Glory describes the essence of God's divinity that requires us to respect and honor God. But glory also points to the visible manifestation of God's invisible presence: for example, in the cloud and pillar of fire leading the Hebrews during the Exodus.

in which are offered now not gold or frankincense or myrrh,*
but he who by them is proclaimed,
sacrificed and received, Jesus Christ.
Who lives and reigns for ever and ever. *Amen.*

PREFACE *(Epiphany, page 20)*

COMMUNION ANTIPHON *(Cf. Matthew 2:2)*
We have seen his star in the East, and have come with gifts to
adore the Lord.

PRAYER AFTER COMMUNION
Go before us with heavenly light, O Lord,
always and everywhere,
that we may perceive with clear sight
and revere with true affection
the mystery in which you have willed us to participate.
Through Christ our Lord. *Amen.*

SOLEMN BLESSING: THE EPIPHANY OF THE LORD *(Optional, page 59)*

BLESSING & DISMISSAL *(page 56)* ✣

• RESPONDING TO THE WORD •

Isaiah feels like the time of darkness is ended.

➡ *How has Christ lit up the darkness in my life?*

Paul rejoices because all persons are included in God's invitation to salvation.

➡ *How can I make others feel more welcome in my Christian community?*

The magi do not fear to do whatever it takes to find Jesus.

➡ *What fears or obstacles do I need to overcome in my search for Jesus?*

January 13

Promises fulfilled

In today's liturgy, Jesus is baptised by John in the river, and God's voice is heard proclaiming Jesus to be the Beloved Son of God with the visible presence of the Holy Spirit bearing witness. Do you remember your baptism? Have you ever witnessed someone else's baptism? What do you recall from these baptismal liturgies? In today's Scriptures, we do well to listen for echoes of our own baptism and the baptisms we have witnessed: water, Spirit, the Trinity, a faith-filled community gathered.

This gospel recounts the final event we celebrate in the Christmas season. The Christmas season looks beyond the baby in Bethlehem. Each feast peels back the layers a little further, each revealing the truth of Jesus of Nazareth from a different perspective. Jesus is the one in whom God keeps the promises made through Isaiah. He will show to the world the glory, justice, power, and abundant love of God.

And us? Through baptism into Christ, we share in his life in God and in his promise-keeping mission in the world. By our baptism we can lay claim to that divine declaration: "You are my beloved Son; with you I am well pleased." Do you celebrate your baptism date anniversary? Today is a fitting time to do so.

■ **MARGARET BICK**

ENTRANCE ANTIPHON *(Cf. Matthew 3:16–17)*

After the Lord was baptized, the heavens were opened, and the Spirit descended upon him like a dove, and the voice of the Father thundered: This is my beloved Son, with whom I am well pleased.

INTRODUCTORY RITES *(page 10)*

COLLECT

Almighty ever-living God,
who, when Christ had been baptized in the River Jordan
and as the Holy Spirit descended upon him,
solemnly declared him your beloved Son,
grant that your children by adoption,
reborn of water and the Holy Spirit,
may always be well pleasing to you.
Through our Lord Jesus Christ, your Son,
who lives and reigns with you in the unity of the Holy Spirit,
one God, for ever and ever. *Amen.*

Or

O God, whose Only Begotten Son
has appeared in our very flesh,
grant, we pray, that we may be inwardly transformed
through him whom we recognize as outwardly like ourselves.
Who lives and reigns with you in the unity of the Holy Spirit,
one God, for ever and ever. *Amen.*

These are the readings for Year C. The first reading, responsorial psalm, and second reading from Year A (Isaiah 42:1-4, 6-7; Psalm 29:1-2, 3-4, 3, 9-10; and Acts 10:34-38) may also be used.

FIRST READING *(Isaiah 40:1-5, 9-11)*

Comfort, give comfort to my people,
    says your God.
Speak tenderly to Jerusalem, and proclaim to her
    that her service is at an end,
    her guilt is expiated;
indeed, she has received from the hand of the LORD
    double for all her sins.

    A voice cries out:
In the desert prepare the way of the LORD!
    Make straight in the wasteland a highway for our God!
Every valley shall be filled in,
    every mountain and hill shall be made low;
the rugged land shall be made a plain,
    the rough country, a broad valley.
Then the glory of the LORD shall be revealed,
    and all people shall see it together;
    for the mouth of the LORD has spoken.

Go up on to a high mountain,
    Zion,* herald of glad tidings;
cry out at the top of your voice,
    Jerusalem, herald of good news!
Fear not to cry out
    and say to the cities of Judah:

Here is your God!
Here comes with power
the Lord GOD,
who rules by a strong arm;
here is his reward with him,
his recompense before him.
Like a shepherd he feeds his flock;
in his arms he gathers the lambs,
carrying them in his bosom,
and leading the ewes with care.

The word of the Lord. *Thanks be to God.*

RESPONSORIAL PSALM *(Psalm 104:1b-2, 3-4, 24-25, 27-28, 29-30)*
R. **O bless the Lord, my soul.**

O LORD, my God, you are great indeed!
You are clothed with majesty and glory,
robed in light as with a cloak.
You have spread out the heavens like a tent-cloth; R.
You have constructed your palace upon the waters.
You make the clouds your chariot;
you travel on the wings of the wind.
You make the winds your messengers,
and flaming fire your ministers. R.
How manifold are your works, O LORD!
In wisdom you have wrought them all—
the earth is full of your creatures;
the sea also, great and wide,
in which are schools without number
of living things both small and great. R.

They look to you to give them food in due time.
When you give it to them, they gather it;
when you open your hand, they are filled with good things. ℟.
If you take away their breath, they perish and return to the dust.
When you send forth your spirit, they are created,
and you renew the face of the earth. ℟.

SECOND READING *(Titus 2:11-14; 3:4-7)*

Beloved: The grace of God has appeared, saving all and training us to reject godless ways and worldly desires and to live temperately, justly, and devoutly in this age, as we await the blessed hope, the appearance of the glory of our great God and savior Jesus Christ, who gave himself for us to deliver us from all lawlessness and to cleanse for himself a people as his own, eager to do what is good.

When the kindness and generous love
    of God our savior appeared,
not because of any righteous deeds we had done
    but because of his mercy,
he saved us through the bath of rebirth
    and renewal by the Holy Spirit,
whom he richly poured out on us
    through Jesus Christ our savior,
so that we might be justified by his grace
    and become heirs in hope of eternal life.

The word of the Lord. ***Thanks be to God.***

ALLELUIA *(See Luke 3:16)*
Alleluia, alleluia. John said: One mightier than I is coming; he will baptize you with the Holy Spirit and with fire. *Alleluia, alleluia.*

GOSPEL *(Luke 3:15-16, 21-22)*

A reading from the holy Gospel according to Luke.
Glory to you, O Lord.

The people were filled with expectation, and all were asking in their hearts whether John might be the Christ. John answered them all, saying, "I am **baptizing you with water,**✝ but one mightier than I is coming. I am not worthy to loosen the thongs of his sandals. He will baptize you with the Holy Spirit and fire."

After all the people had been baptized and Jesus also had been baptized and was praying, heaven was opened and the Holy Spirit descended upon him in bodily form like a dove. And a voice came from heaven, "You are my beloved Son; with you I am well pleased."

The Gospel of the Lord. *Praise to you, Lord Jesus Christ.*

PROFESSION OF FAITH *(page 13)*

PRAYER OF THE FAITHFUL

PREPARATION OF GIFTS *(page 16)*

PRAYER OVER THE OFFERINGS

Accept, O Lord, the offerings
we have brought to honor the revealing of your beloved Son,
so that the oblation of your faithful
may be transformed into the sacrifice of him
who willed in his compassion
to wash away the sins of the world.
Who lives and reigns for ever and ever. *Amen.*

PREFACE: THE BAPTISM OF THE LORD
It is truly right and just, our duty and our salvation,
always and everywhere to give you thanks,
Lord, holy Father, almighty and eternal God.

For in the waters of the Jordan
you revealed with signs and wonders a new Baptism,
so that through the voice that came down from heaven
we might come to believe in your Word dwelling among us,
and by the Spirit's descending in the likeness of a dove
we might know that Christ your Servant
has been anointed with the oil of gladness
and sent to bring the good news to the poor.

And so, with the Powers of heaven,
we worship you constantly on earth,
and before your majesty
without end we acclaim:
Holy, Holy, Holy Lord God of hosts... *(page 35)*

● TAKING A CLOSER LOOK ●

✚ **Baptizing you with water** Baptism means to immerse or wash in water and so becomes a natural sign for ritual purity or holiness. In Judaism, there were many ceremonial washings, either in preparation for celebrating a ritual or as part of a cleansing rite within a ritual. John the Baptist uses a baptism of repentance to symbolize one's desire to put off sinful ways and live as God wants. But for the Christian community, going under the baptismal waters also signified a death to one's whole former life and an emergence into new life in the risen Christ. (Also see **Baptized with the Holy Spirit**, page 374).

COMMUNION ANTIPHON *(John 1:32, 34)*

Behold the One of whom John said: I have seen and testified
that this is the Son of God.

PRAYER AFTER COMMUNION

Nourished with these sacred gifts,
we humbly entreat your mercy, O Lord,
that, faithfully listening to your Only Begotten Son,
we may be your children in name and in truth.
Through Christ our Lord. *Amen.*

BLESSING & DISMISSAL *(page 56)* ❖

❖ RESPONDING TO THE WORD ❖

At his baptism, God
calls Jesus a "beloved
Son."

➲ *How can I thank
God for making me a
beloved child, too?*

Isaiah tells us that
God is like a shep-
herd who gathers the
lambs in his arms.

➲ *What part of my
life shall I entrust to
God's strong arms
today?*

Luke tells us that the
people were filled
with expectation for
the coming of the
Messiah.

➲ *What fills my
heart with expectation
today?*

January 20

Using our gifts for good

What a fizzle the wedding feast might have been had Jesus not intervened! In today's gospel, we see Jesus save the couple's dignity by providing wine when they had run out. Jesus overcomes his reluctance to reveal himself at that moment, and he is exceedingly generous with the quality and quantity of the wine he contributes.

Indeed, Jesus is concerned for the dignity of every person. As I write this, I have come from a Sunday Mass where a newly arrived refugee family was welcomed—a father, mother, and three young girls. Each one of the five said a simple "Thank you" to the congregation which has given generously to help them through their first year in our country.

They were migrants first, fleeing their home in desperation. I tried to imagine what they must have gone through and left behind, the patience and hope they surely needed during their long wait in a camp, and now the courage they will need to settle in a new country and learn a new language.

St. Paul reminds us that we are given the gifts of the Spirit to use for the common good. Today, on the World Day of Prayer for Migrants and Refugees, may we resolve to use our gifts to give others their dignity.

■ BETH PORTER

ENTRANCE ANTIPHON *(Psalm 66 [65]:4)*

All the earth shall bow down before you, O God, and shall sing to you, shall sing to your name, O Most High!

INTRODUCTORY RITES *(page 10)*

COLLECT

Almighty ever-living God,
who govern all things,
both in heaven and on earth,
mercifully hear the pleading of your people
and bestow your peace on our times.
Through our Lord Jesus Christ, your Son,
who lives and reigns with you in the unity of the Holy Spirit,
one God, for ever and ever. *Amen.*

FIRST READING *(Isaiah 62:1-5)*

For Zion's* sake I will not be silent,
for Jerusalem's sake I will not be quiet,
until her vindication shines forth like the dawn
and her victory like a burning torch.

Nations shall behold your vindication,
and all the kings your glory;
you shall be called by a new name
pronounced by the mouth of the LORD.
You shall be a glorious crown in the hand of the LORD,
a royal diadem held by your God.
No more shall people call you "Forsaken,"
or your land "Desolate,"
but you shall be called "My Delight,"
and your land "Espoused."

For the LORD delights in you
and makes your land his spouse.
As a young man marries a virgin,
your Builder shall marry you;
and as a bridegroom rejoices in his bride
so shall your God rejoice in you.

The word of the Lord. *Thanks be to God.*

RESPONSORIAL PSALM *(Psalm 96:1–2, 2–3, 7–8, 9–10)*
℟ **Proclaim his marvelous deeds to all the nations.**

Sing to the LORD a new song;
sing to the LORD, all you lands.
Sing to the LORD; bless his name. ℟
Announce his salvation, day after day.
Tell his glory among the nations;
among all peoples, his wondrous deeds. ℟
Give to the LORD, you families of nations,
give to the LORD glory and praise;
give to the LORD the glory due his name! ℟
Worship the LORD in holy attire.
Tremble before him, all the earth;
say among the nations: The LORD is king.
He governs the peoples with equity. ℟

SECOND READING *(1 Corinthians 12:4–11)*

Brothers and sisters: There are different kinds of **spiritual
gifts**✠ but the same Spirit; there are different forms of service
but the same Lord; there are different workings but the same
God who produces all of them in everyone. To each individual
the manifestation of the Spirit is given for some benefit. To one is
given through the Spirit the expression of wisdom; to another, the

expression of knowledge according to the same Spirit; to another, faith by the same Spirit; to another, gifts of healing by the one Spirit; to another, mighty deeds; to another, prophecy; to another, discernment of spirits; to another, varieties of tongues; to another, interpretation of tongues. But one and the same Spirit produces all of these, distributing them individually to each person as he wishes.

The word of the Lord. *Thanks be to God.*

ALLELUIA *(See 2 Thessalonians 2:14)*
Alleluia, alleluia. God has called us through the Gospel to possess the glory of our Lord Jesus Christ. *Alleluia, alleluia.*

GOSPEL *(John 2:1–11)*
A reading from the holy Gospel according to John.
Glory to you, O Lord.

There was a wedding at Cana in Galilee, and the mother of Jesus was there. Jesus and his disciples were also invited to the wedding. When the wine ran short, the mother of Jesus said to him, "They have no wine." And Jesus said to her, "Woman, how does your concern affect me? My hour has not yet come." His mother said to the servers, "Do whatever he tells you." Now there were six stone water jars there for Jewish ceremonial washings, each holding twenty to thirty gallons. Jesus told them, "Fill the jars with water." So they filled them to the brim. Then he told them, "Draw some out now and take it to the headwaiter." So they took it. And when the headwaiter tasted the water that had become wine, without knowing where it came from—although the servers who had drawn the water knew—, the headwaiter called the bridegroom and said to him, "Everyone serves good wine first, and then when people have drunk freely, an inferior one; but you have kept the good wine until now." Jesus did this as the beginning of his signs at Cana in Galilee and so revealed his glory, and his disciples began to believe in him.

The Gospel of the Lord. *Praise to you, Lord Jesus Christ.*

PROFESSION OF FAITH *(page 13)*

PRAYER OF THE FAITHFUL

PREPARATION OF GIFTS *(page 16)*

PRAYER OVER THE OFFERINGS
Grant us, O Lord, we pray,
that we may participate worthily in these mysteries,
for whenever the memorial of this sacrifice is celebrated
the work of our redemption is accomplished.
Through Christ our Lord. *Amen.*

• TAKING A CLOSER LOOK •

✚ **Spiritual gifts** The Corinthian community was torn by dissension over the nature, apportionment, and use of "spiritual gifts" or spiritual matters (Greek, *pneumatika*). Paul chooses to use the word *charismata* (literally, "gifts of grace") to emphasize that these are free gifts given for service to the community and not just as the possessions of certain individuals for their private enjoyment. The gifts are complementary and meant for the common good. The list of gifts in today's second reading is not exhaustive, for other lists differ (see also 1 Corinthians 12:28-30; Romans 12:6-8; and Ephesians 4:11).

PREFACE *(Sundays in Ordinary Time, pages 28–32)*

COMMUNION ANTIPHON *(Cf. Psalm 23 [22]:5)*
You have prepared a table before me, and how precious is the chalice that quenches my thirst.

Or *(1 John 4:16)*
We have come to know and to believe in the love that God has for us.

PRAYER AFTER COMMUNION
Pour on us, O Lord, the Spirit of your love,
and in your kindness
make those you have nourished
by this one heavenly Bread
one in mind and heart.
Through Christ our Lord. *Amen.*

BLESSING & DISMISSAL *(page 56)* ✤

• RESPONDING TO THE WORD •

Isaiah knows that God delights in us.	Paul recognizes that each of us has special gifts.	Jesus' words transform the ordinary into the extraordinary.
➲ *How have I experienced God's delight in me?*	➲ *What gifts have I been given and how do I use them for good?*	➲ *How have Jesus' words changed my life from the ordinary and expected to the extraordinary and unexpected?*

January 27

Accepting the news we receive

Sharing important news with family and friends can give birth to a feeling greater than the news itself. Bringing news back to our home communities is a more personal celebration of what has been achieved and a recognition of who has helped along the way.

Perhaps this connection to home is what led Jesus to choose Nazareth to proclaim the good news. At this point in the gospel, Jesus was already becoming well known in Galilee for his teaching. The people of Nazareth gathered at the synagogue to see what the carpenter's son may have to say to them, to his friends and family.

Think of a time when someone came to share exciting news with you. What was your response? Conversely, think of a time when someone came to share something that was upsetting or unexpected. Did you respond differently?

Although it can be challenging to always accept the news we receive, we should ask ourselves why that person chose us as the recipient and what our response means to them. 'Tis the season for New Year's resolutions. This year, resolve to show support and acceptance to those who bring us their news.

■ JULIANA DEUTSCHER

ENTRANCE ANTIPHON *(Cf. Psalm 96 [95]:1, 6)*

O sing a new song to the Lord; sing to the Lord, all the earth. In his presence are majesty and splendor, strength and honor in his holy place.

INTRODUCTORY RITES *(page 10)*

COLLECT

Almighty ever-living God,
direct our actions according to your good pleasure,
that in the name of your beloved Son
we may abound in good works.
Through our Lord Jesus Christ, your Son,
who lives and reigns with you in the unity of the Holy Spirit,
one God, for ever and ever. ***Amen.***

FIRST READING *(Nehemiah 8:2–4a, 5–6, 8–10)*

Ezra the priest brought **the law**✝ before the assembly, which consisted of men, women, and those children old enough to understand. Standing at one end of the open place that was before the Water Gate, he read out of the book from daybreak till midday, in the presence of the men, the women, and those children old enough to understand; and all the people listened attentively to the book of the law. Ezra the scribe stood on a wooden platform that had been made for the occasion. He opened the scroll so that all the people might see it—for he was standing higher up than any of the people—; and, as he opened it, all the people rose. Ezra blessed the LORD, the great God, and all the people, their hands raised high, answered, "Amen, amen!" Then they bowed down and prostrated themselves before the LORD, their faces to the ground. Ezra read plainly from the book of the law of God, interpreting it so that all could understand what was read. Then Nehemiah, that is, His Excellency, and Ezra the priest-scribe and the Levites* who were instructing the people said to all the people: "Today is holy to the LORD your God. Do not be sad, and do not weep"—for all the people were weeping as they heard the words of the law. He said further: "Go, eat rich foods and drink sweet drinks, and allot portions to those who had nothing prepared; for today is holy to our LORD. Do not be saddened this day, for rejoicing in the LORD must be your strength!"

The word of the Lord. *Thanks be to God.*

RESPONSORIAL PSALM *(Psalm 19:8, 9, 10, 15)*
R̸ **Your words, Lord, are Spirit and life.**

The law† of the LORD is perfect,
    refreshing the soul;
the decree of the LORD is trustworthy,
    giving wisdom to the simple. R̸
The precepts of the LORD are right,
    rejoicing the heart;
the command of the LORD is clear,
    enlightening the eye. R̸
The fear of the LORD is pure,
    enduring forever;
the ordinances of the LORD are true,
    all of them just. R̸
Let the words of my mouth and the thought of my heart
    find favor before you,
O LORD, my rock and my redeemer. R̸

SECOND READING *(1 Corinthians 12:12-30)*

For the shorter version, omit the indented parts in brackets.

Brothers and sisters: As a body is one though it has many parts, and all the parts of the body, though many, are one body, so also Christ. For in one Spirit we were all baptized into one body, whether Jews or Greeks, slaves or free persons, and we were all given to drink of one Spirit.

Now the body is not a single part, but many.

[If a foot should say, "Because I am not a hand I do not belong to the body," it does not for this reason belong any less to the body. Or if an ear should say, "Because I am not an eye I do not belong to the body," it does not for this reason belong any less to the body. If the whole body were an eye, where would the hearing be? If the whole body were hearing, where would the sense of smell be? But as it is, God placed the parts, each one of them, in the body as he intended. If they were all one part, where would the body be? But as it is, there are many parts, yet one body. The eye cannot say to the hand, "I do not need you," nor again the head to the feet, "I do not need you." Indeed, the parts of the body that seem to be weaker are all the more necessary, and those parts of the body that we consider less honorable we surround with greater honor, and our less presentable parts are treated with greater propriety, whereas our more presentable parts do not need this. But God has so constructed the body as to give greater honor to a part that is without it, so that there may be no division in the body, but that the parts may have the same concern for one another. If one part suffers, all the parts suffer with it; if one part is honored, all the parts share its joy.

Now] you are Christ's body, and individually parts of it. [Some people God has designated in the church to be, first, apostles; second, prophets; third, teachers; then, mighty deeds; then gifts of healing, assistance, administration, and varieties of tongues. Are all apostles? Are all prophets? Are all teachers? Do all work mighty deeds? Do all have gifts of healing? Do all speak in tongues? Do all interpret?]

The word of the Lord. *Thanks be to God.*

ALLELUIA *(See Luke 4:18)*
Alleluia, alleluia. The Lord sent me to bring glad tidings to the poor, and to proclaim liberty to captives. *Alleluia, alleluia.*

GOSPEL *(Luke 1:1–4; 4:14–21)*
A reading from the holy Gospel according to Luke.
Glory to you, O Lord.

Since many have undertaken to compile a narrative of the events that have been fulfilled among us, just as those who were eyewitnesses from the beginning and ministers of the word have handed them down to us, I too have decided, after investigating everything accurately anew, to write it down in an orderly sequence for you, most excellent Theophilus, so that you may realize the certainty of the teachings you have received.

Jesus returned to Galilee in the power of the Spirit, and news of him spread throughout the whole region. He taught in their synagogues and was praised by all.

He came to Nazareth, where he had grown up, and went according to his custom into the synagogue on the sabbath day. He stood up to read and was handed a scroll of the prophet Isaiah. He unrolled the scroll and found the passage where it was written:

The Spirit of the Lord is upon me,
because he has anointed me
to bring glad tidings to the poor.

He has sent me to proclaim liberty to captives
and recovery of sight to the blind,
to let the oppressed go free,
and to proclaim a year acceptable to the Lord.

The Gospel of the Lord. ***Praise to you, Lord Jesus Christ.***

PROFESSION OF FAITH *(page 13)*

PRAYER OF THE FAITHFUL

PREPARATION OF GIFTS *(page 16)*

PRAYER OVER THE OFFERINGS
Accept our offerings, O Lord, we pray,
and in sanctifying them
grant that they may profit us for salvation.
Through Christ our Lord. ***Amen.***

PREFACE *(Sundays in Ordinary Time, pages 28–32)*

• TAKING A CLOSER LOOK •

✛ **The law** The Hebrew Law (*Torah*, instruction) consisted of the first five books of the Old Testament (Genesis, Exodus, Leviticus, Numbers, and Deuteronomy) that tell of God's search for an appropriate covenant partner. Jewish scholars combed these books to discover all of the specific commands given by God and found 613. These became the foundation of their life in community. These laws, although difficult to keep in their entirety, were not considered a burden (as we so often think), but rather as a precious gift because the people knew what God wanted and no longer had to guess what to do in order to please God.

COMMUNION ANTIPHON *(Cf. Psalm 34 [33]:6)*

Look toward the Lord and be radiant; let your faces not be abashed.

Or *(John 8:12)*

I am the light of the world, says the Lord; whoever follows me will not walk in darkness, but will have the light of life.

PRAYER AFTER COMMUNION

Grant, we pray, almighty God,
that, receiving the grace
by which you bring us to new life,
we may always glory in your gift.
Through Christ our Lord. *Amen.*

BLESSING & DISMISSAL *(page 56)* ✤

✦ RESPONDING TO THE WORD ✦

The people adopt a reverent attitude when God's word is read to them.

➡ *What might I do to be more reverent during the readings at Mass?*

Paul knows that we all are joined together into Christ's body.

➡ *When am I most aware of this Christian unity?*

God's Spirit empowers Jesus to proclaim God's presence and release persons from what binds them.

➡ *From what do I want Jesus to free me today?*

February 3

Prophets for the kingdom

In today's gospel, the people of Nazareth refused to renounce their possessive attitude toward Jesus. He was bitterly criticized because he demonstrated great openness of heart, particularly toward people on the peripheries of society. The gospel story shows how difficult it is to attain a universal vision. When we face someone like Jesus, someone with a generous heart, a wide vision, and a great spirit, our reactions are often filled with jealousy, selfishness, and meanness of spirit.

His own people couldn't recognize the holiness of Jesus, because they had never really accepted their own. They were suffering from a form of blindness. They couldn't honor Jesus' relationship with God because they had never fully explored their own sense of belonging to God. Until we see ourselves as people beloved of God, miracles will be scarce, and the prophets and messengers who rise among us will struggle to be heard and accepted for who they are.

Jesus was called to break boundaries and take God's message of salvation to unexpected people and unexpected places. Through our baptism, we are called to be prophets for the kingdom of God. We will encounter many reactions from those to whom we are sent, not all of them positive. Unswerving dedication, bold courage, and deep biblical hope must be our trademarks.

❖ FR. THOMAS ROSICA, CSB

ENTRANCE ANTIPHON *(Psalm 106 [105]:47)*
Save us, O Lord our God! And gather us from the
nations, to give thanks to your holy name, and
make it our glory to praise you.

INTRODUCTORY RITES *(page 10)*

COLLECT
Grant us, Lord our God,
that we may honor you with all our mind,
and love everyone in truth of heart.
Through our Lord Jesus Christ, your Son,
who lives and reigns with you in the unity of the Holy Spirit,
one God, for ever and ever. *Amen.*

FIRST READING *(Jeremiah 1:4-5, 17-19)*
The word of the LORD✝ came to me, saying:
    Before I formed you in the womb I knew you,
        before you were born I dedicated you,
    a prophet to the nations I appointed you.

But do you gird your loins;
    stand up and tell them
    all that I command you.
Be not crushed on their account,
    as though I would leave you crushed before them;
for it is I this day
    who have made you a fortified city,
a pillar of iron, a wall of brass,
    against the whole land:
against Judah's kings and princes,
    against its priests and people.

They will fight against you but not prevail over you,
    for I am with you to deliver you, says the LORD.

The word of the Lord. ***Thanks be to God.***

RESPONSORIAL PSALM *(Psalm 71:1-2, 3-4, 5-6, 15, 17)*
℟ **I will sing of your salvation.**

In you, O **LORD**,✝ I take refuge;
    let me never be put to shame.
In your justice rescue me, and deliver me;
    incline your ear to me, and save me. ℟
Be my rock of refuge,
    a stronghold to give me safety,
    for you are my rock and my fortress.
O my God, rescue me from the hand of the wicked. ℟
For you are my hope, O **LORD**;
    my trust, O God, from my youth.
On you I depend from birth;
    from my mother's womb you are my strength. ℟
My mouth shall declare your justice,
    day by day your salvation.
O God, you have taught me from my youth,
    and till the present I proclaim your wondrous deeds. ℟

SECOND READING *(1 Corinthians 12:31–13:13)*
The shorter version begins at the asterisks.

Brothers and sisters: Strive eagerly for the greatest spiritual
gifts. But I shall show you a still more excellent way.
    If I speak in human and angelic tongues, but do not have love,
I am a resounding gong or a clashing cymbal. And if I have the gift

of prophecy, and comprehend all mysteries and all knowledge; if I have all faith so as to move mountains, but do not have love, I am nothing. If I give away everything I own, and if I hand my body over so that I may boast, but do not have love, I gain nothing.

* * *

(Brothers and sisters:) Love is patient, love is kind. It is not jealous, it is not pompous, it is not inflated, it is not rude, it does not seek its own interests, it is not quick-tempered, it does not brood over injury, it does not rejoice over wrongdoing but rejoices with the truth. It bears all things, believes all things, hopes all things, endures all things.

Love never fails. If there are prophecies, they will be brought to nothing; if tongues, they will cease; if knowledge, it will be brought to nothing. For we know partially and we prophesy partially, but when the perfect comes, the partial will pass away. When I was a child, I used to talk as a child, think as a child, reason as a child; when I became a man, I put aside childish things. At present we see indistinctly, as in a mirror, but then face to face. At present I know partially; then I shall know fully, as I am fully known. So faith, hope, love remain, these three; but the greatest of these is love.

The word of the Lord. *Thanks be to God.*

ALLELUIA *(Luke 4:18)*
Alleluia, alleluia. The Lord sent me to bring glad tidings to the poor, to proclaim liberty to captives. *Alleluia, alleluia.*

GOSPEL *(Luke 4:21–30)*

A reading from the holy Gospel according to Luke.
Glory to you, O Lord.

Jesus began speaking in the synagogue, saying: "Today this Scripture passage is fulfilled in your hearing." And all spoke highly of him and were amazed at the gracious words that came from his mouth. They also asked, "Isn't this the son of Joseph?" He said to them, "Surely you will quote me this proverb, 'Physician, cure yourself,' and say, 'Do here in your native place the things that we heard were done in Capernaum.*'" And he said, "Amen, I say to you, no prophet is accepted in his own native place. Indeed, I tell you, there were many widows in Israel in the days of Elijah when the sky was closed for three and a half years and a severe famine spread over the entire land. It was to none of these that Elijah was sent, but only to a widow in Zarephath* in the land of Sidon.* Again, there were many lepers in Israel during the time of Elisha the prophet; yet not one of them was cleansed, but only Naaman the Syrian." When the people in the synagogue heard this, they were all filled with fury. They rose up, drove him out of the town, and led him to the brow of the hill on which their town had been built, to hurl him down headlong. But Jesus passed through the midst of them and went away.

The Gospel of the Lord. *Praise to you, Lord Jesus Christ.*

PROFESSION OF FAITH *(page 13)*

PRAYER OF THE FAITHFUL

PREPARATION OF GIFTS *(page 16)*

PRAYER OVER THE OFFERINGS

O Lord, we bring to your altar
these offerings of our service:
be pleased to receive them, we pray,
and transform them
into the Sacrament of our redemption.
Through Christ our Lord. *Amen.*

PREFACE *(Sundays in Ordinary Time, pages 28–32)*

❖ TAKING A CLOSER LOOK ❖

✚ **LORD** The New American Bible, used for our Sunday Mass readings, uses LORD in small capital letters to indicate the sacred name of God revealed to Moses and the Israelites—*Yahweh*. This choice is appropriate for two reasons. First, LORD has the same number of letters as God's sacred name: since the Hebrew language wrote only the consonants and not the vowels, God's name was written YHWH (in English). Since God's name was so sacred, the Jews did not speak it aloud but would instead say *Adonai*, the Hebrew word for Lord. In the Bible, when God is addressed as "Lord GOD" (Adonai YHWH), GOD is put in small capital letters.

COMMUNION ANTIPHON *(Cf. Psalm 31 [30]:17-18)*

Let your face shine on your servant. Save me in your merciful love. O Lord, let me never be put to shame, for I call on you.

Or *(Matthew 5:3-4)*

Blessed are the poor in spirit, for theirs is the Kingdom of Heaven. Blessed are the meek, for they shall possess the land.

PRAYER AFTER COMMUNION

Nourished by these redeeming gifts,
we pray, O Lord,
that through this help to eternal salvation
true faith may ever increase.
Through Christ our Lord. *Amen.*

BLESSING & DISMISSAL *(page 56)* ✠

• RESPONDING TO THE WORD •

God calls Jeremiah to a life of witness and promises to support him in times of difficulty.

➡ *When has God helped me when I felt discouraged?*

Paul knows that love is the mark of a genuine Christian life.

➡ *Which of the demands of love do I most need to work on today?*

Jesus' neighbors cannot accept his openness to those not like them.

➡ *How have I been reluctant to recognize God's love for those who are not like me?*

**FEB
10**

February 10

Have faith in love!

I can hear myself in Peter's resigned words to Jesus: "We have worked all night long but have caught nothing. Yet if you say so, I will let down the nets." I have been doing what you are suggesting and it has not worked. Fine, I'll do it again.

So much of the spiritual life is about devoted repetition of the same actions, which sometimes seem to have no effect. I pray the same words day after day and year after year, and I do not see any change. I speak kindly and seem to be ignored. I mess up and say sorry and try to change, and then I mess up again.

On a fishing boat with seasoned fishermen, Jesus' advice is almost laughable: as if they had not thought to put down the nets! What God whispers into our souls is often not the shocking instruction to build an ark, but the ordinary invitation to try love again. Walk beside your people and laugh with them. Respond to those who ask you for help—again. Make something for dinner and share a meal.

And then, when all that habitual love produces something unexpectedly beautiful, do I respond like Peter? *Lord, forgive me for my doubt that loving again will actually change the world. Let me choose faith in love—again.*

■ **LEAH PERRAULT**

ENTRANCE ANTIPHON *(Psalm 95 [94]:6–7)*

O come, let us worship God and bow low before the God who made us, for he is the Lord our God.

INTRODUCTORY RITES *(page 10)*

COLLECT

Keep your family safe, O Lord, with unfailing care,
that, relying solely on the hope of heavenly grace,
they may be defended always by your protection.
Through our Lord Jesus Christ, your Son,
who lives and reigns with you in the unity of the Holy Spirit,
one God, for ever and ever. *Amen.*

FIRST READING *(Isaiah 6:1–2a, 3–8)*

In the year King Uzziah* died, I saw the Lord seated on a high and lofty throne, with the train of his garment filling the temple. Seraphim were stationed above.

They cried one to the other, "**Holy, holy, holy**✝ is the LORD of hosts! All the earth is filled with his glory!" At the sound of that cry, the frame of the door shook and the house was filled with smoke.

Then I said, "Woe is me, I am doomed! For I am a man of unclean lips, living among a people of unclean lips; yet my eyes have seen the King, the LORD of hosts!" Then one of the seraphim flew to me, holding an ember that he had taken with tongs from the altar.

He touched my mouth with it, and said, "See, now that this has touched your lips, your wickedness is removed, your sin purged."

Then I heard the voice of the LORD saying, "Whom shall I send? Who will go for us?" "Here I am," I said; "send me!"

The word of the Lord. *Thanks be to God.*

RESPONSORIAL PSALM *(Psalm 138:1-2, 2-3, 4-5, 7-8)*

℟ **In the sight of the angels I will sing your praises, Lord.**

I will give thanks to you, O LORD, with all my heart,
    for you have heard the words of my mouth;
    in the presence of the angels I will sing your praise;
I will worship at your holy temple
    and give thanks to your name. ℟
Because of your kindness and your truth;
    for you have made great above all things
    your name and your promise.
When I called, you answered me;
    you built up strength within me. ℟
All the kings of the earth shall give thanks to you, O LORD,
    when they hear the words of your mouth;
and they shall sing of the ways of the LORD:
    "Great is the glory of the LORD." ℟
Your right hand saves me.
    The LORD will complete what he has done for me;
your kindness, O LORD, endures forever;
    forsake not the work of your hands. ℟

SECOND READING *(1 Corinthians 15:1-11)*
For the shorter version, omit the indented parts in brackets.

[I am reminding you, brothers and sisters, of the gospel I preached to you, which you indeed received and in which you also stand. Through it you are also being saved, if you hold fast to the word I preached to you, unless you believed in vain. For]
(Brothers and sisters,) I handed on to you as of first importance what I also received: that Christ died for our sins in accordance

with the Scriptures; that he was buried; that he was raised on the third day in accordance with the Scriptures; that he appeared to Cephas,* then to the Twelve. After that, he appeared to more than five hundred brothers at once, most of whom are still living, though some have fallen asleep. After that he appeared to James, then to all the apostles. Last of all, as to one born abnormally, he appeared to me.

[For I am the least of the apostles, not fit to be called an apostle, because I persecuted the church of God. But by the grace of God I am what I am, and his grace to me has not been ineffective. Indeed, I have toiled harder than all of them; not I, however, but the grace of God that is with me.]

Therefore, whether it be I or they, so we preach and so you believed.

The word of the Lord. *Thanks be to God.*

ALLELUIA *(Matthew 4:19)*
Alleluia, alleluia. Come after me and I will make you fishers of men. *Alleluia, alleluia.*

GOSPEL *(Luke 5:1–11)*
A reading from the holy Gospel according to Luke.
Glory to you, O Lord.

While the crowd was pressing in on Jesus and listening to the word of God, he was standing by the Lake of Gennesaret. He saw two boats there alongside the lake; the fishermen had disembarked and were washing their nets. Getting into one of the boats, the one belonging to Simon, he asked him to put out a short distance from the shore. Then he sat down and taught the crowds from the boat. After he had finished speaking, he said to Simon, "Put out into deep water and lower your nets for a catch." Simon said in reply, "Master, we have worked hard all night and have caught nothing, but at your command I will lower the nets." When they had done this, they caught a great number of fish and their nets were tearing. They signaled to their partners in the other boat to come to help them. They came and filled both boats so that the boats were in danger of sinking. When Simon Peter saw this, he fell at the knees of Jesus and said, "Depart from me, Lord, for I am a sinful man." For astonishment at the catch of fish they had made seized him and all those with him, and likewise James and John, the sons of Zebedee, who were partners of Simon. Jesus said to Simon, "Do not be afraid; from now on you will be catching men." When they brought their boats to the shore, they left everything and followed him.

The Gospel of the Lord. *Praise to you, Lord Jesus Christ.*

PROFESSION OF FAITH *(page 13)*

PRAYER OF THE FAITHFUL

PREPARATION OF GIFTS *(page 16)*

PRAYER OVER THE OFFERINGS
O Lord our God,
who once established these created things
to sustain us in our frailty,
grant, we pray,
that they may become for us now
the Sacrament of eternal life.
Through Christ our Lord. *Amen.*

PREFACE *(Sundays in Ordinary Time, pages 28–32)*

COMMUNION ANTIPHON *(Cf. Psalm 107 [106]:8-9)*

Let them thank the Lord for his mercy, his wonders for the children of men, for he satisfies the thirsty soul, and the hungry he fills with good things.

Or *(Matthew 5:5-6)*

Blessed are those who mourn, for they shall be consoled. Blessed are those who hunger and thirst for righteousness, for they shall have their fill.

 ✤ TAKING A CLOSER LOOK ✤

✛ **Holy, holy, holy** Holiness describes the unique quality that makes God divine and thus wholly "other" or separate from all created realities. Strictly speaking, human persons like priests or the community of Israel, and created objects like the Jerusalem temple or altars or sacrificial offerings, only become holy through *contact with God.* God's presence transforms the person or place or thing into something sacred. As Isaiah demonstrates, this quality of holiness demands reverent fear, for to come into contact with God is dangerous because such contact changes whatever is touched.

PRAYER AFTER COMMUNION

O God, who have willed that we be partakers
in the one Bread and the one Chalice,
grant us, we pray, so to live
that, made one in Christ,
we may joyfully bear fruit
for the salvation of the world.
Through Christ our Lord. *Amen.*

BLESSING & DISMISSAL *(page 56)* ✦

● RESPONDING TO THE WORD ●

Isaiah learned that God's holy presence makes us more aware of our lack of holiness.

➡ *From what sinfulness do I want to be cleansed today?*

Paul lists a chain of witnesses to the resurrection to extend it to himself.

➡ *What names would I add to make the chain extend to me?*

Jesus invites Peter to use his fishing skills to bring others to God.

➡ *How can I use my skills to help others find God today?*

February 17

A glimpse of heaven

The world and all its pleasures are temporary. As tempting as these worldly realities are, we are called to conform ourselves to Christ's vision of the good life. In today's gospel, Jesus gives us a glimpse of heaven, and it is a vision which brings both consolation and warning.

In Luke's account of the beatitudes, we witness how Jesus heals all those gathered in body and soul while he teaches the multitudes what it means to live in friendship with God.

Jesus tells of the blessings we can expect, but he doesn't stop there. For those who remain attached to wealth, physical comforts, and the good opinion of others, Jesus reminds us these things will not satisfy the deepest desires of the human heart. Our continued attachment to these things will only cause us misery in this life and the next.

In that light, it is worth considering the words of the prophet Jeremiah from today's first reading. Where do we put our faith? Is our trust in the Lord, or elsewhere? Who (or what) commands our loyalty?

Let us give thanks to God for the wisdom and transformative power of Christ. Through God's grace may we persevere in following Jesus' example, focused on a vision of what truly counts.

■ CHERIDAN SANDERS

ENTRANCE ANTIPHON *(Cf. Psalm 31 [30]:3-4)*
Be my protector, O God, a mighty stronghold to
save me. For you are my rock, my stronghold! Lead
me, guide me, for the sake of your name.

INTRODUCTORY RITES *(page 10)*

COLLECT
O God, who teach us that you abide
in hearts that are just and true,
grant that we may be so fashioned by your grace
as to become a dwelling pleasing to you.
Through our Lord Jesus Christ, your Son,
who lives and reigns with you in the unity of the Holy Spirit,
one God, for ever and ever. ***Amen.***

FIRST READING *(Jeremiah 17:5-8)*

Thus says the LORD:
Cursed is the one who trusts in human beings,
who seeks his strength in flesh,
whose heart turns away from the LORD.
He is like a barren bush in the desert
that enjoys no change of season,
but stands in a lava waste,
a salt and empty earth.
Blessed is the one who trusts in the LORD,
whose hope is the LORD.
He is like a tree planted beside the waters
that stretches out its roots to the stream:
it fears not the heat when it comes;
its leaves stay green;

in the year of drought it shows no distress,
but still bears fruit.

The word of the Lord. *Thanks be to God.*

RESPONSORIAL PSALM *(Psalm 1:1-2, 3, 4, 6)*
R̸ **Blessed are they who hope in the Lord.**

Blessed the man who follows not
the counsel of the wicked,
nor walks in the way of sinners,
nor sits in the company of the insolent,
but delights in the law of the LORD
and meditates on his law day and night. R̸

He is like a tree
planted near running water,
that yields its fruit in due season,
and whose leaves never fade.
Whatever he does, prospers. R̸

Not so the wicked, not so;
they are like chaff which the wind drives away.
For the LORD watches over the way of the just,
but the way of the wicked vanishes. R̸

SECOND READING *(1 Corinthians 15:12, 16-20)*

Brothers and sisters: If Christ is preached as raised from the
dead, how can some among you say there is no resurrection
of the dead? If the dead are not raised, neither has Christ been
raised, and if Christ has not been raised, your faith is vain; you
are still in your sins. Then those who have fallen asleep in Christ
have perished. If for this life only we have hoped in Christ, we
are the most pitiable people of all.

But now Christ has been raised from the dead, the firstfruits of those who have fallen asleep.

The word of the Lord. *Thanks be to God.*

ALLELUIA *(Luke 6:23ab)*
Alleluia, alleluia. Rejoice and be glad; your reward will be great in heaven. *Alleluia, alleluia.*

GOSPEL *(Luke 6:17, 20-26)*
A reading from the holy Gospel according to Luke.
Glory to you, O Lord.

Jesus came down with the Twelve and stood on a stretch of level ground with a great crowd of his disciples and a large number of the people from all Judea and Jerusalem and the coastal region of Tyre and Sidon. And raising his eyes toward his disciples he said:

"Blessed are you who are poor,
for the kingdom of God is yours.
Blessed are you who are now hungry,
for you will be satisfied.
Blessed are you who are now weeping,
for you will laugh.
Blessed are you when people hate you, and when they exclude and insult you, and denounce your name as evil on account of the Son of Man. Rejoice and leap for joy on that day! Behold, your reward will be great in heaven. For their ancestors treated the prophets in the same way. But woe to you who are rich, for you have received your consolation.
Woe to you who are filled now,
for you will be hungry.

Woe to you who laugh now,
for you will grieve and weep.
Woe to you when all speak well of you,
for their ancestors treated the false prophets in this way."

The Gospel of the Lord. *Praise to you, Lord Jesus Christ.*

PROFESSION OF FAITH *(page 13)*

PRAYER OF THE FAITHFUL

PREPARATION OF GIFTS *(page 16)*

PRAYER OVER THE OFFERINGS
May this oblation, O Lord, we pray,
cleanse and renew us
and may it become for those who do your will
the source of eternal reward.
Through Christ our Lord. *Amen.*

PREFACE *(Sundays in Ordinary Time, pages 28-32)*

● TAKING A CLOSER LOOK ●

✝ **The beatitudes** A beatitude (from the Latin *beatus*, meaning blessed or happy) identifies a person and gives the reason why he or she is blessed. In the Old Testament, the blessed are those who receive from God an earthly fulfillment of prosperity, offspring, and long life. In later Jewish writings, the blessings belong to those who will enter the final age of salvation. Jesus offers these future blessings now, for the kingdom is present in him. In his beatitudes (Matthew 5:1-2; Luke 6:20-23), Jesus reveals the characteristics of his followers who wish to enter his kingdom.

COMMUNION ANTIPHON *(Cf. Psalm 78 [77]:29-30)*
They ate and had their fill, and what they craved the Lord gave them; they were not disappointed in what they craved.

Or *(John 3:16)*
God so loved the world that he gave his Only Begotten Son, so that all who believe in him may not perish, but may have eternal life.

PRAYER AFTER COMMUNION
Having fed upon these heavenly delights,
we pray, O Lord,
that we may always long
for that food by which we truly live.
Through Christ our Lord. *Amen.*

BLESSING & DISMISSAL *(page 56)* ✦

✦ RESPONDING TO THE WORD ✦

Jeremiah encourages us to trust in God.

➡ *What fears make it hard for me to trust in God?*

Paul believes that what happened to Jesus in his resurrection will also happen to us.

➡ *How do Paul's words encourage me to believe?*

Jesus' beatitudes and woes reveal his values.

➡ *Which of the beatitudes or woes seems most important to me right now?*

February 24

Understanding and peace

Today's gospel, taken from Luke's version of the Sermon on the Mount, calls us to forgive our enemies. As a person passionate about social justice, I hear this Scripture calling me to also consider empathy and dialogue. Can we identify the humanity and the inherent dignity in those who do wrong to us or to others? Can we love them in a way that also works towards addressing these injustices?

To live and love this way can be difficult. It may be easier to see those who hurt ourselves or others as selfish or as intentionally harmful. Yet, that outlook fosters alienation and isolation instead of community and connection. The gospel recognizes the challenge present here, but encourages us to persist: "If you love those who love you, what credit is that to you? Even sinners love those who love them."

In this gospel, Jesus offers guidance that seems counterintuitive. In the same way, finding common ground with those who oppress others may also be counterintuitive, especially when we are tempted to be angry instead of loving. However, empathy enables us to engage in dialogue, change, and social justice. We can see examples of this in peace processes and efforts towards reconciliation in our country and throughout the world. When we come to a place of understanding, it may also be a place of peace.

■ LANDON TURLOCK

ENTRANCE ANTIPHON *(Psalm 13 [12]:6)*

O Lord, I trust in your merciful love. My heart will rejoice in your salvation. I will sing to the Lord who has been bountiful with me.

INTRODUCTORY RITES *(page 10)*

COLLECT

Grant, we pray, almighty God,
that, always pondering spiritual things,
we may carry out in both word and deed
that which is pleasing to you.
Through our Lord Jesus Christ, your Son,
who lives and reigns with you in the unity of the Holy Spirit,
one God, for ever and ever. *Amen.*

FIRST READING *(1 Samuel 26:2, 7-9, 12-13, 22-23)*

In those days, Saul went down to the desert of Ziph with three thousand picked men of Israel, to search for David in the desert of Ziph. So David and Abishai went among Saul's soldiers by night and found Saul lying asleep within the barricade, with his spear thrust into the ground at his head and Abner and his men sleeping around him.

Abishai whispered to David: "God has delivered your enemy into your grasp this day. Let me nail him to the ground with one thrust of the spear; I will not need a second thrust!" But David said to Abishai, "Do not harm him, for who can lay hands on the LORD's anointed and remain unpunished?" So David took the spear and the water jug from their place at Saul's head, and they got away without anyone's seeing or knowing or awakening. All remained asleep, because the LORD had put them into a deep slumber.

Going across to an opposite slope, David stood on a remote hilltop at a great distance from Abner, son of Ner, and the troops. He said: "Here is the king's spear. Let an attendant come over to get it. The LORD will reward each man for his justice and faithfulness. Today, though the LORD delivered you into my grasp, I would not harm the LORD's anointed."

The word of the Lord. *Thanks be to God.*

RESPONSORIAL PSALM *(Psalm 103:1-2, 3-4, 8, 10, 12-13)*
R. **The Lord is kind and merciful.**

Bless the LORD, O my soul;
    and all my being, bless his holy name.
Bless the LORD, O my soul,
    and forget not all his benefits. R.
He pardons all your iniquities,
    heals all your ills.
He redeems your life from destruction,
    crowns you with kindness and compassion. R.
Merciful and gracious is the LORD,
    slow to anger and abounding in kindness.
Not according to our sins does he deal with us,
    nor does he requite us according to our crimes. R.
As far as the east is from the west,
    so far has he put our transgressions from us.
As a father has compassion on his children,
    so the LORD has compassion on those who fear him. R.

SECOND READING *(1 Corinthians 15:45-49)*

Brothers and sisters: It is written, *The first man, Adam, became a living being*, the last Adam a life-giving spirit. But the spiritual was not first; rather the natural and then the spiritual. The first man was from the earth, earthly; the second man, from heaven. As was the earthly one, so also are the earthly, and as is the heavenly one, so also are the heavenly. Just as we have borne the image of the earthly one, we shall also bear the image of the heavenly one.

The word of the Lord. *Thanks be to God.*

ALLELUIA *(John 13:34)*
Alleluia, alleluia. I give you a new commandment, says the Lord: love one another as I have loved you. *Alleluia, alleluia.*

GOSPEL *(Luke 6:27–38)*
A reading from the holy Gospel according to Luke.
Glory to you, O Lord.

Jesus said to his disciples: "To you who hear I say, love your enemies, do good to those who hate you, bless those who curse you, pray for those who mistreat you. To the person who strikes you on one cheek, offer the other one as well, and from the person who takes your cloak, do not withhold even your tunic. Give to everyone who asks of you, and from the one who takes what is yours do not demand it back. **Do to others as you would have them do to you.** ✣ For if you love those who love you, what credit is that to you? Even sinners love those who love them. And if you do good to those who do good to you, what credit is that to you? Even sinners do the same. If you lend money to those from whom you expect repayment, what credit is that to you? Even sinners lend to sinners, and get back the same amount. But rather, love your enemies and do good to them, and lend expecting nothing back; then your reward will be great and you will be children of the Most High, for he himself is kind to the ungrateful and the wicked. Be merciful, just as your Father is merciful. "Stop judging and you will not be judged. Stop condemning and you will not be condemned. Forgive and you will be forgiven. Give, and gifts will be given to you; a good measure, packed together, shaken down, and overflowing, will be poured into your lap. For the measure with which you measure will in return be measured out to you."

The Gospel of the Lord. *Praise to you, Lord Jesus Christ.*

PROFESSION OF FAITH *(page 13)*

PRAYER OF THE FAITHFUL

PREPARATION OF GIFTS *(page 16)*

PRAYER OVER THE OFFERINGS
As we celebrate your mysteries, O Lord,
with the observance that is your due,
we humbly ask you,
that what we offer to the honor of your majesty

• TAKING A CLOSER LOOK •

✦ **Do to others as you would have them do to you.**
These words of Jesus (also expressed in Matthew 7:12) sum up the basic principle of the Golden Rule. But Jesus uses a positive form of an already held moral principle that was usually expressed in a negative form (such as in Tobit 4:15: "Do to no one what you yourself hate"). Loving both our neighbors and our enemies requires more than simply *avoiding doing bad things* to others, as people had previously said; Jesus insists on an active, loving discipleship in which we *do good things* for others, as we would like them to do for us.

may profit us for salvation.
Through Christ our Lord. *Amen.*

PREFACE *(Sundays in Ordinary Time, pages 28–32)*

COMMUNION ANTIPHON *(Psalm 9:2-3)*
I will recount all your wonders, I will rejoice in you and be glad,
and sing psalms to your name, O Most High.

Or *(Jn 11: 27)*
Lord, I have come to believe that you are the Christ, the Son of
the living God, who is coming into this world.

PRAYER AFTER COMMUNION
Grant, we pray, almighty God,
that we may experience the effects of the salvation
which is pledged to us by these mysteries.
Through Christ our Lord. *Amen.*

BLESSING & DISMISSAL *(page 56)* ✣

● RESPONDING TO THE WORD ●

David says the Lord rewards those who are just and faithful.

➔ *How can I be a more faithful servant of the Lord?*

As with Adam, one day our human bodies will die.

➔ *How am I preparing for eternal life with Christ?*

Jesus asks us to love our enemies.

➔ *How can I respond to Jesus' difficult request today?*

March 3

The Lord frees us!

I was once on a cave exploration trip. Using ropes and special ladders, we explored a huge 300-yard-deep cave with a maze of passageways. One guide and I wanted to get to the very bottom. At one point, deep down in the cave, we stopped for a snack. My guide took off his glasses to adjust his helmet. It was complete, utter darkness and dead silence down there. Shortly after leaving our snack spot, my guide noticed he had left his glasses behind. We never found the glasses, and he struggled as he tried to guide me.

In today's gospel, Jesus says when it comes to really knowing what is in a person's heart, we are like blind guides. We really don't see, even if we think we do. Our eyesight is blocked by our own weaknesses and faults. Jesus invites us: "Remove the wooden beam from your eye first." This is about a conversion of heart, grounded in an ongoing prayer life.

The Lord wants to free us of our burdens. We repent, and God forgives us and helps us change our ways. What joy and freedom! Thus, with the psalmist, we want to proclaim God's "kindness at dawn," and God's "faithfulness throughout night."

▪ **EMMANUEL MARTEL**

ENTRANCE ANTIPHON *(Cf. Psalm 18 [17]:19-20)*

The Lord became my protector. He brought me
out to a place of freedom; he saved me because he
delighted in me.

INTRODUCTORY RITES *(page 10)*

COLLECT

Grant us, O Lord, we pray,
that the course of our world
may be directed by your peaceful rule
and that your Church may rejoice,
untroubled in her devotion.
Through our Lord Jesus Christ, your Son,
who lives and reigns with you in the unity of the Holy Spirit,
one God, for ever and ever. ***Amen.***

FIRST READING *(Sirach 27:4-7)*†

When a sieve is shaken, the husks appear;
   so do one's faults when one speaks.
As the test of what the potter molds is in the furnace,
   so in tribulation is the test of the just.
The fruit of a tree shows the care it has had;
   so too does one's speech disclose the bent of one's mind.
Praise no one before he speaks,
   for it is then that people are tested.

The word of the Lord. ***Thanks be to God.***

RESPONSORIAL PSALM *(Psalm 92:2-3, 13-14, 15-16)*

℟ **Lord, it is good to give thanks to you.**

It is good to give thanks to the LORD,
　to sing praise to your name, Most High,
to proclaim your kindness at dawn
　and your faithfulness throughout the night. ℟

The just one shall flourish like the palm tree,
　like a cedar of Lebanon shall he grow.
They that are planted in the house of the LORD
　shall flourish in the courts of our God. ℟

They shall bear fruit even in old age;
　vigorous and sturdy shall they be,
declaring how just is the LORD,
　my rock, in whom there is no wrong. ℟

SECOND READING *(1 Corinthians 15:54-58)*

Brothers and sisters: When this which is corruptible clothes itself with incorruptibility and this which is mortal clothes itself with immortality, then the word that is written shall come about:

Death is swallowed up in victory.
Where, O death, is your victory?
Where, O death, is your sting?

The sting of death is sin, and the power of sin is the law. But thanks be to God who gives us the victory through our Lord Jesus Christ.

Therefore, my beloved brothers and sisters, be firm, steadfast, always fully devoted to the work of the Lord, knowing that in the Lord your labor is not in vain.

The word of the Lord. *Thanks be to God.*

ALLELUIA *(Philippians 2:15d, 16a)*
Alleluia, alleluia. Shine like lights in the world as you hold on to the word of life. *Alleluia, alleluia.*

GOSPEL *(Luke 6:39–45)*
A reading from the holy Gospel according to Luke.
Glory to you, O Lord.

Jesus told his disciples a parable, "Can a blind person guide a blind person? Will not both fall into a pit? No disciple is superior to the teacher; but when fully trained, every disciple will be like his teacher. Why do you notice the splinter in your brother's eye, but do not perceive the wooden beam in your own? How can you say to your brother, 'Brother, let me remove that splinter in your eye,' when you do not even notice the wooden beam in your own eye? You hypocrite! Remove the wooden beam from your eye first; then you will see clearly to remove the splinter in your brother's eye.

"A good tree does not bear rotten fruit, nor does a rotten tree bear good fruit. For every tree is known by its own fruit. For people do not pick figs from thornbushes, nor do they gather grapes from brambles. A good person out of the store of goodness in his heart produces good, but an evil person out of a store of evil produces evil; for from the fullness of the heart the mouth speaks."

The Gospel of the Lord. *Praise to you, Lord Jesus Christ.*

PROFESSION OF FAITH *(page 13)*

PRAYER OF THE FAITHFUL

PREPARATION OF GIFTS *(page 16)*

PRAYER OVER THE OFFERINGS

O God, who provide gifts to be offered to your name
and count our oblations as signs
of our desire to serve you with devotion,
we ask of your mercy
that what you grant as the source of merit
may also help us to attain merit's reward.
Through Christ our Lord. *Amen.*

PREFACE *(Sundays in Ordinary Time, pages 28–32)*

• TAKING A CLOSER LOOK •

✚ **Sirach** Also known as Ecclesiasticus, the Book of Sirach was written around 180 BC and is a deuterocanonical book that appears as one of the "wisdom" books in the Old Testament of Catholic Bibles; it is a collection of ethical teachings and one of the longest books in the Bible. The book's author, Ben Sira, was a scribe and teacher from Jerusalem who devoted his life to studying Jewish Law and running an academy for young Jewish men. There is little order to the various topics addressed by Ben Sira, as the book is essentially a compilation of his notes taken over the years as a student and teacher. In today's first reading, Ben Sira emphasizes the importance of speech as a reflection of a person's character; like the fruit produced by a tree, speech discloses one's level of self-discipline.

COMMUNION ANTIPHON *(Cf. Psalm 13 [12]:6)*
I will sing to the Lord who has been bountiful with me, sing psalms to the name of the Lord Most High.

Or *(Matthew 28:20)*
Behold, I am with you always, even to the end of the age, says the Lord.

PRAYER AFTER COMMUNION
Nourished by your saving gifts,
we beseech your mercy, Lord,
that by this same Sacrament
with which you feed us in the present age,
you may make us partakers of life eternal.
Through Christ our Lord. *Amen.*

BLESSING & DISMISSAL *(page 56)* ✣

✦ RESPONDING TO THE WORD ✦

Our words reflect what is in our hearts.

➡ *How might my words better reflect the Christian values I hold in my heart?*

Paul reminds us to devote ourselves to serving the Lord.

➡ *What work is Jesus calling me to do for him today?*

Jesus tells us we must remove the wooden beam in our own eye before trying to remove the splinter in another's eye.

➡ *What beam in my eye do I need to work on removing right now?*

Christ lights our darkness

We may be surprised to hear that the Church's liturgy reminds us that Lent is meant to be a joyful season.

> For by your gracious gift each year
> your faithful await the sacred paschal feasts
> with the joy of minds made pure...
> PREFACE 1 OF LENT

The season of Lent finds its meaning and origin in Easter, the annual celebration of our Lord's resurrection and our salvation. As the Church's time to prepare for the high point of the Christian year, it is the most appropriate time for persons to enter into Christ's new life through baptism. How can it not be a time of joy?

Over the centuries, Lent has become a special time for fasting, abstinence, communal and private prayer, self-discipline, serving others, study, reflection, and penance. With the whole Church we re-examine our priorities, leaving sin and self behind and intensifying our love and service of God and our neighbors.

The joy of this time of preparation is all about the surprise of new life coming from what may have appeared dead—just as fresh buds break through each spring on trees that seemed dead during the long winter.

If we use these forty days of Lent for honest examination and careful "pruning" of our lives, we will be ready to celebrate the great feast of Easter with our risen Lord and to be joyful witnesses of the power of his resurrection in our world so broken by sin.

Praying and living the Lenten season

It's a common practice to "give things up" for Lent. But when we give something up, we create an empty space into which we must then put some new form of loving behavior.

Give yourself and each household member an index card. Either divide the card into five weeks or, better, use a new card each week. Invite everyone to write on one side what they want to give up to create space for something new, and on the other side what they want to fill the space with.

For example, giving up calories by fasting creates a space for feeling a little of the hunger that haunts millions of the world's poor. The money we save from fasting can also be donated to groups that help feed the hungry. Giving up some television time as a household creates space for spending time together in conversation, prayer, or even playing games. Giving up an attitude of complaining makes space for a more cooperative approach to fixing dinners or doing chores.

When everyone is finished, take the cards and place them in the center of the dinner table or in your household Lenten prayer space. Light a candle and pray together:

> God, giver of all gifts,
> you have given us so much.
> Now we want to give up something
> so that we might experience
> the emptiness that reminds us
> how much we want to be filled
> by your loving presence.
> May our sacrifice show our willingness
> to change our lives this Lent.
> Amen.

March 6

Beginning Lent with humility

The traditional spiritual disciplines of Lent—prayer, fasting, and almsgiving—open us to encounter the mercy of our gracious God, providing we undertake them with the right attitude.

Jesus warns three times in today's gospel against showy displays of piety; these are not pleasing to the Father, "who sees in secret." Instead, when giving alms, he instructs, "Do not let your left hand know what your right hand is doing"; when praying, "go to your inner room, close the door"; and when fasting, "anoint your head and wash your face." From these words of Jesus, we learn that discretion and humility are hallmarks of discipleship and the proper disposition for Lenten penitence.

The rewards to which Jesus refers in today's gospel are spiritual, not material. Acts of charity, prayer, and fasting won't bring wealth and fame, but they will help us grow closer to God. As we draw nearer to God, we are moved to ask for the reward of "a clean heart" and "a steadfast spirit," and our gracious God will respond with mercy.

May we enter into this Lenten season with the spiritual discretion and humility that please the Father and to which Jesus calls those who would be his disciples.

■ LOUISE MCEWAN

ENTRANCE ANTIPHON *(Wisdom 11:24, 25, 27)*
You are merciful to all, O Lord, and despise nothing
that you have made. You overlook people's sins, to
bring them to repentance, and you spare them, for
you are the Lord our God.

INTRODUCTORY RITES *(page 10)*

COLLECT
Grant, O Lord, that we may begin with holy fasting
this campaign of Christian service,
so that, as we take up battle against spiritual evils,
we may be armed with weapons of self-restraint.
Through our Lord Jesus Christ, your Son,
who lives and reigns with you in the unity of the Holy Spirit,
one God, for ever and ever. *Amen.*

FIRST READING *(Joel 2:12–18)*
Even now, says the LORD,
return to me with your whole heart,
   with fasting, and weeping, and mourning;
Rend your hearts, not your garments,
   and return to the LORD, your God.
For gracious and merciful is he,
   slow to anger, rich in kindness,
   and relenting in punishment.
Perhaps he will again relent
   and leave behind him a blessing,
Offerings and libations
   for the LORD, your God.

Blow the trumpet in Zion!*
    proclaim a fast,
    call an assembly;
Gather the people,
    notify the congregation;
Assemble the elders,
    gather the children
    and the infants at the breast;
Let the bridegroom quit his room
    and the bride her chamber.
Between the porch and the altar
    let the priests, the ministers of the LORD, weep,
And say, "Spare, O LORD, your people,
    and make not your heritage a reproach,
    with the nations ruling over them!
Why should they say among the peoples,
    'Where is their God?' "

Then the LORD was stirred to concern for his land
    and took pity on his people.

The word of the Lord. *Thanks be to God.*

RESPONSORIAL PSALM *(Psalm 51:3-4, 5-6ab, 12-13, 14, 17)*
℟ **Be merciful, O Lord, for we have sinned.**

Have mercy on me, O God, in your goodness;
    in the greatness of your compassion wipe out my offense.
Thoroughly wash me from my guilt
    and of my sin cleanse me. ℟
For I acknowledge my offense,
    and my sin is before me always:

"Against you only have I sinned,
  and done what is evil in your sight." ℟

A clean heart create for me, O God,
  and a steadfast spirit renew within me.

Cast me not out from your presence,
  and your Holy Spirit take not from me. ℟

Give me back the joy of your salvation,
  and a willing spirit sustain in me.

O Lord, open my lips,
  and my mouth shall proclaim your praise. ℟

SECOND READING *(2 Corinthians 5:20—6:2)*

Brothers and sisters: We are ambassadors for Christ, as if God were appealing through us. We implore you on behalf of Christ, be reconciled to God. For our sake he made him to be sin who did not know sin, so that we might become the righteousness of God in him.

Working together, then, we appeal to you not to receive the grace of God in vain. For he says:

In an acceptable time I heard you,
  and on the day of salvation I helped you.

Behold, now is a very acceptable time; behold, now is the day of salvation.

The word of the Lord. *Thanks be to God.*

VERSE BEFORE THE GOSPEL *(See Psalm 95:8)*

Glory and praise to you, Lord Jesus Christ! If today you hear his voice, harden not your hearts. *Glory and praise to you, Lord Jesus Christ!*

GOSPEL *(Matthew 6:1–6, 16–18)*

A reading from the holy Gospel according to Matthew.
Glory to you, O Lord.

Jesus said to his disciples: "Take care not to perform righteous deeds in order that people may see them; otherwise, you will have no recompense from your heavenly Father. When you give alms, do not blow a trumpet before you, as the hypocrites do in the synagogues and in the streets to win the praise of others. Amen, I say to you, they have received their reward. But when you give alms, do not let your left hand know what your right is doing, so that your almsgiving may be secret. And your Father who sees in secret will repay you.

"When you pray, do not be like the hypocrites, who love to stand and pray in the synagogues and on street corners so that others may see them. Amen, I say to you, they have received their reward. But when you pray, go to your inner room, close the door, and pray to your Father in secret. And your Father who sees in secret will repay you.

"When you fast, do not look gloomy like the **hypocrites**.✝ They neglect their appearance, so that they may appear to others to be fasting. Amen, I say to you, they have received their reward. But when you fast, anoint your head and wash your face, so that you may not appear to be fasting, except to your Father who is hidden. And your Father who sees what is hidden will repay you."

The Gospel of the Lord. *Praise to you, Lord Jesus Christ.*

BLESSING AND DISTRIBUTION OF ASHES

After the homily, the priest, standing with hands joined, says:

Dear brethren (brothers and sisters), let us humbly ask God
    our Father
that he be pleased to bless with the abundance of his grace
these ashes, which we will put on our heads in penitence.

After a brief prayer in silence he continues:

O God, who are moved by acts of humility
and respond with forgiveness to works of penance,
lend your merciful ear to our prayers
and in your kindness pour out the grace of your blessing
on your servants who are marked with these ashes,
that, as they follow the Lenten observances,
they may be worthy to come with minds made pure
to celebrate the Paschal Mystery of your Son.
Who lives and reigns for ever and ever. *Amen.*

Or

O God, who desire not the death of sinners,
but their conversion,
mercifully hear our prayers
and in your kindness be pleased to bless these ashes,
which we intend to receive upon our heads,
that we, who acknowledge we are but ashes
and shall return to dust,
may, through a steadfast observance of Lent,
gain pardon for sins and newness of life
after the likeness of your Risen Son.
Who lives and reigns for ever and ever. *Amen.*

The priest sprinkles the ashes with holy water, places ashes on the heads of all those present who come to him, and says to each one:

Repent, and believe in the Gospel.

Or

Remember that you are dust, and to dust you shall return.

PRAYER OF THE FAITHFUL

PREPARATION OF GIFTS *(page 16)*

PRAYER OVER THE OFFERINGS
As we solemnly offer
the annual sacrifice for the beginning of Lent,
we entreat you, O Lord,
that, through works of penance and charity,
we may turn away from harmful pleasures
and, cleansed from our sins, may become worthy
to celebrate devoutly the Passion of your Son.
Who lives and reigns for ever and ever. ***Amen.***

● TAKING A CLOSER LOOK ●

✢ **Hypocrites** *Hypocrite* is a Greek word that means an actor in the theater. Since the audiences of Greek plays were at a distance, actors wore large stereotyped masks to identify their characters. So in popular usage, a hypocrite was someone who pretended to be something that he or she was not, and hypocrisy described the general mismatch between one's external appearance and one's internal attitudes or intentions. Just as the actor hid behind a mask and performed a role, so the hypocrite hides something behind a pleasing external appearance. To avoid being a hypocrite, we can use Lent to align our inner attitudes and our outer actions.

PREFACE *(Lent 3–4, page 22)*

COMMUNION ANTIPHON *(Cf. Psalm 1:2–3)*
He who ponders the law of the Lord day and night will yield
fruit in due season.

PRAYER AFTER COMMUNION
May the Sacrament we have received sustain us, O Lord,
that our Lenten fast may be pleasing to you
and be for us a healing remedy.
Through Christ our Lord. *Amen.*

PRAYER OVER THE PEOPLE
Pour out a spirit of compunction, O God,
on those who bow before your majesty,
and by your mercy may they merit the rewards you promise
to those who do penance.
Through Christ our Lord. *Amen.*

BLESSING & DISMISSAL *(page 56)* ✣

• RESPONDING TO THE WORD •

Joel wants us to change on the inside and not just externally.	Paul says that now is the acceptable time to be an ambassador of Christ.	Jesus warns against hypocritical behavior.
➡ *What change of attitude do I most want to make this Lent?*	➡ *With whom will I share the good news of salvation today?*	➡ *What do I need to do to match my words with my actions?*

March 10

Firmly rooted in God

When we were landscaping our yard a few years ago, we decided to get rid of a juniper tree, thinking it would be a simple process. Wrong! We dug, we chopped, we pulled. Nothing! It was so firmly rooted we ended up pulling it out with a truck.

I think of that juniper today when reflecting on Jesus' temptations in the desert. No matter what the devil said or offered, Jesus remained firmly rooted in God's word. The lure of comfort and wealth and power was no match for what Jesus knew to be ultimately true as revealed in Scripture.

Many people view Lent negatively—as a time of deprivation and denial. Today's gospel reminds us instead that Lent is a time to become more solidly grounded in our faith. Making more time for prayer and Scripture, fasting from things in our lives that keep us from giving ourselves wholeheartedly to God, giving of ourselves in service to others: far from depriving us, these are the tools we can use to ensure that we are firmly rooted in the things of God.

As we continue our Lenten journey, may we be strengthened to follow in the footsteps of the One who unflinchingly stood up to evil and ultimately triumphed over it.

▪ **Teresa Whalen Lux**

Parishes engaged in the Rite of Christian Initiation of Adults (RCIA) may celebrate the Rite of Election today.

ENTRANCE ANTIPHON *(Cf. Psalm 91 [90]:15-16)*
When he calls on me, I will answer him; I will deliver him and give him glory, I will grant him length of days.

INTRODUCTORY RITES *(page 10)*

COLLECT
Grant, almighty God,
through the yearly observances of holy Lent,
that we may grow in understanding
of the riches hidden in Christ
and by worthy conduct pursue their effects.
Through our Lord Jesus Christ, your Son,
who lives and reigns with you in the unity of the Holy Spirit,
one God, for ever and ever. *Amen.*

FIRST READING *(Deuteronomy 26:4-10)*
Moses spoke to the people, saying: "The priest shall receive the basket from you and shall set it in front of the altar of the LORD, your God. Then you shall declare before the LORD, your God, 'My father was a wandering Aramean* who went down to Egypt with a small household and lived there as an alien. But there he became a nation great, strong, and numerous. When the Egyptians maltreated and oppressed us, imposing hard labor upon us, we cried to the LORD, the God of our fathers, and he heard our cry and saw our affliction, our toil, and our oppression. He brought us out of Egypt with his strong hand and outstretched arm, with terrifying power, with **signs and wonders**;✝ and

bringing us into this country, he gave us this land flowing with milk and honey. Therefore, I have now brought you the firstfruits of the products of the soil which you, O LORD, have given me.' And having set them before the LORD, your God, you shall bow down in his presence."

The word of the Lord. *Thanks be to God.*

RESPONSORIAL PSALM *(Psalm 91:1-2, 10-11, 12-13, 14-15)*
℟ **Be with me, Lord, when I am in trouble.**

You who dwell in the shelter of the Most High,
  who abide in the shadow of the Almighty,
say to the LORD, "My refuge and fortress,
  my God in whom I trust." ℟
No evil shall befall you,
  nor shall affliction come near your tent,
for to his angels he has given command about you,
  that they guard you in all your ways. ℟
Upon their hands they shall bear you up,
  lest you dash your foot against a stone.
You shall tread upon the asp and the viper;
  you shall trample down the lion and the dragon. ℟
Because he clings to me, I will deliver him;
  I will set him on high because he acknowledges my name.
He shall call upon me, and I will answer him;
  I will be with him in distress;
I will deliver him and glorify him. ℟

SECOND READING *(Romans 10:8-13)*

Brothers and sisters: What does Scripture say?
The word is near you,

> *in your mouth and in your heart—*

that is, the word of faith that we preach—, for, if you confess with your mouth that Jesus is Lord and believe in your heart that God raised him from the dead, you will be saved. For one believes with the heart and so is justified, and one confesses with the mouth and so is saved. For the Scripture says, *No one who believes in him will be put to shame.* For there is no distinction between Jew and Greek; the same Lord is Lord of all, enriching all who call upon him. For "everyone who calls on the name of the Lord will be saved."

The word of the Lord. *Thanks be to God.*

VERSE BEFORE THE GOSPEL *(Matthew 4:4)*
Glory and praise to you, Lord Jesus Christ! One does not live on bread alone, but on every word that comes forth from the mouth of God. *Glory and praise to you, Lord Jesus Christ!*

GOSPEL *(Luke 4:1-13)*
A reading from the holy Gospel according to Luke.
Glory to you, O Lord.

Filled with the Holy Spirit, Jesus returned from the Jordan and was led by the Spirit into the desert for forty days, to be tempted by the devil. He ate nothing during those days, and when they were over he was hungry. The devil said to him, "If you are the Son of God, command this stone to become bread." Jesus answered him, "It is written, *One does not live on bread alone.*" Then he took him up and showed him all the kingdoms of the world in a single instant. The devil said to him, "I shall give to you all this power and glory; for it has been handed over to me, and I may give it to whomever I wish. All this will be yours, if you worship me." Jesus said to him in reply, "It is written:

> *You shall worship the Lord, your God,*

and him alone shall you serve."

Then he led him to Jerusalem, made him stand on the parapet of the temple, and said to him, "If you are the Son of God, throw yourself down from here, for it is written:

He will command his angels concerning you, to guard you,

and:

With their hands they will support you,
lest you dash your foot against a stone."

Jesus said to him in reply, "It also says, *You shall not put the Lord, your God, to the test.*" When the devil had finished every temptation, he departed from him for a time.

The Gospel of the Lord. ***Praise to you, Lord Jesus Christ.***

[RITE OF ELECTION]

PROFESSION OF FAITH *(page 13)*

PRAYER OF THE FAITHFUL

PREPARATION OF GIFTS *(page 16)*

PRAYER OVER THE OFFERINGS
Give us the right dispositions, O Lord, we pray,
to make these offerings,
for with them we celebrate the beginning
of this venerable and sacred time.
Through Christ our Lord. ***Amen.***

PREFACE: THE TEMPTATION OF THE LORD
It is truly right and just, our duty and our salvation,
always and everywhere to give you thanks,
Lord, holy Father, almighty and eternal God,
through Christ our Lord.

By abstaining forty long days from earthly food,
he consecrated through his fast
the pattern of our Lenten observance
and, by overturning all the snares of the ancient serpent,
taught us to cast out the leaven of malice,
so that, celebrating worthily the Paschal Mystery,
we might pass over at last to the eternal paschal feast.

And so, with the company of Angels and Saints,
we sing the hymn of your praise,
as without end we acclaim:
Holy, Holy, Holy Lord God of hosts... (page 35)

COMMUNION ANTIPHON (Matthew 4:4)
One does not live by bread alone, but by every word that comes
forth from the mouth of God.

Or (Cf. Psalm 91 [90]:4)
The Lord will conceal you with his pinions, and under his wings
you will trust.

• TAKING A CLOSER LOOK •

✣ **Signs and wonders** Although we use the word "miracles" to describe these events, the biblical writers used the terms "deeds of power," "signs," and "wonders." These are God's actions to reorder our world from the domination of Satan and evil powers that frustrate God's plan for a covenant community. Jesus' deeds of power are directly related to his kingdom message. They are the first signs (his resurrection to new life will be the final sign) that God is reordering our world. Like Jesus' parables and meals, Jesus' cures, exorcisms, resuscitations, and nature wonders are signs of God's presence breaking into our world to change it forever.

PRAYER AFTER COMMUNION

Renewed now with heavenly bread,
by which faith is nourished, hope increased,
and charity strengthened,
we pray, O Lord,
that we may learn to hunger for Christ,
the true and living Bread,
and strive to live by every word
which proceeds from your mouth.
Through Christ our Lord. *Amen.*

PRAYER OVER THE PEOPLE

May bountiful blessing, O Lord, we pray,
come down upon your people,
that hope may grow in tribulation,
virtue be strengthened in temptation,
and eternal redemption be assured.
Through Christ our Lord. *Amen.*

BLESSING & DISMISSAL *(page 56)* ✥

• RESPONDING TO THE WORD •

Moses thanks God for God's loving actions for the people.	God is near us through God's own word in Scripture and in our hearts.	The devil tempts Jesus to use his relation as God's Son for his own benefit.
➲ *For what actions of God do I want to give thanks?*	➲ *How can I be more attentive to how God might want to communicate with me today?*	➲ *How can I help others without demanding anything for myself?*

March 17

MAR
17

Finding God in sacred moments

The journey towards strengthening our faith can be disconcerting. Take Abraham, for example. He put his trust in forging a covenant with God to father his people. He demonstrated an unshakable conviction in believing God's incredible promise. Abraham and the disciples in today's readings are our examples. The gift of faith becomes their guiding light from darkness that leads them closer to God.

In today's gospel, the apostles Peter, John, and James witness a series of divine events. They experience the holiness of Jesus in his transfiguration. His appearance changes while he prays on the mountain and meets Elijah and Moses. To cap it off, God directly commands the apostles to listen to Jesus, his Son and Chosen One. These extraordinary events confirm what Jesus had revealed to his faithful followers about his death and resurrection, and his identity as the Son of God.

These readings can strengthen our own faith. Like his disciples, we are asked to trust Jesus and follow him in our spiritual journey. The readings show the possibility of experiencing God through sacred moments. As ordinary followers, we can find God in prayer, Scripture, and our everyday lives.

As our light and salvation, Jesus will give us the courage, hope, and strength to overcome our trials. Ultimately, faith will help us fulfill God's will.

■ **CHRISTL DABU**

ENTRANCE ANTIPHON *(Cf. Psalm 27 [26]:8–9)*

Of you my heart has spoken: Seek his face. It is your face,
O Lord, that I seek; hide not your face from me.

Or *(Cf. Psalm 25 [24]:6, 2, 22)*

Remember your compassion, O Lord, and your merciful love, for
they are from of old. Let not our enemies exult over us. Redeem
us, O God of Israel, from all our distress.

INTRODUCTORY RITES *(page 10)*

COLLECT

O God, who have commanded us
to listen to your beloved Son,
be pleased, we pray,
to nourish us inwardly by your word,
that, with spiritual sight made pure,
we may rejoice to behold your glory.
Through our Lord Jesus Christ, your Son,
who lives and reigns with you in the unity of the Holy Spirit,
one God, for ever and ever. ***Amen.***

FIRST READING *(Genesis 15:5–12, 17–18)*

The Lord God took Abram outside and said, "Look up at the
sky and count the stars, if you can. Just so," he added, "shall
your descendants be." Abram put his faith in the LORD, who
credited it to him as an act of righteousness.

He then said to him, "I am the LORD who brought you from
Ur of the Chaldeans* to give you this land as a possession." "O
Lord GOD," he asked, "how am I to know that I shall possess it?"
He answered him, "Bring me a three-year-old heifer, a three-
year-old she-goat, a three-year-old ram, a turtledove, and a young

pigeon." Abram brought him all these, split them in two, and placed each half opposite the other; but the birds he did not cut up. Birds of prey swooped down on the carcasses, but Abram stayed with them. As the sun was about to set, a trance fell upon Abram, and a deep, terrifying darkness enveloped him.

When the sun had set and it was dark, there appeared a smoking fire pot and a flaming torch, which passed between those pieces. It was on that occasion that the LORD made a **covenant**✝ with Abram, saying: "To your descendants I give this land, from the Wadi of Egypt to the Great River, the Euphrates."

The word of the Lord. *Thanks be to God.*

RESPONSORIAL PSALM *(Psalm 27:1, 7-8, 8-9, 13-14)*
℟ The Lord is my light and my salvation.

The LORD is my light and my salvation;
    whom should I fear?
The LORD is my life's refuge;
    of whom should I be afraid? ℟
Hear, O LORD, the sound of my call;
    have pity on me, and answer me.
Of you my heart speaks; you my glance seeks. ℟
Your presence, O LORD, I seek.
    Hide not your face from me;
do not in anger repel your servant.
    You are my helper: cast me not off. ℟
I believe that I shall see the bounty of the LORD
    in the land of the living.
Wait for the LORD with courage;
    be stouthearted, and wait for the LORD. ℟

SECOND READING *(Philippians 3:17–4:1)*
For the shorter version, omit the indented part in brackets.

[Join with others in being imitators of me, brothers and sisters, and observe those who thus conduct themselves according to the model you have in us. For many, as I have often told you and now tell you even in tears, conduct themselves as enemies of the cross of Christ. Their end is destruction. Their God is their stomach; their glory is in their "shame." Their minds are occupied with earthly things. But]
(Brothers and sisters:) Our citizenship is in heaven, and from it we also await a savior, the Lord Jesus Christ. He will change our lowly body to conform with his glorified body by the power that enables him also to bring all things into subjection to himself.

Therefore, my brothers and sisters, whom I love and long for, my joy and crown, in this way stand firm in the Lord, (beloved).

The word of the Lord. *Thanks be to God.*

VERSE BEFORE THE GOSPEL *(See Matthew 17:5)*
Glory and praise to you, Lord Jesus Christ! From the shining cloud the Father's voice is heard: This is my beloved Son, listen to him. *Glory and praise to you, Lord Jesus Christ!*

GOSPEL *(Luke 9:28b-36)*
A reading from the holy Gospel according to Luke.
Glory to you, O Lord.
Jesus took Peter, John, and James and went up the mountain to pray. While he was praying his face changed in appearance and his clothing became dazzling white. And behold, two men were conversing with him, Moses and Elijah, who appeared in glory and spoke of his exodus that he was going to accomplish in Jerusalem.

Peter and his companions had been overcome by sleep, but becoming fully awake, they saw his glory and the two men standing with him. As they were about to part from him, Peter said to Jesus, "Master, it is good that we are here; let us make three tents, one for you, one for Moses, and one for Elijah." But he did not know what he was saying. While he was still speaking, a cloud came and cast a shadow over them, and they became frightened when they entered the cloud. Then from the cloud came a voice that said, "This is my chosen Son; listen to him." After the voice had spoken, Jesus was found alone. They fell silent and did not at that time tell anyone what they had seen.

The Gospel of the Lord. *Praise to you, Lord Jesus Christ.*

PROFESSION OF FAITH *(page 13)*

PRAYER OF THE FAITHFUL

PREPARATION OF GIFTS *(page 16)*

PRAYER OVER THE OFFERINGS
May this sacrifice, O Lord, we pray,
cleanse us of our faults
and sanctify your faithful in body and mind
for the celebration of the paschal festivities.
Through Christ our Lord. *Amen.*

PREFACE: THE TRANSFIGURATION OF THE LORD

It is truly right and just, our duty and our salvation,
always and everywhere to give you thanks,
Lord, holy Father, almighty and eternal God,
through Christ our Lord.

For after he had told the disciples of his coming Death,
on the holy mountain he manifested to them his glory,
to show, even by the testimony of the law and the prophets,
that the Passion leads to the glory of the Resurrection.

And so, with the Powers of heaven,
we worship you constantly on earth,
and before your majesty
without end we acclaim:
Holy, Holy, Holy Lord God of hosts... *(page 35)*

COMMUNION ANTIPHON *(Matthew 17:5)*

This is my beloved Son, with whom I am well pleased; listen to him.

• TAKING A CLOSER LOOK •

✠ **Covenant** A covenant is a voluntary, formal agreement between two parties that spells out the obligations of their relationship. In the biblical world, the expectations were modeled on the customs that guided relationships between persons of unequal honor, status, and wealth. The covenant bound the parties in mutual and reciprocal obligations. The "patron" or more powerful person (like God) promised to provide for and protect the less powerful "clients" (from the Latin word for dependents). In return, to enhance the honor and reputation of the patron, the clients offered respect, praise, gratitude, and other favors when requested.

PRAYER AFTER COMMUNION

As we receive these glorious mysteries,
we make thanksgiving to you, O Lord,
for allowing us while still on earth
to be partakers even now of the things of heaven.
Through Christ our Lord. *Amen.*

PRAYER OVER THE PEOPLE

Bless your faithful, we pray, O Lord,
with a blessing that endures for ever,
and keep them faithful
to the Gospel of your Only Begotten Son,
so that they may always desire and at last attain
that glory whose beauty he showed in his own Body,
to the amazement of his Apostles.
Through Christ our Lord. *Amen.*

BLESSING & DISMISSAL *(page 56)* ✣

✦ RESPONDING TO THE WORD ✦

Abraham trusts that God will do what God promises.

🡒 *What helps me to trust in God's promises?*

Paul knows we are being transformed as Christ was.

🡒 *What new life from Christ is transforming me this Lent?*

The divine voice tells us to listen to Jesus.

🡒 *What am I doing this Lent to be more attentive to Jesus' voice in the Scriptures and in my life?*

March 24

May our lives be fruitful

"May your life be fruitful." Years ago, these words were solemnly and sincerely spoken to me. In our own way, each of us receives this same blessing. During Lent, we are invited to reflect on the fruitfulness of our lives. Every one of us is created to do more than take up space in the garden.

Jesus, in telling the parable of the barren fig tree, teaches us something important. As gardener, he takes an active role in our lives, promising to rework and renew the soil. Gardeners know these unglamorous tasks are essential for producing abundant fruit.

Jesus lovingly commits himself to the troubles and trials of our lives. The wise gardener, he knows when and how to amend the soil. Tended carefully, even the least appealing aspects of our lives offer essential nutrients for healthy growth. We can be transformed; our lives can become ever more fruitful.

Our "yes" to this growth lies in our personal willingness to repent. Twice in this gospel, Jesus emphasizes his lack of concern over who is a worse sinner or a worse offender. He simply looks for our willingness to be renewed.

At every Eucharist, we renew our "yes." We pray, acknowledging our need for our Lord: "Only say the word and my soul shall be healed."

May our lives be fruitful.

■ **BRENDA MERK HILDEBRAND**

Parishes engaged in the Rite of Christian Initiation of Adults (RCIA) may celebrate the First Scrutiny today (see page 217).

ENTRANCE ANTIPHON *(Cf. Psalm 25 [24]:15-16)*

My eyes are always on the Lord, for he rescues my feet from the snare. Turn to me and have mercy on me, for I am alone and poor.

Or *(Cf. Ezekiel 36:23-26)*

When I prove my holiness among you,
I will gather you from all the foreign lands; and I will pour clean water upon you and cleanse you from all your impurities, and I will give you a new spirit, says the Lord.

INTRODUCTORY RITES *(page 10)*

COLLECT

O God, author of every mercy and of all goodness,
who in fasting, prayer and almsgiving
have shown us a remedy for sin,
look graciously on this confession of our lowliness,
that we, who are bowed down by our conscience,
may always be lifted up by your mercy.
Through our Lord Jesus Christ, your Son,
who lives and reigns with you in the unity of the Holy Spirit,
one God, for ever and ever. ***Amen.***

The readings for Year A may be used in place of these (see page 217).

FIRST READING *(Exodus 3:1-8a, 13-15)*

Moses was tending the flock of his father-in-law Jethro, the priest of Midian.* Leading the flock across the desert, he came to Horeb,* the mountain of God. There an angel of the

LORD appeared to Moses in fire flaming out of a bush. As he looked on, he was surprised to see that the bush, though on fire, was not consumed. So Moses decided, "I must go over to look at this remarkable sight, and see why the bush is not burned."

When the LORD saw him coming over to look at it more closely, God called out to him from the bush, "Moses! Moses!" He answered, "Here I am." God said, "Come no nearer! Remove the sandals from your feet, for the place where you stand is holy ground. I am the God of your fathers," he continued, "the God of Abraham, the God of Isaac, the God of Jacob." Moses hid his face, for he was afraid to look at God. But the LORD said, "I have witnessed the affliction of my people in Egypt and have heard their cry of complaint against their slave drivers, so I know well what they are suffering. Therefore I have come down to rescue them from the hands of the Egyptians and lead them out of that land into a good and spacious land, a land flowing with milk and honey."

Moses said to God, "But when I go to the Israelites and say to them, 'The God of your fathers has sent me to you,' if they ask me, 'What is his name?' what am I to tell them?" God replied, "I am who am." Then he added, "This is what you shall tell the Israelites: **I AM**✝ sent me to you."

God spoke further to Moses, "Thus shall you say to the Israelites: The LORD, the God of your fathers, the God of Abraham, the God of Isaac, the God of Jacob, has sent me to you.

"This is my name forever;
   thus am I to be remembered through all generations."

The word of the Lord. ***Thanks be to God.***

RESPONSORIAL PSALM *(Psalm 103:1-2, 3-4, 6-7, 8, 11)*

℟ **The Lord is kind and merciful.**

Bless the LORD, O my soul;
    and all my being, bless his holy name.
Bless the LORD, O my soul,
    and forget not all his benefits. ℟
He pardons all your iniquities,
    heals all your ills.
He redeems your life from destruction,
    crowns you with kindness and compassion. ℟
The LORD secures justice
    and the rights of all the oppressed.
He has made known his ways to Moses,
    and his deeds to the children of Israel. ℟
Merciful and gracious is the LORD,
    slow to anger and abounding in kindness.
For as the heavens are high above the earth,
    so surpassing is his kindness toward those who fear him. ℟

SECOND READING *(1 Corinthians 10:1-6, 10-12)*

I do not want you to be unaware, brothers and sisters, that our ancestors were all under the cloud and all passed through the sea, and all of them were baptized into Moses in the cloud and in the sea. All ate the same spiritual food, and all drank the same spiritual drink, for they drank from a spiritual rock that followed them, and the rock was the Christ. Yet God was not pleased with most of them, for they were struck down in the desert.

These things happened as examples for us, so that we might not desire evil things, as they did. Do not grumble as some of them did, and suffered death by the destroyer. These things happened to them as an example, and they have been written down as a warning to us, upon whom the end of the ages has come. Therefore, whoever thinks he is standing secure should take care not to fall.

The word of the Lord. ***Thanks be to God.***

VERSE BEFORE THE GOSPEL *(Matthew 4:17)*
Glory and praise to you, Lord Jesus Christ! Repent, says the Lord; the kingdom of heaven is at hand. ***Glory and praise to you, Lord Jesus Christ!***

GOSPEL *(Luke 13:1-9)*
A reading from the holy Gospel according to Luke.
Glory to you, O Lord.

Some people told Jesus about the Galileans whose blood Pilate had mingled with the blood of their sacrifices. Jesus said to them in reply, "Do you think that because these Galileans suffered in this way they were greater sinners than all other Galileans? By no means! But I tell you, if you do not repent, you will all perish as they did! Or those eighteen people who were killed when the tower at Siloam fell on them—do you think they were more guilty than everyone else who lived in Jerusalem? By no means! But I tell you, if you do not repent, you will all perish as they did!"

And he told them this parable: "There once was a person who had a fig tree planted in his orchard, and when he came in search of fruit on it but found none, he said to the gardener, 'For three years now I have come in search of fruit on this fig tree but have found none. So cut it down. Why should it exhaust the soil?' He said to him in reply, 'Sir, leave it for this year also, and I shall cultivate the ground around it and fertilize it; it may bear fruit in the future. If not you can cut it down.'"

The Gospel of the Lord. ***Praise to you, Lord Jesus Christ.***

PROFESSION OF FAITH *(page 13)*

PRAYER OF THE FAITHFUL

PREPARATION OF GIFTS *(page 16)*

PRAYER OVER THE OFFERINGS
Be pleased, O Lord, with these sacrificial offerings,
and grant that we who beseech pardon for our own sins,
may take care to forgive our neighbor.
Through Christ our Lord. *Amen.*

PREFACE *(Lent 1–2, page 21)*

COMMUNION ANTIPHON *(Cf. Psalm 84 [83]:4-5)*
The sparrow finds a home, and the swallow a nest for her young:
by your altars, O Lord of hosts, my King and my God. Blessed
are they who dwell in your house, for ever singing your praise.

• Taking a Closer Look •

✤ **I AM** Like so many things in John's gospel, the words of
Jesus have multiple levels of meaning. In everyday conversation,
Jesus' statement "I am he" (John 4:26, *see page 221*) would simply
identify him. The "I AM" of Exodus 3:14 (in capital letters in the
translation) is God's personal name, *Yahweh*, which was closely
related to the verb "I am." When Jesus utters these words in the
gospels, he is saying that he shares God's power over evil and, as
he says later to Pilate (John 19:11), others have no power over him
unless he willingly permits it.

PRAYER AFTER COMMUNION

As we receive the pledge
of things yet hidden in heaven
and are nourished while still on earth
with the Bread that comes from on high,
we humbly entreat you, O Lord,
that what is being brought about in us in mystery
may come to true completion.
Through Christ our Lord. *Amen.*

PRAYER OVER THE PEOPLE

Direct, O Lord, we pray, the hearts of your faithful,
and in your kindness grant your servants this grace:
that, abiding in the love of you and their neighbor,
they may fulfill the whole of your commands.
Through Christ our Lord. *Amen.*

BLESSING & DISMISSAL *(page 56)* ✦

✦ RESPONDING TO THE WORD ✦

Moses learns that where God is present is holy ground.	Paul warns of being overconfident in our relation to God.	Jesus tells us that God is always at work, like a patient gardener, caring for us.
➡ *Where have I most experienced God's presence creating a holy place or situation?*	➡ *What might I need to do to take more care with my relationship to God?*	➡ *What work of pruning is God doing in me so I might bear more fruit?*

CHRISTIAN INITIATION:
FIRST SCRUTINY

The Mass prayers and readings below are for use
in parishes celebrating the First Scrutiny.

ENTRANCE ANTIPHON *(Ezekiel 36:23-26)*

When I prove my holiness among you, I will gather you from
all the foreign lands and I will pour clean water upon you and
cleanse you from all your impurities, and I will give you a new
spirit, says the Lord.

Or *(Cf. Isaiah 55:1)*

Come to the waters, you who are thirsty, says the Lord; you who
have no money, come and drink joyfully.

COLLECT

Grant, we pray, O Lord,
that these chosen ones may come worthily and wisely
to the confession of your praise,
so that in accordance with that first dignity
which they lost by original sin
they may be fashioned anew through your glory.
Through our Lord Jesus Christ, your Son,
who lives and reigns with you in the unity of the Holy Spirit,
one God, for ever and ever. *Amen.*

FIRST READING *(Exodus 17:3-7)*

In those days, in their thirst for water, the people grumbled
against Moses, saying, "Why did you ever make us leave Egypt?
Was it just to have us die here of thirst with our children and our
livestock?" So Moses cried out to the LORD, "What shall I do with
this people? A little more and they will stone me!" The LORD
answered Moses, "Go over there in front of the people, along with

some of the elders of Israel, holding in your hand, as you go, the
staff with which you struck the river. I will be standing there in
front of you on the rock in Horeb.* Strike the rock, and the water
will flow from it for the people to drink." This Moses did, in the
presence of the elders of Israel. The place was called Massah* and
Meribah,* because the Israelites quarreled there and tested the
Lord, saying, "Is the LORD in our midst or not?"

The word of the Lord. *Thanks be to God.*

RESPONSORIAL PSALM *(Psalm 95:1-2, 6-7, 8-9)*
℟ If today you hear his voice, harden not your hearts.

Come, let us sing joyfully to the LORD;
    let us acclaim the Rock of our salvation.
Let us come into his presence with thanksgiving;
    let us joyfully sing psalms to him. ℟
Come, let us bow down in worship;
    let us kneel before the LORD who made us.
For he is our God,
    and we are the people he shepherds, the flock he guides. ℟
Oh, that today you would hear his voice:
    "Harden not your hearts as at Meribah,*
    as in the day of Massah* in the desert,
where your fathers tempted me;
    they tested me though they had seen my works." ℟

SECOND READING *(Romans 5:1-2, 5-8)*
Brothers and sisters: Since we have been justified by faith,
we have peace with God through our Lord Jesus Christ,
through whom we have gained access by faith to this grace in
which we stand, and we boast in hope of the glory of God.
    And hope does not disappoint, because the love of God has

been poured out into our hearts through the Holy Spirit who has been given to us. For Christ, while we were still helpless, died at the appointed time for the ungodly. Indeed, only with difficulty does one die for a just person, though perhaps for a good person one might even find courage to die. But God proves his love for us in that while we were still sinners Christ died for us.

The word of the Lord. *Thanks be to God.*

VERSE BEFORE THE GOSPEL *(See John 4:42, 15)*
Glory and praise to you, Lord Jesus Christ! Lord, you are truly the Savior of the world; give me living water, that I may never thirst again. *Glory and praise to you, Lord Jesus Christ!*

GOSPEL *(John 4:5–42)*
For the shorter version, omit the indented parts in brackets.

A reading from the holy Gospel according to John.
Glory to you, O Lord.

J esus came to a town of Samaria* called Sychar,* near the plot of land that Jacob had given to his son Joseph. Jacob's well was there. Jesus, tired from his journey, sat down there at the well. It was about noon.

A woman of Samaria came to draw water. Jesus said to her, "Give me a drink." His disciples had gone into the town to buy food. The Samaritan woman said to him, "How can you, a Jew, ask me, a Samaritan woman, for a drink?"—For Jews use nothing in common with Samaritans.—Jesus answered and said to her, "If you knew the gift of God and who is saying to you, 'Give me a drink,' you would have asked him and he would have given you living water." The woman said to him, "Sir, you do not even have a bucket and the cistern is deep; where then can you get this living water? Are you greater than our father Jacob, who gave us this cistern and drank from it himself with his children and his flocks?" Jesus answered and said to her, "Everyone who drinks this water will be thirsty again; but whoever drinks the water I shall give will never thirst; the water I shall give will become in him a spring of water welling up to eternal life." The woman said to him, "Sir, give me this water, so that I may not be thirsty or have to keep coming here to draw water."

[Jesus said to her, "Go call your husband and come back." The woman answered and said to him, "I do not have a husband." Jesus answered her, "You are right in saying, 'I do not have a husband.' For you have had five husbands, and the one you have now is not your husband. What you have said is true." The woman said to him, "Sir,]

"I can see that you are a prophet. Our ancestors worshiped on this mountain; but you people say that the place to worship is in Jerusalem." Jesus said to her, "Believe me, woman, the hour is coming when you will worship the Father neither on this mountain nor in Jerusalem. You people worship what you do not understand; we worship what we understand, because salvation is from the Jews. But the hour is coming, and is now here, when true worshipers will worship the Father in Spirit and truth; and indeed the Father seeks such people to worship him. God is Spirit, and those who worship him must worship in Spirit and truth." The woman said to him, "I know that the Messiah is coming, the one called the Christ; when he comes, he will tell us everything." Jesus said to her, "I am he, the one speaking with you."

[At that moment his disciples returned, and were amazed that he was talking with a woman, but still no one said, "What are you looking for?" or "Why are you talking with her?" The woman left her water jar and went into the town and said to the people, "Come see a man who told me everything I have done.

Could he possibly be the Christ?" They went out of the town and came to him. Meanwhile, the disciples urged him, "Rabbi, eat." But he said to them, "I have food to eat of which you do not know." So the disciples said to one another, "Could someone have brought him something to eat?" Jesus said to them, "My food is to do the will of the one who sent me and to finish his work. Do you not say, 'In four months the harvest will be here'? I tell you, look up and see the fields ripe for the harvest. The reaper is already receiving payment and gathering crops for eternal life, so that the sower and reaper can rejoice together. For here the saying is verified that 'One sows and another reaps.' I sent you to reap what you have not worked for; others have done the work, and you are sharing the fruits of their work."]

Many of the Samaritans of that town began to believe in him [because of the word of the woman who testified, "He told me everything I have done."] When the Samaritans came to him, they invited him to stay with them; and he stayed there two days. Many more began to believe in him because of his word, and they said to the woman, "We no longer believe because of your word; for we have heard for ourselves, and we know that this is truly the savior of the world."

The Gospel of the Lord. *Praise to you, Lord Jesus Christ.*

PRAYER OVER THE OFFERINGS

May your merciful grace prepare your servants, O Lord,
for the worthy celebration of these mysteries
and lead them to it by a devout way of life.
Through Christ our Lord. *Amen.*

PREFACE : THE SAMARITAN WOMAN

It is truly right and just, our duty and our salvation,

always and everywhere to give you thanks,
Lord, holy Father, almighty and eternal God,
through Christ our Lord.

For when he asked the Samaritan woman for water to drink,
he had already created the gift of faith within her
and so ardently did he thirst for her faith,
that he kindled in her the fire of divine love.

And so we, too, give you thanks
and with the Angels
praise your mighty deeds, as we acclaim:
Holy, Holy, Holy Lord God of hosts... (page 35)

COMMUNION ANTIPHON (Cf. John 4:13-14)
For anyone who drinks it, says the Lord, the water I shall give
will become in him a spring welling up to eternal life.

PRAYER AFTER COMMUNION
Give help, O Lord, we pray,
by the grace of your redemption
and be pleased to protect and prepare
those you are to initiate
through the Sacraments of eternal life.
Through Christ our Lord. *Amen.*

PRAYER OVER THE PEOPLE
Direct, O Lord, we pray, the hearts of your faithful,
and in your kindness grant your servants this grace:
that, abiding in the love of you and their neighbor,
they may fulfill the whole of your commands.
Through Christ our Lord. *Amen.*

BLESSING & DISMISSAL (page 56) ✠

March 31

MAR 31

"Living the dream"

My brother, Pat, has a favorite expression. If asked how he is, he often says "Living the dream." I suspect the younger brother in the parable of the prodigal son thought he too was living the dream when he took his share of his father's estate. Sadly for him, it didn't work out well, and he had to come grovelling home. It was his good fortune that his father was a godly man and received his son with open arms and even a celebration.

The parable's focus then shifts to the older son. Many would commiserate with him; he had slaved for his father and was never disobedient. But now he sees the party for his younger brother, and he indulges in what is poison for the soul—resentment. What he has forgotten is that he already has a deep, abiding relationship with his father; he has riches beyond compare.

Often we too forget. We who have received the gift of faith take for granted the sacrifice of Jesus and the wonder of the sacraments. We must strive to remain mindful of God's enduring love for us and to live virtuous lives. We must also accept hardships and seek to transform our suffering into concern and generosity towards those in need.

Father, help us always to return to your open arms and your merciful heart. Amen.

■ **HARRY McAVOY**

Parishes engaged in the Rite of Christian Initiation of Adults (RCIA) may celebrate the Second Scrutiny today (see page 230).

ENTRANCE ANTIPHON *(Cf. Isaiah 66:10–11)*

Rejoice, Jerusalem, and all who love her. Be joyful, all who were in mourning; exult and be satisfied at her consoling breast.

INTRODUCTORY RITES *(page 10)*

COLLECT

O God, who through your Word
reconcile the human race to yourself in a wonderful way,
grant, we pray,
that with prompt devotion and eager faith
the Christian people may hasten
toward the solemn celebrations to come.
Through our Lord Jesus Christ, your Son,
who lives and reigns with you in the unity of the Holy Spirit,
one God, for ever and ever. ***Amen.***

The readings for Year A may be used in place of these (see page 230).

FIRST READING *(Joshua 5:9a, 10–12)*

The LORD said to Joshua, "Today I have removed the reproach of Egypt from you."

While the Israelites were encamped at Gilgal on the plains of Jericho,* they celebrated the Passover on the evening of the fourteenth of the month. On the day after the Passover, they ate of the produce of the land in the form of unleavened cakes and parched grain. On that same day after the Passover, on which they ate of the produce of the land, the manna ceased. No longer was there manna for the Israelites, who that year ate of the yield of the land of Canaan.

The word of the Lord. ***Thanks be to God.***

RESPONSORIAL PSALM *(Psalm 34:2-3, 4-5, 6-7)*
℟ **Taste and see the goodness of the Lord.**

I will bless the LORD at all times;
   his praise shall be ever in my mouth.
Let my soul glory in the LORD;
   the lowly will hear me and be glad. ℟
Glorify the LORD with me,
   let us together extol his name.
I sought the LORD, and he answered me
   and delivered me from all my fears. ℟
Look to him that you may be radiant with joy,
   and your faces may not blush with shame.
When the poor one called out, the LORD heard,
   and from all his distress he saved him. ℟

SECOND READING *(2 Corinthians 5:17-21)*

Brothers and sisters: Whoever is in Christ is a new creation: the old things have passed away; behold, new things have come. And all this is from God, who has **reconciled**✝ us to himself through Christ and given us the ministry of reconciliation, namely, God was reconciling the world to himself in Christ, not counting their trespasses against them and entrusting to us the message of reconciliation. So we are ambassadors for Christ, as if God were appealing through us. We implore you on behalf of Christ, be reconciled to God. For our sake he made him to be sin who did not know sin, so that we might become the righteousness of God in him.

The word of the Lord. *Thanks be to God.*

Glory and praise to you, Lord Jesus Christ! I will get up and go to my Father and shall say to him: Father, I have sinned against heaven and against you. *Glory and praise to you, Lord Jesus Christ!*

A reading from the holy Gospel according to Luke.
Glory to you, O Lord.

Tax collectors and sinners were all drawing near to listen to Jesus, but the Pharisees and scribes began to complain, saying, "This man welcomes sinners and eats with them." So to them Jesus addressed this parable: "A man had two sons, and the younger son said to his father, 'Father give me the share of your estate that should come to me.' So the father divided the property between them. After a few days, the younger son collected all his belongings and set off to a distant country where he squandered his inheritance on a life of dissipation. When he had freely spent everything, a severe famine struck that country, and he found himself in dire need. So he hired himself out to one of the local citizens who sent him to his farm to tend the swine. And he longed to eat his fill of the pods on which the swine fed, but nobody gave him any. Coming to his senses he thought, 'How many of my father's hired workers have more than enough food to eat, but here am I, dying from hunger. I shall get up and go to my father and I shall say to him, "Father, I have sinned against heaven and against you. I no longer deserve to be called your son; treat me as you would treat one of your hired workers." ' So he got up and went back to his father. While he was still a long way off, his father caught sight of him, and was filled with compassion. He ran to his son, embraced him and kissed him. His son said to him, 'Father, I have sinned against heaven and against you; I no longer deserve to be called your son.' But his father ordered his servants, 'Quickly bring the finest robe and put it on him; put a ring on his finger and sandals on his feet. Take the fattened calf and slaughter it. Then let us celebrate with a feast, because this son of mine was dead, and has come to life again; he was lost, and has been found.' Then the celebration began. Now the older son had been out in the field and, on his way back, as he neared the house, he heard the sound of music and dancing. He called one of the servants and asked what this might mean. The servant said to him, 'Your brother has returned and your father has slaughtered the fattened calf because he has him back safe and sound.' He became angry, and when he refused to enter the house, his father came out and pleaded with him. He said to his father in reply, 'Look, all these years I served you and not once did I disobey your orders; yet you never gave me even a young goat to feast on with my friends. But when your son returns who swallowed up your property with prostitutes, for him you slaughter the fattened calf.' He said to him, 'My son, you are here with me always; everything I have is yours. But now we must celebrate and rejoice, because your brother was dead and has come to life again; he was lost and has been found.' "

The Gospel of the Lord. ***Praise to you, Lord Jesus Christ.***

PROFESSION OF FAITH *(page 13)*

PRAYER OF THE FAITHFUL

PREPARATION OF GIFTS *(page 16)*

PRAYER OVER THE OFFERINGS
We place before you with joy these offerings,
which bring eternal remedy, O Lord,
praying that we may both faithfully revere them
and present them to you, as is fitting,
for the salvation of all the world.
Through Christ our Lord. *Amen.*

PREFACE *(Lent 1–2, page 21)*

COMMUNION ANTIPHON *(Luke 15:32)*
You must rejoice, my son, for your brother was dead and has
come to life; he was lost and is found.

• TAKING A CLOSER LOOK •

✣ **Reconciled** Reconciliation is a common Christian image for the experience of salvation, in which God overcomes the breakdown in our relationship caused by sin and makes the relationship right. Reconciliation presumes that an existing relationship has broken down, and it describes the process by which it is restored or made right again. Paul describes salvation as God's initiative—while we were still sinners—working in Christ to reconcile us and then giving us a ministry of reconciliation (2 Corinthians 5:17-21). We carry on this ministry in our everyday lives as "ambassadors of Christ" and celebrate it especially in the sacrament of reconciliation.

PRAYER AFTER COMMUNION

O God, who enlighten everyone who comes into this world,
illuminate our hearts, we pray,
with the splendor of your grace,
that we may always ponder
what is worthy and pleasing to your majesty
and love you in all sincerity.
Through Christ our Lord. *Amen.*

PRAYER OVER THE PEOPLE

Look upon those who call to you, O Lord,
and sustain the weak;
give life by your unfailing light
to those who walk in the shadow of death,
and bring those rescued by your mercy from every evil
to reach the highest good.
Through Christ our Lord. *Amen.*

BLESSING & DISMISSAL *(page 56)* ✦

✦ RESPONDING TO THE WORD ✦

God's gift of the manna ceased when the people could feed themselves in their new land.

➡ *What temporary help from God do I no longer need?*

As Christians we are reconciled with God and become ministers of reconciliation.

➡ *How might I be a minister of reconciliation this week?*

In Jesus' parable, both sons have problems with their father.

➡ *Which son am I most like?*

CHRISTIAN INITIATION:
SECOND SCRUTINY

*The Mass prayers and readings below are for use
in parishes celebrating the Second Scrutiny.*

ENTRANCE ANTIPHON *(Cf. Psalm 25 [24]:15-16)*

My eyes are always on the Lord, for he rescues my feet from the snare. Turn to me and have mercy on me, for I am alone and poor.

COLLECT

Almighty ever-living God,
give to your Church an increase in spiritual joy,
so that those once born of earth
may be reborn as citizens of heaven.
Through our Lord Jesus Christ, your Son,
who lives and reigns with you in the unity of the Holy Spirit,
one God, for ever and ever. ***Amen.***

FIRST READING *(1 Samuel 16:1b, 6-7, 10-13a)*

The LORD said to Samuel: "Fill your horn with oil, and be on your way. I am sending you to Jesse of Bethlehem, for I have chosen my king from among his sons."

As Jesse and his sons came to the sacrifice, Samuel looked at Eliab and thought, "Surely the LORD's anointed is here before him." But the LORD said to Samuel: "Do not judge from his appearance or from his lofty stature, because I have rejected him. Not as man sees does God see, because man sees the appearance but the LORD looks into the heart." In the same way Jesse presented seven sons before Samuel, but Samuel said to Jesse, "The LORD has not chosen any one of these." Then Samuel asked Jesse, "Are these all the sons you have?" Jesse replied, "There is still the youngest, who is tending the sheep." Samuel said to Jesse, "Send for him; we will not begin the sacrificial banquet until he arrives here." Jesse sent and had the young man brought to them. He was ruddy, a youth handsome to behold and making a splendid appearance. The LORD said, "There—anoint him, for this is the one!" Then Samuel, with the horn of oil in hand, anointed David in the presence of his brothers; and from that day on, the spirit of the LORD rushed upon David.

The word of the Lord. *Thanks be to God.*

RESPONSORIAL PSALM *(Psalm 23:1–3a, 3b–4, 5, 6)*

R. **The Lord is my shepherd; there is nothing I shall want.**

The LORD is my shepherd; I shall not want.
    In verdant pastures he gives me repose;
beside restful waters he leads me;
    he refreshes my soul. R.
He guides me in right paths
    for his name's sake.
Even though I walk in the dark valley
    I fear no evil; for you are at my side
with your rod and your staff
    that give me courage. R.
You spread the table before me
    in the sight of my foes;
you anoint my head with oil;
    my cup overflows. R.
Only goodness and kindness follow me
    all the days of my life;
and I shall dwell in the house of the LORD
    for years to come. R.

SECOND READING *(Ephesians 5:8-14)*

Brothers and sisters: You were once darkness, but now you are light in the Lord. Live as children of light, for light produces every kind of goodness and righteousness and truth. Try to learn what is pleasing to the Lord. Take no part in the fruitless works of darkness; rather expose them, for it is shameful even to mention the things done by them in secret; but everything exposed by the light becomes visible, for everything that becomes visible is light. Therefore, it says:

"Awake, O sleeper,
and arise from the dead,
and Christ will give you light."

The word of the Lord. *Thanks be to God.*

VERSE BEFORE THE GOSPEL *(John 8:12)*

Glory and praise to you, Lord Jesus Christ! I am the light of the world, says the Lord; whoever follows me will have the light of life. *Glory and praise to you, Lord Jesus Christ!*

GOSPEL *(John 9:1–41)*

For the shorter version, omit the indented parts in brackets.

A reading from the holy Gospel according to John.
Glory to you, O Lord.

As Jesus passed by he saw a man blind from birth. [His disciples asked him, "Rabbi, who sinned, this man or his parents, that he was born blind?" Jesus answered, "Neither he nor his parents sinned; it is so that the works of God might be made visible through him. We have to do the works of the one who sent me while it is day. Night is coming when no one can work. While I am in the world, I am the light of the

world." When he had said this,]
he spat on the ground and made clay with the saliva, and
smeared the clay on his eyes, and said to him, "Go wash in the
Pool of Siloam"—which means Sent—. So he went and washed,
and came back able to see.

His neighbors and those who had seen him earlier as a beggar
said, "Isn't this the one who used to sit and beg?" Some said, "It
is," but others said, "No, he just looks like him." He said, "I am."
[So they said to him, "How were your eyes opened?" He replied, "The man called Jesus made clay and anointed my eyes
and told me, 'Go to Siloam and wash.' So I went there and
washed and was able to see." And they said to him, "Where is
he?" He said, "I don't know."]
They brought the one who was once blind to the Pharisees. Now
Jesus had made clay and opened his eyes on a sabbath. So then the
Pharisees also asked him how he was able to see. He said to them,
"He put clay on my eyes, and I washed, and now I can see." So
some of the Pharisees said, "This man is not from God, because
he does not keep the sabbath." But others said, "How can a sinful
man do such signs?" And there was a division among them. So
they said to the blind man again, "What do you have to say about
him, since he opened your eyes?" He said, "He is a prophet."

[Now the Jews did not believe that he had been blind and
gained his sight until they summoned the parents of the one
who had gained his sight. They asked them, "Is this your son,
who you say was born blind? How does he now see?" His
parents answered and said, "We know that this is our son and
that he was born blind. We do not know how he sees now,
nor do we know who opened his eyes. Ask him, he is of age;
he can speak for himself." His parents said this because they

were afraid of the Jews, for the Jews had already agreed that if anyone acknowledged him as the Christ, he would be expelled from the synagogue. For this reason his parents said, "He is of age; question him."

So a second time they called the man who had been blind and said to him, "Give God the praise! We know that this man is a sinner." He replied, "If he is a sinner, I do not know. One thing I do know is that I was blind and now I see." So they said to him, "What did he do to you? How did he open your eyes?" He answered them, "I told you already and you did not listen. Why do you want to hear it again? Do you want to become his disciples, too?" They ridiculed him and said, "You are that man's disciple; we are disciples of Moses! We know that God spoke to Moses, but we do not know where this one is from." The man answered and said to them, "This is what is so amazing, that you do not know where he is from, yet he opened my eyes. We know that God does not listen to sinners, but if one is devout and does his will, he listens to him. It is unheard of that anyone ever opened the eyes of a person born blind. If this man were not from God, he would not be able to do anything."]

They answered and said to him, "You were born totally in sin, and are you trying to teach us?" Then they threw him out.

When Jesus heard that they had thrown him out, he found him and said, "Do you believe in the Son of Man?" He answered and said, "Who is he, sir, that I may believe in him?" Jesus said to him, "You have seen him, the one speaking with you is he." He said, "I do believe, Lord," and he worshiped him.

[Then Jesus said, "I came into this world for judgment, so that those who do not see might see, and those who do see might become blind."

Some of the Pharisees who were with him heard this and said to him, "Surely we are not also blind, are we?" Jesus said to them, "If you were blind, you would have no sin; but now you are saying, 'We see,' so your sin remains."]

The Gospel of the Lord. *Praise to you, Lord Jesus Christ.*

PRAYER OVER THE OFFERINGS

We place before you with joy these offerings,
which bring eternal remedy, O Lord,
praying that we may both faithfully revere them
and present them to you, as is fitting,
for those who seek salvation.
Through Christ our Lord. *Amen.*

PREFACE: THE MAN BORN BLIND

It is truly right and just, our duty and our salvation,
always and everywhere to give you thanks,
Lord, holy Father, almighty and eternal God,
through Christ our Lord.

By the mystery of the Incarnation,
he has led the human race that walked in darkness
into the radiance of the faith
and has brought those born in slavery to ancient sin
through the waters of regeneration
to make them your adopted children.

Therefore, all creatures of heaven and earth
sing a new song in adoration,
and we, with all the host of Angels,
cry out, and without end acclaim:
Holy, Holy, Holy Lord God of hosts... (page 35)

COMMUNION ANTIPHON *(Cf. John 9:11, 38)*

The Lord anointed my eyes; I went, I washed, I saw and I believed in God.

PRAYER AFTER COMMUNION

Sustain your family always in your kindness,
O Lord, we pray,
correct them, set them in order,
graciously protect them under your rule,
and in your unfailing goodness
direct them along the way of salvation.
Through Christ our Lord. *Amen.*

PRAYER OVER THE PEOPLE

Look upon those who call to you, O Lord,
and sustain the weak;
give life by your unfailing light
to those who walk in the shadow of death,
and bring those rescued by your mercy from every evil
to reach the highest good.
Through Christ our Lord. *Amen.*

BLESSING & DISMISSAL *(page 56)* ✢

April 7

APR
7

Receiving Jesus' forgiveness

Leaving old ways behind is not easy. Today's readings remind us that breaking away from the past is essential to obtaining eternal life with Jesus Christ.

After the Pharisees and scribes accuse a woman of committing adultery, Jesus provides them with the opportunity to examine their consciences and begin a new life centered on forgiveness. They choose to walk away, silently rejecting this invitation.

It is the woman who gains freedom from her past. With her accusers gone, she is no longer bound by their punishment. But her true freedom comes from the forgiveness

Jesus gives her. She is left alone with this man who gives her a new chance at life. Her only instruction is to go on her way and not sin again.

Never sinning again is impossible, as we often repeat past mistakes. However, the Lord's mercy is infinite and if we continue to seek forgiveness for our sins, he grants it. In this way we can work on our transgressions, leaving them behind and entering into a Christ-centered life. This work is hard, but by keeping our hearts open, we can receive Jesus' forgiveness as well as strength to begin anew.

◼ ELIZABETH CHESLEY-JEWELL

Parishes engaged in the Rite of Christian Initiation of Adults (RCIA) may celebrate the Third Scrutiny today (see page 244).

ENTRANCE ANTIPHON *(Cf. Psalm 43 [42]:1-2)*

Give me justice, O God, and plead my cause against a nation that is faithless. From the deceitful and cunning rescue me, for you, O God, are my strength.

INTRODUCTORY RITES *(page 10)*

COLLECT

By your help, we beseech you, Lord our God,
may we walk eagerly in that same charity
with which, out of love for the world,
your Son handed himself over to death.
Through our Lord Jesus Christ, your Son,
who lives and reigns with you in the unity of the Holy Spirit,
one God, for ever and ever. *Amen.*

The readings for Year A may be used in place of these (see page 244).

FIRST READING *(Isaiah 43:16-21)*

Thus says the LORD,
    who opens a way in the sea
        and a path in the mighty waters,
who leads out chariots and horsemen,
        a powerful army,
till they lie prostrate together, never to rise,
        snuffed out and quenched like a wick.
Remember not the events of the past,
        the things of long ago consider not;
see, I am doing something new!

Now it springs forth, do you not perceive it?
In the desert I make a way,
   in the wasteland, rivers.
Wild beasts honor me,
   jackals and ostriches,
for I put water in the desert
   and rivers in the wasteland
   for my chosen people to drink,
the people whom I formed for myself,
   that they might announce my praise.

The word of the Lord. *Thanks be to God.*

RESPONSORIAL PSALM *(Psalm 126:1-2, 2-3, 4-5, 6)*
℟ **The Lord has done great things for us; we are filled with joy.**

When the LORD brought back the captives of Zion,*
   we were like men dreaming.
Then our mouth was filled with laughter,
   and our tongue with rejoicing. ℟

Then they said among the nations,
   "The LORD has done great things for them."
The LORD has done great things for us;
   we are glad indeed. ℟

Restore our fortunes, O LORD,
   like the torrents in the southern desert.
Those that sow in tears
   shall reap rejoicing. ℟

Although they go forth weeping,
   carrying the seed to be sown,
they shall come back rejoicing,
   carrying their sheaves. ℟

SECOND READING *(Philippians 3:8-14)*

Brothers and sisters: I consider everything as a loss because of the supreme good of knowing Christ Jesus my Lord. For his sake I have accepted the loss of all things and I consider them so much rubbish, that I may gain Christ and be found in him, not having any righteousness of my own based on the law but that which comes through faith in Christ, the righteousness from God, depending on faith to know him and the power of his resurrection and the sharing of his sufferings by being conformed to his death, if somehow I may attain the resurrection from the dead.

It is not that I have already taken hold of it or have already attained perfect maturity, but I continue my pursuit in hope that I may possess it, since I have indeed been taken possession of by Christ Jesus. Brothers and sisters, I for my part do not consider myself to have taken possession. Just one thing: forgetting what lies behind but straining forward to what lies ahead, I continue my pursuit toward the goal, the prize of God's upward calling, in Christ Jesus.

The word of the Lord. *Thanks be to God.*

VERSE BEFORE THE GOSPEL *(Joel 2:12-13)*
Glory and praise to you, Lord Jesus Christ! Even now, says the Lord, return to me with your whole heart; for I am gracious and merciful. *Glory and praise to you, Lord Jesus Christ!*

GOSPEL *(John 8:1–11)*

A reading from the holy Gospel according to John.

Glory to you, O Lord.

Jesus went to the Mount of Olives. But early in the morning he arrived again in the temple area, and all the people started coming to him, and he sat down and taught them. Then **the scribes and the Pharisees**✝ brought a woman who had been caught in adultery and made her stand in the middle. They said to him, "Teacher, this woman was caught in the very act of committing adultery. Now in the law, Moses commanded us to stone such women. So what do you say?" They said this to test him, so that they could have some charge to bring against him. Jesus bent down and began to write on the ground with his finger. But when they continued asking him, he straightened up and said to them, "Let the one among you who is without sin be the first to throw a stone at her." Again he bent down and wrote on the ground. And in response, they went away one by one, beginning with the elders. So he was left alone with the woman before him. Then Jesus straightened up and said to her, "Woman, where are they? Has no one condemned you?" She replied, "No one, sir." Then Jesus said, "Neither do I condemn you. Go, and from now on do not sin any more."

The Gospel of the Lord. *Praise to you, Lord Jesus Christ.*

PROFESSION OF FAITH *(page 13)*

PRAYER OF THE FAITHFUL

PREPARATION OF GIFTS *(page 16)*

PRAYER OVER THE OFFERINGS
Hear us, almighty God,
and, having instilled in your servants
the teachings of the Christian faith,
graciously purify them
by the working of this sacrifice.
Through Christ our Lord. *Amen.*

PREFACE *(Lent 1–2, page 21)*

COMMUNION ANTIPHON *(John 8:10–11)*
Has no one condemned you, woman? No one, Lord. Neither shall I condemn you. From now on, sin no more.

• TAKING A CLOSER LOOK •

✢ **The scribes and the Pharisees** The scribes were the Jewish biblical scholars (often called *Rabbi* or teacher) who were experts in interpreting the meaning of the Law (*Torah*). The Pharisees were a lay group, not priests, characterized by their zeal for the Jewish Law. In Jesus' time, they were influential among the ordinary people because they were living examples of what every Jew was called upon to do. They believed that since the Law was God's revealed guideline for them, it should be followed as perfectly as possible in every detail of ordinary life. They recognized as authoritative not only the written Law (in the first five books of the Bible or Pentateuch) but also the many interpretations of this written Law given by generations of scholarly commentators.

PRAYER AFTER COMMUNION

We pray, almighty God,
that we may always be counted among the members of Christ,
in whose Body and Blood we have communion.
Who lives and reigns for ever and ever. *Amen.*

PRAYER OVER THE PEOPLE

Bless, O Lord, your people,
who long for the gift of your mercy,
and grant that what, at your prompting, they desire
they may receive by your generous gift.
Through Christ our Lord. *Amen.*

BLESSING & DISMISSAL *(page 56)* ✠

✠ RESPONDING TO THE WORD ✠

Isaiah proclaims that God is doing something new.

➡ *What new thing is God doing in me this Lent?*

Paul's losses seem small when compared with his gain of having Christ in his life.

➡ *What have I already gained by seeking Christ this Lent?*

Jesus is reluctant to condemn the woman, though her sin seems obvious.

➡ *When have I been quick to condemn others instead of letting God be the one to judge them?*

CHRISTIAN INITIATION: THIRD SCRUTINY

*The Mass prayers and readings below are for use
in parishes celebrating the Third Scrutiny.*

ENTRANCE ANTIPHON *(Cf. Psalm 18 [17]:5-7)*
The waves of death rose about me; the pains of the netherworld surrounded me. In my anguish I called to the Lord; and from his holy temple he heard my voice.

COLLECT
Grant, O Lord, to these chosen ones
that, instructed in the holy mysteries,
they may receive new life at the font of Baptism
and be numbered among the members of your Church.
Through our Lord Jesus Christ, your Son,
who lives and reigns with you in the unity of the Holy Spirit,
one God, for ever and ever. *Amen.*

FIRST READING *(Ezekiel 37:12-14)*
Thus says the Lord GOD: O my people, I will open your graves and have you rise from them, and bring you back to the land of Israel. Then you shall know that I am the LORD, when I open your graves and have you rise from them, O my people! I will put my spirit in you that you may live, and I will settle you upon your land; thus you shall know that I am the LORD. I have promised, and I will do it, says the LORD.

The word of the Lord. *Thanks be to God.*

RESPONSORIAL PSALM *(Psalm 130:1-2, 3-4, 5-6, 7-8)*

R. With the Lord there is mercy and fullness of redemption.

Out of the depths I cry to you, O LORD;
   LORD, hear my voice!
Let your ears be attentive
   to my voice in supplication. R.

If you, O LORD, mark iniquities,
   LORD, who can stand?
But with you is forgiveness,
   that you may be revered. R.

I trust in the LORD;
   my soul trusts in his word.
More than sentinels wait for the dawn,
   let Israel wait for the LORD. R.

For with the LORD is kindness
   and with him is plenteous redemption;
and he will redeem Israel
   from all their iniquities. R.

SECOND READING *(Romans 8:8-11)*

Brothers and sisters: Those who are in the flesh cannot please God. But you are not in the flesh; on the contrary, you are in the spirit, if only the Spirit of God dwells in you. Whoever does not have the Spirit of Christ does not belong to him. But if Christ is in you, although the body is dead because of sin, the spirit is alive because of righteousness. If the Spirit of the One who raised Jesus from the dead dwells in you, the One who raised Christ from the dead will give life to your mortal bodies also, through his Spirit dwelling in you.

The word of the Lord. *Thanks be to God.*

VERSE BEFORE THE GOSPEL *(John 11:25, 26)*
Glory and praise to you, Lord Jesus Christ! I am the resurrection and the life, says the Lord; whoever believes in me, even if he dies, will never die. *Glory and praise to you, Lord Jesus Christ!*

GOSPEL *(John 11:1–45)*
For the shorter version, omit the indented text in brackets and add words in parentheses.

A reading from the holy Gospel according to John.
Glory to you, O Lord.

[Now a man was ill, Lazarus from Bethany,* the village of Mary and her sister Martha. Mary was the one who had anointed the Lord with perfumed oil and dried his feet with her hair; it was her brother Lazarus who was ill. So] The sisters (of Lazarus) sent word to Jesus saying, "Master, the one you love is ill." When Jesus heard this he said, "This illness is not to end in death, but is for the glory of God, that the Son of God may be glorified through it." Now Jesus loved Martha and her sister and Lazarus. So when he heard that he was ill, he remained for two days in the place where he was. Then after this he said to his disciples, "Let us go back to Judea."

[The disciples said to him, "Rabbi, the Jews were just trying to stone you, and you want to go back there?" Jesus answered, "Are there not twelve hours in a day? If one walks during the day, he does not stumble, because he sees the light of this world. But if one walks at night, he stumbles, because the light is not in him." He said this, and then told them, "Our friend Lazarus is asleep, but I am going to awaken him." So the disciples said to him, "Master, if he is asleep, he will be saved." But Jesus was talking about his death, while they thought that he meant ordinary sleep. So then Jesus said to them clearly, "Lazarus has died. And

I am glad for you that I was not there, that you may believe. Let us go to him." So Thomas, called Didymus,* said to his fellow disciples, "Let us also go to die with him."]

When Jesus arrived, he found that Lazarus had already been in the tomb for four days.

[Now Bethany was near Jerusalem, only about two miles away. And many of the Jews had come to Martha and Mary to comfort them about their brother.]

When Martha heard that Jesus was coming, she went to meet him; but Mary sat at home. Martha said to Jesus, "Lord, if you had been here, my brother would not have died. But even now I know that whatever you ask of God, God will give you." Jesus said to her, "Your brother will rise." Martha said to him, "I know he will rise, in the resurrection on the last day." Jesus told her, "I am the resurrection and the life; whoever believes in me, even if he dies, will live, and everyone who lives and believes in me will never die. Do you believe this?" She said to him, "Yes, Lord. I have come to believe that you are the Christ, the Son of God, the one who is coming into the world."

[When she had said this, she went and called her sister Mary secretly, saying, "The teacher is here and is asking for you." As soon as she heard this, she rose quickly and went to him. For Jesus had not yet come into the village, but was still where Martha had met him. So when the Jews who were with her in the house comforting her saw Mary get up quickly and go out, they followed her, presuming that she was going to the tomb to weep there. When Mary came to where Jesus was and saw him, she fell at his feet and said to him, "Lord, if you had been here, my brother would not have died." When Jesus saw her weeping and the Jews who had come with her weeping,] he became perturbed and deeply troubled, and said, "Where have you laid him?" They said to him, "Sir, come and see." And Jesus wept. So the Jews said, "See how he loved him." But some of them said, "Could not the one who opened the eyes of the blind man have done something so that this man would not have died?"

So Jesus, perturbed again, came to the tomb. It was a cave, and a stone lay across it. Jesus said, "Take away the stone." Martha, the dead man's sister, said to him, "Lord, by now there will be a stench; he has been dead for four days." Jesus said to her, "Did I not tell you that if you believe you will see the glory of God?" So they took away the stone. And Jesus raised his eyes and said, "Father, I thank you for hearing me. I know that you always hear me; but because of the crowd here I have said this, that they may believe that you sent me." And when he had said this, he cried out in a loud voice, "Lazarus, come out!" The dead man came out, tied hand and foot with burial bands, and his face was wrapped in a cloth. So Jesus said to them, "Untie him and let him go."

Now many of the Jews who had come to Mary and seen what he had done began to believe in him.

The Gospel of the Lord. *Praise to you, Lord Jesus Christ.*

PRAYER OVER THE OFFERINGS

Hear us, almighty God,
and, having instilled in your servants
the first fruits of the Christian faith,
graciously purify them by the working of this sacrifice.
Through Christ our Lord. *Amen.*

PREFACE: LAZARUS

It is truly right and just, our duty and our salvation,
always and everywhere to give you thanks,
Lord, holy Father, almighty and eternal God,
through Christ our Lord.

For as true man he wept for Lazarus his friend
and as eternal God raised him from the tomb,
just as, taking pity on the human race,
he leads us by sacred mysteries to new life.

Through him the host of Angels adores your majesty
and rejoices in your presence for ever.
May our voices, we pray, join with theirs
in one chorus of exultant praise, as we acclaim:
Holy, Holy, Holy Lord God of hosts... *(page 35)*

COMMUNION ANTIPHON *(Cf. John 11:26)*
Everyone who lives and believes in me will not die for ever, says
the Lord.

PRAYER AFTER COMMUNION
May your people be at one, O Lord, we pray,
and in wholehearted submission to you
may they obtain this grace:
that, safe from all distress,
they may readily live out their joy at being saved
and remember in loving prayer those to be reborn.
Through Christ our Lord. *Amen.*

PRAYER OVER THE PEOPLE
Bless, O Lord, your people,
who long for the gift of your mercy,
and grant that what, at your prompting, they desire
they may receive by your generous gift.
Through Christ our Lord. *Amen.*

BLESSING & DISMISSAL *(page 56)* ✠

April 14

Jesus took his place

Every year, the Church opens a window into Christ's suffering, so we understand the love that compelled him. "Jesus took his place at table with the apostles." I was struck that these are words that begin the telling of the passion of Christ in Luke's gospel. Jesus is taking his place, in place of us.

He took his place as the sacrificial lamb during the passover meal. Then, he took his place in humble service. He took his place being counted among the wicked, losing all his social standing. He took his place interceding for us, then in undergoing scurrilous insults. He took his place in being convicted while innocent.

As the painful description of our Lord's suffering continues, we see something else unfold. He received.

He received help, care, even pity. This, our Lord God, Savior and Redeemer, did. He received the final punishment with its nails and the crown of thorns. While he received the judgment of the world upon himself, he received the repentant sinner, hung alongside him. This is how our Savior lived—and died.

When you receive Christ in the Eucharist today, do so gratefully, humbly, and confidently. For God so loved the world that God gave all. For you.

▦ JOHANNE BROWNRIGG

THE COMMEMORATION
OF THE LORD'S ENTRANCE
INTO JERUSALEM

FIRST FORM: THE PROCESSION

INTRODUCTION

The assembly, carrying palm branches, gather in a place distinct from the church to which the procession will move. They may sing Hosanna! or another hymn.

Dear brethren (brothers and sisters),
since the beginning of Lent until now
we have prepared our hearts by penance and charitable works.
Today we gather together to herald with the whole Church
the beginning of the celebration
of our Lord's Paschal Mystery,
that is to say, of his Passion and Resurrection.
For it was to accomplish this mystery
that he entered his own city of Jerusalem.
Therefore, with all faith and devotion,
let us commemorate
the Lord's entry into the city for our salvation,
following in his footsteps,
so that, being made by his grace partakers of the Cross,
we may have a share also in his Resurrection and in his life.

Let us pray:

Almighty ever-living God,
sanctify these branches with your blessing,
that we, who follow Christ the King in exultation,

may reach the eternal Jerusalem through him.
Who lives and reigns for ever and ever. *Amen.*

Or

Increase the faith of those who place their hope in you, O God,
and graciously hear the prayers of those who call on you,
that we, who today hold high these branches
to hail Christ in his triumph,
may bear fruit for you by good works accomplished in him.
Who lives and reigns for ever and ever. *Amen.*

GOSPEL *(Luke 19:28–40)*
A reading from the holy Gospel according to Luke.
Glory to you, O Lord.

Jesus proceeded on his journey up to Jerusalem. As he drew
near to Bethphage* and Bethany* at the place called the
Mount of Olives, he sent two of his disciples. He said, "Go into
the village opposite you, and as you enter it you will find a colt
tethered on which no one has ever sat. Untie it and bring it here.
And if anyone should ask you, 'Why are you untying it?' you will
answer, 'The Master has need of it.'" So those who had been sent
went off and found everything just as he had told them. And as
they were untying the colt, its owners said to them, "Why are
you untying this colt?" They answered, "The Master has need of
it." So they brought it to Jesus, threw their cloaks over the colt,
and helped Jesus to mount. As he rode along, the people were
spreading their cloaks on the road; and now as he was approaching the slope of the Mount of Olives, the whole multitude of his
disciples began to praise God aloud with joy for all the mighty
deeds they had seen. They proclaimed:
    "Blessed is the king who comes

in the name of the Lord.
  Peace in heaven
    and glory in the highest."
Some of the Pharisees in the crowd said to him, "Teacher, rebuke
your disciples." He said in reply, "I tell you, if they keep silent,
the stones will cry out!"
  The Gospel of the Lord. *Praise to you, Lord Jesus Christ.*

PROCESSION
Dear brethren (brothers and sisters),
like the crowds who acclaimed Jesus in Jerusalem,
let us go forth in peace.

*All process to the church singing a hymn in honor of Christ the King. Mass
continues with the Collect.*

SECOND FORM: THE SOLEMN ENTRANCE
*The blessing of branches and proclamation of the gospel take place, as
above, but in the church. After the gospel, the celebrant moves solemnly
through the church to the sanctuary, while all sing. Mass continues with the
Collect.*

THIRD FORM: THE SIMPLE ENTRANCE
*The people gather in the church as usual. While the celebrant goes to the
altar, the following entrance antiphon or a suitable hymn is sung.*

ENTRANCE ANTIPHON *(Cf. John 12:1, 12-13; Psalm 24 [23]:9-10)*
Six days before the Passover, when the Lord came into the city
of Jerusalem, the children ran to meet him; in their hands they
carried palm branches and with a loud voice cried out: Hosanna

in the highest! Blessed are you, who have come in your abundant mercy!

O gates, lift high your heads; grow higher, ancient doors. Let him enter, the king of glory! Who is this king of glory? He, the Lord of hosts, he is the king of glory. Hosanna in the highest! Blessed are you, who have come in your abundant mercy!

INTRODUCTORY RITES *(page 10)*

COLLECT
Almighty ever-living God,
who as an example of humility for the human race to follow
caused our Savior to take flesh and submit to the Cross,
graciously grant that we may heed his lesson of patient suffering
and so merit a share in his Resurrection.
Who lives and reigns with you in the unity of the Holy Spirit,
one God, for ever and ever. *Amen.*

FIRST READING *(Isaiah 50:4–7)*

The Lord God has given me
a well-trained tongue,
that I might know how to speak to the weary
a word that will rouse them.
Morning after morning
he opens my ear that I may hear;
and I have not rebelled,
have not turned back.
I gave my back to those who beat me,
my cheeks to those who plucked my beard;
my face I did not shield
from buffets and spitting.

The Lord God is my help,
>   therefore I am not disgraced;
I have set my face like flint,
>   knowing that I shall not be put to shame.

The word of the Lord. *Thanks be to God.*

RESPONSORIAL PSALM *(Psalm 22:8-9, 17-18, 19-20, 23-24)*
℞ **My God, my God, why have you abandoned me?**

All who see me scoff at me;
>   they mock me with parted lips, they wag their heads:
"He relied on the Lord; let him deliver him,
>   let him rescue him, if he loves him." ℞
Indeed, many dogs surround me,
>   a pack of evildoers closes in upon me;
they have pierced my hands and my feet;
>   I can count all my bones. ℞
They divide my garments among them,
>   and for my vesture they cast lots.
But you, O Lord, be not far from me;
>   O my help, hasten to aid me. ℞
I will proclaim your name to my brethren;
>   in the midst of the assembly I will praise you:
"You who fear the Lord, praise him;
>   all you descendants of Jacob, give glory to him;
>   revere him, all you descendants of Israel!" ℞

SECOND READING *(Philippians 2:6-11)*

Christ Jesus, though he was in the form of God,
did not regard equality with God
something to be grasped.

Rather, he emptied himself,
taking the form of a slave,
coming in human likeness;
and found human in appearance,
he humbled himself,
becoming obedient to the point of death,
even death on a cross.
Because of this, God greatly exalted him
and bestowed on him the name
which is above every name,
that at the name of Jesus
every knee should bend,
of those in heaven and on earth and under the earth,
and every tongue confess that
Jesus Christ is Lord,
to the glory of God the Father.

The word of the Lord. ***Thanks be to God.***

VERSE BEFORE THE GOSPEL *(Philippians 2:8–9)*
Glory and praise to you, Lord Jesus Christ! Christ became
obedient to the point of death, even death on a cross. Because
of this, God greatly exalted him and bestowed on him the name
which is above every name. ***Glory and praise to you, Lord Jesus
Christ!***

GOSPEL *(Luke 22:14–23:56)*
*Several readers may proclaim the passion narrative today. (**N**) indicates
the narrator, (**✝**) the words of Jesus, (**V**) a voice, and (**C**) the crowd. The
shorter version begins (page 262) and ends (page 266) at the asterisks.*

N The Passion of our Lord Jesus Christ according to Luke.

When the hour came, Jesus took his place at table with the apostles. He said to them,

✝ "I have eagerly desired to eat this **Passover**✝ with you before I suffer, for, I tell you, I shall not eat it again until there is fulfillment in the kingdom of God."

N Then he took a cup, gave thanks, and said,

✝ "Take this and share it among yourselves; for I tell you that from this time on I shall not drink of the fruit of the vine until the kingdom of God comes."

N Then he took the bread, said the blessing, broke it, and gave it to them, saying,

✝ "This is my body, which will be given for you; do this in memory of me."

N And likewise the cup after they had eaten, saying,

✝ "This cup is the new covenant in my blood, which will be shed for you.

"And yet behold, the hand of the one who is to betray me is with me on the table; for the Son of Man indeed goes as it has been determined; but woe to that man by whom he is betrayed."

N And they began to debate among themselves who among them would do such a deed.

Then an argument broke out among them about which of them should be regarded as the greatest. He said to them,

✝ "The kings of the Gentiles lord it over them and those in

authority over them are addressed as 'Benefactors'; but among you it shall not be so. Rather, let the greatest among you be as the youngest, and the leader as the servant. For who is greater: the one seated at table or the one who serves? Is it not the one seated at table? I am among you as the one who serves. It is you who have stood by me in my trials; and I confer a kingdom on you, just as my Father has conferred one on me, that you may eat and drink at my table in my kingdom; and you will sit on thrones judging the twelve tribes of Israel.

"Simon, Simon, behold Satan has demanded to sift all of you like wheat, but I have prayed that your own faith may not fail; and once you have turned back, you must strengthen your brothers."

N   He said to him,

V "Lord, I am prepared to go to prison and to die with you."

N But he replied,

✝ "I tell you, Peter, before the cock crows this day, you will deny three times that you know me."

N   He said to them,

✝ "When I sent you forth without a money bag or a sack or sandals, were you in need of anything?"

C "No, nothing,"

N they replied. He said to them,

✝ "But now one who has a money bag should take it, and likewise a sack, and one who does not have a sword should sell his cloak and buy one. For I tell you that this Scripture must be fulfilled in me, namely, *He was counted among the wicked*; and indeed what is written about me is coming to fulfillment."

N Then they said,

C "Lord, look, there are two swords here."

N But he replied,

† "It is enough!"

N   Then going out, he went, as was his custom, to the Mount of Olives, and the disciples followed him. When he arrived at the place he said to them,

† "Pray that you may not undergo the test."

N After withdrawing about a stone's throw from them and kneeling, he prayed, saying,

† "Father, if you are willing, take this cup away from me; still, not my will but yours be done."

N And to strengthen him an angel from heaven appeared to him. He was in such agony and he prayed so fervently that his sweat became like drops of blood falling on the ground. When he rose from prayer and returned to his disciples, he found them sleeping from grief. He said to them,

† "Why are you sleeping? Get up and pray that you may not undergo the test."

N   While he was still speaking, a crowd approached and in front was one of the Twelve, a man named Judas. He went up to Jesus to kiss him. Jesus said to him,

† "Judas, are you betraying the Son of Man with a kiss?"

N His disciples realized what was about to happen, and they asked,

C **"Lord, shall we strike with a sword?"**

N And one of them struck the high priest's servant and cut off his right ear. But Jesus said in reply,

✝ "Stop, no more of this!"

N Then he touched the servant's ear and healed him. And Jesus said to the chief priests and temple guards and elders who had come for him,

✝ "Have you come out as against a robber, with swords and clubs? Day after day I was with you in the temple area, and you did not seize me; but this is your hour, the time for the power of darkness."

N   After arresting him they led him away and took him into the house of the high priest; Peter was following at a distance. They lit a fire in the middle of the courtyard and sat around it, and Peter sat down with them. When a maid saw him seated in the light, she looked intently at him and said,

C **"This man too was with him."**

N But he denied it saying,

V "Woman, I do not know him."

N A short while later someone else saw him and said,

C **"You too are one of them"**;

N but Peter answered,

V "My friend, I am not."

N About an hour later, still another insisted,

C **"Assuredly, this man too was with him, for he also is a Galilean."**

N But Peter said,

V "My friend, I do not know what you are talking about."

N Just as he was saying this, the cock crowed, and the Lord turned and looked at Peter; and Peter remembered the word of the Lord, how he had said to him, "Before the cock crows today, you will deny me three times." He went out and began to weep bitterly. The men who held Jesus in custody were ridiculing and beating him. They blindfolded him and questioned him, saying,

C **"Prophesy! Who is it that struck you?"**

N And they reviled him in saying many other things against him. When day came the council of elders of the people met, both chief priests and scribes, and they brought him before their Sanhedrin.* They said,

C **"If you are the Christ, tell us,"**

N but he replied to them,

✝ "If I tell you, you will not believe, and if I question, you will not respond. But from this time on the Son of Man will be seated at the right hand of the power of God."

N They all asked,

C **"Are you then the Son of God?"**

N He replied to them,

† "You say that I am."

N Then they said,

C "What further need have we for testimony? We have heard it from his own mouth."

* * *

N   Then the whole assembly of them (The elders of the people, chief priests and scribes,) arose and brought him before Pilate. They brought charges against him, saying,

C "We found this man misleading our people; he opposes the payment of taxes to Caesar* and maintains that he is the Christ, a king."

N Pilate asked him,

V "Are you the king of the Jews?"

N He said to him in reply,

† "You say so."

N Pilate then addressed the chief priests and the crowds,

V "I find this man not guilty."

N But they were adamant and said,

C "He is inciting the people with his teaching throughout all Judea, from Galilee where he began even to here."

N   On hearing this, Pilate asked if the man was a Galilean; and upon learning that he was under Herod's jurisdiction, he sent him to Herod who was in Jerusalem at that time. Herod was very glad to see Jesus; he had been wanting to see him for a long time, for he had heard about him and had been hoping to see him perform some sign. He questioned him at length, but he gave him no answer. The chief priests and scribes, meanwhile, stood by accusing him harshly. Herod and his soldiers treated him contemptuously and mocked him, and after clothing him in resplendent garb, he sent him back to Pilate. Herod and Pilate became friends that very day, even though they had been enemies formerly. Pilate then summoned the chief priests, the rulers, and the people and said to them,

V "You brought this man to me and accused him of inciting the people to revolt. I have conducted my investigation in your presence and have not found this man guilty of the charges you have brought against him, nor did Herod, for he sent him back to us. So no capital crime has been committed by him. Therefore I shall have him flogged and then release him."

N   But all together they shouted out,

C "Away with this man! Release Barabbas* to us."

N —Now Barabbas had been imprisoned for a rebellion that had taken place in the city and for murder.—Again Pilate addressed them, still wishing to release Jesus, but they continued their shouting,

C "Crucify him! Crucify him!"

N Pilate addressed them a third time,

V "What evil has this man done? I found him guilty of no capital crime. Therefore I shall have him flogged and then release him."

N With loud shouts, however, they persisted in calling for his crucifixion, and their voices prevailed. The verdict of Pilate was that their demand should be granted. So he released the man who had been imprisoned for rebellion and murder, for whom they asked, and he handed Jesus over to them to deal with as they wished.

As they led him away they took hold of a certain Simon, a Cyrenian,* who was coming in from the country; and after laying the cross on him, they made him carry it behind Jesus. A large crowd of people followed Jesus, including many women who mourned and lamented him. Jesus turned to them and said,

✝ "Daughters of Jerusalem, do not weep for me; weep instead for yourselves and for your children for indeed, the days are coming when people will say, 'Blessed are the barren, the wombs that never bore and the breasts that never nursed.' At that time people will say to the mountains, 'Fall upon us!' and to the hills, 'Cover us!' for if these things are done when the wood is green what will happen when it is dry?"

N Now two others, both criminals, were led away with him to be executed.

When they came to the place called the Skull, they crucified him and the criminals there, one on his right, the other on his left. Then Jesus said,

✝ "Father, forgive them, they know not what they do."

N They divided his garments by casting lots. The people stood by and watched; the rulers, meanwhile, sneered at him and said,

C "He saved others, let him save himself if he is the chosen one, the Christ of God."

N Even the soldiers jeered at him. As they approached to offer him wine they called out,

C **"If you are King of the Jews, save yourself."**

N Above him there was an inscription that read, "This is the King of the Jews."

   Now one of the criminals hanging there reviled Jesus, saying,

V "Are you not the Christ? Save yourself and us."

N The other, however, rebuking him, said in reply,

V "Have you no fear of God, for you are subject to the same condemnation? And indeed, we have been condemned justly, for the sentence we received corresponds to our crimes, but this man has done nothing criminal."

N Then he said,

V "Jesus, remember me when you come into your kingdom."

N He replied to him,

† "Amen, I say to you, today you will be with me in Paradise."

N   It was now about noon and darkness came over the whole land until three in the afternoon because of an eclipse of the sun. Then the veil of the temple was torn down the middle. Jesus cried out in a loud voice,

† "Father, into your hands I commend my spirit";

N and when he had said this he breathed his last.

(Here all kneel and pause for a short time.)

N The centurion who witnessed what had happened glorified God and said,

V "This man was innocent beyond doubt."

N When all the people who had gathered for this spectacle saw what had happened, they returned home beating their breasts; but all his acquaintances stood at a distance, including the women who had followed him from Galilee and saw these events.

* * *

N Now there was a virtuous and righteous man named Joseph who, though he was a member of the council, had not consented to their plan of action. He came from the Jewish town of Arimathea and was awaiting the kingdom of God. He went to Pilate and asked for the body of Jesus. After he had taken the body down, he wrapped it in a linen cloth and laid him in a rock-hewn tomb in which no one had yet been buried. It was the day of preparation, and the sabbath was about to begin. The women who had come from Galilee with him followed behind, and when they had seen the tomb and the way in which his body was laid in it, they returned and prepared spices and perfumed oils. Then they rested on the sabbath according to the commandment.

The Gospel of the Lord. *Praise to you, Lord Jesus Christ.*

PROFESSION OF FAITH *(page 13)*

PRAYER OF THE FAITHFUL

PREPARATION OF GIFTS *(page 16)*

PRAYER OVER THE OFFERINGS
Through the Passion of your Only Begotten Son, O Lord,

may our reconciliation with you be near at hand,
so that, though we do not merit it by our own deeds,
yet by this sacrifice made once for all,
we may feel already the effects of your mercy.
Through Christ our Lord. *Amen.*

PREFACE: THE PASSION OF THE LORD
It is truly right and just, our duty and our salvation,
always and everywhere to give you thanks,
Lord, holy Father, almighty and eternal God,
through Christ our Lord.

For, though innocent, he suffered willingly for sinners
and accepted unjust condemnation to save the guilty.
His Death has washed away our sins,
and his Resurrection has purchased our justification.

And so, with all the Angels,
we praise you, as in joyful celebration we acclaim:
Holy, Holy, Holy Lord God of hosts... (page 35)

● TAKING A CLOSER LOOK ●

✤ **Passover** Passover (Greek, *ta pascha*) was the annual Jewish family celebration remembering God's deliverance of Israel from Egypt. In particular, the term recalls God's striking down of every Egyptian firstborn, both children and animals, and "passing over" those of the Hebrews (see Exodus 12). To this feast was joined an eight-day period when only unleavened bread could be eaten. Their leaven was not like our powdered yeast, but rather a fermentation agent as is used in making sourdough bread today. Thus leavened bread contained a corrupting agent that would render it "unclean" for ritual use on this most sacred feast.

COMMUNION ANTIPHON *(Matthew 26:42)*

Father, if this chalice cannot pass without my drinking it, your will be done.

PRAYER AFTER COMMUNION

Nourished with these sacred gifts,
we humbly beseech you, O Lord,
that, just as through the death of your Son
you have brought us to hope for what we believe,
so by his Resurrection
you may lead us to where you call.
Through Christ our Lord. *Amen.*

PRAYER OVER THE PEOPLE

Look, we pray, O Lord, on this your family,
for whom our Lord Jesus Christ
did not hesitate to be delivered into the hands of the wicked
and submit to the agony of the Cross.
Who lives and reigns for ever and ever.

BLESSING & DISMISSAL *(page 56)* ❖

❖ RESPONDING TO THE WORD ❖

God's servant desires to speak an encouraging word to the weary.

➡ *Who needs to hear a good word from me today?*

Jesus did not grasp at glory but emptied himself in service.

➡ *For whom can I empty myself in service today?*

Even in his own suffering, Jesus encourages others.

➡ *How can I forget my troubles and help someone in need today?*

The Triduum (Latin for "three days") comes at the end of Holy Week and comprises the three-day period of prayer leading to the Easter feast, the fulfillment of the whole liturgical year.

Holy Thursday

On Holy Thursday (also called Maundy Thursday), the Church celebrates the Lord's Supper and the institution of the Eucharist. The word "Maundy" stems from the Latin word *mandatum*, meaning "commandment," and refers to the new commandment of love that Jesus gave his disciples that night.

Most parishes now observe the custom of foot-washing, recalling how Jesus washed his disciples' feet at the Last Supper (John 13:1-20). After the liturgy, the consecrated bread is transferred to a side altar and kept in the tabernacle of repose. Then the altar is stripped.

Good Friday

Good Friday is the only day of the year on which Mass is not celebrated. The altar is bare, and the liturgy consists of proclaiming John's passion account, intercessions, veneration of the cross, and a communion service.

Many churches, in addition to the liturgy of Good Friday, have a meditation on the Way of the Cross commemorating the events of Jesus' passion. Some parishes have also introduced Good Friday meditations on the "seven last words" of Christ on the cross taken from all four gospels.

The Great Vigil of Easter

Only the Eucharist itself is older than the liturgy of the Easter Vigil. This service re-enacts the passage from death into life. On this night, we celebrate our deliverance by Christ our Passover and look forward to the day when we shall see him face to face. During the Easter Vigil, as the Roman Missal explains, "the Church, keeping watch, awaits the Resurrection of Christ and celebrates it in the Sacraments" (*Universal Norms on the Liturgical Year and the General Roman Calendar*, n. 21).

The liturgy begins in a darkened church. The paschal candle is lighted as the "Light of Christ" is proclaimed and praised. In many churches, small candles held by the worshipers provide the only light for this part of the service. These candles are lighted from the paschal candle.

Several readings from the Old Testament summarize the story of salvation, telling of God's work of creation, the calling of the Hebrews to be God's people, their deliverance in the Exodus, and God's constant care until Christ came. An air of expectancy surrounds the prayers and singing of canticles that follow each reading.

Then the altar candles are lighted from the paschal candle, and, in a blaze of light and triumphant music, the first Easter Eucharist begins. Our risen Lord comes, in word and sacrament, into the darkness of our lives with the light of his risen life.

Baptisms follow the Scripture readings. Easter Eve has always been the traditional time for baptisms and, in ancient times, for the laying-on of hands by the bishop. If there are no candidates for baptism, the congregation joins in the renewal of baptismal promises. Thus is recalled the time when we died and were buried with Christ and were raised with him to newness of life.

Praying and living Holy Week

When a Jewish household gathers for its Passover meal, the youngest child begins the reminiscing by asking: "Why is this night different from all other nights?" So likewise, we Christians might ask, "Why are these three days of the Triduum different from all other days?" The answer, of course, is that they encapsulate the deepest meaning of the story of our salvation. Through his death and resurrection, Jesus brings us all into the right relationships with God and with others.

During Holy Week and the Triduum, in order to recall the story of our salvation, individuals and family members might read the Scriptures appointed for each day or, if there are young children, read the events of Holy Week from a Bible storybook.

But knowing the story is only half the challenge. We need to connect its life-giving possibilities with our own lives. Use the following questions (based on Exodus 14:15–15:1, see page 316) as a way for household members to discover the "exodus" character of their own lives.

- Tell a story of your experience of freedom and deliverance. What part did God play in this experience?

- When did you escape your own form of slavery and head for the promised land of freedom?

- When did you pass through the waters of your Red Sea and dance like Miriam on the other side?

- Tell a story of your passing over from some form of death to new life.

April 18

Sharing in the paschal mystery

Although Peter would have been familiar with foot washing as an act of hospitality towards weary travelers, he was initially uncomfortable allowing Jesus to wash his feet. Had we attended the Last Supper, we might also have protested, because of the incongruity of a master washing a disciple's feet.

Post-resurrection, though, and with the aid of the Spirit, we disciples now understand the many dimensions of this sign. We recognize in Jesus' humble action yet another example of his self-sacrificial love, laying down both his outer garb and his very life, as Paschal Lamb, for our sake. We are reminded, too, of the many ways in which we today share in the paschal mystery: through the entire sacramental life of the Church and in the myriad other ways in which the ordained and common priesthoods share in Christ's priestly, prophetic, and royal offices. We acknowledge with gratitude Jesus' act of hospitality, welcoming us into his eternal home.

Still, becoming comfortable with and accepting the unfailing Divine Love at the core of stories about the relationship between God and human beings is a lifelong effort. Renewing our "share" with Jesus, may our Triduum celebrations free us to love others as Jesus loves us.

■ CHRISTINE MADER

ENTRANCE ANTIPHON *(Cf. Galatians 6:14)*

We should glory in the Cross of our Lord Jesus Christ,
in whom is our salvation, life and resurrection, through
whom we are saved and delivered.

INTRODUCTORY RITES *(page 10)*

COLLECT

O God, who have called us to participate
in this most sacred Supper,
in which your Only Begotten Son,
when about to hand himself over to death,
entrusted to the Church a sacrifice new for all eternity,
the banquet of his love,
grant, we pray,
that we may draw from so great a mystery,
the fullness of charity and of life.
Through our Lord Jesus Christ, your Son,
who lives and reigns with you in the unity of the Holy Spirit,
one God, for ever and ever. *Amen.*

FIRST READING *(Exodus 12:1-8, 11-14)*

The LORD said to Moses and Aaron in the land of Egypt,
"This month shall stand at the head of your calendar;
you shall reckon it the first month of the year. Tell the whole
community of Israel: On the tenth of this month every one of
your families must procure for itself a lamb, one apiece for each
household. If a family is too small for a whole lamb, it shall join
the nearest household in procuring one and shall share in the
lamb in proportion to the number of persons who partake of
it. The lamb must be a year-old male and without blemish. You
may take it from either the sheep or the goats. You shall keep it

until the fourteenth day of this month, and then, with the whole assembly of Israel present, it shall be slaughtered during the evening twilight. They shall take some of its blood and apply it to the two doorposts and the lintel of every house in which they partake of the lamb. That same night they shall eat its roasted flesh with unleavened bread and bitter herbs.

"This is how you are to eat it: with your loins girt, sandals on your feet and your staff in hand, you shall eat like those who are in flight. It is the Passover of the LORD. For on this same night I will go through Egypt, striking down every firstborn of the land, both man and beast, and executing judgment on all the gods of Egypt—I, the LORD! But the blood will mark the houses where you are. Seeing the blood, I will pass over you; thus, when I strike the land of Egypt, no destructive blow will come upon you.

"This day shall be a memorial feast for you, which all your generations shall celebrate with pilgrimage to the LORD, as a perpetual institution."

The word of the Lord. *Thanks be to God.*

RESPONSORIAL PSALM *(Psalm 116:12-13, 15-16bc, 17-18)*
℟ **Our blessing-cup is a communion with the Blood of Christ.**

How shall I make a return to the LORD
   for all the good he has done for me?
The cup of salvation I will take up,
   and I will call upon the name of the LORD. ℟
Precious in the eyes of the LORD
   is the death of his faithful ones.
I am your servant, the son of your handmaid;
   you have loosed my bonds. ℟

To you will I offer sacrifice of thanksgiving,
    and I will call upon the name of the LORD.
My vows to the LORD I will pay
    in the presence of all his people. ℟

SECOND READING *(1 Corinthians 11:23–26)*

Brothers and sisters: I received from the Lord what I also handed on to you, that the Lord Jesus, on the night he was handed over, took bread, and, after he had given thanks, broke it and said, "This is my body that is for you. Do this in remembrance of me." In the same way also the cup, after supper, saying, "This cup is the new covenant in my blood. Do this, as often as you drink it, in remembrance of me." For as often as you eat this bread and drink the cup, you proclaim the death of the Lord until he comes.

The word of the Lord. *Thanks be to God.*

VERSE BEFORE THE GOSPEL *(John 13:34)*
Glory and praise to you, Lord Jesus Christ! I give you a new commandment, says the Lord: love one another as I have loved you. *Glory and praise to you, Lord Jesus Christ!*

GOSPEL *(John 13:1-15)*
A reading from the holy Gospel according to John.
Glory to you, O Lord.

Before the feast of Passover, Jesus knew that his hour had come to pass from this world to the Father. He loved his own in the world and he loved them to the end. The devil had already induced Judas, son of Simon the Iscariot, to hand him over. So, during supper, fully aware that the Father had put everything into his power and that he had come from God and was returning to God, he rose from supper and took off his outer garments. He took a towel and tied it around his waist. Then he poured water into a basin and began to **wash the disciples' feet**✝ and dry them with the towel around his waist. He came to Simon Peter, who said to him, "Master, are you going to wash my feet?" Jesus answered and said to him, "What I am doing, you do not understand now, but you will understand later." Peter said to him, "You will never wash my feet." Jesus answered him, "Unless I wash you, you will have no inheritance with me." Simon Peter said to him, "Master, then not only my feet, but my hands and head as well." Jesus said to him, "Whoever has bathed has no need except to have his feet washed, for he is clean all over; so you are clean, but not all." For he knew who would betray him; for this reason, he said, "Not all of you are clean."

So when he had washed their feet and put his garments back on and reclined at table again, he said to them, "Do you realize what I have done for you? You call me 'teacher' and 'master,' and rightly so, for indeed I am. If I, therefore, the master and teacher, have washed your feet, you ought to wash one another's feet. I have given you a model to follow, so that as I have done for you, you should also do."

The Gospel of the Lord. *Praise to you, Lord Jesus Christ.*

THE WASHING OF FEET
During the washing of feet, the assembly may sing an appropriate song.

PRAYER OF THE FAITHFUL

PREPARATION OF GIFTS *(page 16)*

PRAYER OVER THE OFFERINGS

Grant us, O Lord, we pray,
that we may participate worthily in these mysteries,
for whenever the memorial of this sacrifice is celebrated
the work of our redemption is accomplished.
Through Christ our Lord. *Amen.*

PREFACE *(Most Holy Eucharist 1, page 32)*

COMMUNION ANTIPHON *(1 Corinthians 11:24–25)*

This is the Body that will be given up for you; this is the Chalice
of the new covenant in my Blood, says the Lord; do this, whenever you receive it, in memory of me.

PRAYER AFTER COMMUNION

Grant, almighty God,
that, just as we are renewed
by the Supper of your Son in this present age,
so we may enjoy his banquet for all eternity.
Who lives and reigns for ever and ever. *Amen.*

❖ TAKING A CLOSER LOOK ❖

✝ **Wash the disciples' feet** Footwashing was not part of
the Passover ritual, but for John it is clearly an acting out of the
deepest meaning of Eucharist—giving oneself in loving service for
others. In the biblical world, sandals did not keep the dirt away. So
a customary sign of hospitality upon entering a house was to provide water for guests to wash their feet. This was usually the task of
a servant. So, when Jesus assumes the role of the servant instead
of the master that he is, what would normally be considered undig-
nified and humiliating becomes a sign of his love for his disciples.

The Blessing and Dismissal are omitted tonight.

TRANSFER OF THE MOST BLESSED SACRAMENT
The consecrated eucharistic bread is carried through the church in procession to the place of repose. During the procession, the hymn "Pange lingua" or some other eucharistic song is sung.

When the procession reaches the place of repose, the celebrant incenses the eucharistic bread, while the "Tantum ergo" (stanzas 5-6 of the "Pange lingua") is sung. The tabernacle of repose is then closed.

After a few moments of silent adoration, the priests and ministers of the altar leave. The faithful are encouraged to continue adoration before the Blessed Sacrament for a suitable period of time through the evening and night, but there should be no solemn adoration after midnight. ✛

• RESPONDING TO THE WORD •

God tells the Israelites to make their family meal holy.

➔ *How might I make my household meals more holy?*

Jesus gives his body as a sign of his willingness to give himself up in relation to us.

➔ *How can I give myself for others who are in need today?*

The disciples are told to imitate Jesus' service in relation to one another.

➔ *Who most needs my help today?*

April 19

APR 19

Cross the bridge!

Today's gospel is fundamental in many ways. The entire history of the world, from the moment Adam and Eve ate the apple, has led to this moment. From the Great Flood, to the Exodus, to the Ten Commandments, to the kings and prophets of old—all is in preparation for this moment.

For today, God fulfills his promise from long ago. When Adam and Eve sinned, an immeasurable separation was made between humanity and God, one that we could never fix. However, God never abandons God's children. Jesus shows himself for who he truly is and why he came to the earth.

Jesus is so much more than a prophet, a king, a teacher, a healer, an exorcist or a miracle worker. He is God, our Savior.

The day our first parents fell, God promised to save us. In his suffering and death on the cross, Jesus fulfills this promise and restores our relationship with God. This is the purpose of his life. Jesus is the bridge between heaven and earth. If you haven't crossed it, God invites you to do so now. All you have to do is have faith in Jesus Christ and repent of your sins. There is no better time to give your life to Jesus. May you do so now.

■ **CONNOR BROWNRIGG**

No Mass is celebrated today. The celebration of the Lord's Passion consists of three parts: the Liturgy of the Word, the Adoration of the Holy Cross, and the Reception of Holy Communion.

PRAYER

Remember your mercies, O Lord,
and with your eternal protection sanctify your servants,
for whom Christ your Son,
by the shedding of his Blood,
established the Paschal Mystery.
Who lives and reigns for ever and ever. *Amen.*

Or

O God, who by the Passion of Christ your Son, our Lord,
abolished the death inherited from ancient sin
by every succeeding generation,
grant that just as, being conformed to him,
we have borne by the law of nature
the image of the man of earth,
so by the sanctification of grace
we may bear the image of the Man of heaven.
Through Christ our Lord. *Amen.*

LITURGY OF THE WORD

FIRST READING *(Isaiah 52:13–53:12)*

See, my servant shall prosper,
he shall be raised high and greatly exalted.
Even as many were amazed at him—
so marred was his look beyond human semblance

and his appearance beyond that of the sons of man—
so shall he startle many nations,
  because of him kings shall stand speechless;
for those who have not been told shall see,
  those who have not heard shall ponder it.

Who would believe what we have heard?
  To whom has the arm of the LORD been revealed?
He grew up like a sapling before him,
  like a shoot from the parched earth;
there was in him no stately bearing to make us look at him,
  nor appearance that would attract us to him.
He was spurned and avoided by people,
  a man of suffering, accustomed to infirmity,
one of those from whom people hide their faces,
  spurned, and we held him in no esteem.

Yet it was our infirmities that he bore,
  our sufferings that he endured,
while we thought of him as stricken,
  as one smitten by God and afflicted.
But he was pierced for our offenses,
  crushed for our sins;
upon him was the chastisement that makes us whole,
  by his stripes we were healed.
We had all gone astray like sheep,
  each following his own way;
but the LORD laid upon him
  the guilt of us all.

Though he was harshly treated, he submitted
  and opened not his mouth;

like a lamb led to the slaughter
    or a sheep before the shearers,
    he was silent and opened not his mouth.
Oppressed and condemned, he was taken away,
    and who would have thought any more of his destiny?
When he was cut off from the land of the living,
    and smitten for the sin of his people,
a grave was assigned him among the wicked
    and a burial place with evildoers,
though he had done no wrong
    nor spoken any falsehood.
But the LORD was pleased
    to crush him in infirmity.

If he gives his life as an offering for sin,
    he shall see his descendants in a long life,
    and the will of the LORD shall be accomplished through him.

Because of his affliction
    he shall see the light in fullness of days;
through his suffering, my servant shall justify many,
    and their guilt he shall bear.
Therefore I will give him his portion among the great,
    and he shall divide the spoils with the mighty,
because he surrendered himself to death
    and was counted among the wicked;
and he shall take away the sins of many,
    and win pardon for their offenses.

The word of the Lord. *Thanks be to God.*

RESPONSORIAL PSALM *(Psalm 31:2, 6, 12–13, 15–16, 17, 25)*
℞ **Father, into your hands I commend my spirit.**

In you, O LORD, I take refuge;
  let me never be put to shame.
In your justice rescue me.
Into your hands I commend my spirit;
  you will redeem me, O LORD, O faithful God. ℞

For all my foes I am an object of reproach,
  a laughingstock to my neighbors, and a dread to my friends;
  they who see me abroad flee from me.
I am forgotten like the unremembered dead;
  I am like a dish that is broken. ℞

But my trust is in you, O LORD;
  I say, "You are my God.
In your hands is my destiny; rescue me
  from the clutches of my enemies and my persecutors." ℞

Let your face shine upon your servant;
  save me in your kindness.
Take courage and be stouthearted,
  all you who hope in the Lord. ℞

SECOND READING *(Hebrews 4:14–16; 5:7–9)*

Brothers and sisters: Since we have a great high priest who has passed through the heavens, Jesus, the Son of God, let us hold fast to our confession. For we do not have a high priest who is unable to sympathize with our weaknesses, but one who has similarly been tested in every way, yet without sin. So let us confidently approach the throne of grace to receive mercy and to find grace for timely help.

In the days when Christ was in the flesh, he offered prayers and supplications with loud cries and tears to the one who was able to save him from death, and he was heard because of his reverence. Son though he was, he learned obedience from what he suffered; and when he was made perfect, he became the source of eternal salvation for all who obey him.

The word of the Lord. ***Thanks be to God.***

VERSE BEFORE THE GOSPEL *(Philippians 2:8–9)*
Glory and praise to you, Lord Jesus Christ! Christ became obedient to the point of death, even death on a cross. Because of this, God greatly exalted him and bestowed on him the name which is above every other name. ***Glory and praise to you, Lord Jesus Christ!***

GOSPEL *(John 18:1–19:42)*
*Several readers may proclaim the passion narrative today. (**N**) indicates the narrator, (**†**) the words of Jesus, (**V**) a voice, and (**C**) the crowd.*

N The Passion of our Lord Jesus Christ according to John.

Jesus went out with his disciples across the Kidron valley to where there was a garden, into which he and his disciples entered. Judas his betrayer also knew the place, because Jesus had often met there with his disciples. So Judas got a band of soldiers and guards from the chief priests and the Pharisees and went there with lanterns, torches, and weapons. Jesus, knowing everything that was going to happen to him, went out and said to them,

† "Whom are you looking for?"

N They answered him,

C "Jesus the Nazorean."

N He said to them,

† "I AM."

N Judas his betrayer was also with them. When he said to them, "I AM," they turned away and fell to the ground. So he again asked them,

† "Whom are you looking for?"

N They said,

C "Jesus the Nazorean."

N Jesus answered,

† "I told you that I AM. So if you are looking for me, let these men go."

N This was to fulfill what he had said, "I have not lost any of those you gave me." Then Simon Peter, who had a sword, drew it, struck the high priest's slave, and cut off his right ear. The slave's name was Malchus. Jesus said to Peter,

† "Put your sword into its scabbard. Shall I not drink the cup that the Father gave me?"

N　So the band of soldiers, the tribune, and the Jewish guards seized Jesus, bound him, and brought him to Annas first. He was the father-in-law of Caiaphas,* who was high priest that year. It was Caiaphas who had counseled the Jews that it was better that one man should die rather than the people.

　　Simon Peter and another disciple followed Jesus. Now the other disciple was known to the high priest, and he entered the courtyard of the high priest with Jesus. But Peter stood at the gate outside. So the other disciple, the acquaintance of the high priest, went out and spoke to the gatekeeper and brought Peter in. Then the maid who was the gatekeeper said to Peter,

C "You are not one of this man's disciples, are you?"

N He said,

V "I am not."

N Now the slaves and the guards were standing around a charcoal fire that they had made, because it was cold, and were warming themselves. Peter was also standing there keeping warm.

The high priest questioned Jesus about his disciples and about his doctrine. Jesus answered him,

✝ "I have spoken publicly to the world. I have always taught in a synagogue or in the temple area where all the Jews gather, and in secret I have said nothing. Why ask me? Ask those who heard me what I said to them. They know what I said."

N When he had said this, one of the temple guards standing there struck Jesus and said,

V "Is this the way you answer the high priest?"

N Jesus answered him,

✝ "If I have spoken wrongly, testify to the wrong; but if I have spoken rightly, why do you strike me?"

N Then Annas sent him bound to Caiaphas the high priest.

Now Simon Peter was standing there keeping warm. And they said to him,

C "You are not one of his disciples, are you?"

N He denied it and said,

V "I am not."

N One of the slaves of the high priest, a relative of the one whose ear Peter had cut off, said,

C "Didn't I see you in the garden with him?"

N Again Peter denied it. And immediately the cock crowed.
    Then they brought Jesus from Caiaphas to the praetorium. It was morning. And they themselves did not enter the praetorium, in order not to be defiled so that they could eat the Passover. So Pilate came out to them and said,

V "What charge do you bring against this man?"

N They answered and said to him,

C "If he were not a criminal, we would not have handed him over to you."

N At this, Pilate said to them,

V "Take him yourselves, and judge him according to your law."

N The Jews answered him,

C "We do not have the right to execute anyone,"

N in order that the word of Jesus might be fulfilled that he said indicating the kind of death he would die. So Pilate went back into the praetorium and summoned Jesus and said to him,

V "Are you the King of the Jews?"

N Jesus answered,

✝ "Do you say this on your own or have others told you about me?"

N Pilate answered,

V "I am not a Jew, am I? Your own nation and the chief priests handed you over to me. What have you done?"

N Jesus answered,

✝ "My kingdom does not belong to this world. If my kingdom did belong to this world, my attendants would be fighting to keep me from being handed over to the Jews. But as it is, my kingdom is not here."

N So Pilate said to him,

V "Then you are a king?"

N Jesus answered,

✝ "You say I am a king. For this I was born and for this I came into the world, to testify to the truth. Everyone who belongs to the truth listens to my voice."

N Pilate said to him,

V "What is truth?"

N When he had said this, he again went out to the Jews and said to them,

V "I find no guilt in him. But you have a custom that I release one prisoner to you at Passover. Do you want me to release to you the King of the Jews?"

N They cried out again,

C "Not this one but Barabbas!"*

N Now Barabbas was a revolutionary.

Then Pilate took Jesus and had him scourged. And the soldiers wove a crown out of thorns and placed it on his head, and clothed him in a purple cloak, and they came to him and said,

C "Hail, King of the Jews!"

N And they struck him repeatedly. Once more Pilate went out and said to them,

V "Look, I am bringing him out to you, so that you may know that I find no guilt in him."

N So Jesus came out, wearing the crown of thorns and the purple cloak. And Pilate said to them,

V "Behold, the man!"

N When the chief priests and the guards saw him they cried out,

C "Crucify him, crucify him!"

N Pilate said to them,

V "Take him yourselves and crucify him. I find no guilt in him."

N The Jews answered,

C "We have a law, and according to that law he ought to die, because he made himself the Son of God."

N Now when Pilate heard this statement, he became even more afraid, and went back into the praetorium and said to Jesus,

V "Where are you from?"

N Jesus did not answer him. So Pilate said to him,

V "Do you not speak to me? Do you not know that I have power to release you and I have power to crucify you?"

N Jesus answered him,

† "You would have no power over me if it had not been given to you from above. For this reason the one who handed me over to you has the greater sin."

N Consequently, Pilate tried to release him; but the Jews cried out,

C "If you release him, you are not a Friend of Caesar.* Everyone who makes himself a king opposes Caesar."

N When Pilate heard these words he brought Jesus out and seated him on the judge's bench in the place called Stone Pavement, in Hebrew, Gabbatha. It was preparation day for Passover, and it was about noon. And he said to the Jews,

V "Behold, your king!"

N They cried out,

C "Take him away, take him away! Crucify him!"

N Pilate said to them,

V "Shall I crucify your king?"

N The chief priests answered,

C "We have no king but Caesar."

N Then he handed him over to them to be crucified.
      So they took Jesus, and, carrying the cross himself, he went

out to what is called the Place of the Skull, in Hebrew, Golgotha. There **they crucified him**,✝ and with him two others, one on either side, with Jesus in the middle. Pilate also had an inscription written and put on the cross. It read, "Jesus the Nazorean, the King of the Jews." Now many of the Jews read this inscription, because the place where Jesus was crucified was near the city; and it was written in Hebrew, Latin, and Greek. So the chief priests of the Jews said to Pilate,

C "Do not write 'The King of the Jews,' but that he said, 'I am the King of the Jews.'"

N Pilate answered,

V "What I have written, I have written."

N   When the soldiers had crucified Jesus, they took his clothes and divided them into four shares, a share for each soldier. They also took his tunic, but the tunic was seamless, woven in one piece from the top down. So they said to one another,

C "Let's not tear it, but cast lots for it to see whose it will be,"

N in order that the passage of Scripture might be fulfilled that says:

> *They divided my garments among them,*
> *and for my vesture they cast lots.*

This is what the soldiers did. Standing by the cross of Jesus were his mother and his mother's sister, Mary the wife of Clopas, and Mary of Magdala. When Jesus saw his mother and the disciple there whom he loved he said to his mother,

✝ "Woman, behold, your son."

N Then he said to the disciple,

† "Behold, your mother."

N And from that hour the disciple took her into his home.
    After this, aware that everything was now finished, in order
    that the Scripture might be fulfilled, Jesus said,

† "I thirst."

N There was a vessel filled with common wine. So they put a
    sponge soaked in wine on a sprig of hyssop and put it up to his
    mouth. When Jesus had taken the wine, he said,

† "It is finished."

N And bowing his head, he handed over the spirit.

(Here all kneel and pause for a short time.)

N Now since it was preparation day, in order that the bodies
    might not remain on the cross on the sabbath, for the sabbath
    day of that week was a solemn one, the Jews asked Pilate that
    their legs be broken and that they be taken down. So the sol-
    diers came and broke the legs of the first and then of the other
    one who was crucified with Jesus. But when they came to Jesus
    and saw that he was already dead, they did not break his legs,
    but one soldier thrust his lance into his side, and immediately
    blood and water flowed out. An eyewitness has testified, and
    his testimony is true; he knows that he is speaking the truth, so
    that you also may come to believe. For this happened so that
    the Scripture passage might be fulfilled:
        Not a bone of it will be broken.

And again another passage says:

They will look upon him whom they have pierced.

After this, Joseph of Arimathea,* secretly a disciple of Jesus for fear of the Jews, asked Pilate if he could remove the body of Jesus. And Pilate permitted it. So he came and took his body. Nicodemus, the one who had first come to him at night, also came bringing a mixture of myrrh* and aloes weighing about one hundred pounds. They took the body of Jesus and bound it with burial cloths along with the spices, according to the Jewish burial custom. Now in the place where he had been crucified there was a garden, and in the garden a new tomb, in which no one had yet been buried. So they laid Jesus there because of the Jewish preparation day; for the tomb was close by.

The Gospel of the Lord. *Praise to you, Lord Jesus Christ.*

PRAYER OF THE FAITHFUL
For Holy Church

Let us pray, dearly beloved, for the holy Church of God,
that our God and Lord be pleased to give her peace,
to guard her and to unite her throughout the whole world
and grant that, leading our life in tranquility and quiet,
we may glorify God the Father almighty.
(Prayer in silence.)

Almighty ever-living God,
who in Christ revealed your glory to all the nations,
watch over the works of your mercy,
that your Church, spread throughout all the world,
may persevere with steadfast faith in confessing your name.
Through Christ our Lord. *Amen.*

For the Pope
Let us pray also for our most Holy Father Pope N.,
that our God and Lord,
who chose him for the Order of Bishops,
may keep him safe and unharmed for the Lord's holy Church,
to govern the holy People of God.
(Prayer in silence.)
Almighty ever-living God,
by whose decree all things are founded,
look with favor on our prayers
and in your kindness protect the Pope chosen for us,
that, under him, the Christian people,
governed by you their maker,
may grow in merit by reason of their faith.
Through Christ our Lord. *Amen.*

For all orders and degrees of the faithful
Let us pray also for our Bishop N.,
for all Bishops, Priests, and Deacons of the Church
and for the whole of the faithful people.
(Prayer in silence.)
Almighty ever-living God,
by whose Spirit the whole body of the Church
is sanctified and governed,
hear our humble prayer for your ministers,
that, by the gift of your grace,
all may serve you faithfully.
Through Christ our Lord. *Amen.*

For catechumens

Let us pray also for (our) catechumens,
that our God and Lord
may open wide the ears of their inmost hearts
and unlock the gates of his mercy,
that, having received forgiveness of all their sins
through the waters of rebirth,
they, too, may be one with Christ Jesus our Lord.
(Prayer in silence.)
Almighty ever-living God,
who make your Church ever fruitful with new offspring,
increase the faith and understanding of (our) catechumens,
that, reborn in the font of Baptism,
they may be added to the number of your adopted children.
Through Christ our Lord. *Amen.*

For the unity of Christians

Let us pray also for all our brothers and sisters who believe in Christ,
that our God and Lord may be pleased,
as they live the truth,
to gather them together and keep them in his one Church.
(Prayer in silence.)
Almighty ever-living God,
who gather what is scattered
and keep together what you have gathered,
look kindly on the flock of your Son,
that those whom one Baptism has consecrated
may be joined together by integrity of faith
and united in the bond of charity.
Through Christ our Lord. *Amen.*

For the Jewish people

Let us pray also for the Jewish people,
to whom the Lord our God spoke first,
that he may grant them to advance in love of his name
and in faithfulness to his covenant.
(Prayer in silence.)
Almighty ever-living God,
who bestowed your promises on Abraham and his descendants,
graciously hear the prayers of your Church,
that the people you first made your own
may attain the fullness of redemption.
Through Christ our Lord. *Amen.*

For those who do not believe in Christ

Let us pray also for those who do not believe in Christ,
that, enlightened by the Holy Spirit,
they, too, may enter on the way of salvation.
(Prayer in silence.)
Almighty ever-living God,
grant to those who do not confess Christ
that, by walking before you with a sincere heart,
they may find the truth
and that we ourselves, being constant in mutual love
and striving to understand more fully the mystery of your life,
may be made more perfect witnesses to your love in the world.
Through Christ our Lord. *Amen.*

For those who do not believe in God

Let us pray also for those who do not acknowledge God,
that, following what is right in sincerity of heart,

they may find the way to God himself.
(Prayer in silence.)
Almighty ever-living God,
who created all people
to seek you always by desiring you
and, by finding you, come to rest,
grant, we pray,
that, despite every harmful obstacle,
all may recognize the signs of your fatherly love
and the witness of the good works
done by those who believe in you,
and so in gladness confess you,
the one true God and Father of our human race.
Through Christ our Lord. *Amen.*

For those in public office

Let us pray also for those in public office,
that our God and Lord
may direct their minds and hearts according to his will
for the true peace and freedom of all.
(Prayer in silence.)
Almighty ever-living God,
in whose hand lies every human heart
and the rights of peoples,
look with favor, we pray,
on those who govern with authority over us,
that throughout the whole world,
the prosperity of peoples,
the assurance of peace,
and freedom of religion

may through your gift be made secure.
Through Christ our Lord. *Amen.*

For those in tribulation
Let us pray, dearly beloved,
to God the Father almighty,
that he may cleanse the world of all errors,
banish disease, drive out hunger,
unlock prisons, loosen fetters,
granting to travelers safety, to pilgrims return,
health to the sick, and salvation to the dying.
(Prayer in silence.)
Almighty ever-living God,
comfort of mourners, strength of all who toil,
may the prayers of those who cry out in any tribulation
come before you,
that all may rejoice,
because in their hour of need
your mercy was at hand.
Through Christ our Lord. *Amen.*

ADORATION OF THE HOLY CROSS

Three times the celebrant invites the assembly to proclaim its faith:

Behold the wood of the Cross,
on which hung the salvation of the world.
Come, let us adore.

After each response all venerate the cross briefly in silence. After the third response, the people approach to venerate the cross. They make a simple

*genuflection or perform some other appropriate sign of reverence
according to local custom.*

*During the veneration, appropriate songs may be sung. All who have
venerated the cross return to their places and sit. Where large numbers of
people make individual veneration difficult, the celebrant may raise the
cross briefly for all to venerate in silence.*

HOLY COMMUNION

THE LORD'S PRAYER *(page 53)*

PRAYER AFTER COMMUNION
Almighty ever-living God,
who have restored us to life
by the blessed Death and Resurrection of your Christ,
preserve in us the work of your mercy,
that, by partaking of this mystery,

● TAKING A CLOSER LOOK ●

✠ **They crucified him** Crucifixion was the most painful torture the ancient world had devised. Besides the pain from scourging, beating, loss of blood, and lack of vital fluids, when one's arms and legs were fixed to a cross by tying with rope or nailing, the victim began a slow process of asphyxiation. As the muscles of the upper body rigidly tightened in prolonged contraction, breathing became more and more difficult and painful. The only relief was to push oneself up by using one's legs. When the legs could no longer lift the body up, breathing stopped and the victim died. Thus, death could be hastened by breaking the victim's legs (John 19:31-32).

we may have a life unceasingly devoted to you.
Through Christ our Lord. *Amen.*

PRAYER OVER THE PEOPLE
May abundant blessing, O Lord, we pray,
descend upon your people,
who have honored the Death of your Son
in the hope of their resurrection:
may pardon come,
comfort be given,
holy faith increase,
and everlasting redemption be made secure.
Through Christ our Lord. *Amen.*

All depart in silence. ✠

• RESPONDING TO THE WORD •

Through his suffering, God's servant brings blessings to others.

➡ *When have I been blessed by someone who suffered?*

Jesus sympathizes with our weakness.

➡ *What weakness do I want to acknowledge to Jesus today?*

Jesus' pierced heart reveals his great love for us.

➡ *How will I show my love for Jesus during the coming week?*

April 20

Christis risen!

It is easy to think that if we had been present for God's great saving acts, detailed in the readings of the Easter Vigil and culminating in the resurrection, then faith would be easy. If only we had seen, then we would believe. But St. Paul says faith comes from hearing (Romans 10:17). Our resurrection story from Luke supports this idea. Even the first witnesses to the resurrection struggled to understand what their eyes told them. An empty tomb is not, automatically, good news. The women only understood and believed after the angels gave the explanation: "He is not here, but he has been raised."

The women, in turn, tell the disciples. The women had seen, but needed hearing to understand. Now these men have heard, but need to see. Only one even took the time to look. But when Peter did, he found it just as the women had said.

God is active in our lives even today. But we often fail to recognize such action for what it is. Faith, which God gives us through the community of faith and the Church, where we hear the story, gives us the lenses to see what God is doing. If we take the time to look into what we have heard, we might see something that leaves us as amazed as Peter.

■ **BRETT SALKELD**

There is no Mass celebrated during the day on Holy Saturday. But during the night, we anticipate Jesus' resurrection with one of the most ancient rites—a solemn vigil, which leads into the celebration of the 50 days of the Easter Season.

The Easter Vigil is arranged in four parts: the Service of Light (Lucernarium), the Liturgy of the Word, the Liturgy of Baptism, and the Liturgy of the Eucharist.

LUCERNARIUM

BLESSING OF THE FIRE

Dear brethren (brothers and sisters),
on this most sacred night,
in which our Lord Jesus Christ
passed over from death to life,
the Church calls upon her sons and daughters,
scattered throughout the world,
to come together to watch and pray.
If we keep the memorial
of the Lord's paschal solemnity in this way,
listening to his word and celebrating his mysteries,
then we shall have the sure hope
of sharing his triumph over death
and living with him in God.

Let us pray.

O God, who through your Son
bestowed upon the faithful the fire of your glory,

sanctify this new fire, we pray,
and grant that,
by these paschal celebrations,
we may be so inflamed with heavenly desires,
that with minds made pure
we may attain festivities of unending splendor.
Through Christ our Lord. *Amen.*

PREPARATION OF THE CANDLE

The celebrant cuts a cross in the Easter candle and traces the Greek letters alpha (Α) and omega (Ω) and the numerals 2019, saying:

Christ yesterday and today;
the Beginning and the End;
the Alpha; and the Omega.
All time belongs to him;
and all the ages.
To him be glory and power;
through every age and for ever. Amen.

When the marks have been made, the celebrant may insert five grains of incense in the candle, saying:

By his holy and glorious wounds,
may Christ the Lord guard us and protect us. Amen.

LIGHTING OF THE CANDLE

The celebrant lights the Easter candle from the new fire, saying:

May the light of Christ rising in glory
dispel the darkness of our hearts and minds.

PROCESSION WITH THE EASTER CANDLE

The priest or deacon takes the Easter candle and, three times during the procession to the altar, lifts it high and sings alone. Then the people respond.

The Light of Christ.
Thanks be to God.

EASTER PROCLAMATION *(EXSULTET)*

For the shorter version, omit the indented parts in brackets.

Exult, let them exult, the hosts of heaven,
exult, let Angel ministers of God exult,
let the trumpet of salvation
sound aloud our mighty King's triumph!
Be glad, let earth be glad, as glory floods her,
ablaze with light from her eternal King,
let all corners of the earth be glad,
knowing an end to gloom and darkness.
Rejoice, let Mother Church also rejoice,
arrayed with the lightning of his glory,
let this holy building shake with joy,
filled with the mighty voices of the peoples.

[(Therefore, dearest friends,
standing in the awesome glory of this holy light,
invoke with me, I ask you,
the mercy of God almighty,
that he, who has been pleased to number me,
though unworthy, among the Levites,*
may pour into me his light unshadowed,
that I may sing this candle's perfect praises).]

(The Lord be with you.
And with your spirit.)
Lift up your hearts.
We lift them up to the Lord.
Let us give thanks to the Lord our God.
It is right and just.

It is truly right and just,
with ardent love of mind and heart
and with devoted service of our voice,
to acclaim our God invisible, the almighty Father,
and Jesus Christ, our Lord, his Son, his Only Begotten.

Who for our sake paid Adam's debt to the eternal Father,
and, pouring out his own dear Blood,
wiped clean the record of our ancient sinfulness.

These then are the feasts of Passover,
in which is slain the Lamb, the one true Lamb,
whose Blood anoints the doorposts of believers.

This is the night,
when once you led our forebears, Israel's children,
from slavery in Egypt
and made them pass dry-shod through the Red Sea.

This is the night
that with a pillar of fire
banished the darkness of sin.

This is the night
that even now, throughout the world,
sets Christian believers apart from worldly vices

and from the gloom of sin,
leading them to grace
and joining them to his holy ones.

This is the night,
when Christ broke the prison-bars of death
and rose victorious from the underworld.

[Our birth would have been no gain,
had we not been redeemed.]
O wonder of your humble care for us!
O love, O charity beyond all telling,
to ransom a slave you gave away your Son!

O truly necessary sin of Adam,
destroyed completely by the Death of Christ!

O happy fault
that earned so great, so glorious a Redeemer!

[O truly blessed night,
worthy alone to know the time and hour
when Christ rose from the underworld!

This is the night
of which it is written:
The night shall be as bright as day,
dazzling is the night for me,
and full of gladness.]

The sanctifying power of this night
dispels wickedness, washes faults away,
restores innocence to the fallen, and joy to mourners,
[drives out hatred, fosters concord, and brings down the mighty.]

The longer version ending:

On this, your night of grace, O holy Father,
accept this candle, a solemn offering,
the work of bees and of your servants' hands,
an evening sacrifice of praise,
this gift from your most holy Church.

But now we know the praises of this pillar,
which glowing fire ignites for God's honor,
a fire into many flames divided,
yet never dimmed by sharing of its light,
for it is fed by melting wax,
drawn out by mother bees
to build a torch so precious.

O truly blessed night,
when things of heaven are wed to those of earth,
and divine to the human.

Therefore, O Lord,
we pray you that this candle,
hallowed to the honor of your name,
may persevere undimmed,
to overcome the darkness of this night.
Receive it as a pleasing fragrance,
and let it mingle with the lights of heaven.
May this flame be found still burning
by the Morning Star:
the one Morning Star who never sets,
Christ your Son,
who, coming back from death's domain,

has shed his peaceful light on humanity,
and lives and reigns for ever and ever. ***Amen.***

The shorter version ending:

O truly blessed night,
when things of heaven are wed to those of earth
and divine to the human.

On this, your night of grace, O holy Father,
accept this candle, a solemn offering,
the work of bees and of your servants' hands,
an evening sacrifice of praise,
this gift from your most holy Church.

Therefore, O Lord,
we pray you that this candle,
hallowed to the honor of your name,
may persevere undimmed,
to overcome the darkness of this night.
Receive it as a pleasing fragrance,
and let it mingle with the lights of heaven.
May this flame be found still burning
by the Morning Star:
the one Morning Star who never sets,
Christ your Son,
who, coming back from death's domain,
has shed his peaceful light on humanity,
and lives and reigns for ever and ever. ***Amen.***

LITURGY OF THE WORD

....

Dear brethren (brothers and sisters),
now that we have begun our solemn Vigil,
let us listen with quiet hearts to the Word of God.
Let us meditate on how God in times past saved his people
and in these, the last days, has sent us his Son as our Redeemer.
Let us pray that our God may complete this paschal work
    of salvation
by the fullness of redemption.

FIRST READING *(Genesis 1:1—2:2)*
For the shorter version, omit the indented parts in brackets.

In the beginning, when God created the heavens and the earth,
[the earth was a formless wasteland, and darkness covered the
abyss, while a mighty wind swept over the waters.

Then God said, "Let there be light," and there was light. God
saw how good the light was. God then separated the light from
the darkness. God called the light "day," and the darkness he
called "night." Thus evening came, and morning followed—the
first day.

Then God said, "Let there be a dome in the middle of the
waters, to separate one body of water from the other." And so
it happened: God made the dome, and it separated the water
above the dome from the water below it. God called the dome
"the sky." Evening came, and morning followed—the second day.

Then God said, "Let the water under the sky be gathered
into a single basin, so that the dry land may appear." And so
it happened: the water under the sky was gathered into its
basin, and the dry land appeared. God called the dry land "the

earth," and the basin of the water he called "the sea." God saw how good it was. Then God said, "Let the earth bring forth vegetation: every kind of plant that bears seed and every kind of fruit tree on earth that bears fruit with its seed in it." And so it happened: the earth brought forth every kind of plant that bears seed and every kind of fruit tree on earth that bears fruit with its seed in it. God saw how good it was. Evening came, and morning followed—the third day.

Then God said: "Let there be lights in the dome of the sky, to separate day from night. Let them mark the fixed times, the days and the years, and serve as luminaries in the dome of the sky, to shed light upon the earth." And so it happened: God made the two great lights, the greater one to govern the day, and the lesser one to govern the night; and he made the stars. God set them in the dome of the sky, to shed light upon the earth, to govern the day and the night, and to separate the light from the darkness. God saw how good it was. Evening came, and morning followed—the fourth day.

Then God said, "Let the water teem with an abundance of living creatures, and on the earth let birds fly beneath the dome of the sky." And so it happened: God created the great sea monsters and all kinds of swimming creatures with which the water teems, and all kinds of winged birds. God saw how good it was, and God blessed them, saying, "Be fertile, multiply, and fill the water of the seas; and let the birds multiply on the earth." Evening came, and morning followed—the fifth day.

Then God said, "Let the earth bring forth all kinds of living creatures: cattle, creeping things, and wild animals of all kinds." And so it happened: God made all kinds of wild animals, all kinds of cattle, and all kinds of creeping things of the earth. God saw how good it was. Then]

God said: "Let us make man in our image, after our likeness. Let them have dominion over the fish of the sea, the birds of the air, and the cattle, and over all the wild animals and all the creatures that crawl on the ground."

God created man in his image;
in the image of God he created him;
male and female he created them.

God blessed them, saying: "Be fertile and multiply; fill the earth and subdue it. Have dominion over the fish of the sea, the birds of the air, and all the living things that move on the earth." God also said: "See, I give you every seed-bearing plant all over the earth and every tree that has seed-bearing fruit on it to be your food; and to all the animals of the land, all the birds of the air, and all the living creatures that crawl on the ground, I give all the green plants for food." And so it happened. God looked at everything he had made, and he found it very good.

[Evening came, and morning followed—the sixth day.

Thus the heavens and the earth and all their array were completed. Since on the seventh day God was finished with the work he had been doing, he rested on the seventh day from all the work he had undertaken.]

The word of the Lord. ***Thanks be to God.***

An alternate psalm follows.

RESPONSORIAL PSALM *(Psalm 104:1-2, 5-6, 10, 12, 13-14, 24, 35)*
℞ **Lord, send out your Spirit, and renew the face of the earth.**

Bless the LORD, O my soul!
O LORD, my God, you are great indeed!

You are clothed with majesty and glory,
　　robed in light as with a cloak.

℟ **Lord, send out your Spirit, and renew the face of the earth.**

You fixed the earth upon its foundation,
　　not to be moved forever;
with the ocean, as with a garment, you covered it;
　　above the mountains the waters stood. ℟

You send forth springs into the watercourses
　　that wind among the mountains.
Beside them the birds of heaven dwell;
　　from among the branches they send forth their song. ℟

You water the mountains from your palace;
　　the earth is replete with the fruit of your works.
You raise grass for the cattle,
　　and vegetation for man's use,
producing bread from the earth. ℟

How manifold are your works, O LORD!
　　In wisdom you have wrought them all—
the earth is full of your creatures.
　　Bless the LORD, O my soul! ℟

OR

RESPONSORIAL PSALM *(Psalm 33:4-5, 6-7, 12-13, 20 and 22)*

℟ **The earth is full of the goodness of the Lord.**

Upright is the word of the LORD,
　　and all his works are trustworthy.
He loves justice and right;
　　of the kindness of the LORD the earth is full. ℟

By the word of the LORD the heavens were made;
　　by the breath of his mouth all their host.

He gathers the waters of the sea as in a flask;
  in cellars he confines the deep. ℟
Blessed the nation whose God is the LORD,
  the people he has chosen for his own inheritance.
From heaven the LORD looks down;
  he sees all mankind. ℟
Our soul waits for the LORD,
  who is our help and our shield.
May your kindness, O LORD, be upon us
  who have put our hope in you. ℟

PRAYER

Let us pray.

Almighty ever-living God,
who are wonderful in the ordering of all your works,
may those you have redeemed understand
that there exists nothing more marvelous
than the world's creation in the beginning
except that, at the end of the ages,
Christ our Passover has been sacrificed.
Who lives and reigns for ever and ever. *Amen.*

Or

O God, who wonderfully created human nature
and still more wonderfully redeemed it,
grant us, we pray,
to set our minds against the enticements of sin,
that we may merit to attain eternal joys.
Through Christ our Lord. *Amen.*

SECOND READING (*Genesis 22:1–18*)

For the shorter version, omit the indented parts in brackets.

God put Abraham to the test. He called to him, "Abraham!"
"Here I am," he replied. Then God said: "Take your son
Isaac, your only one, whom you love, and go to the land of
Moriah. There you shall offer him up as a holocaust on a height
that I will point out to you."

[Early the next morning Abraham saddled his donkey, took
with him his son Isaac and two of his servants as well, and
with the wood that he had cut for the holocaust, set out for
the place of which God had told him.

On the third day Abraham got sight of the place from afar.
Then he said to his servants: "Both of you stay here with the
donkey, while the boy and I go on over yonder. We will worship and then come back to you." Thereupon Abraham took
the wood for the holocaust and laid it on his son Isaac's shoulders, while he himself carried the fire and the knife. As the two
walked on together, Isaac spoke to his father Abraham: "Father!"
Isaac said. "Yes, son," he replied. Isaac continued, "Here are the
fire and the wood, but where is the sheep for the holocaust?"
"Son," Abraham answered, "God himself will provide the sheep
for the holocaust." Then the two continued going forward.]
When they came to the place of which God had told him,
Abraham built an altar there and arranged the wood on it.

[Next he tied up his son Isaac, and put him on top of the
wood on the altar.]
Then he reached out and took the knife to slaughter his son. But
the LORD's messenger called to him from heaven, "Abraham,
Abraham!" "Here I am," he answered. "Do not lay your hand on

the boy," said the messenger. "Do not do the least thing to him. I know now how devoted you are to God, since you did not withhold from me your own beloved son." As Abraham looked about, he spied a ram caught by its horns in the thicket. So he went and took the ram and offered it up as a holocaust in place of his son.

[Abraham named the site Yahweh-yireh; hence people now say, "On the mountain the LORD will see."]

Again the LORD's messenger called to Abraham from heaven and said: "I swear by myself, declares the LORD, that because you acted as you did in not withholding from me your beloved son, I will bless you abundantly and make your descendants as countless as the stars of the sky and the sands of the seashore; your descendants shall take possession of the gates of their enemies, and in your descendants all the nations of the earth shall find blessing—all this because you obeyed my command."

The word of the Lord. *Thanks be to God.*

RESPONSORIAL PSALM *(Psalm 16:5, 8, 9-10, 11)*
R̷ **You are my inheritance, O Lord.**

O LORD, my allotted portion and my cup,
  you it is who hold fast my lot.
I set the LORD ever before me;
  with him at my right hand I shall not be disturbed. R̷
Therefore my heart is glad and my soul rejoices,
  my body, too, abides in confidence;
because you will not abandon my soul to the netherworld,
  nor will you suffer your faithful one to undergo corruption. R̷
You will show me the path to life,
  fullness of joys in your presence,
  the delights at your right hand forever. R̷

PRAYER

Let us pray.

O God, supreme Father of the faithful,
who increase the children of your promise
by pouring out the grace of adoption
throughout the whole world
and who through the Paschal Mystery
make your servant Abraham father of nations,
as once you swore,
grant, we pray,
that your peoples may enter worthily
into the grace to which you call them.
Through Christ our Lord. *Amen.*

THIRD READING *(Exodus 14:15–15:1)*

The LORD said to Moses, "Why are you crying out to me? Tell the Israelites to go forward. And you, lift up your staff and, with hand outstretched over the sea, split the sea in two, that the Israelites may pass through it on dry land. But I will make the Egyptians so obstinate that they will go in after them. Then I will receive glory through Pharaoh and all his army, his chariots and charioteers. The Egyptians shall know that I am the LORD, when I receive glory through Pharaoh and his chariots and charioteers."

The angel of God, who had been leading Israel's camp, now moved and went around behind them. The column of cloud also, leaving the front, took up its place behind them, so that it came between the camp of the Egyptians and that of Israel. But the cloud now became dark, and thus the night passed without the rival camps coming any closer together all night long. Then Moses stretched out his hand over the sea, and the LORD swept the sea with a strong east wind throughout the night and so turned it into dry land. When the water was thus divided, the Israelites marched into the midst of the sea on dry land, with the water like a wall to their right and to their left.

The Egyptians followed in pursuit; all Pharaoh's horses and chariots and charioteers went after them right into the midst of the sea. In the night watch just before dawn the LORD cast through the column of the fiery cloud upon the Egyptian force a glance that threw it into a panic; and he so clogged their chariot wheels that they could hardly drive. With that the Egyptians sounded the retreat before Israel, because the LORD was fighting for them against the Egyptians.

Then the LORD told Moses, "Stretch out your hand over the sea, that the water may flow back upon the Egyptians, upon their chariots and their charioteers." So Moses stretched out his hand over the sea, and at dawn the sea flowed back to its normal depth. The Egyptians were fleeing head on toward the sea, when the LORD hurled them into its midst. As the water flowed back, it covered the chariots and the charioteers of Pharaoh's whole army which had followed the Israelites into the sea. Not a single one of them escaped. But the Israelites had marched on dry land through the midst of the sea, with the water like a wall to their right and to their left. Thus the LORD saved Israel on that day from the power of the Egyptians. When Israel saw the Egyptians lying dead on the seashore and beheld the great power that the Lord had shown against the Egyptians, they feared the LORD and believed in him and in his servant Moses.

Then Moses and the Israelites sang this song to the LORD:
I will sing to the Lord, for he is gloriously triumphant;
horse and chariot he has cast into the sea.

The word of the Lord. *Thanks be to God.*

RESPONSORIAL CANTICLE *(Exodus 15:1-2, 3-4, 5-6, 17-18)*
℟ **Let us sing to the Lord; he has covered himself in glory.**

I will sing to the LORD, for he is gloriously triumphant;
horse and chariot he has cast into the sea.
My strength and my courage is the LORD,
and he has been my savior.
He is my God, I praise him;
the God of my father, I extol him. ℟
The LORD is a warrior,
LORD is his name!
Pharaoh's chariots and army he hurled into the sea;
the elite of his officers were submerged in the Red Sea. ℟
The flood waters covered them,
they sank into the depths like a stone.
Your right hand, O LORD, magnificent in power,
your right hand, O LORD, has shattered the enemy. ℟
You brought in the people you redeemed
and planted them on the mountain of your inheritance—
the place where you made your seat, O LORD,
the sanctuary, LORD, which your hands established.
The LORD shall reign forever and ever. ℟

PRAYER

Let us pray.

O God, whose ancient wonders
remain undimmed in splendor even in our day,
for what you once bestowed on a single people,
freeing them from Pharaoh's persecution
by the power of your right hand,
now you bring about as the salvation of the nations
through the waters of rebirth,
grant, we pray, that the whole world
may become children of Abraham
and inherit the dignity of Israel's birthright.
Through Christ our Lord. *Amen.*

Or

O God, who by the light of the New Testament
have unlocked the meaning
of wonders worked in former times,
so that the Red Sea prefigures the sacred font
and the nation delivered from slavery
foreshadows the Christian people,
grant, we pray, that all nations,
obtaining the privilege of Israel by merit of faith,
may be reborn by partaking of your Spirit.
Through Christ our Lord. *Amen.*

FOURTH READING *(Isaiah 54:5-14)*

The One who has become your husband is your Maker;
his name is the LORD of hosts;
your redeemer is the Holy One of Israel,
called God of all the earth.

The LORD calls you back,
    like a wife forsaken and grieved in spirit,
    a wife married in youth and then cast off,
    says your God.
For a brief moment I abandoned you,
    but with great tenderness I will take you back.
In an outburst of wrath, for a moment
    I hid my face from you;
but with enduring love I take pity on you,
    says the LORD, your redeemer.
This is for me like the days of Noah,
    when I swore that the waters of Noah
    should never again deluge the earth;
so I have sworn not to be angry with you,
    or to rebuke you.
Though the mountains leave their place
    and the hills be shaken,
my love shall never leave you
    nor my covenant of peace be shaken,
    says the LORD, who has mercy on you.
O afflicted one, storm-battered and unconsoled,
    I lay your pavements in carnelians,
    and your foundations in sapphires;
I will make your battlements of rubies,
    your gates of carbuncles,
    and all your walls of precious stones.
All your children shall be taught by the LORD,
    and great shall be the peace of your children.
In justice shall you be established,

far from the fear of oppression,
where destruction cannot come near you.

The word of the Lord. *Thanks be to God.*

RESPONSORIAL PSALM *(Psalm 30:2, 4, 5-6, 11-12, 13)*
℟ **I will praise you, Lord, for you have rescued me.**

I will extol you, O LORD, for you drew me clear
and did not let my enemies rejoice over me.
O LORD, you brought me up from the netherworld;
you preserved me from among those going down into the pit. ℟
Sing praise to the LORD, you his faithful ones,
and give thanks to his holy name.
For his anger lasts but a moment;
a lifetime, his good will.
At nightfall, weeping enters in,
but with the dawn, rejoicing. ℟
Hear, O LORD, and have pity on me;
O LORD, be my helper.
You changed my mourning into dancing;
O LORD, my God, forever will I give you thanks. ℟

PRAYER
Let us pray.

Almighty ever-living God,
surpass, for the honor of your name,
what you pledged to the Patriarchs by reason of their faith,
and through sacred adoption increase the children of your promise,
so that what the Saints of old never doubted would come to pass
your Church may now see in great part fulfilled.
Through Christ our Lord. *Amen.*

FIFTH READING *(Isaiah 55:1-11)*

Thus says the LORD:
   All you who are thirsty,
     come to the water!
You who have no money,
     come, receive grain and eat;
come, without paying and without cost,
     drink wine and milk!
Why spend your money for what is not bread,
     your wages for what fails to satisfy?
Heed me, and you shall eat well,
     you shall delight in rich fare.
Come to me heedfully,
     listen, that you may have life.
I will renew with you the everlasting covenant,
     the benefits assured to David.
As I made him a witness to the peoples,
     a leader and commander of nations,
so shall you summon a nation you knew not,
     and nations that knew you not shall run to you,
because of the LORD, your God,
     the Holy One of Israel, who has glorified you.

Seek the LORD while he may be found,
     call him while he is near.
Let the scoundrel forsake his way,
     and the wicked man his thoughts;
let him turn to the Lord for mercy;
     to our God, who is generous in forgiving.
For my thoughts are not your thoughts,
     nor are your ways my ways, says the LORD.

As high as the heavens are above the earth,
    so high are my ways above your ways
    and my thoughts above your thoughts.

For just as from the heavens
    the rain and snow come down
and do not return there
    till they have watered the earth,
    making it fertile and fruitful,
giving seed to the one who sows
    and bread to the one who eats,
so shall my word be
    that goes forth from my mouth;
my word shall not return to me void,
    but shall do my will,
    achieving the end for which I sent it.

The word of the Lord. *Thanks be to God.*

RESPONSORIAL CANTICLE *(Isaiah 12:2-3, 4, 5-6)*
℞ **You will draw water joyfully from the springs of salvation.**

God indeed is my savior;
    I am confident and unafraid.
My strength and my courage is the LORD,
    and he has been my savior.
With joy you will draw water
    at the fountain of salvation. ℞
Give thanks to the LORD, acclaim his name;
    among the nations make known his deeds,
    proclaim how exalted is his name. ℞
Sing praise to the LORD for his glorious achievement;
    let this be known throughout all the earth.

Shout with exultation, O city of Zion,*
for great in your midst
is the Holy One of Israel!

R You will draw water joyfully from the springs of salvation.

PRAYER

Let us pray.

Almighty ever-living God,
sole hope of the world,
who by the preaching of your Prophets
unveiled the mysteries of this present age,
graciously increase the longing of your people,
for only at the prompting of your grace
do the faithful progress in any kind of virtue.
Through Christ our Lord. *Amen.*

SIXTH READING (Baruch 3:9-15, 32—4:4)

Hear, O Israel, the commandments of life:
listen, and know prudence!
How is it, Israel,
that you are in the land of your foes,
grown old in a foreign land,
defiled with the dead,
accounted with those destined for the netherworld?
You have forsaken the fountain of wisdom!
Had you walked in the way of God,
you would have dwelt in enduring peace.
Learn where prudence is,
where strength, where understanding;
that you may know also
where are length of days, and life,

where light of the eyes, and peace.
Who has found the place of wisdom,
who has entered into her treasuries?

The One who knows all things knows her;
he has probed her by his knowledge—
The One who established the earth for all time,
and filled it with four-footed beasts;
he who dismisses the light, and it departs,
calls it, and it obeys him trembling;
before whom the stars at their posts
shine and rejoice;
when he calls them, they answer, "Here we are!"
shining with joy for their Maker.
Such is our God;
no other is to be compared to him:
he has traced out the whole way of understanding,
and has given her to Jacob, his servant,
to Israel, his beloved son.

Since then she has appeared on earth,
and moved among people.
She is the book of the precepts of God,
the law that endures forever;
all who cling to her will live,
but those will die who forsake her.
Turn, O Jacob, and receive her:
walk by her light toward splendor.
Give not your glory to another,
your privileges to an alien race.

Blessed are we, O Israel;
for what pleases God is known to us!

The word of the Lord. *Thanks be to God.*

RESPONSORIAL PSALM *(Psalm 19:8, 9, 10, 11)*
℟ **Lord, you have the words of everlasting life.**

The law of the LORD is perfect,
refreshing the soul;
the decree of the LORD is trustworthy,
giving wisdom to the simple. ℟

The precepts of the LORD are right,
rejoicing the heart;
the command of the LORD is clear,
enlightening the eye. ℟

The fear of the LORD is pure,
enduring forever;
the ordinances of the LORD are true,
all of them just. ℟

They are more precious than gold,
than a heap of purest gold;
sweeter also than syrup
or honey from the comb. ℟

PRAYER

Let us pray.

O God, who constantly increase your Church
by your call to the nations,
graciously grant
to those you wash clean in the waters of Baptism

the assurance of your unfailing protection.
Through Christ our Lord. *Amen.*

SEVENTH READING *(Ezekiel 36:16–17a, 18–28)*

The word of the LORD came to me, saying: Son of man, when the house of Israel lived in their land, they defiled it by their conduct and deeds. Therefore I poured out my fury upon them because of the blood that they poured out on the ground, and because they defiled it with idols. I scattered them among the nations, dispersing them over foreign lands; according to their conduct and deeds I judged them. But when they came among the nations wherever they came, they served to profane my holy name, because it was said of them: "These are the people of the LORD, yet they had to leave their land." So I have relented because of my holy name which the house of Israel profaned among the nations where they came. Therefore say to the house of Israel: Thus says the Lord GOD: Not for your sakes do I act, house of Israel, but for the sake of my holy name, which you profaned among the nations to which you came. I will prove the holiness of my great name, profaned among the nations, in whose midst you have profaned it. Thus the nations shall know that I am the LORD, says the Lord GOD, when in their sight I prove my holiness through you. For I will take you away from among the nations, gather you from all the foreign lands, and bring you back to your own land. I will sprinkle clean water upon you to cleanse you from all your impurities, and from all your idols I will cleanse you. I will give you a new heart and place a new spirit within you, taking from your bodies your stony hearts and giving you natural hearts. I will put my spirit within you and make you live by my statutes, careful to observe my decrees. You shall live in the land I gave your fathers; you shall be my people, and I will be your God.

The word of the Lord. ***Thanks be to God.***

When baptism is celebrated, sing Psalm 42/43 (below); when baptism is not celebrated, sing Isaiah 12 (from after the Fifth Reading, page 323) or Psalm 51 (this page).

RESPONSORIAL PSALM *(Psalm 42:3, 5; 43:3, 4)*
℟ **Like a deer that longs for running streams,**
   my soul longs for you, my God.

Athirst is my soul for God, the living God.
   When shall I go and behold the face of God? ℟
I went with the throng
   and led them in procession to the house of God,
amid loud cries of joy and thanksgiving,
   with the multitude keeping festival. ℟
Send forth your light and your fidelity;
   they shall lead me on
and bring me to your holy mountain,
   to your dwelling-place. ℟
Then will I go in to the altar of God,
   the God of my gladness and joy;
then will I give you thanks upon the harp,
   O God, my God! ℟

OR

RESPONSORIAL PSALM *(Psalm 51:12-13, 14-15, 18-19)*
℟ **Create a clean heart in me, O God.**

A clean heart create for me, O God,
   and a steadfast spirit renew within me.

Cast me not out from your presence,
    and your Holy Spirit take not from me. ℟
Give me back the joy of your salvation,
    and a willing spirit sustain in me.
I will teach transgressors your ways,
    and sinners shall return to you. ℟
For you are not pleased with sacrifices;
    should I offer a holocaust, you would not accept it.
My sacrifice, O God, is a contrite spirit;
    a heart contrite and humbled, O God, you will not spurn. ℟

PRAYER

Let us pray.

O God of unchanging power and eternal light,
look with favor on the wondrous mystery of the whole Church
and serenely accomplish the work of human salvation,
which you planned from all eternity;
may the whole world know and see
that what was cast down is raised up,
what had become old is made new,
and all things are restored to integrity through Christ,
just as by him they came into being.
Who lives and reigns for ever and ever. *Amen.*

Or

O God, who by the pages of both Testaments
instruct and prepare us to celebrate the Paschal Mystery,
grant that we may comprehend your mercy,
so that the gifts we receive from you this night
may confirm our hope of the gifts to come.
Through Christ our Lord. *Amen.*

GLORY TO GOD *(page 12)*

COLLECT

Let us pray.

O God, who make this most sacred night radiant
with the glory of the Lord's Resurrection,
stir up in your Church a spirit of adoption,
so that, renewed in body and mind,
we may render you undivided service.
Through our Lord Jesus Christ, your Son,
who lives and reigns with you in the unity of the Holy Spirit,
one God, for ever and ever. *Amen.*

EPISTLE *(Romans 6:3–11)*

Brothers and sisters: Are you unaware that we who were
baptized into Christ Jesus were baptized into his death? We
were indeed buried with him through baptism into death, so
that, just as Christ was raised from the dead by the glory of the
Father, we too might live in newness of life.

For if we have grown into union with him through a death like
his, we shall also be united with him in the **resurrection.** ✠ We
know that our old self was crucified with him, so that our sinful
body might be done away with, that we might no longer be in slavery to sin. For a dead person has been absolved from sin. If, then,
we have died with Christ, we believe that we shall also live with
him. We know that Christ, raised from the dead, dies no more;
death no longer has power over him. As to his death, he died to
sin once and for all; as to his life, he lives for God. Consequently,
you too must think of yourselves as being dead to sin and living for
God in Christ Jesus.

The Gospel of the Lord. *Praise to you, Lord Jesus Christ.*

RESPONSORIAL PSALM *(Psalm 118:1-2, 16-17, 22-23)*

R. Alleluia, alleluia, alleluia.

Give thanks to the LORD, for he is good,
    for his mercy endures forever.
Let the house of Israel say,
    "His mercy endures forever." R.

The right hand of the LORD has struck with power;
    the right hand of the LORD is exalted.
I shall not die, but live,
    and declare the works of the LORD. R.

The stone which the builders rejected
    has become the cornerstone.
By the LORD has this been done;
    it is wonderful in our eyes. R.

GOSPEL *(Luke 24:1-12)*

A reading from the holy Gospel according to Luke.

Glory to you, O Lord.

At daybreak on the first day of the week the women who
had come from Galilee with Jesus took the spices they had
prepared and went to the tomb. They found the stone rolled away
from the tomb; but when they entered, they did not find the body
of the Lord Jesus. While they were puzzling over this, behold, two
men in dazzling garments appeared to them. They were terrified
and bowed their faces to the ground. They said to them, "Why do
you seek the living one among the dead? He is not here, but he has
been raised. Remember what he said to you while he was still in
Galilee, that the Son of Man must be handed over to sinners and
be crucified, and rise on the third day." And they remembered his
words. Then they returned from the tomb and announced all these
things to the eleven and to all the others. The women were Mary

Magdalene, Joanna, and Mary the mother of James; the others who
accompanied them also told this to the apostles, but their story
seemed like nonsense and they did not believe them. But Peter
got up and ran to the tomb, bent down, and saw the burial cloths
alone; then he went home amazed at what had happened.

The Gospel of the Lord. *Praise to you, Lord Jesus Christ.*

LITURGY OF BAPTISM

INVITATION

When baptism is celebrated:

Dearly beloved,
with one heart and one soul, let us by our prayers
come to the aid of these our brothers and sisters
    in their blessed hope,
so that, as they approach the font of rebirth,
the almighty Father may bestow on them
all his merciful help.

When baptism is not celebrated, but the font is blessed:

Dearly beloved,
let us humbly invoke upon this font
the grace of God the almighty Father,
that those who from it are born anew
may be numbered among the children of adoption in Christ.

*If baptism is not celebrated and the font is not blessed, proceed to the
blessing of the water outside of baptism (page 336).*

LITANY OF SAINTS

Lord, have mercy. *Lord, have mercy.*
Christ, have mercy. *Christ, have mercy.*
Lord, have mercy. *Lord, have mercy.*

Holy Mary, Mother of God, *pray for us.*

Saint Michael,
Holy Angels of God,
Saint John the Baptist,
Saint Joseph,
Saint Peter and Saint Paul,
Saint Andrew,
Saint John,
Saint Mary Magdalene,
Saint Stephen,
Saint Ignatius of Antioch,
Saint Lawrence,
Saint Perpetua
    and Saint Felicity,
Saint Agnes,

Saint Gregory,
Saint Augustine,
Saint Athanasius,
Saint Basil,
Saint Martin,
Saint Benedict,
Saint Francis
    and Saint Dominic,
Saint Francis Xavier,
Saint John Vianney,
Saint Catherine of Siena,
Saint Teresa of Jesus,
All holy men and women,
    Saints of God,

Lord, be merciful,
Lord, deliver us, we pray.
From all evil,
From every sin,
From everlasting death,
By your Incarnation,
By your Death and Resurrection,
By the outpouring of the Holy Spirit,

Be merciful to us sinners,
Lord, we ask you, hear our prayer.

When baptism is celebrated add:

Bring these chosen ones to new birth through the grace of Baptism,
Lord, we ask you, hear our prayer.

Or, when baptism is not celebrated:

Make this font holy by your grace for the new birth of your children,
Lord, we ask you, hear our prayer.

Jesus, Son of the living God,
Lord, we ask you, hear our prayer.
Christ, hear us.
Christ, hear us.
Christ, graciously hear us.
Christ, graciously hear us.

When baptism is celebrated, the priest prays:

Almighty ever-living God,
be present by the mysteries of your great love
and send forth the spirit of adoption
to create the new peoples
brought to birth for you in the font of Baptism,
so that what is to be carried out by our humble service
may be brought to fulfillment by your mighty power.
Through Christ our Lord. *Amen.*

BLESSING OF BAPTISMAL WATER
O God, who by invisible power
accomplish a wondrous effect

through sacramental signs
and who in many ways have prepared water, your creation,
to show forth the grace of Baptism;

O God, whose Spirit
in the first moments of the world's creation
hovered over the waters,
so that the very substance of water
would even then take to itself the power to sanctify;

O God, who by the outpouring of the flood
foreshadowed regeneration,
so that from the mystery of one and the same element of water
would come an end to vice and a beginning of virtue;

O God, who caused the children of Abraham
to pass dry-shod through the Red Sea,
so that the chosen people,
set free from slavery to Pharaoh,
would prefigure the people of the baptized;

O God, whose Son,
baptized by John in the waters of the Jordan,
was anointed with the Holy Spirit,
and, as he hung upon the Cross,
gave forth water from his side along with blood,
and after his Resurrection, commanded his disciples:

"Go forth, teach all nations, baptizing them
in the name of the Father and of the Son and of the Holy Spirit,"
look now, we pray, upon the face of your Church
and graciously unseal for her the fountain of Baptism.

May this water receive by the Holy Spirit
the grace of your Only Begotten Son,
so that human nature, created in your image
and washed clean through the Sacrament of Baptism
from all the squalor of the life of old,
may be found worthy to rise to the life of newborn children
through water and the Holy Spirit.

May the power of the Holy Spirit,
O Lord, we pray,
come down through your Son
into the fullness of this font,
so that all who have been buried with Christ
by Baptism into death
may rise again to life with him.
Who lives and reigns with you in the unity of the Holy Spirit,
one God, for ever and ever. *Amen.*

**Springs of water, bless the Lord;
praise and exalt him above all for ever.**

Baptism is now conferred. Adults are then confirmed immediately afterward.

*If there is no baptism and the font is not blessed, the priest blesses the
water and invites the assembly to renew their baptismal commitment:*

THE BLESSING OF WATER *(OUTSIDE OF BAPTISM)*
Dear brothers and sisters,
let us humbly beseech the Lord our God
to bless this water he has created,
which will be sprinkled upon us
as a memorial of our Baptism.
May he graciously renew us,

that we may remain faithful to the Spirit
whom we have received.

Lord our God,
in your mercy be present to your people
who keep vigil on this most sacred night,
and, for us who recall the wondrous work of our creation
and the still greater work of our redemption,
graciously bless this water.
For you created water to make the fields fruitful
and to refresh and cleanse our bodies.
You also made water the instrument of your mercy:
for through water you freed your people from slavery
and quenched their thirst in the desert;
through water the Prophets proclaimed the new covenant
you were to enter upon with the human race;
and last of all,
through water, which Christ made holy in the Jordan,
you have renewed our corrupted nature
in the bath of regeneration.

Therefore, may this water be for us
a memorial of the Baptism we have received,
and grant that we may share
in the gladness of our brothers and sisters,
who at Easter have received their Baptism.
Through Christ our Lord. *Amen.*

*When the Rite of Baptism (and Confirmation) has been completed or, if
this has not taken place, after the blessing of water, all stand, holding
lighted candles in their hands, and renew the promise of baptismal faith,
unless this has already been done together with those to be baptized.*

RENEWAL OF BAPTISMAL PROMISES

Dear brethren (brothers and sisters), through the Paschal Mystery
we have been buried with Christ in Baptism,
so that we may walk with him in newness of life.
And so, now that our Lenten observance is concluded,
let us renew the promises of Holy Baptism,
by which we once renounced Satan and his works
and promised to serve God in the holy Catholic Church.
And so I ask you:

1 Do you renounce Satan? *I do.*
And all his works? *I do.*
And all his empty show? *I do.*

2 Do you renounce sin,
so as to live in the freedom of the children of God? *I do.*
Do you renounce the lure of evil,
so that sin may have no mastery over you? *I do.*
Do you renounce Satan,
the author and prince of sin? *I do.*

PROFESSION OF FAITH

Do you believe in God, the Father almighty,
Creator of heaven and earth? *I do.*

Do you believe in Jesus Christ, his only Son, our Lord,
who was born of the Virgin Mary,
suffered death and was buried,
rose again from the dead
and is seated at the right hand of the Father? *I do.*

Do you believe in the Holy Spirit,
the holy Catholic Church,

the communion of saints,
the forgiveness of sins,
the resurrection of the body,
and life everlasting? *I do.*

And may almighty God, the Father of our Lord Jesus Christ,
who has given us new birth by water and the Holy Spirit
and bestowed on us forgiveness of our sins,
keep us by his grace,
in Christ Jesus our Lord,
for eternal life. *Amen.*

SPRINKLING WITH BAPTISMAL WATER

The priest sprinkles all the people with the blessed baptismal water, while an appropriate song may be sung.

PRAYER OF THE FAITHFUL

LITURGY OF THE EUCHARIST

PREPARATION OF GIFTS *(page 16)*

PRAYER OVER THE OFFERINGS

Accept, we ask, O Lord,
the prayers of your people
with the sacrificial offerings,
that what has begun in the paschal mysteries
may, by the working of your power,
bring us to the healing of eternity.
Through Christ our Lord. *Amen.*

PREFACE *(Easter 1, page 24)*

COMMUNION ANTIPHON *(1 Corinthians 5:7-8)*
Christ our Passover has been sacrificed; therefore let us keep the
feast with the unleavened bread of purity and truth, alleluia.

PRAYER AFTER COMMUNION
Pour out on us, O Lord, the Spirit of your love,
and in your kindness make those you have nourished
by this paschal Sacrament
one in mind and heart.
Through Christ our Lord. *Amen.*

SOLEMN BLESSING: MASS OF THE EASTER VIGIL
May almighty God bless you
through today's Easter Solemnity
and, in his compassion,
defend you from every assault of sin. *Amen.*

• TAKING A CLOSER LOOK •

✣ **Resurrection** What happened on Easter was a complete
surprise to the disciples. The Jesus that they had known and who
had died was suddenly experienced as alive again. This new life, described as resurrection, was not just a restoration of one's former
life—a resuscitation from the dead. The prophets Elijah and Elisha
had brought people back to this life, as had Jesus for the daughter
of Jairus, the son of the widow of Nain, and Jesus' beloved friend
Lazarus. Although their return from the dead left them tempo-
rarily alive, they would die again. Jesus' resurrection was a new
life that would not be subject to death again. It was eternal life—
permanent and undying existence in the presence of God forever.

And may he, who restores you to eternal life
in the Resurrection of his Only Begotten,
endow you with the prize of immortality. *Amen.*

Now that the days of the Lord's Passion have drawn to a close,
may you who celebrate the gladness of the Paschal Feast
come with Christ's help, and exulting in spirit,
to those feasts that are celebrated in eternal joy. *Amen.*

And may the blessing of almighty God,
the Father, and the Son, and the Holy Spirit,
come down on you and remain with you for ever. *Amen.*

DISMISSAL *(page 57)* ✢

✦ RESPONDING TO THE WORD ✦

The Old Testament readings recall God's desire to create a covenant community that would follow God's guidelines.	Paul reminds us that our union with Jesus will bring us to new life.	The disciples are told to seek Jesus among the living, not the dead.
➲ *What word, phrase, or idea in these readings most interested me tonight?*	➲ *What new life has begun in me during this Lent?*	➲ *Where shall I seek Jesus as I go forth from this Easter celebration?*

April 21

From darkness to light!

A dark morning—it seems like the world is ending. Nothing remains, no future, only sadness. Even the tomb is empty. No comfort can be found in grieving. If only time could turn back!

Mary stands, weeping, outside the darkened tomb. She is bereft, hoping against hope, but now she is unable even to gaze on the lifeless body of her beloved Jesus who had been the promise of so much.

Unless we have suffered the loss of someone close, it is impossible to understand death. But this is even worse—a disappearance, obliteration.

Then suddenly, Jesus appears and the darkness engulfing her soul is lifted. We can imagine it is as if light bursts forth from the tomb.

This is Easter, the resurrection. A new world was born that morning when Jesus stepped out of the tomb where he had lain for three days. The sin which brought darkness was obliterated and the world began anew, bathed in the light of the resurrection.

This miracle isn't confined to that historical event some 2,000 years ago. It is alive this Easter morning, and it is alive every Sunday morning when we remember the life, death, and resurrection of Jesus.

This is the miracle: the light of Christ banishes the darkness of hopelessness.

◼ **Patrick M. Doyle**

ENTRANCE ANTIPHON *(Cf. Psalm 139 [138]:18, 5-6)*
I have risen, and I am with you still, alleluia. You
have laid your hand upon me, alleluia. Too wonderful for me, this knowledge, alleluia, alleluia.

Or *(Luke 24:34; cf. Revelation 1:6)*
The Lord is truly risen, alleluia. To him be glory and
power for all the ages of eternity, alleluia, alleluia.

INTRODUCTORY RITES *(page 10)*

COLLECT
O God, who on this day,
through your Only Begotten Son,
have conquered death
and unlocked for us the path to eternity,
grant, we pray, that we who keep
the solemnity of the Lord's Resurrection
may, through the renewal brought by your Spirit,
rise up in the light of life.
Through our Lord Jesus Christ, your Son,
who lives and reigns with you in the unity of the Holy Spirit,
one God, for ever and ever. *Amen.*

FIRST READING *(Acts 10:34a, 37–43)*
Peter proceeded to speak and said: "You know what has happened all over Judea, beginning in Galilee after the baptism
that John preached, how God anointed Jesus of Nazareth with
the Holy Spirit and power. He went about doing good and healing all those oppressed by the devil, for God was with him. We
are witnesses of all that he did both in the country of the Jews
and in Jerusalem. They put him to death by hanging him on a

tree. This man God raised on the third day and granted that he be visible, not to all the people, but to us, the witnesses chosen by God in advance, who ate and drank with him after he rose from the dead. He commissioned us to preach to the people and testify that he is the one appointed by God as judge of the living and the dead. To him all the prophets bear witness, that everyone who believes in him will receive forgiveness of sins through his name."

The word of the Lord. *Thanks be to God.*

RESPONSORIAL PSALM *(Psalm 118:1-2, 16-17, 22-23)*

R̷ **This is the day the Lord has made; let us rejoice and be glad.**
   Or **Alleluia.**

Give thanks to the LORD, for he is good,
   for his mercy endures forever.
Let the house of Israel say,
   "His mercy endures forever." R̷
"The right hand of the LORD has struck with power;
   the right hand of the LORD is exalted.
I shall not die, but live,
   and declare the works of the LORD." R̷
The stone which the builders rejected
   has become the cornerstone.
By the LORD has this been done;
   it is wonderful in our eyes. R̷

An alternate reading follows.

SECOND READING *(Colossians 3:1-4)*

Brothers and sisters: If then you were raised with Christ, seek what is above, where Christ is seated at the right hand of God. Think of what is above, not of what is on earth. For you have died, and your life is hidden with Christ in God. When Christ your life appears, then you too will appear with him in glory.

The word of the Lord. ***Thanks be to God.***

OR

SECOND READING *(1 Corinthians 5:6b-8)*

Brothers and sisters: Do you not know that a little yeast leavens all the dough? Clear out the old yeast, so that you may become a fresh batch of dough, inasmuch as you are unleavened. For our paschal lamb, Christ, has been sacrificed. Therefore, let us celebrate the feast, not with the old yeast, the yeast of malice and wickedness, but with the unleavened bread of sincerity and truth.

The word of the Lord. ***Thanks be to God.***

SEQUENCE

Christians, to the Paschal Victim
    Offer your thankful praises!
A Lamb the sheep redeems;
    Christ, who only is sinless,
    Reconciles sinners to the Father.
Death and life have contended in that combat stupendous:
    The Prince of life, who died, reigns immortal.
Speak, Mary, declaring
    What you saw, wayfaring.

"The tomb of Christ, who is living,
    The glory of Jesus' resurrection;
Bright angels attesting,
    The shroud and napkin resting.
Yes, Christ my hope is arisen;
    To Galilee he goes before you."
Christ indeed from death is risen, our new life obtaining.
    Have mercy, victor King, ever reigning!
    Amen. Alleluia.

ALLELUIA (See 1 Corinthians 5:7b–8a)
Alleluia, alleluia. Christ, our paschal lamb, has been sacrificed;
let us then feast with joy in the Lord. *Alleluia, alleluia.*

*The gospel from the Easter Vigil (page 331) may be read instead. For the
gospel for an afternoon or evening Mass, see next page.*

GOSPEL (John 20:1–9)
A reading from the holy Gospel according to John.
Glory to you, O Lord.

On the first day of the week, Mary of Magdala came to
the tomb✝ early in the morning, while it was still dark,
and saw the stone removed from the tomb. So she ran and went
to Simon Peter and to the other disciple whom Jesus loved, and
told them, "They have taken the Lord from the tomb, and we
don't know where they put him." So Peter and the other disciple
went out and came to the tomb. They both ran, but the other
disciple ran faster than Peter and arrived at the tomb first; he
bent down and saw the burial cloths there, but did not go in.
When Simon Peter arrived after him, he went into the tomb and
saw the burial cloths there, and the cloth that had covered his

head, not with the burial cloths but rolled up in a separate place. Then the other disciple also went in, the one who had arrived at the tomb first, and he saw and believed. For they did not yet understand the Scripture that he had to rise from the dead.

The Gospel of the Lord. ***Praise to you, Lord Jesus Christ.***

Alternate reading for an afternoon or evening Mass:

GOSPEL *(Luke 24:13–35)*
A reading from the holy Gospel according to Luke.
Glory to you, Lord.

That very day, the first day of the week, two of Jesus' disciples were going to a village seven miles from Jerusalem called Emmaus, and they were conversing about all the things that had occurred. And it happened that while they were conversing and debating, Jesus himself drew near and walked with them, but their eyes were prevented from recognizing him. He asked them, "What are you discussing as you walk along?" They stopped, looking downcast. One of them, named Cleopas, said to him in reply, "Are you the only visitor to Jerusalem who does not know of the things that have taken place there in these days?" And he replied to them, "What sort of things?" They said to him, "The things that happened to Jesus the Nazarene, who was a prophet mighty in deed and word before God and all the people, how our chief priests and rulers both handed him over to a sentence of death and crucified him. But we were hoping that he would be the one to redeem Israel; and besides all this, it is now the third day since this took place. Some women from our group, however, have astounded us: they were at **the tomb**✢ early in the morning and did not find his body; they came back and reported that they had indeed seen a vision of angels who announced that he was alive. Then some of those with us went to the tomb and found things just as the women had described, but him they did not see." And he said to them, "Oh, how foolish you are! How slow of heart to believe all that the prophets spoke! Was it not necessary that the Christ should suffer these things and enter into his glory?" Then beginning with Moses and all the prophets, he interpreted to them what referred to him in all the Scriptures. As they approached the village to which they were going, he gave the impression that he was going on farther. But they urged him, "Stay with us, for it is nearly evening and the day is almost over." So he went in to stay with them. And it happened that, while he was with them at table, he took bread, said the blessing, broke it, and gave it to them. With that their eyes were opened and they recognized him, but he vanished from their sight. Then they said to each other, "Were not our hearts burning within us while he spoke to us on the way and opened the Scriptures to us?" So they set out at once and returned to Jerusalem where they found gathered together the eleven and those with them who were saying, "The Lord has truly been raised and has appeared to Simon!" Then the two recounted what had taken place on the way and how he was made known to them in the breaking of bread.

The Gospel of the Lord. *Praise to you, Lord Jesus Christ.*

RENEWAL OF BAPTISMAL PROMISES AND PROFESSION OF FAITH

(See page 338)

In Easter Sunday Masses the rite of the renewal of baptismal promises may take place after the homily, according to the text used at the Easter Vigil.

PRAYER OF THE FAITHFUL

PREPARATION OF GIFTS *(page 16)*

PRAYER OVER THE OFFERINGS

Exultant with paschal gladness, O Lord,
we offer the sacrifice
by which your Church
is wondrously reborn and nourished.
Through Christ our Lord. *Amen.*

❖ TAKING A CLOSER LOOK ❖

✝ **The tomb** It is apparent from the resurrection accounts in the gospels that the meaning of the event was not immediately intelligible. The empty tomb was not a proof of the resurrection but a fact whose meaning needed to be discovered. Finding the empty tomb made Jesus' followers bewildered and confused, grasping for various possible answers to account for it. Only when the disciples experienced the risen Lord did the meaning of the empty tomb become clear. The stone was rolled back not so Jesus could get out, but so we could get in and be assured that his tomb of death will remain empty forever. He is risen!

PREFACE *(Easter 1, page 24)*

COMMUNION ANTIPHON *(1 Corinthians 5:7–8)*

 Christ our Passover has been sacrificed, alleluia; therefore let us keep the feast with the unleavened bread of purity and truth, alleluia, alleluia.

PRAYER AFTER COMMUNION

Look upon your Church, O God,
with unfailing love and favor,
so that, renewed by the paschal mysteries,
she may come to the glory of the resurrection.
Through Christ our Lord. *Amen.*

SOLEMN BLESSING: MASS OF THE EASTER VIGIL *(Optional, page 340)*

BLESSING & DISMISSAL *(page 56)* ✦

✦ RESPONDING TO THE WORD ✦

Peter wants to share his good news about Jesus with others.

➡ *With whom will I share my good news today?*

Paul encourages us to live in a new way because of our relationship with Christ.

➡ *What new behaviors will I adopt to be more like Jesus?*

The disciples seek Jesus, who disguises himself in many forms.

➡ *How have I discovered Christ hidden in others?*

These fifty days are like one great Sunday

The season of Easter is actually a celebration of fifty days, from Easter until Pentecost. The word "Pentecost" means "fiftieth" and is the Greek translation of the Hebrew word *Shavuot*. *Shavuot*, the Jewish Feast of Weeks, began as a harvest festival in Canaan, coming approximately seven weeks after the first day of Passover.

What Sunday is to our Christian week, the Easter season is to the whole liturgical year. The fifty days of Easter have been observed longer than any other season of the Christian year. In the early Church, it was celebrated as an "unbroken Sunday," a week of weeks (7 times 7, or 49 days) plus the eighth day of the new creation. During these fifty days of joy, we are called upon in our life and worship to proclaim the lordship of Jesus revealed through his resurrection, ascension, and the outpouring of the Holy Spirit.

This season is a time to grow in our understanding of the paschal mystery and to make it part of our lives through our renewed attentiveness to God's word that we hear each Sunday and talk about in our households, through our fuller participation in the Eucharist, and through our renewed dedication to acts of charity and justice.

As we celebrate this season, we become more deeply aware of Christ's abiding but hidden presence with us that is daily transforming us into the image of Jesus.

Praying and living the Easter season

Since the Easter season is fifty days long, it will take some effort on our part to extend its celebration for the full seven weeks until Pentecost.

As Christians we each share in the Easter experience because we have in one way or another met the risen Christ and so become connected to the community that witnesses to the good news of his resurrection.

One way to make Easter into a season of celebrations and keep its spirit alive is to adopt the daily practice of using the Collect for Sunday as the gathering prayer for a household meal.

Another practice is to connect ourselves to the long chain of Christian witnesses that have preceded us. Gather your household or faith-sharing group and explain that when Paul locates himself in the Christian tradition, he creates a chain of witnesses connecting those who experienced Christ's first Easter appearance to himself.

Invite the household to bring this chain of witnesses from Paul's time down to our present time by naming those who have been most important in handing on the living tradition (e.g., family, relatives, friends, mentors, spiritual persons you have admired, patron saints, etc.).

Write down the names to create your household's or group's unique connection to the Easter tradition. To express your solidarity, share a sign of peace with one another. Then conclude by praying the Lord's Prayer together.

April 28

The gift of welcome

In today's gospel, Thomas' act of doubt reveals an important aspect of faith. Faith is rooted not only in a supernatural virtue, but in the experience of inclusion.

Imagine how Thomas felt when the other disciples joyfully told him of their encounter with the risen Lord. The pain of exclusion can be heard in his declaration, "I will not believe." Thomas has missed out on one of the most important events his companions had ever experienced. The disciples have been elevated to a new level of awareness about Jesus. Thomas, however, has not. He feels excluded.

His is a normal human reaction. We don't like to miss out on the action. Absent from some great event, we may seek to minimize the experience of those who were present. But in doing so, we erect walls around our hearts and barriers between ourselves and others.

Jesus breaks through Thomas' feeling of exclusion. He welcomes Thomas by inviting him to put his hand in Jesus' side. "Do not be unbelieving but believe," Jesus says.

Thomas has been given the gift of welcome. Jesus has healed Thomas' wound, the wound of being left on the outside. Perhaps we can do as Jesus did with those we see sitting on the sidelines. It may strengthen their faith—and ours.

■ GLEN ARGAN

ENTRANCE ANTIPHON *(1 Peter 2:2)*

Like newborn infants, you must long for the pure, spiritual milk,
that in him you may grow to salvation, alleluia.

Or *(4 Esdras 2:36-37)*

Receive the joy of your glory, giving thanks to God, who has
called you into the heavenly kingdom, alleluia.

INTRODUCTORY RITES *(page 10)*

COLLECT

God of everlasting mercy,
who in the very recurrence of the paschal feast
kindle the faith of the people you have made your own,
increase, we pray, the grace you have bestowed,
that all may grasp and rightly understand
in what font they have been washed,
by whose Spirit they have been reborn,
by whose Blood they have been redeemed.
Through our Lord Jesus Christ, your Son,
who lives and reigns with you in the unity of the Holy Spirit,
one God, for ever and ever. *Amen.*

FIRST READING *(Acts 5:12-16)*

Many signs and wonders were done among the people at the
hands of the apostles. They were all together in Solomon's
portico. None of the others dared to join them, but the people
esteemed them. Yet more than ever, believers in the Lord, great
numbers of men and women, were added to them. Thus they even
carried the sick out into the streets and laid them on cots and mats
so that when Peter came by, at least his shadow might fall on one
or another of them. A large number of people from the towns in

the vicinity of Jerusalem also gathered, bringing the sick and those disturbed by unclean spirits, and they were all cured.

The word of the Lord. *Thanks be to God.*

RESPONSORIAL PSALM *(Psalm 118:2-4, 13-15, 22-24)*

R̂ **Give thanks to the Lord for he is good, his love is everlasting.** *Or* **Alleluia.**

Let the house of Israel say,
    "His **mercy endures forever."**✝
Let the house of Aaron say,
    "His mercy endures forever."
Let those who fear the LORD say,
    "His mercy endures forever." R̂

I was hard pressed and was falling,
    but the LORD helped me.
My strength and my courage is the LORD,
    and he has been my savior.
The joyful shout of victory
    in the tents of the just. R̂

The stone which the builders rejected
    has become the cornerstone.
By the LORD has this been done;
    it is wonderful in our eyes.
This is the day the LORD has made;
    let us be glad and rejoice in it. R̂

SECOND READING *(Revelation 1:9-11a, 12-13, 17-19)*

I, John, your brother, who share with you the distress, the kingdom, and the endurance we have in Jesus, found myself on the island called Patmos because I proclaimed God's word and gave testimony to Jesus. I was caught up in spirit on the Lord's day and heard behind me a voice as loud as a trumpet, which said, "Write on a scroll what you see." Then I turned to see whose voice it was that spoke to me, and when I turned, I saw seven gold lampstands and in the midst of the lampstands one like a son of man, wearing an ankle-length robe, with a gold sash around his chest.

When I caught sight of him, I fell down at his feet as though dead. He touched me with his right hand and said, "Do not be afraid. I am the first and the last, the one who lives. Once I was dead, but now I am alive forever and ever. I hold the keys to death and the netherworld. Write down, therefore, what you have seen, and what is happening, and what will happen afterwards."

The word of the Lord. *Thanks be to God.*

ALLELUIA *(John 20:29)*
Alleluia, alleluia. You believe in me, Thomas, because you have seen me, says the Lord; blessed are they who have not seen me, but still believe! *Alleluia, alleluia.*

GOSPEL *(John 20:19–31)*
A reading from the holy Gospel according to John.
Glory to you, O Lord.

On the evening of that first day of the week, when the doors were locked, where the disciples were, for fear of the Jews, Jesus came and stood in their midst and said to them, "Peace be with you." When he had said this, he showed them his hands and his side. The disciples rejoiced when they saw the Lord. Jesus said to them again, "Peace be with you. As the Father has sent me, so I send you." And when he had said this, he breathed on them and said to them, "Receive the Holy Spirit. Whose sins you forgive are forgiven them, and whose sins you retain are retained."

Thomas, called Didymus,* one of the Twelve, was not with them when Jesus came. So the other disciples said to him, "We have seen the Lord." But he said to them, "Unless I see the mark of the nails in his hands and put my finger into the nailmarks and put my hand into his side, I will not believe."

Now a week later his disciples were again inside and Thomas was with them. Jesus came, although the doors were locked, and stood in their midst and said, "Peace be with you." Then he said to Thomas, "Put your finger here and see my hands, and bring your hand and put it into my side, and do not be unbelieving, but believe." Thomas answered and said to him, "My Lord and my God!" Jesus said to him, "Have you come to believe because you have seen me? Blessed are those who have not seen and have believed."

Now Jesus did many other signs in the presence of his disciples that are not written in this book. But these are written that you may come to believe that Jesus is the Christ, the Son of God, and that through this belief you may have life in his name.

The Gospel of the Lord. *Praise to you, Lord Jesus Christ.*

PROFESSION OF FAITH *(page 13)*

PRAYER OF THE FAITHFUL

PREPARATION OF GIFTS *(page 16)*

PRAYER OVER THE OFFERINGS

Accept, O Lord, we pray,
the oblations of your people
(and of those you have brought to new birth),
that, renewed by confession of your name and by Baptism,
they may attain unending happiness.
Through Christ our Lord. *Amen.*

PREFACE *(Easter 1, page 24)*

COMMUNION ANTIPHON *(Cf. John 20:27)*

Bring your hand and feel the place of the nails, and do not be
unbelieving but believing, alleluia.

• TAKING A CLOSER LOOK •

✝ **Mercy endures forever** In the Old Testament, mercy
(Hebrew, *hesed*) usually identifies a complex Hebrew idea that
describes God's special covenant love. God's desire to be in communion with us as covenant partners reveals an attitude of divine
love and faithfulness that includes loyalty, compassion, dependability, trustworthiness, and an eagerness to help when situations
turn bad. And once God commits to the people in covenant fidelity,
there is no question of God ever retracting that commitment. God's
covenant love will never end.

PRAYER AFTER COMMUNION

Grant, we pray, almighty God,
that our reception of this paschal Sacrament
may have a continuing effect
in our minds and hearts.
Through Christ our Lord. *Amen.*

SOLEMN BLESSING: EASTER TIME *(Optional, page 60)*

BLESSING & DISMISSAL *(page 56)* ✤

• RESPONDING TO THE WORD •

The apostles continue Jesus' healing work.	The risen Jesus tells John not to be afraid.	Thomas voices his doubts yet overcomes them with faith.
⮑ *Who might need my healing actions or words today?*	⮑ *What fears about Christ's presence to me must I overcome?*	⮑ *What doubts about Jesus require more faith on my part?*

May 5

Share the good news!

God lovingly pursues us, calling us far beyond our own safety zones to share the good news of salvation. We see this clearly in the life of the apostle Peter.

He was chosen for discipleship by Jesus but he had a hard time. When Jesus was brought before the high priest, Peter was so afraid that he denied three times that he was Christ's disciple. After he saw Jesus' empty tomb, he went home and locked all the doors. When it looked like the great adventure with Jesus was a miserable failure, he went back to what he knew: his fishing boat.

However, the promise of Easter was genuine. Jesus really did rise from the dead. He met Simon Peter on his own territory, when he was fishing, and called him again. Call and response were unmistakable. Three times, Jesus asks "Do you love me?" Peter's answer was "Yes," "Yes," and "Yes I do, and I already told you I did."

Jesus tells Peter to take care of the flock, prepare for difficult times, and "Follow me." Peter did that. So today, all around the world, we are still responding to God's call, still daring to take risks in service to the proclamation of God's unending love. We are compelled to share the good news of Jesus Christ, risen from the dead. Alleluia!

■ MARILYN J. SWEET

ENTRANCE ANTIPHON *(Cf. Psalm 66 [65]:1-2)*

Cry out with joy to God, all the earth; O sing to the
glory of his name. O render him glorious praise,
alleluia.

INTRODUCTORY RITES *(page 10)*

COLLECT

May your people exult for ever, O God,
in renewed youthfulness of spirit,
so that, rejoicing now in the restored glory of our adoption,
we may look forward in confident hope
to the rejoicing of the day of resurrection.
Through our Lord Jesus Christ, your Son,
who lives and reigns with you in the unity of the Holy Spirit,
one God, for ever and ever. *Amen.*

FIRST READING *(Acts 5:27-32, 40b-41)*

When the captain and the court officers had brought the
apostles in and made them stand before the **Sanhedrin,**＊✝
the high priest questioned them, "We gave you strict orders,
did we not, to stop teaching in that name? Yet you have filled
Jerusalem with your teaching and want to bring this man's blood
upon us." But Peter and the apostles said in reply, "We must
obey God rather than men. The God of our ancestors raised
Jesus, though you had him killed by hanging him on a tree. God
exalted him at his right hand as leader and savior to grant Israel
repentance and forgiveness of sins. We are witnesses of these
things, as is the Holy Spirit whom God has given to those who
obey him."

The Sanhedrin ordered the apostles to stop speaking in the
name of Jesus, and dismissed them. So they left the presence of

the Sanhedrin, rejoicing that they had been found worthy to suffer dishonor for the sake of the name.

The word of the Lord. *Thanks be to God.*

RESPONSORIAL PSALM *(Psalm 30:2, 4, 5-6, 11-12, 13)*
R̸ **I will praise you, Lord, for you have rescued me.** *Or* **Alleluia.**

I will extol you, O LORD, for you drew me clear
　　and did not let my enemies rejoice over me.
O LORD, you brought me up from the netherworld;
　　you preserved me from among those going down into the pit. R̸

Sing praise to the LORD, you his faithful ones,
　　and give thanks to his holy name.
For his anger lasts but a moment;
　　a lifetime, his good will.
At nightfall, weeping enters in,
　　but with the dawn, rejoicing. R̸

Hear, O LORD, and have pity on me;
　　O LORD, be my helper.
You changed my mourning into dancing;
　　O LORD, my God, forever will I give you thanks. R̸

SECOND READING *(Revelation 5:11-14)*

I, John, looked and heard the voices of many angels who surrounded the throne and the living creatures and the elders. They were countless in number, and they cried out in a loud voice:
　　"Worthy is the Lamb that was slain
　　　　to receive power and riches, wisdom and strength,
　　　　honor and glory and blessing."
Then I heard every creature in heaven and on earth and under the earth and in the sea, everything in the universe, cry out:

"To the one who sits on the throne and to the Lamb
be blessing and honor, glory and might,
forever and ever."
The four living creatures answered, "Amen," and the elders fell
down and worshiped.

The word of the Lord. *Thanks be to God.*

ALLELUIA
Alleluia, alleluia. Christ is risen, creator of all; he has shown
pity on all people. *Alleluia, alleluia.*

GOSPEL *(John 21:1-19)*
The shorter reading ends at the asterisks.

A reading from the holy Gospel according to John.
Glory to you, O Lord.

At that time, Jesus revealed himself again to his disciples
at the Sea of Tiberias. He revealed himself in this way.
Together were Simon Peter, Thomas called Didymus,* Nathanael
from Cana in Galilee, Zebedee's sons, and two others of his disciples. Simon Peter said to them, "I am going fishing." They said
to him, "We also will come with you." So they went out and got
into the boat, but that night they caught nothing. When it was
already dawn, Jesus was standing on the shore; but the disciples
did not realize that it was Jesus. Jesus said to them, "Children,
have you caught anything to eat?" They answered him, "No."
So he said to them, "Cast the net over the right side of the boat
and you will find something." So they cast it, and were not able
to pull it in because of the number of fish. So the disciple whom
Jesus loved said to Peter, "It is the Lord." When Simon Peter
heard that it was the Lord, he tucked in his garment, for he was

lightly clad, and jumped into the sea. The other disciples came in
the boat, for they were not far from shore, only about a hundred
yards, dragging the net with the fish. When they climbed out
on shore, they saw a charcoal fire with fish on it and bread. Jesus
said to them, "Bring some of the fish you just caught." So Simon
Peter went over and dragged the net ashore full of one hundred
fifty-three large fish. Even though there were so many, the net
was not torn. Jesus said to them, "Come, have breakfast." And
none of the disciples dared to ask him, "Who are you?" because
they realized it was the Lord. Jesus came over and took the bread
and gave it to them, and in like manner the fish. This was now
the third time Jesus was revealed to his disciples after being
raised from the dead.

* * *

When they had finished breakfast, Jesus said to Simon Peter,
"Simon, son of John, do you love me more than these?" Simon
Peter answered him, "Yes, Lord, you know that I love you."
Jesus said to him, "Feed my lambs." He then said to Simon
Peter a second time, "Simon, son of John, do you love me?"
Simon Peter answered him, "Yes, Lord, you know that I love
you." Jesus said to him, "Tend my sheep." Jesus said to him the
third time, "Simon, son of John, do you love me?" Peter was
distressed that Jesus had said to him a third time, "Do you
love me?" and he said to him, "Lord, you know everything;
you know that I love you." Jesus said to him, "Feed my sheep.
Amen, amen, I say to you, when you were younger, you used to
dress yourself and go where you wanted; but when you grow
old, you will stretch out your hands, and someone else will
dress you and lead you where you do not want to go." He said

this signifying by what kind of death he would glorify God. And when he had said this, he said to him, "Follow me."

The Gospel of the Lord. *Praise to you, Lord Jesus Christ.*

PROFESSION OF FAITH *(page 13)*

PRAYER OF THE FAITHFUL

PREPARATION OF GIFTS *(page 16)*

PRAYER OVER THE OFFERINGS
Receive, O Lord, we pray,
these offerings of your exultant Church,
and, as you have given her cause for such great gladness,
grant also that the gifts we bring
may bear fruit in perpetual happiness.
Through Christ our Lord. *Amen.*

PREFACE *(Easter 1–5, pages 24-26)*

✣ Taking a Closer Look ✣

✠ **Sanhedrin** The *Sanhedrin* (Greek, "council") was the official group of Jewish leaders in Jerusalem that functioned as a court both to decide cases and to determine disputed points of the law. Because religious and political concerns were not separate in the biblical world, the council dealt with both political and religious matters. Although its exact makeup is hard to determine, at the time of Jesus its members included representatives of all the various Jewish parties—Sadducees, Pharisees, priests, scribes, and elders of the chief families—and worked closely with the high priest, as is evident both in Jesus' trial and in the trials of the apostles (Acts 4 and 5).

COMMUNION ANTIPHON (Luke 24:35)

The disciples recognized the Lord Jesus in the breaking of the bread, alleluia.

Or (Cf. John 21:12–13)

Jesus said to his disciples: Come and eat. And he took bread and gave it to them, alleluia.

PRAYER AFTER COMMUNION

Look with kindness upon your people, O Lord,
and grant, we pray,
that those you were pleased to renew by eternal mysteries
may attain in their flesh
the incorruptible glory of the resurrection.
Through Christ our Lord. *Amen.*

SOLEMN BLESSING: EASTER TIME (Optional, page 60)

BLESSING & DISMISSAL (page 56) ❖

❖ RESPONDING TO THE WORD ❖

The apostles obey Jesus' command to spread the good news rather than the human command to stop.

➥ What can I do today to be more courageous in my witness to my life in Christ?

John describes the heavenly praise of God and of Jesus, the Lamb of God.

➥ How can I add my praise to theirs today?

When Peter recognizes Jesus, nothing can hold him back.

➥ What might be holding me back from being with Jesus?

May 12

Respond to the call!

Once, when out hiking in the forest, my wife and I lost track of our little girl. Holding our son close and shouting out our daughter's name, we spent anxious moments frantically searching for her in the bush. Only a parent can know the relief we felt upon discovering her to be safe and sound. Or, perhaps, could a shepherd also be familiar with such emotion?

Jesus, the Good Shepherd, says "My sheep hear my voice." The first step on the road to follow Jesus is to listen. To have familiarity, even intimacy, with the voice of the Good Shepherd means to spend time listening to the Word of God.

But Jesus' teaching on the Good Shepherd suggests more is then required of us: "I know them, and they follow me." After listening, we must respond to the embrace of the Good Shepherd. Discerning our own specific vocation, we ask how this journey can take us yet closer to God.

Paul's and Barnabas's vocation was to preach the Word, even when opposed. Jesus found his own message contested and contradicted by the religious authorities; they even wanted to stone him. While it is unlikely this would happen to us today, it is always good to ask: how I can respond to the loving call of the Good Shepherd through my actions this week?

■ JOE GUNN

ENTRANCE ANTIPHON *(Cf. Psalm 33 [32]:5-6)*
The merciful love of the Lord fills the earth; by the word of the
Lord the heavens were made, alleluia.

INTRODUCTORY RITES *(page 10)*

COLLECT
Almighty ever-living God,
lead us to a share in the joys of heaven,
so that the humble flock may reach
where the brave Shepherd has gone before.
Who lives and reigns with you in the unity of the Holy Spirit,
one God, for ever and ever. *Amen.*

FIRST READING *(Acts 13:14, 43-52)*

Paul and Barnabas continued on from Perga and reached
Antioch in Pisidia.* On the sabbath they entered the synagogue and took their seats. Many Jews and worshipers who were
converts to Judaism followed Paul and Barnabas, who spoke to
them and urged them to remain faithful to the grace of God.

On the following sabbath almost the whole city gathered to
hear the word of the Lord. When the Jews saw the crowds, they
were filled with jealousy and with violent abuse contradicted
what Paul said. Both Paul and Barnabas spoke out boldly and
said, "It was necessary that the word of God be spoken to you
first, but since you reject it and condemn yourselves as unworthy
of **eternal life,**✝ we now turn to the Gentiles. For so the Lord has
commanded us, *I have made you a light to the Gentiles, that you
may be an instrument of salvation to the ends of the earth."*

The Gentiles were delighted when they heard this and glorified the word of the Lord. All who were destined for eternal life
came to believe, and the word of the Lord continued to spread

through the whole region. The Jews, however, incited the women of prominence who were worshipers and the leading men of the city, stirred up a persecution against Paul and Barnabas, and expelled them from their territory. So they shook the dust from their feet in protest against them, and went to Iconium.* The disciples were filled with joy and the Holy Spirit.

The word of the Lord. *Thanks be to God.*

RESPONSORIAL PSALM *(Psalm 100:1-2, 3, 5)*

℟. **We are his people, the sheep of his flock.** *Or* **Alleluia.**

Sing joyfully to the LORD, all you lands;
  serve the LORD with gladness;
  come before him with joyful song. ℟.
Know that the LORD is God;
  he made us, his we are;
  his people, the flock he tends. ℟.
The LORD is good:
  his kindness endures forever,
  and his faithfulness, to all generations. ℟.

SECOND READING *(Revelation 7:9, 14b-17)*

I, John, had a vision of a great multitude, which no one could count, from every nation, race, people, and tongue. They stood before the throne and before the Lamb, wearing white robes and holding palm branches in their hands.

Then one of the elders said to me, "These are the ones who have survived the time of great distress; they have washed their robes and made them white in the blood of the Lamb.

"For this reason they stand before God's throne
  and worship him day and night in his temple.

The one who sits on the throne will shelter them.
They will not hunger or thirst anymore,
    nor will the sun or any heat strike them.
For the Lamb who is in the center of the throne
    will shepherd them
    and lead them to springs of life-giving water,
    and God will wipe away every tear from their eyes."

The word of the Lord. *Thanks be to God.*

ALLELUIA (*John 10:14*)
Alleluia, alleluia. I am the good shepherd, says the Lord;
I know my sheep, and mine know me. *Alleluia, alleluia.*

GOSPEL (*John 10:27-30*)
A reading from the holy Gospel according to John.
Glory to you, O Lord.

Jesus said: "My sheep hear my voice; I know them, and they
follow me. I give them **eternal life**,✝ and they shall never perish. No one can take them out of my hand. My Father, who has
given them to me, is greater than all, and no one can take them
out of the Father's hand. The Father and I are one."

The Gospel of the Lord. *Praise to you, Lord Jesus Christ.*

PROFESSION OF FAITH (*page 13*)

PRAYER OF THE FAITHFUL

PREPARATION OF GIFTS (*page 16*)

PRAYER OVER THE OFFERINGS

Grant, we pray, O Lord,
that we may always find delight in these paschal mysteries,
so that the renewal constantly at work within us
may be the cause of our unending joy.
Through Christ our Lord. *Amen.*

PREFACE *(Easter 1–5, pages 24–26)*

COMMUNION ANTIPHON

The Good Shepherd has risen, who laid down his life for his
sheep and willingly died for his flock, alleluia.

• TAKING A CLOSER LOOK •

✢ **Eternal life** John's gospel describes the destiny of believers as eternal life, that is, a life that shares in the divine type of
life that has no visible beginning or ending. It is a permanent
and undying existence in the presence of God forever. Human
life ends with death, but though death ends our physical life, our
relationship with God continues because God chooses to share
the divine life with us. Eternal life, then, is qualitatively different
from natural life for it is a life that death cannot destroy. Eternal
life is our future destiny, but it begins here and now in us by our
association with Jesus and through God's Holy Spirit.

PRAYER AFTER COMMUNION

Look upon your flock, kind Shepherd,
and be pleased to settle in eternal pastures
the sheep you have redeemed
by the Precious Blood of your Son.
Who lives and reigns for ever and ever. ***Amen.***

SOLEMN BLESSING: EASTER TIME *(Optional, page 60)*

BLESSING & DISMISSAL *(page 56)* ✦

✦ RESPONDING TO THE WORD ✦

Despite problems, the disciples were filled with joy.	God will wipe away our tears of sadness.	Jesus speaks to us and invites us to follow him.
➧ *What joy have I felt during this Easter season?*	➧ *What sadness do I want Jesus to lift today?*	➧ *How has Jesus been calling me to follow him in new ways during Lent and Easter?*

May 19

Honoring Christ's sacrifice

Today's readings share essential Christian themes of death, redeeming sacrifice, and eternal life. In the book of Revelation, early Christians learned "there shall be no more death." During the Easter season, we Christians more than ever know this to be true.

The Mass enables us to witness Christ's prevailing sacrifice that perpetually prevents evil from ever triumphing over good. Again, and again, and again, at every Mass the Lord Jesus Christ, through the priest, makes the ultimate sacrifice for his children on earth.

What can we do to honor his sacrifice? In today's gospel, the Lord asks us to love one another: "As I have loved you, you also should love one another." Jesus points out that this kind of love is what makes us Christians: "This is how all will know that you are my disciples, if you have love for one another."

The suffering we inevitably endure in life can be transformative. If our sacrifices are fueled by love for one another, they will bring us closer to God. When we are in a state of grace we can fully experience the Eucharist, God's incredible love for us. When we try to understand just an ounce of that love, it can profoundly change the way we interact with one another and how we live our lives daily.

■ **DANA KENNY**

ENTRANCE ANTIPHON *(Cf. Psalm 98 [97]:1–2)*

O sing a new song to the Lord, for he has worked wonders; in
the sight of the nations he has shown his deliverance, alleluia.

INTRODUCTORY RITES *(page 10)*

COLLECT

Almighty ever-living God,
constantly accomplish the Paschal Mystery within us,
that those you were pleased to make new in Holy Baptism
may, under your protective care, bear much fruit
and come to the joys of life eternal.
Through our Lord Jesus Christ, your Son,
who lives and reigns with you in the unity of the Holy Spirit,
one God, for ever and ever. *Amen.*

FIRST READING *(Acts 14:21–27)*

After Paul and Barnabas had proclaimed the good news to that
city and made a considerable number of disciples, they returned to Lystra* and to Iconium* and to Antioch. They strengthened the spirits of the disciples and exhorted them to persevere in
the faith, saying, "It is necessary for us to undergo many hardships
to enter the kingdom of God." They appointed elders for them
in each church and, with prayer and fasting, commended them
to the Lord in whom they had put their faith. Then they traveled
through Pisidia* and reached Pamphylia.* After proclaiming the
word at Perga they went down to Attalia.* From there they sailed to
Antioch, where they had been commended to the grace of God for
the work they had now accomplished. And when they arrived, they
called the church together and reported what God had done with
them and how he had opened the door of faith to the Gentiles.

The word of the Lord. *Thanks be to God.*

RESPONSORIAL PSALM *(Psalm 145:8-9, 10-11, 12-13)*

℟. I will praise your name forever, my king and my God. *Or* Alleluia.

The LORD is gracious and merciful,
 slow to anger and of great kindness.
The LORD is good to all
 and compassionate toward all his works. ℟.
Let all your works give you thanks, O LORD,
 and let your faithful ones bless you.
Let them discourse of the glory of your kingdom
 and speak of your might. ℟.
Let them make known your might to the children of Adam,
 and the glorious splendor of your kingdom.
Your kingdom is a kingdom for all ages,
 and your dominion endures through all generations. ℟.

SECOND READING *(Revelation 21:1-5a)*

Then I, John, saw **a new heaven and a new earth.** ✣ The
former heaven and the former earth had passed away, and
the sea was no more. I also saw the holy city, a new Jerusalem,
coming down out of heaven from God, prepared as a bride
adorned for her husband. I heard a loud voice from the throne
saying, "Behold, God's dwelling is with the human race. He will
dwell with them and they will be his people and God himself
will always be with them as their God. He will wipe every tear
from their eyes, and there shall be no more death or mourning,
wailing or pain, for the old order has passed away."

The One who sat on the throne said, "Behold, I make all
things new."

The word of the Lord. *Thanks be to God.*

ALLELUIA *(John 13:34)*
Alleluia, alleluia. I give you a new commandment, says the Lord: love one another as I have loved you. *Alleluia, alleluia.*

GOSPEL *(John 13:31-33a, 34-35)*
A reading from the holy Gospel according to John.
Glory to you, O Lord.

When Judas had left them, Jesus said, "Now is the Son of Man glorified, and God is glorified in him. If God is glorified in him, God will also glorify him in himself, and God will glorify him at once. My children, I will be with you only a little while longer. I give you a new commandment: love one another. As I have loved you, so you also should love one another. This is how all will know that you are my disciples, if you have love for one another."

The Gospel of the Lord. *Praise to you, Lord Jesus Christ.*

PROFESSION OF FAITH *(page 13)*

PRAYER OF THE FAITHFUL

PREPARATION OF GIFTS *(page 16)*

• TAKING A CLOSER LOOK •

✠ **A new heaven and a new earth** The early Christians awaited God's triumph over evil and the foundation of a new order—a new creation (heaven and earth)—free from oppression, violence, and suffering. Contrary to what is often thought about the Book of Revelation, it is not about the end of our world by divinely induced catastrophe, but rather the end of the world as we know it—dominated by evil and destructive empires. Revelation's ending describes a new world in which God dwells in our midst and evil is no longer found.

PRAYER OVER THE OFFERINGS

O God, who by the wonderful exchange effected in this sacrifice
have made us partakers of the one supreme Godhead,
grant, we pray,
that, as we have come to know your truth,
we may make it ours by a worthy way of life.
Through Christ our Lord. *Amen.*

PREFACE *(Easter 1–5, pages 24–26)*

COMMUNION ANTIPHON *(Cf. John 15:1, 5)*

I am the true vine and you are the branches, says the Lord. Whoever
remains in me, and I in him, bears fruit in plenty, alleluia.

PRAYER AFTER COMMUNION

Graciously be present to your people, we pray, O Lord,
and lead those you have imbued with heavenly mysteries
to pass from former ways to newness of life.
Through Christ our Lord. *Amen.*

SOLEMN BLESSING: EASTER TIME *(Optional, page 60)*

BLESSING & DISMISSAL *(page 56)* ❖

● RESPONDING TO THE WORD ●

Paul and Barnabas encourage their fellow workers.	The world is transformed when God comes to dwell with us.	Jesus declares that his followers will be known by their love.
➲ *Who might need my encouragement today?*	➲ *Where have I experienced God's presence recently?*	➲ *Who has shown me the self-sacrificing love of Jesus?*

May 26

A final message

Jesus is "going away," we are told in today's gospel as we near the end of the Easter season. Imagine how upset the apostles felt. Also reflect on Jesus' human desire to comfort and reassure them. As is usually the case when anyone approaches a final goodbye, Jesus wants to impart his most important message.

As I reflect on this, I remember visiting my father for a weekend shortly before he died. He slept most of the time as I read or prayed while sitting by his bed. One moment he woke up, looked right at me and said quietly, "It wasn't always easy for your mom and me to raise such a large family. I hope you understand." He quickly fell back asleep. At the time, I did understand, and now, after many more years of parenthood, I have even greater understanding. I remain grateful for this last message that conveyed what he held in his heart for me.

Jesus' final message was that the Father would send his gifts of the Holy Spirit and peace. Can we receive these gifts with gratitude? Perhaps we will also be moved to offer a special message to someone dear who needs a word of love and comfort.

■ JOE EGAN

ENTRANCE ANTIPHON *(Cf. Isaiah 48:20)*
Proclaim a joyful sound and let it be heard;
proclaim to the ends of the earth: The Lord has
freed his people, alleluia.

INTRODUCTORY RITES *(page 10)*

COLLECT
Grant, almighty God,
that we may celebrate with heartfelt devotion these days of joy,
which we keep in honor of the risen Lord,
and that what we relive in remembrance
we may always hold to in what we do.
Through our Lord Jesus Christ, your Son,
who lives and reigns with you in the unity of the Holy Spirit,
one God, for ever and ever. *Amen.*

FIRST READING *(Acts 15:1-2, 22-29)*
Some who had come down from Judea were instructing the
brothers, "Unless you are circumcised according to the
Mosaic practice, you cannot be saved." Because there arose no
little dissension and debate by Paul and Barnabas with them, it
was decided that Paul, Barnabas, and some of the others should
go up to Jerusalem to the apostles and elders about this question.

The apostles and elders, in agreement with the whole church,
decided to choose representatives and to send them to Antioch
with Paul and Barnabas. The ones chosen were Judas, who was
called Barsabbas, and Silas, leaders among the brothers. This is
the letter delivered by them:

"The apostles and the elders, your brothers, to the brothers in
Antioch, Syria, and Cilicia* of Gentile origin: greetings. Since
we have heard that some of our number who went out without

any mandate from us have upset you with their teachings and disturbed your peace of mind, we have with one accord decided to choose representatives and to send them to you along with our beloved Barnabas and Paul, who have dedicated their lives to the name of our Lord Jesus Christ. So we are sending Judas and Silas who will also convey this same message by word of mouth: 'It is the decision of the Holy Spirit and of us not to place on you any burden beyond these necessities, namely, to abstain from meat sacrificed to idols, from blood, from meats of strangled animals, and from unlawful marriage. If you keep free of these, you will be doing what is right. Farewell.' "

The word of the Lord. *Thanks be to God.*

RESPONSORIAL PSALM *(Psalm 67:2-3, 5, 6, 8)*
℟ **O God, let all the nations praise you!** *Or* **Alleluia.**

May God have pity on us and bless us;
   may he let his face shine upon us.
So may your way be known upon earth;
   among all nations, your salvation. ℟
May the nations be glad and exult
   because you rule the peoples in equity;
   the nations on the earth you guide. ℟
May the peoples praise you, O God;
   may all the peoples praise you!
May God bless us,
   and may all the ends of the earth fear him! ℟

SECOND READING *(Revelation 21:10-14, 22-23)*
The angel took me in spirit to a great, high mountain and showed me the holy city Jerusalem coming down out of

heaven from God. It gleamed with the splendor of God. Its radiance was like that of a precious stone, like jasper, clear as crystal. It had a massive, high wall, with twelve gates where twelve angels were stationed and on which names were inscribed, the names of the twelve tribes of the Israelites. There were three gates facing east, three north, three south, and three west. The wall of the city had twelve courses of stones as its foundation, on which were inscribed the twelve names of the twelve apostles of the Lamb.

I saw no temple in the city for its temple is the Lord God almighty and the Lamb. The city had no need of sun or moon to shine on it, for the glory of God gave it light, and its lamp was the Lamb.

The word of the Lord. *Thanks be to God.*

ALLELUIA *(John 14:23)*
Alleluia, alleluia. Whoever loves me will keep my word, says the Lord, and my Father will love him and we will come to him. *Alleluia, alleluia.*

GOSPEL *(John 14:23–29)*
A reading from the holy Gospel according to John.
Glory to you, O Lord.

Jesus said to his disciples: "Whoever loves me will keep my word, and my Father will love him, and we will come to him and make our dwelling with him. Whoever does not love me does not keep my words; yet the word you hear is not mine but that of the Father who sent me.

"I have told you this while I am with you. **The Advocate,**✝ the Holy Spirit, whom the Father will send in my name, will teach you everything and remind you of all that I told you. Peace I leave with you; my peace I give to you. Not as the world gives do

I give it to you. Do not let your hearts be troubled or afraid. You heard me tell you, 'I am going away and I will come back to you.' If you loved me, you would rejoice that I am going to the Father; for the Father is greater than I. And now I have told you this before it happens, so that when it happens you may believe."

The Gospel of the Lord. *Praise to you, Lord Jesus Christ.*

PROFESSION OF FAITH *(page 13)*

PRAYER OF THE FAITHFUL

PREPARATION OF GIFTS *(page 16)*

PRAYER OVER THE OFFERINGS
May our prayers rise up to you, O Lord,
together with the sacrificial offerings,
so that, purified by your graciousness,
we may be conformed to the mysteries of your mighty love.
Through Christ our Lord. *Amen.*

• TAKING A CLOSER LOOK •

✣ **The Advocate** Jesus responds with the promise of an indwelling presence to those who keep his commandments. That presence is described variously as being of both the Father and Jesus, of the Holy Spirit, or that of Jesus himself. Jesus' abiding presence with the disciples after his return to the Father is accomplished in and through the Advocate (Greek, *parakletos*, Paraclete), as John usually identifies the Holy Spirit. The idea of an "advocate," which is taken from the law courts, identifies one who, like a lawyer, comes to stand by the side of the one in need and speak in his or her defense.

PREFACE *(Easter 1–5, pages 24–26)*

COMMUNION ANTIPHON *(John 14:15–16)*
If you love me, keep my commandments, says the Lord, and I will ask the Father and he will send you another Paraclete, to abide with you for ever, alleluia.

PRAYER AFTER COMMUNION
Almighty ever-living God,
who restore us to eternal life in the Resurrection of Christ,
increase in us, we pray, the fruits of this paschal Sacrament
and pour into our hearts the strength of this saving food.
Through Christ our Lord. *Amen.*

SOLEMN BLESSING: EASTER TIME *(Optional, page 60)*

BLESSING & DISMISSAL *(page 56)* ✤

● RESPONDING TO THE WORD ●

The apostles decide to not burden believers beyond necessities.

➡ *What can I do today to follow this advice and help to lighten others' burdens?*

John envisions a city with no temple because God's presence is everywhere.

➡ *Where do I look for God's presence?*

Though he will no longer be visible, Jesus promises to be with us in Spirit.

➡ *When have I felt Jesus' presence with me recently?*

May 30

All U.S. dioceses, except those within the ecclesiastical provinces of Boston, Hartford, New York, Newark, Philadelphia, and Omaha, transfer the celebration of the Ascension of the Lord from Thursday to this coming Sunday.

If the Ascension is celebrated on Thursday in your diocese, see the Mass for the Ascension on page 385. Then on Sunday use the Mass for the Seventh Sunday of Easter, page 392.

June 2

"You are witnesses of these things"

Imagine learning about Scripture from our Lord. Imagine sitting at Jesus' feet while he discusses the prophets. Such an exercise in imagination can change our lives. We will want to witness to this experience, to state with confidence that our lives have been changed. Witnessing to a personal transformation can be a powerful means of communication.

"You are witnesses of these things," Jesus tells his disciples in today's gospel account of his ascension. The power of witness can be transformative, especially if we touch someone's life when they need encouragement in facing a challenge. Our witness could strengthen their faith; it may give them the courage to witness to their own experience of the Lord. When the actions of others support and validate our own experience, it becomes easier to believe. An upward spiral in faith occurs; each person's witnessing builds upon and strengthens the faith of others. When many see the same thing, it can help us overcome the tendency to doubt.

Today, reflect on the power of both being a witness and experiencing the witness of others. With praise and thanksgiving, be grateful for the witness provided by those around you. Imagine the power of communicating the risen Lord to others in your life.

■ JOHN O'BRIEN

(MASS DURING THE DAY)

ENTRANCE ANTIPHON *(Acts 1:11)*

Men of Galilee, why gaze in wonder at the heavens? This Jesus whom you saw ascending into heaven will return as you saw him go, alleluia.

INTRODUCTORY RITES *(page 10)*

COLLECT

Gladden us with holy joys, almighty God,
and make us rejoice with devout thanksgiving,
for the Ascension of Christ your Son
is our exaltation,
and, where the Head has gone before in glory,
the Body is called to follow in hope.
Through our Lord Jesus Christ, your Son,
who lives and reigns with you in the unity of the Holy Spirit,
one God, for ever and ever. *Amen.*

Or

Grant, we pray, almighty God,
that we, who believe that your Only Begotten Son,
    our Redeemer,
ascended this day to the heavens,
may in spirit dwell already in heavenly realms.
Who lives and reigns with you in the unity of the Holy Spirit,
one God, for ever and ever. *Amen.*

FIRST READING *(Acts 1:1–11)*

In the first book, Theophilus, I dealt with all that Jesus did and taught until the day he was taken up, after giving instructions through the Holy Spirit to the apostles whom he had chosen. He presented himself alive to them by many proofs after he had suffered, appearing to them during forty days and speaking about the kingdom of God. While meeting with them, he enjoined them not to depart from Jerusalem, but to wait for "the promise of the Father about which you have heard me speak; for John baptized with water, but in a few days you will be **baptized with the Holy Spirit**."✝

When they had gathered together they asked him, "Lord, are you at this time going to restore the kingdom to Israel?" He answered them, "It is not for you to know the times or seasons that the Father has established by his own authority. But you will receive power when the Holy Spirit comes upon you, and you will be my witnesses in Jerusalem, throughout Judea and Samaria,* and to the ends of the earth." When he had said this, as they were looking on, he was lifted up, and a cloud took him from their sight. While they were looking intently at the sky as he was going, suddenly two men dressed in white garments stood beside them. They said, "Men of Galilee, why are you standing there looking at the sky? This Jesus who has been taken up from you into heaven will return in the same way you have seen him going into heaven."

The word of the Lord. *Thanks be to God.*

RESPONSORIAL PSALM *(Psalm 47:2–3, 6–7, 8–9)*

℟ **God mounts his throne to shouts of joy: a blare of trumpets for the Lord.** *Or* **Alleluia.**

All you peoples, clap your hands,
    shout to God with cries of gladness,

for the LORD, the Most High, the awesome,
  is the great king over all the earth.

℟ **God mounts his throne to shouts of joy: a blare of trumpets
  for the Lord.** *Or* **Alleluia.**

God mounts his throne amid shouts of joy;
  the LORD, amid trumpet blasts.

Sing praise to God, sing praise;
  sing praise to our king, sing praise. ℟

For king of all the earth is God;
  sing hymns of praise.

God reigns over the nations,
  God sits upon his holy throne. ℟

An alternate reading follows.

SECOND READING *(Ephesians 1:17-23)*

Brothers and sisters: May the God of our Lord Jesus Christ, the Father of glory, give you a Spirit of wisdom and revelation resulting in knowledge of him. May the eyes of your hearts be enlightened, that you may know what is the hope that belongs to his call, what are the riches of glory in his inheritance among the holy ones, and what is the surpassing greatness of his power for us who believe, in accord with the exercise of his great might: which he worked in Christ, raising him from the dead and seating him at his right hand in the heavens, far above every principality, authority, power, and dominion, and every name that is named not only in this age but also in the one to come. And he put all things beneath his feet and gave him as head over all things to the church, which is his body, the fullness of the one who fills all things in every way.

The word of the Lord. *Thanks be to God.*

OR

SECOND READING *(Hebrews 9:24-28; 10:19-23)*

Christ did not enter into a sanctuary made by hands, a copy of the true one, but heaven itself, that he might now appear before God on our behalf. Not that he might offer himself repeatedly, as the high priest enters each year into the sanctuary with blood that is not his own; if that were so, he would have had to suffer repeatedly from the foundation of the world. But now once for all he has appeared at the end of the ages to take away sin by his sacrifice. Just as it is appointed that men and women die once, and after this the judgment, so also Christ, offered once to take away the sins of many, will appear a second time, not to take away sin but to bring salvation to those who eagerly await him.

Therefore, brothers and sisters, since through the blood of Jesus we have confidence of entrance into the sanctuary by the new and living way he opened for us through the veil, that is, his flesh, and since we have "a great priest over the house of God," let us approach with a sincere heart and in absolute trust, with our hearts sprinkled clean from an evil conscience and our bodies washed in pure water. Let us hold unwaveringly to our confession that gives us hope, for he who made the promise is trustworthy.

The word of the Lord. *Thanks be to God.*

ALLELUIA *(Matthew 28:19a, 20b)*
Alleluia, alleluia. Go and teach all nations, says the Lord; I am with you always, until the end of the world. *Alleluia, alleluia.*

GOSPEL *(Luke 24:46-53)*
A reading from the holy Gospel according to Luke.
Glory to you, O Lord.

J esus said to his disciples: "Thus it is written that the Christ would suffer and rise from the dead on the third day and that repentance, for the forgiveness of sins, would be preached in his name to all the nations, beginning from Jerusalem. You are witnesses of these things. And behold I am sending the promise of my Father upon you; but stay in the city until you are clothed with power from on high."

Then he led them out as far as Bethany,* raised his hands, and blessed them. As he blessed them he parted from them and was taken up to heaven. They did him homage and then returned to Jerusalem with great joy, and they were continually in the temple praising God.

The Gospel of the Lord. *Praise to you, Lord Jesus Christ.*

PROFESSION OF FAITH *(page 10)*

PRAYER OF THE FAITHFUL

PREPARATION OF GIFTS *(page 13)*

PRAYER OVER THE OFFERINGS
We offer sacrifice now in supplication, O Lord,

• TAKING A CLOSER LOOK •

✝ **Baptized with the Holy Spirit** For early Christians, there were two great signs of God's saving activity that would bring new life: the resurrection of Jesus and the outpouring of the Holy Spirit. Jesus compares this outpouring of God's Spirit (the power of life associated with breathing) to a baptismal washing that purifies the person and signifies one's desire to change and be more united with God's saving activity. Once empowered by the indwelling of the Spirit, the disciples will be able to carry on the mission and ministry of Jesus in our world.

to honor the wondrous Ascension of your Son:
grant, we pray,
that through this most holy exchange
we, too, may rise up to the heavenly realms.
Through Christ our Lord. *Amen.*

PREFACE *(Ascension of the Lord 1–2, page 27)*

COMMUNION ANTIPHON *(Matthew 28:20)*
Behold, I am with you always, even to the end of the age, alleluia.

PRAYER AFTER COMMUNION
Almighty ever-living God,
who allow those on earth to celebrate divine mysteries,
grant, we pray,
that Christian hope may draw us onward
to where our nature is united with you.
Through Christ our Lord. *Amen.*

SOLEMN BLESSING: THE ASCENSION OF THE LORD *(Optional, page 61)*

BLESSING & DISMISSAL *(page 56)* ⁑

● RESPONDING TO THE WORD ●

Though Jesus departs, he promises empowerment by the Holy Spirit.

⇨ *When have I felt most empowered by the Holy Spirit?*

Our minds are enlightened and our hearts are renewed with hope.

⇨ *What new hopes have I felt during this Easter season?*

Jesus wants us to be witnesses of the new way he has opened for life in God's presence.

⇨ *How can I share my experience of the risen Christ with someone?*

SEVENTH SUNDAY OF EASTER

ENTRANCE ANTIPHON *(Cf. Psalm 27 [26]:7-9)*

O Lord, hear my voice, for I have called to you; of you my heart has spoken: Seek his face; hide not your face from me, alleluia.

INTRODUCTORY RITES *(page 10)*

COLLECT

Graciously hear our supplications, O Lord,
so that we, who believe that the Savior of the human race
is with you in your glory,
may experience, as he promised,
until the end of the world,
his abiding presence among us.
Who lives and reigns with you in the unity of the Holy Spirit,
one God, for ever and ever. *Amen.*

FIRST READING *(Acts 7:55-60)*

Stephen, filled with the Holy Spirit, looked up intently to heaven and saw the glory of God and Jesus standing at the right hand of God, and Stephen said, "Behold, I see the heavens opened and the Son of Man standing at the right hand of God." But they cried out in a loud voice, covered their ears, and rushed upon him together. They threw him out of the city, and began to stone him. The witnesses laid down their cloaks at the feet of a young man named Saul. As they were stoning Stephen, he called out, "Lord Jesus, receive my spirit." Then he fell to his knees and cried out in a loud voice, "Lord, do not hold this sin against them"; and when he said this, he fell asleep.

The word of the Lord. *Thanks be to God.*

RESPONSORIAL PSALM *(Psalm 97:1-2, 6-7, 9)*

R̷ **The Lord is king, the most high over all the earth.**
   Or **Alleluia.**

The LORD is king; let the earth rejoice;
   let the many islands be glad.
Justice and judgment are the foundation of his throne. R̷
The heavens proclaim his justice,
   and all peoples see his glory.
All gods are prostrate before him. R̷
You, O LORD, are the Most High over all the earth,
   exalted far above all gods. R̷

SECOND READING *(Revelation 22:12-14, 16-17, 20)*

I, John, heard a voice saying to me: "Behold, I am coming
   soon. I bring with me the recompense I will give to each
according to his deeds. I am the Alpha and the Omega, the first
and the last, the beginning and the end."

   Blessed are they who wash their robes so as to have the right
to the tree of life and enter the city through its gates.

   "I, Jesus, sent my angel to give you this testimony for the
churches. I am the root and offspring of David, the bright morning star."

   The Spirit and the bride say, "Come." Let the hearer say,
"Come." Let the one who thirsts come forward, and the one who
wants it receive the gift of life-giving water.

   The one who gives this testimony says, "Yes, I am coming
soon." Amen! Come, Lord Jesus!

The word of the Lord. *Thanks be to God.*

ALLELUIA *(See John 14:18)*

Alleluia, alleluia. I will not leave you orphans, says the Lord.
I will come back to you, and your hearts will rejoice. *Alleluia,*
alleluia.

GOSPEL *(John 17:20–26)*

A reading from the holy Gospel according to John.
Glory to you, O Lord.

Lifting up his eyes to heaven, Jesus prayed, saying: "Holy
Father, I pray not only for them, but also for those who will
believe in me through their word, so that they may all be one,
as you, Father, are in me and I in you, that they also may be in
us, that **the world** ✠ may believe that you sent me. And I have
given them the glory you gave me, so that they may be one, as
we are one, I in them and you in me, that they may be brought
to perfection as one, that the world may know that you sent me,
and that you loved them even as you loved me. Father, they are
your gift to me. I wish that where I am they also may be with me,
that they may see my glory that you gave me, because you loved
me before the foundation of the world. Righteous Father, the
world also does not know you, but I know you, and they know
that you sent me. I made known to them your name and I will
make it known, that the love with which you loved me may be in
them and I in them."

The Gospel of the Lord. *Praise to you, Lord Jesus Christ.*

PROFESSION OF FAITH *(page 13)*

PRAYER OF THE FAITHFUL

PREPARATION OF GIFTS *(page 16)*

PRAYER OVER THE OFFERINGS
Accept, O Lord, the prayers of your faithful
with the sacrificial offerings,
that through these acts of devotedness
we may pass over to the glory of heaven.
Through Christ our Lord. *Amen.*

PREFACE *(Easter 1–5, pages 24–26, or Ascension 1–2, page 27)*

COMMUNION ANTIPHON *(John 17:22)*
Father, I pray that they may be one as we also are one, alleluia.

• Taking a Closer Look •

✛ **The world** Many terms in John's gospel and letters have two levels of meaning. Usually "the world" (Greek, *cosmos*) would describe the ordered quality of God's creation. But John also uses "the world" to refer to the forces that resist God's reordering of creation and community. Though the world is hostile to God, God is not hostile to the world but sends Jesus "into the world" for its salvation. Another way of describing those saved is found in today's Collect—"the human race" (Greek, *genos*; Latin, *genus*)— meaning all human beings as the descendants of a common ancestor, loosely interpreted as a single entity—in this case, all of humanity understood as descended from Adam and Eve.

PRAYER AFTER COMMUNION

Hear us, O God our Savior,
and grant us confidence,
that through these sacred mysteries
there will be accomplished in the body of the whole Church
what has already come to pass in Christ her Head.
Who lives and reigns for ever and ever. *Amen.*

SOLEMN BLESSING: EASTER TIME *(Optional, page 60)*
OR THE ASCENSION *(Optional, page 61)*

BLESSING & DISMISSAL *(page 56)* ✦

✦ RESPONDING TO THE WORD ✦

Like Jesus, Stephen prays for his persecutors.

➡ *For which of my persecutors ought I to pray today?*

Jesus invites the one who thirsts to come to him.

➡ *For what spiritual good am I thirsting today?*

Jesus desires that all may be one in him.

➡ *What barrier to unity might I need to break down so that others can more easily come to Christ?*

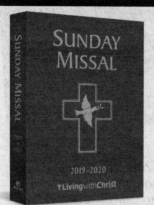
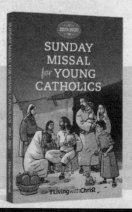

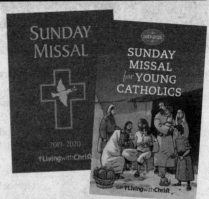

Witnesses of the good news

As the gospels show, every time the disciples experience the risen and ascended Christ, they are told to share this with others. Being a Christian can never be just a "me and Jesus" experience. We must continue the ministry and mission of Jesus in our world. Pentecost reminds us of this task and invites us to take the Easter message of Christ's resurrection and spread this good news to our world.

The remainder of the Church's year is called "ordinary time." This does not mean that this time is not important, but rather that it is "ordered" by our ever-deepening appreciation of how the mystery of our faith must be lived in our everyday lives.

During this time, Sunday by Sunday, we listen and respond to the Scripture readings and thus deepen our awareness of Jesus' life and teaching. As we better understand who he was, we also better understand who we are as his followers today.

Jesus' message was a new way to relate to God and to others, and this is what we share with our family, our friends, our fellow-parishioners, and all those with whom we work and play. As individuals and communities, we begin to live right now as the kingdom community that Christ envisioned. We must dare to create communities based on justice and right relationships with one another, built on love and respect for each person as a beloved child of God, communities of harmony and peace.

Praying and living Pentecost all year

Find a time to pray quietly or gather the household. (You may wish to do this several times between Pentecost and the end of the liturgical year.) Pray this prayer to the Holy Spirit:

Come, Holy Spirit, fill the hearts of your faithful
and enkindle in them the fire of your love.
Send forth your Spirit and they shall be created,
and you shall renew the face of the earth.

The Holy Spirit has given each of us personal gifts to use for building the Christian community. Consider the following questions (if you are with others, reflect and share together):
- What are the Holy Spirit's gifts to me?
- What situation or event illustrates how each gift helps others?
- In what other ways might I use my gifts?

If you are with others, invite each person to proceed around the circle, laying a hand on each person's head, while saying:

May you use your gifts in the service of God and others.

When all have had a chance to bless and be blessed, pray:

O God, help us to use your gifts
to make the world a better place—
more filled with your presence,
more in keeping with your desires,
and more aligned with your will.
Send your Holy Spirit upon us now
so that we can recognize the gifts you have given,
more eagerly make them our own,
and more willingly share them with others.
Amen.

June 9

JUN 9

A universal language

Locked doors and locked hearts do not deter the risen Lord. Literally and figuratively, the apostles were locked behind closed doors. They were locked in the upper room, fearful of the authorities. They were also locked inside their own fear, anger, guilt, and grief. And Jesus broke through it all.

He appeared suddenly in their midst and shared with them the first gifts of the resurrection: forgiveness and peace. He commissioned them to share those gifts with others. He sent them out, as the Father had sent him.

The peace of the risen Lord, and all the gifts of his Spirit, would unlock the door of the upper room—and also unlock the disciples' hearts and lives.

We see this in Acts, where the peace and joy they have received are communicated to others: Jews and non-Jews, strangers from many countries, people of many languages. The gifts the apostles received were sharable—more than that, contagious—and they were available for everyone. Not just a select few. *Everyone.*

The apostles spoke a universal language on Pentecost: the language of love, peace, forgiveness, and hope—the story of God's mighty deeds, the call to discipleship, to a life of love and self-giving. This call could be heard and understood by everyone: a call into relationship with Christ and with one another.

■ **Dinah Simmons**

MASS DURING THE DAY

ENTRANCE ANTIPHON *(Wisdom 1:7)*
The Spirit of the Lord has filled the whole world and that which contains all things understands what is said, alleluia.

Or *(Romans 5:5; cf. 8:11)*
The love of God has been poured into our hearts through the Spirit of God dwelling within us, alleluia.

INTRODUCTORY RITES *(page 10)*

COLLECT
O God, who by the mystery of today's great feast
sanctify your whole Church in every people and nation,
pour out, we pray, the gifts of the Holy Spirit
across the face of the earth
and, with the divine grace that was at work
when the Gospel was first proclaimed,
fill now once more the hearts of believers.
Through our Lord Jesus Christ, your Son,
who lives and reigns with you in the unity of the Holy Spirit,
one God, for ever and ever. *Amen.*

FIRST READING *(Acts 2:1-11)*
When the time for **Pentecost**✝ was fulfilled, they were all in one place together. And suddenly there came from the sky a noise like a strong driving wind, and it filled the entire house in which they were. Then there appeared to them tongues as of fire, which parted and came to rest on each one of them. And they were all filled with the Holy Spirit and began to speak in different tongues, as the Spirit enabled them to proclaim.

Now there were devout Jews from every nation under heaven staying in Jerusalem. At this sound, they gathered in a large crowd, but they were confused because each one heard them speaking in his own language. They were astounded, and in amazement they asked, "Are not all these people who are speaking Galileans? Then how does each of us hear them in his native language? We are Parthians,* Medes,* and Elamites,* inhabitants of Mesopotamia,* Judea and Cappadocia,* Pontus and Asia, Phrygia* and Pamphylia,* Egypt and the districts of Libya near Cyrene, as well as travelers from Rome, both Jews and converts to Judaism, Cretans and Arabs, yet we hear them speaking in our own tongues of the mighty acts of God."

The word of the Lord. *Thanks be to God.*

RESPONSORIAL PSALM *(Psalm 104:1, 24, 29–30, 31, 34)*
R̶ **Lord, send out your Spirit, and renew the face of the earth.**
    Or **Alleluia.**

Bless the LORD, O my soul!
    O LORD, my God, you are great indeed!
How manifold are your works, O LORD!
    The earth is full of your creatures. R̶
If you take away their breath, they perish
    and return to their dust.
When you send forth your spirit, they are created,
    and you renew the face of the earth. R̶
May the glory of the Lord endure forever;
    may the LORD be glad in his works!
Pleasing to him be my theme;
    I will be glad in the LORD. R̶

An alternate reading follows.

SECOND READING *(1 Corinthians 12:3b-7, 12-13)*

Brothers and sisters: No one can say, "Jesus is Lord," except by the Holy Spirit.

There are different kinds of spiritual gifts but the same Spirit; there are different forms of service but the same Lord; there are different workings but the same God who produces all of them in everyone. To each individual the manifestation of the Spirit is given for some benefit.

As a body is one though it has many parts, and all the parts of the body, though many, are one body, so also Christ. For in one Spirit we were all baptized into one body, whether Jews or Greeks, slaves or free persons, and we were all given to drink of one Spirit.

The word of the Lord. ***Thanks be to God.***

OR

SECOND READING *(Romans 8:8-17)*

Brothers and sisters: Those who are in the flesh cannot please God. But you are not in the flesh; on the contrary, you are in the spirit, if only the Spirit of God dwells in you. Whoever does not have the Spirit of Christ does not belong to him. But if Christ is in you, although the body is dead because of sin, the spirit is alive because of righteousness. If the Spirit of the one who raised Jesus from the dead dwells in you, the one who raised Christ from the dead will give life to your mortal bodies also, through his Spirit that dwells in you. Consequently, brothers and sisters, we are not debtors to the flesh, to live according to the flesh. For if you live according to the flesh, you will die, but if by the Spirit you put to death the deeds of the body, you will live.

For those who are led by the Spirit of God are sons of God. For you did not receive a spirit of slavery to fall back into fear, but you received a Spirit of adoption, through whom we cry, "Abba, Father!" The Spirit himself bears witness with our spirit that we are children of God, and if children, then heirs, heirs of God and joint heirs with Christ, if only we suffer with him so that we may also be glorified with him.

The word of the Lord. ***Thanks be to God.***

SEQUENCE *(Veni, Sancte Spiritus)*
Come, Holy Spirit, come!
And from your celestial home
   Shed a ray of light divine!
Come, Father of the poor!
Come, source of all our store!
   Come, within our bosoms shine.
You, of comforters the best;
You, the soul's most welcome guest;
   Sweet refreshment here below.
In our labor, rest most sweet;
Grateful coolness in the heat;
   Solace in the midst of woe.
O most blessed Light divine,
Shine within these hearts of yours,
   And our inmost being fill!
Where you are not, we have naught,
Nothing good in deed or thought,
   Nothing free from taint of ill.
Heal our wounds, our strength renew;
On our dryness pour your dew;
   Wash the stains of guilt away.

Bend the stubborn heart and will;
Melt the frozen, warm the chill;
  Guide the steps that go astray.
On the faithful, who adore
And confess you, evermore
  In your sevenfold gift descend.
Give them virtue's sure reward;
Give them your salvation, Lord;
  Give them joys that never end. Amen.
  Alleluia.

ALLELUIA
Alleluia, alleluia. Come, Holy Spirit, fill the hearts of your faithful and kindle in them the fire of your love. *Alleluia, alleluia.*

An alternate reading follows.

GOSPEL *(John 20:19–23)*
A reading from the holy Gospel according to John.
Glory to you, O Lord.

On the evening of that first day of the week, when the doors were locked, where the disciples were, for fear of the Jews, Jesus came and stood in their midst and said to them, "Peace be with you." When he had said this, he showed them his hands and his side. The disciples rejoiced when they saw the Lord. Jesus said to them again, "Peace be with you. As the Father has sent me, so I send you." And when he had said this, he breathed on them and said to them, "Receive the Holy Spirit. Whose sins you forgive are forgiven them, and whose sins you retain are retained."

The Gospel of the Lord. *Praise to you, Lord Jesus Christ.*

OR

GOSPEL *(John 14:15–16, 23b–26)*
A reading from the holy Gospel according to John.
Glory to you, O Lord.

Jesus said to his disciples: "If you love me, you will keep my commandments. And I will ask the Father, and he will give you another Advocate to be with you always.

"Whoever loves me will keep my word, and my Father will love him, and we will come to him and make our dwelling with him. Those who do not love me do not keep my words; yet the word you hear is not mine but that of the Father who sent me.

"I have told you this while I am with you. The Advocate, the Holy Spirit whom the Father will send in my name, will teach you everything and remind you of all that I told you."

The Gospel of the Lord. *Praise to you, Lord Jesus Christ.*

PROFESSION OF FAITH *(page 13)*

PRAYER OF THE FAITHFUL

PREPARATION OF GIFTS *(page 16)*

PRAYER OVER THE OFFERINGS
Grant, we pray, O Lord,
that, as promised by your Son,
the Holy Spirit may reveal to us more abundantly
the hidden mystery of this sacrifice
and graciously lead us into all truth.
Through Christ our Lord. *Amen.*

PREFACE: THE MYSTERY OF PENTECOST

It is truly right and just, our duty and our salvation,
always and everywhere to give you thanks,
Lord, holy Father, almighty and eternal God.

For, bringing your Paschal Mystery to completion,
you bestowed the Holy Spirit today
on those you made your adopted children
by uniting them to your Only Begotten Son.
This same Spirit, as the Church came to birth,
opened to all peoples the knowledge of God
and brought together the many languages of the earth
in profession of the one faith.

Therefore, overcome with paschal joy,
every land, every people exults in your praise
and even the heavenly Powers, with the angelic hosts,
sing together the unending hymn of your glory,
as they acclaim:
Holy, Holy, Holy Lord God of hosts... *(page 35)*

• TAKING A CLOSER LOOK •

✛ **Pentecost** Pentecost (Greek, the "fiftieth day") was the Jewish feast (also called "Weeks" or *Shavuot*) that came fifty days after Passover. It celebrated the spring grain harvest and the offering to God of the firstfruits of the crop (Exodus 23:14-17). One of the three major Jewish feast days, over the centuries the feast became associated with the giving of the Law (or *Torah*) and focused more on covenant renewal. In the New Testament, this feast day echoes the Jewish themes with the descent of the Holy Spirit to form the Christian community and to harvest the firstfruits of its universal mission.

COMMUNION ANTIPHON *(Acts 2:4, 11)*

They were all filled with the Holy Spirit and spoke of the marvels of God, alleluia.

PRAYER AFTER COMMUNION

O God, who bestow heavenly gifts upon your Church,
safeguard, we pray, the grace you have given,
that the gift of the Holy Spirit poured out upon her
may retain all its force
and that this spiritual food
may gain her abundance of eternal redemption.
Through Christ our Lord. *Amen.*

SOLEMN BLESSING: THE HOLY SPIRIT *(Optional, page 62)*

BLESSING & DISMISSAL *(page 56)* ✤

• RESPONDING TO THE WORD •

The Holy Spirit helps us to communicate with others about the gift that Jesus is for us.

➦ *With whom would I like to speak about Christ today?*

We have all been gifted by the Holy Spirit.

➦ *What spiritual gifts have I been given, and how am I using them?*

Peace and the Holy Spirit are gifts of the risen Christ.

➦ *What spiritual peace have I experienced recently?*

June 16

Three in One

The Trinity is a foundational Christian doctrine. It is also difficult to understand. For some it is a math puzzle: how can there be three within one? On the other hand, although most people can correctly state that there are three persons in one God, when they explain what that means, it sometimes sounds like three gods.

We might have an easier time saying what the Trinity is *not* than what it is. It can be easier to recognize a challenge to the belief in one God or the belief that there are three within that one God.

The Bible may not state that there are three persons in one God, but the three persons of the Trinity are frequently found together. Today's gospel, an excerpt from Jesus' Last Supper discourse, is one such place. The Spirit will come to communicate Jesus' message, not a new one. And since what Jesus has, the Father also has, the Spirit will continue the revelation of the one God.

When we worship together, we celebrate things rather than define them. Thus, we affirm our belief in the Trinity each Sunday in the Creed, as well as when we invoke the Father, Son, and Holy Spirit throughout the liturgy.

■ JOHN L. MCLAUGHLIN

ENTRANCE ANTIPHON

Blest be God the Father, and the Only Begotten Son
of God, and also the Holy Spirit, for he has shown us
his merciful love.

INTRODUCTORY RITES *(page 10)*

COLLECT

God our Father, who by sending into the world
the Word of truth and the Spirit of sanctification
made known to the human race your wondrous mystery,
grant us, we pray, that in professing the true faith,
we may acknowledge the Trinity of eternal glory
and adore your Unity, powerful in majesty.
Through our Lord Jesus Christ, your Son,
who lives and reigns with you in the unity of the Holy Spirit,
one God, for ever and ever. *Amen.*

FIRST READING *(Proverbs 8:22-31)*

Thus says the wisdom of God:
    "The LORD possessed me, the beginning of his ways,
        the forerunner of his prodigies of long ago;
from of old I was poured forth,
    at the first, before the earth.
When there were no depths I was brought forth,
    when there were no fountains or springs of water;
before the mountains were settled into place,
    before the hills, I was brought forth;
while as yet the earth and fields were not made,
    nor the first clods of the world.

"When the Lord established the heavens I was there,

when he marked out the **vault**✝ over the face of the deep;
when he made firm the skies above,
    when he fixed fast the foundations of the earth;
when he set for the sea its limit,
    so that the waters should not transgress his command;
then was I beside him as his craftsman,
    and I was his delight day by day,
playing before him all the while,
    playing on the surface of his earth;
    and I found delight in the human race."

The word of the Lord. *Thanks be to God.*

RESPONSORIAL PSALM *(Psalm 8:4-5, 6-7, 8-9)*
℟ **O Lord, our God, how wonderful your name in all the earth!**

When I behold your heavens, the work of your fingers,
    the moon and the stars which you set in place—
What is man that you should be mindful of him,
    or the son of man that you should care for him? ℟
You have made him little less than the angels,
    and crowned him with glory and honor.
You have given him rule over the works of your hands,
    putting all things under his feet: ℟
All sheep and oxen,
    yes, and the beasts of the field,
The birds of the air, the fishes of the sea,
    and whatever swims the paths of the seas. ℟

SECOND READING *(Romans 5:1-5)*

Brothers and sisters: Therefore, since we have been justified
by faith, we have peace with God through our Lord Jesus

Christ, through whom we have gained access by faith to this grace in which we stand, and we boast in hope of the glory of God. Not only that, but we even boast of our afflictions, knowing that affliction produces endurance, and endurance, proven character, and proven character, hope, and hope does not disappoint, because the love of God has been poured out into our hearts through the Holy Spirit that has been given to us.

The word of the Lord. *Thanks be to God.*

ALLELUIA *(See Revelation 1:8)*
Alleluia, alleluia. Glory to the Father, the Son, and the Holy Spirit; to God who is, who was, and who is to come. *Alleluia, alleluia.*

GOSPEL *(John 16:12-15)*
A reading from the holy Gospel according to John.
Glory to you, O Lord.
Jesus said to his disciples: "I have much more to tell you, but you cannot bear it now. But when he comes, the Spirit of truth, he will guide you to all truth. He will not speak on his own, but he will speak what he hears, and will declare to you the things that are coming. He will glorify me, because he will take from what is mine and declare it to you. Everything that the Father has is mine; for this reason I told you that he will take from what is mine and declare it to you."

The Gospel of the Lord. *Praise to you, Lord Jesus Christ.*

PROFESSION OF FAITH *(page 13)*

PRAYER OF THE FAITHFUL

PREPARATION OF GIFTS *(page 16)*

PRAYER OVER THE OFFERINGS

Sanctify by the invocation of your name,
we pray, O Lord our God,
this oblation of our service,
and by it make of us an eternal offering to you.
Through Christ our Lord. *Amen.*

PREFACE: THE MYSTERY OF THE MOST HOLY TRINITY

It is truly right and just, our duty and our salvation,
always and everywhere to give you thanks,
Lord, holy Father, almighty and eternal God.

For with your Only Begotten Son and the Holy Spirit
you are one God, one Lord:
not in the unity of a single person,
but in a Trinity of one substance.

For what you have revealed to us of your glory
we believe equally of your Son
and of the Holy Spirit,

• TAKING A CLOSER LOOK •

✝ **Vault (of the heavens)** In the ancient world, the heavens were imagined as a great vault or dome (the sky) that covered the earth, dividing the heavenly waters above it from those below (Genesis 1:6-7). God divided these waters by creating this vault and thus allowing the earth to have dry land. A kind of thinly beaten metallic plate or bowl (the "firmament") kept the waters above the heavens from inundating the earth except through doors that, when opened (Genesis 7:11), allowed the wind, rain, snow, and hail stored in heaven (Job 37:9, 38:22, 37) to descend to earth.

so that, in the confessing of the true and eternal Godhead,
you might be adored in what is proper to each Person,
their unity in substance,
and their equality in majesty.

For this is praised by Angels and Archangels,
Cherubim, too, and Seraphim,
who never cease to cry out each day,
as with one voice they acclaim:
Holy, holy, holy, Lord God of hosts... (page 35)

COMMUNION ANTIPHON *(Galatians 4:6)*
Since you are children of God, God has sent into your hearts the
Spirit of his Son, the Spirit who cries out: Abba, Father.

PRAYER AFTER COMMUNION
May receiving this Sacrament, O Lord our God,
bring us health of body and soul,
as we confess your eternal holy Trinity and undivided Unity.
Through Christ our Lord. *Amen.*

BLESSING & DISMISSAL *(page 56)* ✳

● RESPONDING TO THE WORD ●

Wisdom infused
God's creative work.

🡒 *Which wonders of
creation inspire me to
marvel and praise God
the Creator?*

Paul even boasts of
his afflictions because
they build character
and reveal God's love.

🡒 *What hardships
have revealed God's
love for me?*

The Holy Spirit will
guide us to all truth.

🡒 *With what dif-
ficulties do I most need
the Spirit's guidance
today?*

June 23

What is Jesus asking of us?

The disciples knew the immense gathering was growing hungry. "Dismiss the crowd," they urged Jesus, hoping the people would find food elsewhere. But Jesus said, "Give them some food yourselves." Think about that. Jesus could have turned the stones into bread; he could have made it rain manna. Instead, he made it the disciples' responsibility to meet the crowd's need.

How did they respond? Faithfulness. Logic may have said the task was impossible, but they stepped out in faith—because Jesus asked. They gave it their all, and even though their all wasn't nearly enough, they still brought it in faith—because Jesus asked.

What "impossible task" might Jesus ask of us this week? To whom is he asking us to give? How will we respond?

If we focus on our few loaves and fish, we see only what is lacking. We feel unprepared, ill-equipped, and eventually we talk ourselves out of acting. It isn't enough anyway. What difference would I make?

But if we focus on Jesus, and give him our all, we become part of the difference he will make. In today's celebration, bring Jesus your fish and loaves. Give him your all, and trust that in him all are fed, that all are filled.

◾ CAROLINE PIGNAT

ENTRANCE ANTIPHON *(Cf. Psalm 81 [80]:17)*
He fed them with the finest wheat and satisfied
them with honey from the rock.

INTRODUCTORY RITES *(page 10)*

COLLECT
O God, who in this wonderful Sacrament
have left us a memorial of your Passion,
grant us, we pray,
so to revere the sacred mysteries of your Body and Blood
that we may always experience in ourselves
the fruits of your redemption.
Who live and reign with God the Father
in the unity of the Holy Spirit,
one God, for ever and ever. *Amen.*

FIRST READING *(Genesis 14:18-20)*
In those days, Melchizedek, king of Salem, brought out bread
and wine, and being a priest of God Most High, he blessed
Abram with these words:
   "Blessed be Abram by God Most High,
      the creator of heaven and earth;
   and blessed be God Most High,
      who delivered your foes into your hand."
Then Abram gave him a tenth of everything.

The word of the Lord. *Thanks be to God.*

RESPONSORIAL PSALM *(Psalm 110:1, 2, 3, 4)*

℟ **You are a priest forever, in the line of Melchizedek.**

The LORD said to my Lord: "Sit at my right hand
    till I make your enemies your footstool." ℟
The scepter of your power the LORD will stretch forth from Zion:*
    "Rule in the midst of your enemies." ℟
"Yours is princely power in the day of your birth, in holy splendor;
    before the daystar, like the dew, I have begotten you." ℟
The LORD has sworn, and he will not repent:
    "You are a priest forever, according to the order
      of Melchizedek." ℟

SECOND READING *(1 Corinthians 11:23–26)*

Brothers and sisters: I received from the Lord what I also handed on to you, that the Lord Jesus, on the night he was handed over, took bread, and, after he had given thanks, broke it and said, "This is my body that is for you. Do this in remembrance of me." In the same way also the cup, after supper, saying, "This cup is the new **covenant in my blood**.✝ Do this, as often as you drink it, in remembrance of me." For as often as you eat this bread and drink the cup, you proclaim the death of the Lord until he comes.

The word of the Lord. *Thanks be to God.*

SEQUENCE

The shorter version begins at the asterisks.

Laud, O Zion,* your salvation,
Laud with hymns of exultation,
   Christ, your king and shepherd true:

Bring him all the praise you know,
He is more than you bestow.
   Never can you reach his due.

Special theme for glad thanksgiving
Is the quick'ning and the living
   Bread today before you set:

From his hands of old partaken,
As we know, by faith unshaken,
   Where the Twelve at supper met.

Full and clear ring out your chanting,
Joy nor sweetest grace be wanting,
   From your heart let praises burst:

For today the feast is holden,
When the institution olden
   Of that supper was rehearsed.

Here the new law's new oblation,
By the new king's revelation,
   Ends the form of ancient rite:

Now the new the old effaces,
Truth away the shadow chases,
   Light dispels the gloom of night.

What he did at supper seated,
Christ ordained to be repeated,
  His memorial ne'er to cease:

And his rule for guidance taking,
Bread and wine we hallow, making
  Thus our sacrifice of peace.

This the truth each Christian learns,
Bread into his flesh he turns,
  To his precious blood the wine:

Sight has fail'd, nor thought conceives,
But a dauntless faith believes,
  Resting on a pow'r divine.

Here beneath these signs are hidden
Priceless things·to sense forbidden;
  Sign, not things are all we see:

Blood is poured and flesh is broken,
Yet in either wondrous token
  Christ entire we know to be.

Whoso of this food partakes,
Does not rend the Lord nor breaks;
  Christ is whole to all that tastes:

Thousands are, as one, receivers,
One, as thousands of believers,
  Eats of him who cannot waste.

Bad and good the feast are sharing,
Of what divers dooms preparing,
    Endless death, or endless life.

Life to these, to those damnation,
See how like participation
    Is with unlike issues rife.

When the sacrament is broken,
Doubt not, but believe 'tis spoken,
    That each sever'd outward token
        doth the very whole contain.

Nought the precious gift divides,
Breaking but the sign betides
    Jesus still the same abides,
        still unbroken does remain.

* * *

The shorter form of the sequence begins here.

Lo! the angel's food is given
To the pilgrim who has striven;
    See the children's bread from heaven,
        which on dogs may not be spent.

Truth the ancient types fulfilling,
Isaac bound, a victim willing,
    Paschal lamb, its lifeblood spilling,
        manna to the fathers sent.

Very bread, good shepherd, tend us,
Jesu, of your love befriend us,
    You refresh us, you defend us,
    Your eternal goodness send us
In the land of life to see.

You who all things can and know,
Who on earth such food bestow,
    Grant us with your saints, though lowest,
    Where the heav'nly feast you show,
Fellow heirs and guests to be. Amen. Alleluia.

ALLELUIA *(John 6:51)*
Alleluia, alleluia. I am the living bread that came down from heaven, says the Lord; whoever eats this bread will live forever. *Alleluia, alleluia.*

GOSPEL *(Luke 9:11b–17)*
A reading from the holy Gospel according to Luke.
Glory to you, O Lord.

Jesus spoke to the crowds about the kingdom of God, and he healed those who needed to be cured. As the day was drawing to a close, the Twelve approached him and said, "Dismiss the crowd so that they can go to the surrounding villages and farms and find lodging and provisions; for we are in a deserted place here." He said to them, "Give them some food yourselves." They replied, "Five loaves and two fish are all we have, unless we ourselves go and buy food for all these people." Now the men there numbered about five thousand. Then he said to his disciples, "Have them sit down in groups of about fifty." They did so and made them all sit down. Then taking the five loaves and the two fish, and looking up to heaven, he said the blessing over them, broke them, and gave them to the disciples to set before the crowd. They all ate and were satisfied. And when the leftover fragments were picked up, they filled twelve wicker baskets.

The Gospel of the Lord. *Praise to you, Lord Jesus Christ.*

PROFESSION OF FAITH *(page 13)*

PRAYER OF THE FAITHFUL

PREPARATION OF GIFTS *(page 16)*

PRAYER OVER THE OFFERINGS
Grant your Church, O Lord, we pray,
the gifts of unity and peace,
whose signs are to be seen in mystery
in the offerings we here present.
Through Christ our Lord. *Amen.*

• TAKING A CLOSER LOOK •

✛ **Covenant in my blood** Blood is the carrier of life, and its power is bestowed by God, who gives life to all beings. Thus in sacrificial rituals, the animal's blood represents its life. When the covenant was ritually sealed through a sacrifice, the blood was partially sprinkled on the altar (for God) and partially on the people. This symbolized that through this covenant bond they would share a common life together. So when shared in the Eucharist, Jesus' blood bonds us into communion with him for eternal life.

PREFACE *(Most Holy Eucharist 1–2, pages 32–33)*

COMMUNION ANTIPHON *(John 6:57)*

Whoever eats my flesh and drinks my blood remains in me and I in him, says the Lord.

PRAYER AFTER COMMUNION

Grant, O Lord, we pray,
that we may delight for all eternity
in that share in your divine life,
which is foreshadowed in the present age
by our reception of your precious Body and Blood.
Who live and reign for ever and ever. *Amen.*

BLESSING & DISMISSAL *(page 56)* ✣

• RESPONDING TO THE WORD •

After Melchizedek's blessing, Abram gives him a gift.

➲ *What gift can I offer today for God's blessings on me?*

Jesus asks us to remember his gift when we celebrate Eucharist.

➲ *How might I thank Jesus today for the gift of his abiding presence?*

The wondrous sharing of Jesus' bread is continued in our Eucharist.

➲ *How might I share myself more with others?*

GUARANTEED LOWEST PRICES OF THE SEASON

- **GREAT GIFT** FOR YOUR LOVED ONES!

- **DISCOUNTS TO PARISHES** FOR MULTIPLE COPIES!

Order By July 31 To Take Advantage Of Our Prepublication Special Pricing

HOW TO ORDER

 Call us at **1-800-321-0411** (Please refer to LSM18P2-PVB when placing your order)

 Online at **www.livingwithchrist.us/2missal**

Missals will ship in October—in time for the first Sunday of Advent. Orders shipped and billed to a parish/institution will be invoiced when the missals ship. All other orders must prepay.

Prepare ▪ Participate ▪ Reflect

Living with Christ is published by Bayard, Inc.   LSM18P2-PVB

June 30

The invitation still stands

I find myself challenged by today's gospel. Jesus calls two men and says, "Follow me." Though neither refuses, both find reasons not to follow right away.

Jesus' response to their requests sounds harsh. At this point, these men did not know what we, as Christians, know. They didn't understand that the man who was asking them to give up everything in their lives and follow him was none other than the Son of God.

How many times have we responded to God in the same way? God is calling us, but it can be hard to recognize him. We may already have plans, important things we want to do, and although we hear the call, we do not make following it a priority.

However, no matter how many times we've delayed responding to God's call, the invitation still stands. And even though we've gone our own way, Christ finds us where we are and requests our company on his mission.

Being a disciple of Christ is not easy. It implies a leap of faith. It requires us to freely choose, every single day, to live for something greater than ourselves.

■ **Myriam Dupuis**

ENTRANCE ANTIPHON *(Psalm 47 [46]:2)*

All peoples, clap your hands. Cry to God with
shouts of joy!

INTRODUCTORY RITES *(page 10)*

COLLECT

O God, who through the grace of adoption
chose us to be children of light,
grant, we pray,
that we may not be wrapped in the darkness of error
but always be seen to stand in the bright light of truth.
Through our Lord Jesus Christ, your Son,
who lives and reigns with you in the unity of the Holy Spirit,
one God, for ever and ever. *Amen.*

FIRST READING *(1 Kings 19:16b, 19–21)*

T he LORD said to Elijah: "You shall anoint Elisha, son of
Shaphat* of Abel-meholah,* as **prophet**⁺ to succeed you."

Elijah set out and came upon Elisha, son of Shaphat, as he
was plowing with twelve yoke of oxen; he was following the
twelfth. Elijah went over to him and threw his cloak over him.
Elisha left the oxen, ran after Elijah, and said, "Please, let me
kiss my father and mother goodbye, and I will follow you."
Elijah answered, "Go back! Have I done anything to you?"
Elisha left him, and taking the yoke of oxen, slaughtered them;
he used the plowing equipment for fuel to boil their flesh, and
gave it to his people to eat. Then Elisha left and followed Elijah
as his attendant.

The word of the Lord. *Thanks be to God.*

RESPONSORIAL PSALM *(Psalm 16:1-2, 5, 7-8, 9-10, 11)*

℟ You are my inheritance, O Lord.

Keep me, O God, for in you I take refuge;
  I say to the LORD, "My Lord are you.
O LORD, my allotted portion and my cup,
  you it is who hold fast my lot." ℟
I bless the LORD who counsels me;
  even in the night my heart exhorts me.
I set the LORD ever before me;
  with him at my right hand I shall not be disturbed. ℟
Therefore my heart is glad and my soul rejoices,
  my body, too, abides in confidence
because you will not abandon my soul to the netherworld,
  nor will you suffer your faithful one to undergo corruption. ℟
You will show me the path to life,
  fullness of joys in your presence,
  the delights at your right hand forever. ℟

SECOND READING *(Galatians 5:1, 13-18)*

Brothers and sisters: For freedom Christ set us free; so stand firm and do not submit again to the yoke of slavery.

For you were called for freedom, brothers and sisters. But do not use this freedom as an opportunity for the flesh; rather, serve one another through love. For the whole law is fulfilled in one statement, namely, *You shall love your neighbor as yourself*. But if you go on biting and devouring one another, beware that you are not consumed by one another.

I say, then: live by the Spirit and you will certainly not gratify the desire of the flesh. For the flesh has desires against the Spirit, and the Spirit against the flesh; these are opposed to each other, so that you may not do what you want. But if you are guided by the Spirit, you are not under the law.

The word of the Lord. *Thanks be to God.*

ALLELUIA *(1 Samuel 3:9; John 6:68c)*
Alleluia, alleluia. Speak, Lord, your servant is listening; you have the words of everlasting life. *Alleluia, alleluia.*

GOSPEL *(Luke 9:51-62)*
A reading from the holy Gospel according to Luke.
Glory to you, O Lord.

When the days for Jesus' being taken up were fulfilled, he resolutely determined to journey to Jerusalem, and he sent messengers ahead of him. On the way they entered a Samaritan village to prepare for his reception there, but they would not welcome him because the destination of his journey was Jerusalem. When the disciples James and John saw this they asked, "Lord, do you want us to call down fire from heaven to consume them?" Jesus turned and rebuked them, and they journeyed to another village.

As they were proceeding on their journey someone said to him, "I will follow you wherever you go." Jesus answered him, "Foxes have dens and birds of the sky have nests, but the Son of Man has nowhere to rest his head."

And to another he said, "Follow me." But he replied, "Lord, let me go first and bury my father." But he answered him, "Let the dead bury their dead. But you, go and proclaim the kingdom of God." And another said, "I will follow you, Lord, but first let me say farewell to my family at home." To him Jesus said, "No one who sets a hand to the plow and looks to what was left behind is fit for the kingdom of God."

The Gospel of the Lord. ***Praise to you, Lord Jesus Christ.***

PROFESSION OF FAITH *(page 13)*

PRAYER OF THE FAITHFUL

PREPARATION OF GIFTS *(page 16)*

PRAYER OVER THE OFFERINGS
O God, who graciously accomplish
the effects of your mysteries,
grant, we pray,
that the deeds by which we serve you
may be worthy of these sacred gifts.
Through Christ our Lord. ***Amen.***

PREFACE *(Sundays in Ordinary Time, pages 28–32)*

• TAKING A CLOSER LOOK •

✝ **Prophet** Biblical prophets (Greek, "to speak for or on behalf of someone") spoke as God's intermediaries to the king and to the covenant people. Rulers tended to forget that they were to rule according to God's covenant law and not for their own interests. The prophets spoke on behalf of God, reminding the people of God's agenda and encouraging them to trust in God rather than in human power and wisdom. While their words were often taken as predicting the future, their predictive power was a consequence of their belief that God always comes in judgment to punish evil and in mercy to reward good.

COMMUNION ANTIPHON *(Cf. Psalm 103 [102]:1)*
Bless the Lord, O my soul, and all within me, his holy name.

Or *(John 17:20–21)*
O Father, I pray for them, that they may be one in us, that the world may believe that you have sent me, says the Lord.

PRAYER AFTER COMMUNION
May this divine sacrifice we have offered and received
fill us with life, O Lord, we pray,
so that, bound to you in lasting charity,
we may bear fruit that lasts for ever.
Through Christ our Lord. *Amen.*

BLESSING & DISMISSAL *(page 56)* ❖

❖ RESPONDING TO THE WORD ❖

Elisha has to leave those he loves to become a prophet.	Paul claims that freedom is service to others in love.	Jesus says that he has nowhere to rest.
➲ *What have I had to leave behind lately to follow Christ?*	➲ *How has my service to others made me more free?*	➲ *How might I invite Jesus to come and rest in me?*

July 7

Jesus calls us to discipleship

The 70 disciples demonstrate courage and strength when Jesus appoints and sends them on their first mission. It will be a difficult task. In our time, they would have been asked to carry no wallet, no backpack, and certainly no cellphone. They are being sent " like lambs among wolves."

Upon entering any house, they are to offer God's gift of peace and to trust in God and in people's hospitality. They are to trust this new way of life where love accepts generously the gifts of others and ministers to the sick. Yet when the disciples return, they rejoice. Why? Perhaps they have come to experience and see that out of so little so much is being given.

Jesus knows the suffering of God's people is great. God knows our needs require God's love and mercy to heal a suffering world. Jesus calls us to discipleship—to be his body, his hands, and his heart to care, to listen, and to love in a way that serves and reveals the kingdom of God. We are asked to trust in this new way of being: giving ourselves to Jesus' love when we respond to the needs of others.

We have a choice: will we be voiceless bystanders in our world or trusting, rejoicing bearers of the mercy and love of God?

■ JULIE CACHIA

ENTRANCE ANTIPHON *(Cf. Psalm 48 [47]:10-11)*

Your merciful love, O God, we have received in the
midst of your temple. Your praise, O God, like your
name, reaches the ends of the earth; your right hand
is filled with saving justice.

INTRODUCTORY RITES *(page 10)*

COLLECT

O God, who in the abasement of your Son
have raised up a fallen world,
fill your faithful with holy joy,
for on those you have rescued from slavery to sin
you bestow eternal gladness.
Through our Lord Jesus Christ, your Son,
who lives and reigns with you in the unity of the Holy Spirit,
one God, for ever and ever. *Amen.*

FIRST READING *(Isaiah 66:10-14c)*

Thus says the LORD:
    Rejoice with Jerusalem and be glad because of her,
        all you who love her;
exult, exult with her,
        all you who were mourning over her!
Oh, that you may suck fully
        of the milk of her comfort,
that you may nurse with delight
        at her abundant breasts!
        For thus says the LORD:
Lo, I will spread prosperity over Jerusalem like a river,
        and the wealth of the nations like an overflowing torrent.
As nurslings, you shall be carried in her arms,

and fondled in her lap;
as a mother comforts her child,
   so will I comfort you;
   in Jerusalem you shall find your comfort.

When you see this, your heart shall rejoice
   and your bodies flourish like the grass;
the LORD's power shall be known to his servants.

The word of the Lord. *Thanks be to God.*

RESPONSORIAL PSALM *(Psalm 66:1-3, 4-5, 6-7, 16, 20)*
℟ **Let all the earth cry out to God with joy.**

Shout joyfully to God, all the earth,
   sing praise to the glory of his name;
   proclaim his glorious praise.
Say to God, "How tremendous are your deeds!" ℟
"Let all on earth worship and sing praise to you,
   sing praise to your name!"
Come and see the works of God,
   his tremendous deeds among the children of Adam. ℟
He has changed the sea into dry land;
   through the river they passed on foot;
   therefore let us rejoice in him.
He rules by his might forever. ℟
Hear now, all you who fear God, while I declare
   what he has done for me.
Blessed be God who refused me not
   my prayer or his kindness! ℟

SECOND READING *(Galatians 6:14-18)*

Brothers and sisters: May I never boast except in the cross of our Lord Jesus Christ, through which the world has been crucified to me, and I to the world. For neither does circumcision mean anything, nor does uncircumcision, but only a new creation. **Peace**✝ and mercy be to all who follow this rule and to the Israel of God.

From now on, let no one make troubles for me; for I bear the marks of Jesus on my body.

The grace of our Lord Jesus Christ be with your spirit, brothers and sisters. Amen.

The word of the Lord. *Thanks be to God.*

ALLELUIA *(Colossians 3:15a, 16a)*

Alleluia, alleluia. Let the peace of Christ control your hearts; let the word of Christ dwell in you richly. *Alleluia, alleluia.*

GOSPEL *(Luke 10:1-12, 17-20)*
For the shorter version, omit the indented parts in brackets.

A reading from the holy Gospel according to Luke.
Glory to you, O Lord.

At that time the Lord appointed seventy-two others whom he sent ahead of him in pairs to every town and place he intended to visit. He said to them, "The harvest is abundant but the laborers are few; so ask the master of the harvest to send out laborers for his harvest. Go on your way; behold, I am sending you like lambs among wolves. Carry no money bag, no sack, no sandals; and greet no one along the way. Into whatever house you enter, first say, 'Peace✝ to this household.' If a peaceful person lives there, your peace will rest on him; but if not, it will return to you. Stay in the same house and eat and drink what is offered to you, for the laborer deserves his payment. Do not move about from one house to another. Whatever town you enter and they welcome you, eat what is set before you, cure the sick in it and say to them, 'The kingdom of God is at hand for you.'

[Whatever town you enter and they do not receive you, go out into the streets and say, 'The dust of your town that clings to our feet, even that we shake off against you.' Yet know this: the kingdom of God is at hand. I tell you, it will be more tolerable for Sodom on that day than for that town."

The seventy-two returned rejoicing, and said, "Lord, even the demons are subject to us because of your name." Jesus said, "I have observed Satan fall like lightning from the sky. Behold, I have given you the power to 'tread upon serpents' and scorpions and upon the full force of the enemy and nothing will harm you. Nevertheless, do not rejoice because the spirits are subject to you, but rejoice because your names are written in heaven."]

The Gospel of the Lord. ***Praise to you, Lord Jesus Christ.***

PROFESSION OF FAITH *(page 13)*

PRAYER OF THE FAITHFUL

PREPARATION OF GIFTS *(page 16)*

PRAYER OVER THE OFFERINGS

May this oblation dedicated to your name
purify us, O Lord,
and day by day bring our conduct
closer to the life of heaven.
Through Christ our Lord. *Amen.*

PREFACE *(Sundays in Ordinary Time, pages 28–32)*

COMMUNION ANTIPHON *(Psalm 34 [33]:9)*

Taste and see that the Lord is good; blessed the man who seeks
refuge in him.

Or *(Matthew 11:28)*

Come to me, all who labor and are burdened, and I will refresh
you, says the Lord.

● TAKING A CLOSER LOOK ●

✢ **Peace** Peace (Hebrew, *shalom*) describes the experience
of fullness or completeness—lacking nothing that one needs for
a full and happy life. Peace is a gift that comes with God's presence. Thus it is also the goal for the life of the covenant community. The way to peace is justice—establishing and maintain-
ing rightly ordered relationships for the covenant community
according to God's guidelines. As a greeting, peace is a wish for
fullness of life, for union with God, and for harmony with others
leading to happiness for all.

PRAYER AFTER COMMUNION

Grant, we pray, O Lord,
that, having been replenished by such great gifts,
we may gain the prize of salvation
and never cease to praise you.
Through Christ our Lord. *Amen.*

BLESSING & DISMISSAL *(page 56)* ✢

• RESPONDING TO THE WORD •

God promises to comfort us as a mother comforts a child.

➡ *What comfort would I seek from God today?*

Old status markers like circumcision mean nothing to Paul because of his relation to Christ.

➡ *How has my faith made me rethink worldly honors?*

Jesus offers several guidelines for his disciples to follow as they embark on their ministry.

➡ *Which of these is most challenging for me right now?*

July 14

Love generously!

The story of the good Samaritan is so familiar that we almost take it for granted. Of course we want to be the good Samaritan!

It is easy to see the priest and the Levite as villains, walking by on the other side, but they followed the customs of class and the precautions of safety on a dangerous road. When someone has car trouble or asks me for change on the side of the street, I calculate my time and money, weigh the risks, and decide whether I can spare the time, money, and risk to help.

The good Samaritan is willing to care even at a cost to himself. He takes the risk of being victimized, gives his time and his money, and perhaps most importantly defies social and class customs to do so. Mercy does not offer love that is convenient, expected, or easy; it offers loving care when it is unconventional, over the top, or even costly.

God has planted this law of mercy inside us: "in your mouths and in your hearts; you have only to carry it out." May we be so in touch with God dwelling inside each of us that we love generously without counting the cost. May we be more faithful to God's laws than the external rules and customs which become our excuses.

■ **LEAH PERRAULT**

ENTRANCE ANTIPHON *(Cf. Psalm 17 [16]:15)*
As for me, in justice I shall behold your face; I shall be filled with the vision of your glory.

INTRODUCTORY RITES *(page 10)*

COLLECT
O God, who show the light of your truth
to those who go astray,
so that they may return to the right path,
give all who for the faith they profess
are accounted Christians
the grace to reject whatever is contrary to the name of Christ
and to strive after all that does it honor.
Through our Lord Jesus Christ, your Son,
who lives and reigns with you in the unity of the Holy Spirit,
one God, for ever and ever. *Amen.*

FIRST READING *(Deuteronomy 30:10–14)*

Moses said to the people: "If only you would heed the voice of the LORD, your God, and keep his **commandments and statutes**⁺ that are written in this book of the law, when you return to the LORD, your God, with all your heart and all your soul.

"For this command that I enjoin on you today is not too mysterious and remote for you. It is not up in the sky, that you should say, 'Who will go up in the sky to get it for us and tell us of it, that we may carry it out?' Nor is it across the sea, that you should say, 'Who will cross the sea to get it for us and tell us of it, that we may carry it out?' No, it is something very near to you, already in your mouths and in your hearts; you have only to carry it out."

The word of the Lord. *Thanks be to God.*

An alternate psalm follows.

RESPONSORIAL PSALM *(Psalm 69:14, 17, 30–31, 33–34, 36, 37)*
R̥ **Turn to the Lord in your need, and you will live.**

I pray to you, O LORD,
   for the time of your favor, O God!
In your great kindness answer me
   with your constant help.
Answer me, O LORD, for bounteous is your kindness:
   in your great mercy turn toward me. R̥
I am afflicted and in pain;
   let your saving help, O God, protect me.
I will praise the name of God in song,
   and I will glorify him with thanksgiving. R̥
"See, you lowly ones, and be glad;
   you who seek God, may your hearts revive!
For the LORD hears the poor,
   and his own who are in bonds he spurns not." R̥
For God will save Zion*
   and rebuild the cities of Judah.
The descendants of his servants shall inherit it,
   and those who love his name shall inhabit it. R̥

OR

RESPONSORIAL PSALM *(Psalm 19:8, 9, 10, 11)*
R̥ **Your words, Lord, are Spirit and life.**

The law of the LORD is perfect,
   refreshing the soul;
the decree of the LORD is trustworthy,
   giving wisdom to the simple. R̥

The precepts of the LORD are right,
    rejoicing the heart;
the command of the LORD is clear,
    enlightening the eye.

R. **Your words, Lord, are Spirit and life.**

The fear of the LORD is pure,
    enduring forever;
the ordinances of the LORD are true,
    all of them just. R.

They are more precious than gold,
    than a heap of purest gold;
sweeter also than syrup
    or honey from the comb. R.

SECOND READING *(Colossians 1:15-20)*

Christ Jesus is the image of the invisible God,
    the firstborn of all creation.
For in him were created all things in heaven and on earth,
    the visible and the invisible,
        whether thrones or dominions or principalities or powers;
    all things were created through him and for him.
He is before all things,
    and in him all things hold together.
He is the head of the body, the church.
He is the beginning, the firstborn from the dead,
    that in all things he himself might be preeminent.
For in him all the fullness was pleased to dwell,
    and through him to reconcile all things for him,
    making peace by the blood of his cross
    through him, whether those on earth or those in heaven.

The word of the Lord. ***Thanks be to God.***

ALLELUIA *(See John 6:63c, 68c)*
Alleluia, alleluia. Your words, Lord, are Spirit and life; you have the words of everlasting life. *Alleluia, alleluia.*

GOSPEL *(Luke 10:25-37)*
A reading from the holy Gospel according to Luke.
Glory to you, O Lord.

There was a scholar of the law who stood up to test him and said, "Teacher, what must I do to inherit eternal life?" Jesus said to him, "What is written in the law? How do you read it?" He said in reply, *"You shall love the Lord, your God, with all your heart, with all your being, with all your strength, and with all your mind, and your neighbor as yourself."* He replied to him, "You have answered correctly; do this and you will live."

But because he wished to justify himself, he said to Jesus, "And who is my neighbor?" Jesus replied, "A man fell victim to robbers as he went down from Jerusalem to Jericho.* They stripped and beat him and went off leaving him half-dead. A priest happened to be going down that road, but when he saw him, he passed by on the opposite side. Likewise a Levite* came to the place, and when he saw him, he passed by on the opposite side. But a Samaritan traveler who came upon him was moved with compassion at the sight. He approached the victim, poured oil and wine over his wounds and bandaged them. Then he lifted him up on his own animal, took him to an inn, and cared for him. The next day he took out two silver coins and gave them to the innkeeper with the instruction, 'Take care of him. If you spend more than what I have given you, I shall repay you on my way back.' Which of these three, in your opinion, was neighbor to the robbers' victim?" He answered, "The one who treated him with mercy." Jesus said to him, "Go and do likewise."

The Gospel of the Lord. *Praise to you, Lord Jesus Christ.*

PROFESSION OF FAITH *(page 13)*

PRAYER OF THE FAITHFUL

PREPARATION OF GIFTS *(page 16)*

PRAYER OVER THE OFFERINGS
Look upon the offerings of the Church, O Lord,
as she makes her prayer to you,
and grant that, when consumed by those who believe,
they may bring ever greater holiness.
Through Christ our Lord. *Amen.*

PREFACE *(Sundays in Ordinary Time, pages 28–32)*

• TAKING A CLOSER LOOK •

✢ **Commandments and statutes** These two words summarize God's directives or basic guidelines for the Hebrew covenant community's life with one another. They identify the basic attitudes and actions that must be followed to fulfill God's desires. "Commandments" refers to the ten basic "words" that God spoke directly to Moses and the community on Mount Sinai (Exodus 20:1-17). When the people are overcome by fear, they request that in the future God not speak to them directly but only through Moses. "Statutes" describes this further teaching through Moses that makes specific applications of the ten commandments.

COMMUNION ANTIPHON *(Cf. Psalm 84 [83]:4-5)*

The sparrow finds a home, and the swallow a nest for her young: by your altars, O Lord of hosts, my King and my God. Blessed are they who dwell in your house, for ever singing your praise.

Or *(John 6:57)*

Whoever eats my flesh and drinks my blood remains in me and I in him, says the Lord.

PRAYER AFTER COMMUNION

Having consumed these gifts, we pray, O Lord,
that, by our participation in this mystery,
its saving effects upon us may grow.
Through Christ our Lord. *Amen.*

BLESSING & DISMISSAL *(page 56)* ❖

❖ RESPONDING TO THE WORD ❖

Moses knows it is much easier to know God's commandments than to keep them.

➡ *Which commandment is most problematic for me now?*

Jesus' presence throughout creation allows him to reconcile all things in himself.

➡ *How might I imitate Jesus' reconciling work today?*

Jesus praises the one who overcame his prejudices and acted out of compassion.

➡ *How can I recognize and overcome my prejudices in order to help someone in need?*

July 21

Frame today around Jesus

When I was a young bride, we lived in an old Victorian home that really came to life when the dining room was filled with people. My husband was the better cook, so most of the meal preparation was his to do. I specialized in setting a wonderful table with our beautiful wedding gifts. As the years went by, everything became simpler, many wedding gifts gathered dust, and the joy of sharing hospitality at our table with friends and family deepened.

The tradition of welcoming the stranger and the friend at the dinner table runs deep in human history. It is a good thing. We see Abraham engaging the entire household in the rushed preparations to serve unexpected guests. We see Martha bustling about. We see Mary sitting at the feet of Jesus. Then Martha engages Jesus in getting Mary's help with the preparations, and it does not turn out the way she hopes!

Luke does not say how Martha responded. However, we can choose to hear Christ's words spoken not as a rebuke, but as a tender invitation to approach more closely, live more deeply, and love more richly. Each of us can make the conscious choice to frame today around Jesus Christ, and then we will experience the rest of our world take shape around that choice. Tomorrow we can make the same choice again.

■ MARILYN SWEET

ENTRANCE ANTIPHON *(Psalm 54 [53]:6, 8)*

See, I have God for my help. The Lord sustains my soul. I will sacrifice to you with willing heart, and praise your name, O Lord, for it is good.

INTRODUCTORY RITES *(page 10)*

COLLECT

Show favor, O Lord, to your servants
and mercifully increase the gifts of your grace,
that, made fervent in hope, faith and charity,
they may be ever watchful in keeping your commands.
Through our Lord Jesus Christ, your Son,
who lives and reigns with you in the unity of the Holy Spirit,
one God, for ever and ever. *Amen.*

FIRST READING *(Genesis 18:1–10a)*

The LORD appeared to Abraham by the terebinth of Mamre, as he sat in the entrance of his tent, while the day was growing hot. Looking up, Abraham saw three men standing nearby. When he saw them, he ran from the entrance of the tent to greet them; and bowing to the ground, he said: "Sir, if I may ask you this favor, please do not go on past your servant. Let some water be brought, that you may bathe your feet, and then rest yourselves under the tree. Now that you have come this close to your servant, let me bring you a little food, that you may refresh yourselves; and afterward you may go on your way." The men replied, "Very well, do as you have said."

Abraham hastened into the tent and told Sarah, "Quick, three measures of fine flour! Knead it and make rolls." He ran to the herd, picked out a tender, choice steer, and gave it to a servant, who quickly prepared it. Then Abraham got some curds and milk, as well as the steer that had been prepared, and set these before the three men; and he waited on them under the tree while they ate.

They asked Abraham, "Where is your wife Sarah?" He replied, "There in the tent." One of them said, "I will surely return to you about this time next year, and Sarah will then have a son."

The word of the Lord. ***Thanks be to God.***

RESPONSORIAL PSALM *(Psalm 15:2–3, 3–4, 5)*

℟ **He who does justice will live in the presence of the Lord.**

One who walks blamelessly and does justice;
    who thinks the truth in his heart
    and slanders not with his tongue. ℟
Who harms not his fellow man,
    nor takes up a reproach against his neighbor;
by whom the reprobate is despised,
    while he honors those who fear the LORD. ℟
Who lends not his money at usury
    and accepts no bribe against the innocent.
One who does these things
    shall never be disturbed. ℟

SECOND READING *(Colossians 1:24–28)*

Brothers and sisters: Now I rejoice in my sufferings for your sake, and in my flesh I am filling up what is lacking in the afflictions of Christ on behalf of his body, which is the church, of which I am a minister in accordance with God's stewardship given to me to bring to completion for you the word of God, the **mystery**✠ hidden from ages and from generations past. But now it has been manifested to his holy ones, to whom God chose to make known the riches of the glory of this mystery among the Gentiles; it is Christ in you, the hope for glory. It is he whom we proclaim, admonishing everyone and teaching everyone with all wisdom, that we may present everyone perfect in Christ.

The word of the Lord. *Thanks be to God.*

ALLELUIA *(See Luke 8:15)*
Alleluia, alleluia. Blessed are they who have kept the word with a generous heart and yield a harvest through perseverance. *Alleluia, alleluia.*

GOSPEL *(Luke 10:38–42)*
A reading from the holy Gospel according to Luke.
Glory to you, O Lord.

Jesus entered a village where a woman whose name was Martha welcomed him. She had a sister named Mary who sat beside the Lord at his feet listening to him speak. Martha, burdened with much serving, came to him and said, "Lord, do you not care that my sister has left me by myself to do the serving? Tell her to help me." The Lord said to her in reply, "Martha, Martha, you are anxious and worried about many things. There is need of only one thing. Mary has chosen the better part and it will not be taken from her."

The Gospel of the Lord. *Praise to you, Lord Jesus Christ.*

PROFESSION OF FAITH *(page 13)*

PRAYER OF THE FAITHFUL

PREPARATION OF GIFTS *(page 16)*

PRAYER OVER THE OFFERINGS

O God, who in the one perfect sacrifice
brought to completion varied offerings of the law,
accept, we pray, this sacrifice from your faithful servants
and make it holy, as you blessed the gifts of Abel,
so that what each has offered to the honor of your majesty
may benefit the salvation of all.
Through Christ our Lord. *Amen.*

PREFACE *(Sundays in Ordinary Time, pages 28–32)*

COMMUNION ANTIPHON *(Psalm 111 [110]:4-5)*
The Lord, the gracious, the merciful, has made a memorial of his
wonders; he gives food to those who fear him.

• TAKING A CLOSER LOOK •

✦ **Mystery** In the Greek world of early Christianity, "mystery"
(singular) pointed to that which is hidden or secret and cannot be
talked about openly. For Christians like Paul, mystery points to what
is hidden and cannot be known unless God reveals it. Paul identifies this revealed mystery as God's surprising desire to unite all humanity—both Jew and Gentile—into one community in Christ. Of
course, this mystery cannot be kept hidden but becomes the core
of Paul's Christian message. In later theological terminology, a mystery, strictly speaking, is a revealed truth about God that can be af-
firmed in faith but never completely and adequately expressed in
abstract concepts or rational explanations. The primary Christian
theological mysteries are the Trinity and the Incarnation.

Or *(Revelation 3:20)*
Behold, I stand at the door and knock, says the Lord. If anyone
hears my voice and opens the door to me, I will enter his house
and dine with him, and he with me.

PRAYER AFTER COMMUNION
Graciously be present to your people, we pray, O Lord,
and lead those you have imbued with heavenly mysteries
to pass from former ways to newness of life.
Through Christ our Lord. *Amen.*

BLESSING & DISMISSAL *(page 56)* ✛

✛ RESPONDING TO THE WORD ✛

Abraham's generous
hospitality is pleasing
to his surprise divine
visitor.

➡ *How might I be
more hospitable to
those who come unex-
pectedly to me today?*

Paul claims that the
mystery revealed is
"Christ in you" (a
plural form, meaning
the whole commu-
nity).

➡ *When have I expe-
rienced Christ's pres-
ence in the gathered
community at Mass?*

Martha and Mary
show two ways of
being in Christ's
presence.

➡ *Which of these
sisters am I most like?
Why?*

July 28

We are God's children!

Our two-year-old friend came to visit and, as we don't have a resident toddler, it was a treat to have him over. Before long he had us crawling on the floor making train tracks out of green painter's tape.

Who has not witnessed a small child ask again and again for something they want? When the child is quite young and innocent their requests are simple. Persistent and maybe not timely, but with complete earnestness they ask for love, for drinks, for food, for protection, and for play. They ask over and over.

Why, then, do we not also ask in this way for the things we need? Are we too shy? Do we fear rejection? Do we feel we do not deserve them? Little children do not have these feelings; they just ask and they receive. How happy we are to give! How thrilled that we were asked!

Sometimes we need to be reminded that we also are children, God's children. We have a loving, giving Father who is waiting for us to ask. One who welcomes our persistence too. In today's gospel, Jesus shows us how to ask—through prayer. Reaffirming our place as faithful children, God encourages us to say "Our Father" and to know that we too will receive.

■ **LIZ SUMMERS**

ENTRANCE ANTIPHON *(Cf. Psalm 68 [67]:6-7, 36)*
God is in his holy place, God who unites those
who dwell in his house; he himself gives might
and strength to his people.

INTRODUCTORY RITES *(page 10)*

COLLECT
O God, protector of those who hope in you,
without whom nothing has firm foundation, nothing is holy,
bestow in abundance your mercy upon us
and grant that, with you as our ruler and guide,
we may use the good things that pass
in such a way as to hold fast even now
to those that ever endure.
Through our Lord Jesus Christ, your Son,
who lives and reigns with you in the unity of the Holy Spirit,
one God, for ever and ever. *Amen.*

FIRST READING *(Genesis 18:20-32)*

I n those days, the LORD said: "The outcry against Sodom and
Gomorrah is so great, and their sin so grave, that I must go
down and see whether or not their actions fully correspond to
the cry against them that comes to me. I mean to find out."

While Abraham's visitors walked on farther toward Sodom,
the LORD remained standing before Abraham. Then Abraham
drew nearer and said: "Will you sweep away the innocent with the
guilty? Suppose there were fifty innocent people in the city; would
you wipe out the place, rather than spare it for the sake of the fifty
innocent people within it? Far be it from you to do such a thing,
to make the innocent die with the guilty so that the innocent and
the guilty would be treated alike! Should not the judge of all the

world act with justice?" The LORD replied, "If I find fifty innocent people in the city of Sodom, I will spare the whole place for their sake." Abraham spoke up again: "See how I am presuming to speak to my LORD, though I am but dust and ashes! What if there are five less than fifty innocent people? Will you destroy the whole city because of those five?" He answered, "I will not destroy it, if I find forty-five there." But Abraham persisted, saying "What if only forty are found there?" He replied, "I will forbear doing it for the sake of the forty." Then Abraham said, "Let not my LORD grow impatient if I go on. What if only thirty are found there?" He replied, "I will forbear doing it if I can find but thirty there." Still Abraham went on, "Since I have thus dared to speak to my LORD, what if there are no more than twenty?" The LORD answered, "I will not destroy it, for the sake of the twenty." But he still persisted: "Please, let not my LORD grow angry if I speak up this last time. What if there are at least ten there?" He replied, "For the sake of those ten, I will not destroy it."

The word of the Lord. *Thanks be to God.*

RESPONSORIAL PSALM *(Psalm 138:1–2, 2–3, 6–7, 7–8)*
℟ **Lord, on the day I called for help, you answered me.**

I will give thanks to you, O LORD, with all my heart,
 for you have heard the words of my mouth;
 in the presence of the angels I will sing your praise;
I will worship at your holy temple
 and give thanks to your name. ℟
Because of your kindness and your truth;
 for you have made great above all things
 your name and your promise.
When I called you answered me;

you built up strength within me. ℟·
The LORD is exalted, yet the lowly he sees,
   and the proud he knows from afar.
Though I walk amid distress, you preserve me;
   against the anger of my enemies you raise your hand. ℟·
Your right hand saves me.
The LORD will complete what he has done for me;
your kindness, O LORD, endures forever;
   forsake not the work of your hands. ℟·

SECOND READING *(Colossians 2:12-14)*

Brothers and sisters: You were buried with him in baptism,
in which you were also raised with him through faith in the
power of God, who raised him from the dead. And even when
you were dead in transgressions and the uncircumcision of your
flesh, he brought you to life along with him, having forgiven us
all our transgressions; obliterating the bond against us, with its
legal claims, which was opposed to us, he also removed it from
our midst, nailing it to the cross.

The word of the Lord. *Thanks be to God.*

ALLELUIA *(Romans 8:15bc)*
Alleluia, alleluia. You have received a Spirit of adoption,
through which we cry, Abba, Father. *Alleluia, alleluia.*

GOSPEL *(Luke 11:1-13)*
A reading from the holy Gospel according to Luke.
Glory to you, O Lord.

Jesus was praying in a certain place, and when he had finished,
one of his disciples said to him, "Lord, teach us to pray just as
John taught his disciples." He said to them, "**When you pray, say:**✝

Father, hallowed be your name,
    your kingdom come.
    Give us each day our daily bread
    and forgive us our sins
    for we ourselves forgive everyone in debt to us,
    and do not subject us to the final test.'"

And he said to them, "Suppose one of you has a friend to whom he goes at midnight and says, 'Friend, lend me three loaves of bread, for a friend of mine has arrived at my house from a journey and I have nothing to offer him,' and he says in reply from within, 'Do not bother me; the door has already been locked and my children and I are already in bed. I cannot get up to give you anything.' I tell you, if he does not get up to give the visitor the loaves because of their friendship, he will get up to give him whatever he needs because of his persistence.

"And I tell you, ask and you will receive; seek and you will find; knock and the door will be opened to you. For everyone who asks, receives; and the one who seeks, finds; and to the one who knocks, the door will be opened. What father among you would hand his son a snake when he asks for a fish? Or hand him a scorpion when he asks for an egg? If you then, who are wicked, know how to give good gifts to your children, how much more will the Father in heaven give the Holy Spirit to those who ask him?"

The Gospel of the Lord. ***Praise to you, Lord Jesus Christ.***

PROFESSION OF FAITH *(page 13)*

PRAYER OF THE FAITHFUL

PREPARATION OF GIFTS *(page 16)*

PRAYER OVER THE OFFERINGS

Accept, O Lord, we pray, the offerings
which we bring from the abundance of your gifts,
that through the powerful working of your grace
these most sacred mysteries may sanctify our present way of life
and lead us to eternal gladness.
Through Christ our Lord. *Amen.*

PREFACE *(Sundays in Ordinary Time, pages 28–32)*

COMMUNION ANTIPHON *(Psalm 103 [102]: 2)*

Bless the Lord, O my soul, and never forget all his benefits.

Or *(Matthew 5:7–8)*

Blessed are the merciful, for they shall receive mercy. Blessed are
the clean of heart, for they shall see God.

● TAKING A CLOSER LOOK ●

✚ **The Lord's Prayer** In this simple Lukan form (the more
familiar one is from Matthew's gospel), the Lord's Prayer reflects
the expectations and obligations in the relationship of a benevolent patron (a father of a household, a king, or a master) to his
dependents. The first set of petitions indicate how we, as God's
dependents, will fulfill our part of the relationship: by respecting
the holiness of God's person (or "name") and by making our own
God's aim of creating the kingdom community here on earth. The
second set of petitions asks God to fulfill the obligations of a patron by providing food ("our daily bread"), forgiving our offenses
(conditioned, of course, on our forgiveness of others), and protecting us from evil.

PRAYER AFTER COMMUNION

We have consumed, O Lord, this divine Sacrament,
the perpetual memorial of the Passion of your Son;
grant, we pray, that this gift,
which he himself gave us with love beyond all telling,
may profit us for salvation.
Through Christ our Lord. *Amen.*

BLESSING & DISMISSAL *(page 56)* ✢

• RESPONDING TO THE WORD •

Abraham pushes God to greater and greater mercy through his persistent requests on behalf of the innocent.	Jesus brought us to life when we were cut off from God's life by our sinfulness.	Jesus encourages persistence in our prayer.
➡ *For whom might I ask God's mercy in my prayer today?*	➡ *How can I thank Jesus for his loving mercy to me?*	➡ *For what have I been asking over and over from God?*

August 4

**AUG
4**

How do we measure our success?

The parable of the rich fool—the man who tore down his barns and built larger ones to store his crops—always reminds me of my parents' teaching on success. They continually reminded my siblings and me that our success would not be measured on earth, but rather in our heavenly home.

No matter what we do in life, whatever our role, education, vocation, titles, responsibilities or material goods, everything must encourage us to serve our sisters and brothers in need and ultimately strengthen our relationship with our Creator. When something stands in the way of this call to service and faithfulness, we have a duty to consider whether we are working towards our human potential and revealing the image of God engraved on each of our souls.

Of course, my folks' teachings are a radical departure from society's definition of success and obsession with material accumulation. Living the Christian life is not for the fainthearted. Sharing our time, talent, and treasure with each other might deplete our bank accounts and leisure time, but it will ensure we encounter abundance in the life to come.

Unlike the rich fool in today's gospel, may we measure success by our constant service to those in need, and through the growth of our spiritual life and personal relationship with Jesus Christ.

■ **Fr. Matthew Durham, CSB**

ENTRANCE ANTIPHON *(Psalm 70 [69]:2, 6)*
O God, come to my assistance; O Lord, make haste to help me!
You are my rescuer, my help; O Lord, do not delay.

INTRODUCTORY RITES *(page 10)*

COLLECT
Draw near to your servants, O Lord,
and answer their prayers with unceasing kindness,
that, for those who glory in you as their Creator and guide,
you may restore what you have created
and keep safe what you have restored.
Through our Lord Jesus Christ, your Son,
who lives and reigns with you in the unity of the Holy Spirit,
one God, for ever and ever. *Amen.*

FIRST READING *(Ecclesiastes 1:2; 2:21-23)*

Vanity✝ of vanities, says Qoheleth,*
vanity of vanities! All things are vanity!
Here is one who has labored with wisdom and knowledge and
skill, and yet to another who has not labored over it, he must leave
property. This also is vanity and a great misfortune. For what profit
comes to man from all the toil and anxiety of heart with which he
has labored under the sun? All his days sorrow and grief are his oc-
cupation; even at night his mind is not at rest. This also is vanity.

The word of the Lord. *Thanks be to God.*

RESPONSORIAL PSALM *(Psalm 90:3-4, 5-6, 12-13, 14 and 17)*
℟ **If today you hear his voice, harden not your hearts.**

You turn man back to dust,
  saying, "Return, O children of men."
For a thousand years in your sight
  are as yesterday, now that it is past,
  or as a watch of the night. ℟

You make an end of them in their sleep;
  the next morning they are like the changing grass,
Which at dawn springs up anew,
  but by evening wilts and fades. ℟

Teach us to number our days aright,
  that we may gain wisdom of heart.
Return, O LORD! How long?
  Have pity on your servants! ℟

Fill us at daybreak with your kindness,
  that we may shout for joy and gladness all our days.
And may the gracious care of the LORD our God be ours;
  prosper the work of our hands for us!
  Prosper the work of our hands! ℟

SECOND READING *(Colossians 3:1-5, 9-11)*

Brothers and sisters: If you were raised with Christ, seek what is above, where Christ is seated at the right hand of God. Think of what is above, not of what is on earth. For you have died, and your life is hidden with Christ in God. When Christ your life appears, then you too will appear with him in glory.

Put to death, then, the parts of you that are earthly: immorality, impurity, passion, evil desire, and the greed that is idolatry. Stop lying to one another, since you have taken off the old self with its practices and have put on the new self, which is being renewed, for knowledge, in the image of its creator. Here there is not Greek and Jew, circumcision and uncircumcision, barbarian, Scythian, slave, free; but Christ is all and in all.

The word of the Lord. *Thanks be to God.*

ALLELUIA *(Matthew 5:3)*
Alleluia, alleluia. Blessed are the poor in spirit, for theirs is the kingdom of heaven. *Alleluia, alleluia.*

GOSPEL *(Luke 12:13–21)*
A reading from the holy Gospel according to Luke.
Glory to you, O Lord.

Someone in the crowd said to Jesus, "Teacher, tell my brother to share the inheritance with me." He replied to him, "Friend, who appointed me as your judge and arbitrator?" Then he said to the crowd, "Take care to guard against all greed, for though one may be rich, one's life does not consist of possessions."

Then he told them a parable. "There was a rich man whose land produced a bountiful harvest. He asked himself, 'What shall I do, for I do not have space to store my harvest?' And he said, 'This is what I shall do: I shall tear down my barns and build larger ones. There I shall store all my grain and other goods and I shall say to myself, "Now as for you, you have so many good things stored up for many years, rest, eat, drink, be merry!" ' But God said to him, 'You fool, this night your life will be demanded of you; and the things you have prepared, to whom will they belong?' Thus will it be for all who store up treasure for themselves but are not rich in what matters to God."

The Gospel of the Lord. *Praise to you, Lord Jesus Christ.*

PROFESSION OF FAITH *(page 13)*

PRAYER OF THE FAITHFUL

PREPARATION OF GIFTS *(page 16)*

PRAYER OVER THE OFFERINGS
Graciously sanctify these gifts, O Lord, we pray,
and, accepting the oblation of this spiritual sacrifice,
make of us an eternal offering to you.
Through Christ our Lord. *Amen.*

PREFACE *(Sundays in Ordinary Time, pages 28–32)*

• TAKING A CLOSER LOOK •

✛ **Vanity** The word "vanity" (Hebrew, *hebel*) describes something that is not substantial and lasting, but ephemeral and passing (like fog that evaporates quickly as the sun rises)—and so worthless, empty of meaning, purpose, and content. As the author probes the meaning of life, he is overwhelmed by its transitory character over which he has no control. The result is a rather pessimistic assessment that not only is life fleeting, but our efforts to change things and to secure our future are useless. In the end, life passes by and the endless grind of work changes nothing. Our Christian belief in life with God after death radically changes this assessment.

COMMUNION ANTIPHON *(Wisdom 16:20)*

You have given us, O Lord, bread from heaven, endowed with all delights and sweetness in every taste.

Or *(John 6:35)*

I am the bread of life, says the Lord; whoever comes to me will not hunger and whoever believes in me will not thirst.

PRAYER AFTER COMMUNION

Accompany with constant protection, O Lord,
those you renew with these heavenly gifts
and, in your never-failing care for them,
make them worthy of eternal redemption.
Through Christ our Lord. *Amen.*

BLESSING & DISMISSAL *(page 56)* ✣

✦ RESPONDING TO THE WORD ✦

Qoheleth feels like life passes quickly and often seems meaningless.	Paul urges us to put off our old self and put on a new self that is like Jesus.	Jesus warns us to guard against greed and the amassing of possessions.
➡ *What has made my life most meaningful?*	➡ *What can I do this week to change my words and actions to be more like those of Jesus?*	➡ *What can I give away this week to help those who are poor and in need?*

August 11

AUG
11

Preparing for the future

Long, lazy summer days offer kids a chance for imaginative play. They act out their favorite stories and recreate the exploits of their heroines and heroes. This play has a purpose. It provides our young with the opportunity to prepare themselves for their futures.

Every Sunday we are called on to reflect on our own futures through stories, parables, and admonitions. We hear in the passage from the Book of Wisdom, authored possibly as late as the first century, of a people enslaved in Egypt preparing for their liberation. They trusted in the promises of God for "the salvation of the just and the destruction of their foes." Do we?

The Letter to the Hebrews reminds us of the lives of great women and men of the Old Testament. It shows us how their faith sustained them no matter what challenges they faced. Abraham continued to believe, even when asked to sacrifice his only son, Isaac. Have we developed such a wholehearted trust in God?

Luke's parables of the alert slave and faithful manager call us to ready ourselves for any contingency. Where is our treasure? Where is our heart? These weekly passages and our daily actions at play or work continually prepare us to live God's word.

■ MICHAEL DOUGHERTY

ENTRANCE ANTIPHON *(Cf. Psalm 74 [73]:20, 19, 22, 23)*

Look to your covenant, O Lord, and forget not the life of your poor ones for ever. Arise, O God, and defend your cause, and forget not the cries of those who seek you.

INTRODUCTORY RITES *(page 10)*

COLLECT

Almighty ever-living God,
whom, taught by the Holy Spirit,
we dare to call our Father,
bring, we pray, to perfection in our hearts
the spirit of adoption as your sons and daughters,
that we may merit to enter into the inheritance
which you have promised.
Through our Lord Jesus Christ, your Son,
who lives and reigns with you in the unity of the Holy Spirit,
one God, for ever and ever. *Amen.*

FIRST READING *(Wisdom 18:6-9)*

The night of the passover was known beforehand to our
fathers,
    that, with sure knowledge of the oaths in which they put
        their faith,✝
    they might have courage.
Your people awaited the salvation of the just
    and the destruction of their foes.
For when you punished our adversaries,
    in this you glorified us whom you had summoned.
For in secret the holy children of the good were offering sacrifice
    and putting into effect with one accord the divine institution.

The word of the Lord. *Thanks be to God.*

RESPONSORIAL PSALM *(Psalm 33:1, 12, 18–19, 20–22)*

℟ Blessed the people the Lord has chosen to be his own.

Exult, you just, in the LORD;
    praise from the upright is fitting.
Blessed the nation whose God is the LORD,
    the people he has chosen for his own inheritance. ℟
See, the eyes of the LORD are upon those who fear him,
    upon those who hope for his kindness,
to deliver them from death
    and preserve them in spite of famine. ℟
Our soul waits for the LORD,
    who is our help and our shield.
May your kindness, O LORD, be upon us
    who have put our hope in you. ℟

SECOND READING *(Hebrews 11:1–2, 8–19)*
The shorter version ends at the asterisks.

Brothers and sisters: **Faith**✝ is the realization of what is
hoped for and evidence of things not seen. Because of it the
ancients were well attested.

By faith Abraham obeyed when he was called to go out to a
place that he was to receive as an inheritance; he went out, not
knowing where he was to go. By faith he sojourned in the promised land as in a foreign country, dwelling in tents with Isaac and
Jacob, heirs of the same promise; for he was looking forward to
the city with foundations, whose architect and maker is God. By
faith he received power to generate, even though he was past the
normal age—and Sarah herself was sterile—for he thought that
the one who had made the promise was trustworthy. So it was
that there came forth from one man, himself as good as dead,

descendants as numerous as the stars in the sky and as countless as the sands on the seashore.

* * *

All these died in faith. They did not receive what had been promised but saw it and greeted it from afar and acknowledged themselves to be strangers and aliens on earth, for those who speak thus show that they are seeking a homeland. If they had been thinking of the land from which they had come, they would have had opportunity to return. But now they desire a better homeland, a heavenly one. Therefore, God is not ashamed to be called their God, for he has prepared a city for them.

By faith Abraham, when put to the test, offered up Isaac, and he who had received the promises was ready to offer his only son, of whom it was said, "Through Isaac descendants shall bear your name." He reasoned that God was able to raise even from the dead, and he received Isaac back as a symbol.

The word of the Lord. *Thanks be to God.*

ALLELUIA *(See Matthew 24:42a, 44)*
Alleluia, alleluia. Stay awake and be ready! For you do not know on what day your Lord will come. *Alleluia, alleluia.*

GOSPEL *(Luke 12:32–48)*
For the shorter version, omit the indented parts in brackets.

A reading from the holy Gospel according to Luke.
Glory to you, O Lord.

Jesus said to his disciples:
["Do not be afraid any longer, little flock, for your Father is pleased to give you the kingdom. Sell your belongings and give alms. Provide money bags for yourselves that do not

wear out, an inexhaustible treasure in heaven that no thief can reach nor moth destroy. For where your treasure is, there also will your heart be.]

"Gird your loins and light your lamps and be like servants who await their master's return from a wedding, ready to open immediately when he comes and knocks. Blessed are those servants whom the master finds vigilant on his arrival. Amen, I say to you, he will gird himself, have them recline at table, and proceed to wait on them. And should he come in the second or third watch and find them prepared in this way, blessed are those servants. Be sure of this: if the master of the house had known the hour when the thief was coming, he would not have let his house be broken into. You also must be prepared, for at an hour you do not expect, the Son of Man will come."

[Then Peter said, "Lord, is this parable meant for us or for everyone?" And the Lord replied, "Who, then, is the faithful and prudent steward whom the master will put in charge of his servants to distribute the food allowance at the proper time? Blessed is that servant whom his master on arrival finds doing so. Truly, I say to you, the master will put the servant in charge of all his property. But if that servant says to himself, 'My master is delayed in coming,' and begins to beat the menservants and the maidservants, to eat and drink and get drunk, then that servant's master will come on an unexpected day and at an unknown hour and will punish the servant severely and assign him a place with the unfaithful. That servant who knew his master's will but did not make preparations nor act in accord with his will shall be beaten severely; and the servant who was ignorant of his master's will but acted in a way deserving of a severe beating shall be beaten only lightly.

Much will be required of the person entrusted with much, and still more will be demanded of the person entrusted with more."]

The Gospel of the Lord. *Praise to you, Lord Jesus Christ.*

PROFESSION OF FAITH *(page 13)*

PRAYER OF THE FAITHFUL

PREPARATION OF GIFTS *(page 16)*

PRAYER OVER THE OFFERINGS
Be pleased, O Lord, to accept the offerings of your Church,
for in your mercy you have given them to be offered
and by your power you transform them
into the mystery of our salvation.
Through Christ our Lord. *Amen.*

⬤ TAKING A CLOSER LOOK ⬤

✠ **Faith** Although today we tend to identify faith as an *intellectual assent* in relation to doctrines, in Jesus' time it was not so narrowly understood. Faith describes the basic trust on which a relationship can be built. It recognizes that the other person is trustworthy and dependable and so can be relied on with confidence. So those who trust in Jesus accept him for what he claims to be and expect him to do what he promises—both heal illness and forgive sins. In the gospels, this basic faith is often contrasted with its opposite, fear, which keeps a relationship from being established or continuing.

PREFACE *(Sundays in Ordinary Time, pages 28–32)*

COMMUNION ANTIPHON *(Psalm 147:12, 14)*

O Jerusalem, glorify the Lord, who gives you your fill of finest wheat.

Or *(Cf. John 6:51)*

The bread that I will give, says the Lord, is my flesh for the life of the world.

PRAYER AFTER COMMUNION

May the communion in your Sacrament
that we have consumed, save us, O Lord,
and confirm us in the light of your truth.
Through Christ our Lord. *Amen.*

BLESSING & DISMISSAL *(page 56)* ✣

• RESPONDING TO THE WORD •

The Jewish Passover was a time of hope for God's rescue from their difficult situation.

❯ *How have I tried to rescue someone from a situation that they thought was hopeless?*

By faith, we trust that God will give us new life just as God has promised.

❯ *How have I encouraged others to trust God more fully?*

Jesus warns us to be vigilant because we never know when he will surprise us with his presence.

❯ *When has Jesus surprised me by his coming?*

August 15

Sing with Mary!

Luke's gospel today beckons us to follow Mary as she eagerly sets out to the beautiful hill country of Judea in service of her cousin Elizabeth. Expectant mothers, both women are filled with the Holy Spirit as they engage in a dialogue of faith that reflects their joy and readiness to serve God's plan of salvation for the world. Mary's Magnificat reveals her deep, prayerful understanding of God's long-awaited promise that is now being fulfilled, to restore all the descendants of Abraham to harmony with God.

So freely and totally did Mary respond to God's grace throughout her life, that in death she was divinely honored. In declaring the dogma of the Assumption, the Church proclaims and celebrates that in Mary there was no obstacle to deny her immediate passing through death and becoming the first after her Son to be raised body and soul to fullness of life with God.

Today's feast of the Assumption of Mary celebrates the summit of her journey as God's most humble and faithful servant. As we reflect on this joyful feast, we realize that she is teaching us to sing the Magnificat with her to the world. We too are invited to proclaim in joy and humble service the compassion and justice of God. Like Mary, in serving the reign of God, we too will one day share in her destiny.

■ **REV. MICHAEL TRAHER, SFM**

MASS DURING THE DAY

ENTRANCE ANTIPHON *(Cf. Revelation 12:1)*

A great sign appeared in heaven: a woman clothed
with the sun, and the moon beneath her feet, and
on her head a crown of twelve stars.

Or

Let us all rejoice in the Lord, as we celebrate the feast day in honor of the Virgin Mary, at whose Assumption the Angels rejoice
and praise the Son of God.

INTRODUCTORY RITES *(page 10)*

COLLECT

Almighty ever-living God,
who assumed the Immaculate Virgin Mary, the Mother of your Son,
body and soul into heavenly glory,
grant, we pray,
that, always attentive to the things that are above,
we may merit to be sharers of her glory.
Through our Lord Jesus Christ, your Son,
who lives and reigns with you in the unity of the Holy Spirit,
one God, for ever and ever. ***Amen.***

FIRST READING *(Revelation 11:19a; 12:1-6a, 10ab)*

God's temple in heaven was opened, and the ark of his covenant could be seen in the temple.

A great sign appeared in the sky, **a woman clothed with the sun,** ✝ with the moon under her feet, and on her head a crown of twelve stars. She was with child and wailed aloud in pain as she labored to give birth. Then another sign appeared in the sky; it was a huge red dragon, with seven heads and ten horns, and on its heads were seven diadems. Its tail swept away a third of the stars in the sky and hurled them down to the earth. Then the dragon stood before the woman about to give birth, to devour her child when she gave birth. She gave birth to a son, a male child, destined to rule all the nations with an iron rod. Her child was caught up to God and his throne. The woman herself fled into the desert where she had a place prepared by God.

Then I heard a loud voice in heaven say:

"Now have salvation and power come,
    and the Kingdom of our God
    and the authority of his Anointed One."

The word of the Lord. *Thanks be to God.*

RESPONSORIAL PSALM *(Psalm 45:10, 11, 12, 16)*

℟ **The queen stands at your right hand, arrayed in gold.**

The queen takes her place at your right hand in gold of Ophir. ℟
Hear, O daughter, and see; turn your ear,
    forget your people and your father's house. ℟
So shall the king desire your beauty;
    for he is your lord. ℟
They are borne in with gladness and joy;
    they enter the palace of the king. ℟

SECOND READING *(1 Corinthians 15:20–27)*

Brothers and sisters: Christ has been raised from the dead, the firstfruits of those who have fallen asleep. For since death came through man, the resurrection of the dead came also through man. For just as in Adam all die, so too in Christ shall all be brought to life, but each one in proper order: Christ the firstfruits;

then, at his coming, those who belong to Christ; then comes the end, when he hands over the Kingdom to his God and Father, when he has destroyed every sovereignty and every authority and power. For he must reign until he has put all his enemies under his feet. The last enemy to be destroyed is death, for "he subjected everything under his feet."

The word of the Lord. *Thanks be to God.*

ALLELUIA

Alleluia, alleluia. Mary is taken up to heaven; a chorus of angels exults. *Alleluia, alleluia.*

GOSPEL *(Luke 1:39–56)*

A reading from the holy Gospel according to Luke.

Glory to you, O Lord.

Mary set out and traveled to the hill country in haste to a town of Judah, where she entered the house of Zechariah* and greeted Elizabeth. When Elizabeth heard Mary's greeting, the infant leaped in her womb, and Elizabeth, filled with the Holy Spirit, cried out in a loud voice and said, "Blessed are you among women, and blessed is the fruit of your womb. And how does this happen to me, that the mother of my Lord should come to me? For at the moment the sound of your greeting reached my ears, the infant in my womb leaped for joy. Blessed are you who believed that what was spoken to you by the Lord would be fulfilled."

And Mary said:

"My soul proclaims the greatness of the Lord;
    my spirit rejoices in God my Savior
    for he has looked with favor on his lowly servant.

From this day all generations will call me blessed:
　　the Almighty has done great things for me
　　and holy is his Name.
He has mercy on those who fear him
　　in every generation.
He has shown the strength of his arm,
　　and has scattered the proud in their conceit.
He has cast down the mighty from their thrones,
　　and has lifted up the lowly.
He has filled the hungry with good things,
　　and the rich he has sent away empty.
He has come to the help of his servant Israel
　　for he has remembered his promise of mercy,
　　the promise he made to our fathers,
　　to Abraham and his children forever."

Mary remained with her about three months and then returned to her home.

The Gospel of the Lord. ***Praise to you, Lord Jesus Christ.***

PROFESSION OF FAITH *(page 13)*

PRAYER OF THE FAITHFUL

PREPARATION OF GIFTS *(page 16)*

PRAYER OVER THE OFFERINGS

May this oblation, our tribute of homage,
rise up to you, O Lord,
and, through the intercession of the most Blessed Virgin Mary,
whom you assumed into heaven,
may our hearts, aflame with the fire of love,

constantly long for you.
Through Christ our Lord. *Amen.*

PREFACE: THE GLORY OF MARY ASSUMED INTO HEAVEN

It is truly right and just, our duty and our salvation,
always and everywhere to give you thanks,
Lord, holy Father, almighty and eternal God,
through Christ our Lord.

For today the Virgin Mother of God
was assumed into heaven
as the beginning and image
of your Church's coming to perfection
and a sign of sure hope and comfort to your pilgrim people;
rightly you would not allow her
to see the corruption of the tomb
since from her own body she marvelously brought forth
your incarnate Son, the Author of all life.

• TAKING A CLOSER LOOK •

✝ **A woman clothed with the sun** Today's reading portrays the conflict between Christ and the power of evil (Satan) through the symbolic conflict of a huge red dragon and a celestial woman clothed with the sun, the moon, and twelve stars. The woman could represent God's people—either as Israel giving birth to the Messiah or as the Church being persecuted by Satan—or Mary, enduring the pain of birth for a son, "who is to rule all the nations" (12:5).

And so, in company with the choirs of Angels,
we praise you, and with joy we proclaim:
Holy, Holy, Holy Lord God of hosts... *(page 35)*

COMMUNION ANTIPHON *(Luke 1:48–49)*
All generations will call me blessed, for he who is mighty has
done great things for me.

PRAYER AFTER COMMUNION
Having received the Sacrament of salvation,
we ask you to grant, O Lord,
that, through the intercession of the Blessed Virgin Mary,
whom you assumed into heaven,
we may be brought to the glory of the resurrection.
Through Christ our Lord. ***Amen.***

SOLEMN BLESSING: THE BLESSED VIRGIN MARY *(Optional, page 62)*

BLESSING & DISMISSAL *(page 56)* ❖

● RESPONDING TO THE WORD ●

The woman at the center of the struggle between good and evil receives God's protection.

➡ *When has God protected me in my struggle with evil?*

Christ has conquered death and is risen to new life.

➡ *How have I experienced this new life recently?*

Mary prays that God's presence will transform our world and reverse the impact of evil and injustice.

➡ *What injustice does God most want me to help change?*

August 18

The road to eternity

Sometimes we hesitate doing what God asks for fear of rejection. Jeremiah gives a clear picture of what can happen when we stand with the Lord. Thrown down a well to die, he is humiliated and persecuted for speaking God's truth to a stubborn, corrupt king. Yet he stays dedicated to what God has asked.

On August 9, 1991, Polish Franciscans Michał Tomaszek and Zbigniew Strzałkowski were killed by Peru's Shining Path guerrillas. They were targeted because of their pastoral work among the people of the Andes. The two friars are now numbered among the great cloud of witnesses, people of faith who gave their lives for the gospel.

In today's gospel, Jesus says he will bring division, not peace. When we face a hostile reaction because for following Jesus, we are challenged to go deeper into the heart of Jesus. How do we contend with the cross of insults, gossip, broken relationships, and family squabbles? The writer of Hebrews says it clearly: look to Jesus, the perfecter of our faith. Jesus presents us blameless before his Father via the furnace of humiliation. This is the road to eternity.

The Holy Spirit provides us the navigating skills and prayer to stay the course. Our suffering has redemptive value in God's economy. If we fully embrace this, we can do all things through Christ.

■ **DENIS GRADY, OFS**

ENTRANCE ANTIPHON *(Psalm 84 [83]:10-11)*

Turn your eyes, O God, our shield; and look on the
face of your anointed one; one day within your courts
is better than a thousand elsewhere.

INTRODUCTORY RITES *(page 10)*

COLLECT

O God, who have prepared for those who love you
good things which no eye can see,
fill our hearts, we pray, with the warmth of your love,
so that, loving you in all things and above all things,
we may attain your promises,
which surpass every human desire.
Through our Lord Jesus Christ, your Son,
who lives and reigns with you in the unity of the Holy Spirit,
one God, for ever and ever. *Amen.*

FIRST READING *(Jeremiah 38:4-6, 8-10)*

In those days, the princes said to the king: "Jeremiah ought
to be put to death; he is demoralizing the soldiers who are
left in this city, and all the people, by speaking such things to
them; he is not interested in the welfare of our people, but in
their ruin." King Zedekiah answered: "He is in your power";
for the king could do nothing with them. And so they took
Jeremiah and threw him into the cistern of Prince Malchiah,
which was in the quarters of the guard, letting him down
with ropes. There was no water in the cistern, only mud, and
Jeremiah sank into the mud.

Ebed-melech,* a court official, went there from the palace
and said to him: "My lord king, these men have been at fault

in all they have done to the prophet Jeremiah, casting him into the cistern. He will die of famine on the spot, for there is no more food in the city." Then the king ordered Ebed-melech the Cushite to take three men along with him, and draw the prophet Jeremiah out of the cistern before he should die.

The word of the Lord. *Thanks be to God.*

RESPONSORIAL PSALM *(Psalm 40:2, 3, 4, 18)*

R Lord, come to my aid!

I have waited, waited for the LORD,
  and he stooped toward me. R
The LORD heard my cry.
He drew me out of the pit of destruction,
  out of the mud of the swamp;
he set my feet upon a crag;
  he made firm my steps. R
And he put a new song into my mouth,
  a hymn to our God.
Many shall look on in awe
  and trust in the LORD. R
Though I am afflicted and poor,
  yet the LORD thinks of me.
You are my help and my deliverer;
  O my God, hold not back! R

SECOND READING *(Hebrews 12:1–4)*

Brothers and sisters: Since we are surrounded by so great a cloud of witnesses, let us rid ourselves of every burden and sin that clings to us and persevere in running the race that lies before us while keeping our eyes fixed on Jesus, the leader and perfecter of faith. For the sake of the joy that lay before him he endured the cross, despising its shame, and has taken his seat at the right of the throne of God. Consider how he endured such opposition from sinners, in order that you may not grow weary and lose heart. In your struggle against sin you have not yet resisted to the point of shedding blood.

The word of the Lord. *Thanks be to God.*

ALLELUIA *(John 10:27)*
Alleluia, alleluia. My sheep hear my voice, says the Lord; I know them, and they follow me. *Alleluia, alleluia.*

GOSPEL *(Luke 12:49–53)*
A reading from the holy Gospel according to Luke.
Glory to you, O Lord.

Jesus said to his disciples: "I have come to set the earth on fire, and how I wish it were already blazing! There is a baptism with which I must be baptized, and how great is my anguish until it is accomplished! Do you think that I have come to establish peace on the earth? No, I tell you, but rather **division.** ✠ From now on a household of five will be divided, three against two and two against three; a father will be divided against his son and a son against his father, a mother against her daughter and a daughter against her mother, a mother-in-law against her daughter-in-law and a daughter-in-law against her mother-in-law."

The Gospel of the Lord. *Praise to you, Lord Jesus Christ.*

PROFESSION OF FAITH *(page 13)*

PRAYER OF THE FAITHFUL

PREPARATION OF GIFTS *(page 16)*

PRAYER OVER THE OFFERINGS

Receive our oblation, O Lord,
by which is brought about a glorious exchange,
that, by offering what you have given,
we may merit to receive your very self.
Through Christ our Lord. *Amen.*

PREFACE *(Sundays in Ordinary Time, pages 28-32)*

• TAKING A CLOSER LOOK •

✚ **Division** The coming of the kingdom of God will bring a time of judgment, and while Jesus' words in today's gospel seem harsh, they are intended to urge us to seriously consider our choices and their consequences. Being Christians requires our loyalty to Jesus Christ, and this loyalty must be honored—over all of our other relationships. Jesus challenges his disciples to take a closer look at where their love and loyalty lies, because his true followers are those who love God above all and are willing to forsake everything for Jesus Christ.

COMMUNION ANTIPHON *(Psalm 130 [129]:7)*
With the Lord there is mercy; in him is plentiful redemption.

Or *(John 6:51–52)*
I am the living bread that came down from heaven, says the Lord. Whoever eats of this bread will live for ever.

PRAYER AFTER COMMUNION
Made partakers of Christ through these Sacraments,
we humbly implore your mercy, Lord,
that, conformed to his image on earth,
we may merit also to be his coheirs in heaven.
Who lives and reigns for ever and ever. *Amen.*

BLESSING & DISMISSAL *(page 56)* ❖

❖ RESPONDING TO THE WORD ❖

The princes of Judah would not accept Jeremiah's message.

➔ *What is Jesus saying to me today that I am having trouble accepting?*

"We are surrounded by so great a cloud of witnesses."

➔ *Who in my life right now is witnessing to the power and goodness of God?*

Jesus tells us his life and message will bring division.

➔ *What side of the divide am I choosing? How do I know?*

August 25

AUG
25

God's loving discipline

My husband and I love our baby girl. Because we love our daughter, we don't always let her get her own way. Instead, we teach our child discipline and reward good behavior. This can be a challenge in a society where children receive too much power without having the emotional and intellectual maturity to go with it.

Children look to their parents to discover who they are and that they are loved. We are God's children and God loves us infinitely more than we can imagine. God is a faithful parent and disciplines us because God wants to heal us. We are called to strive for holiness, to enter through the narrow door. The way to heaven isn't easy, but walking the path is fruitful and worth the effort. The author of the letter to the Hebrews writes that we should not be discouraged or lose hope during God's loving discipline, but rather receive it with the knowledge that it's for our own benefit and healing.

During today's eucharistic celebration, thank the Lord for endlessly loving us. Look to God and talk with God as children speak with their parents. Pray for the wisdom to recognize God's loving discipline and the strength to accept it.

■ **SARAH ESCOBAR**

ENTRANCE ANTIPHON *(Cf. Psalm 86 [85]:1-3)*

Turn your ear, O Lord, and answer me; save the servant who trusts in you, my God. Have mercy on me, O Lord, for I cry to you all the day long.

INTRODUCTORY RITES *(page 10)*

COLLECT

O God, who cause the minds of the faithful
to unite in a single purpose,
grant your people to love what you command
and to desire what you promise,
that, amid the uncertainties of this world,
our hearts may be fixed on that place
where true gladness is found.
Through our Lord Jesus Christ, your Son,
who lives and reigns with you in the unity of the Holy Spirit,
one God, for ever and ever. *Amen.*

FIRST READING *(Isaiah 66:18-21)*

Thus says the LORD: I know their works and their thoughts, and I come to gather nations of every language; they shall come and see my glory. I will set a sign among them; from them I will send fugitives to the nations: to Tarshish,* Put and Lud, Mosoch,* Tubal* and Javan,* to the distant coastlands that have never heard of my fame, or seen my glory; and they shall proclaim my glory among the nations. They shall bring all your brothers and sisters from all the nations as an offering to the LORD, on horses and in chariots, in carts, upon mules and dromedaries, to Jerusalem, my holy mountain, says the LORD, just as the Israelites bring their offering to the house of the LORD in clean vessels. Some of these I will take as priests and Levites,* says the LORD.

The word of the Lord. *Thanks be to God.*

RESPONSORIAL PSALM *(Psalm 117:1, 2)*
℟ **Go out to all the world and tell the Good News.** *Or* **Alleluia.**

Praise the LORD, all you nations;
    glorify him, all you peoples! ℟
For steadfast is his kindness toward us,
    and the fidelity of the LORD endures forever. ℟

SECOND READING *(Hebrews 12:5-7, 11-13)*

Brothers and sisters, You have forgotten the exhortation addressed to you as children: "My son, do not disdain the discipline of the Lord or lose heart when reproved by him; for whom the Lord loves, he disciplines; he scourges every son he acknowledges." Endure your trials as "discipline"; God treats you as sons. For what "son" is there whom his father does not discipline? At the time, all discipline seems a cause not for joy but for pain, yet later it brings the peaceful fruit of righteousness to those who are trained by it.

So strengthen your drooping hands and your weak knees. Make straight paths for your feet, that what is lame may not be disjointed but healed.

The word of the Lord. *Thanks be to God.*

ALLELUIA *(John 14:6)*
Alleluia, alleluia. I am the way, the truth and the life, says the Lord; no one comes to the Father, except through me. *Alleluia, alleluia.*

GOSPEL *(Luke 13:22–30)*

A reading from the holy Gospel according to Luke.
Glory to you, O Lord.

Jesus passed through towns and villages, teaching as he went and making his way to Jerusalem. Someone asked him, "Lord, will only a few people be saved?" He answered them, "Strive to enter through the narrow gate, for many, I tell you, will attempt to enter but will not be strong enough. After the master of the house has arisen and locked the door, then will you stand outside knocking and saying, 'Lord, open the door for us.' He will say to you in reply, 'I do not know where you are from.' And you will say, 'We ate and drank in your company and you taught in our streets.' Then he will say to you, 'I do not know where you are from. Depart from me, all you evildoers!' And there will be wailing and grinding of teeth when you see Abraham, Isaac, and Jacob and all the prophets in the **kingdom of God**✝ and you yourselves cast out. And people will come from the east and the west and from the north and the south and will recline at table in the kingdom of God. For behold, some are last who will be first, and some are first who will be last."

The Gospel of the Lord. *Praise to you, Lord Jesus Christ.*

PROFESSION OF FAITH *(page 13)*

PRAYER OF THE FAITHFUL

PREPARATION OF GIFTS *(page 16)*

PRAYER OVER THE OFFERINGS

O Lord, who gained for yourself a people by adoption
through the one sacrifice offered once for all,
bestow graciously on us, we pray,
the gifts of unity and peace in your Church.
Through Christ our Lord. *Amen.*

PREFACE *(Sundays in Ordinary Time, pages 28–32)*

COMMUNION ANTIPHON *(Cf. Psalm 104 [103]:13–15)*

The earth is replete with the fruits of your work, O Lord; you
bring forth bread from the earth and wine to cheer the heart.

Or *(Cf. John 6:54)*

Whoever eats my flesh and drinks my blood has eternal life, says
the Lord, and I will raise him up on the last day.

⸻ ✦ TAKING A CLOSER LOOK ✦ ⸻

✦ **Kingdom of God** In his teaching and preaching, Jesus
identifies God's ideal community as the kingdom of God—both
the *place* where God rules and the *people* who live as God desires.
This community is to be characterized by a new way of living
together that includes everyone (both Jew and Gentile) who, as
brothers and sisters, will relate to God as their Father and as their
King, whose benevolent rule over them guides every moment of
their lives. The kingdom is inaugurated by Jesus and continues
today in the Christian community that daily strives to make God's
ideal of community a reality.

PRAYER AFTER COMMUNION

Complete within us, O Lord, we pray,
the healing work of your mercy
and graciously perfect and sustain us,
so that in all things we may please you.
Through Christ our Lord. *Amen.*

BLESSING & DISMISSAL *(page 56)* ❖

❖ RESPONDING TO THE WORD ❖

God gathers all nations together so they might worship.	God gives us the strength to endure our trials.	Those who act rightly learn to know Jesus and will recline with him in the kingdom of God.
➲ *Who might I invite to worship with me this week?*	➲ *How has God helped me endure my trials?*	➲ *What am I doing to increase my knowledge of Jesus and share it with others?*

September 1

Move away from self-centeredness!

In bookstores today, shelves are lined with titles on self-improvement, building self-esteem and assertiveness skills, and how to win. Smartphones put the world at our fingertips. We get impatient when we don't immediately get what we want or have to wait in line. Jesus says that in his kingdom the last will be first and those who pushed their way to the front will be relegated to the cheap seats.

Jesus is radical in his challenge as he faces the power-brokers of his time. Put others ahead of yourself and reach out to those who can't necessarily reciprocate. As I try to apply this teaching, I realize it's asking a lot of me.

How I operate socially and whom I invite to dinner indicate the type of person I am. How I move from self-centeredness to being other-centered is a challenge. As my relationship with God grows, I realize God loves me. I am developing a healthier acceptance of my strengths and limitations. At this Eucharist I give thanks that God dwells within me. I don't need to be first in line; I don't need the best seat in the house. The knowledge that God loves me unconditionally allows me to let others cut in front without my getting upset.

◼ **GERRI SOBIE**

ENTRANCE ANTIPHON *(Cf. Psalm 86 [85]:3, 5)*

Have mercy on me, O Lord, for I cry to you all the day long.
O Lord, you are good and forgiving, full of mercy to all who
call to you.

INTRODUCTORY RITES *(page 10)*

COLLECT

God of might, giver of every good gift,
put into our hearts the love of your name,
so that, by deepening our sense of reverence,
you may nurture in us what is good
and, by your watchful care,
keep safe what you have nurtured.
Through our Lord Jesus Christ, your Son,
who lives and reigns with you in the unity of the Holy Spirit,
one God, for ever and ever. *Amen.*

FIRST READING *(Sirach 3:17-18, 20, 28-29)*

My child, conduct your affairs with humility,
and you will be loved more than a giver of gifts.
Humble yourself the more, the greater you are,
    and you will find favor with God.
What is too sublime for you, seek not,
    into things beyond your strength search not.
The mind of a sage appreciates proverbs,
    and an attentive ear is the joy of the wise.
Water quenches a flaming fire,
    and alms atone for sins.

The word of the Lord. *Thanks be to God.*

RESPONSORIAL PSALM *(Psalm 68:4-5, 6-7, 10-11)*

℞ **God, in your goodness, you have made a home for the poor.**

The just rejoice and exult before God;
    they are glad and rejoice.
Sing to God, chant praise to his name;
    whose name is the LORD. ℞

The father of orphans and the defender of widows
    is God in his holy dwelling.
God gives a home to the forsaken;
    he leads forth prisoners to prosperity. ℞

A bountiful rain you showered down, O God, upon your
    inheritance;
    you restored the land when it languished;
your flock settled in it;
    in your goodness, O God, you provided it for the needy. ℞

SECOND READING *(Hebrews 12:18-19, 22-24a)*

Brothers and sisters: You have not approached that which
could be touched and a blazing fire and gloomy darkness
and storm and a trumpet blast and a voice speaking words such
that those who heard begged that no message be further addressed to them. No, you have approached Mount Zion* and
the city of the living God, the heavenly Jerusalem, and countless angels in festal gathering, and the assembly of the firstborn
enrolled in heaven, and God the judge of all, and the spirits of
the just made perfect, and Jesus, the mediator of a new covenant,
and the sprinkled blood that speaks more eloquently than that
of Abel.

The word of the Lord. *Thanks be to God.*

ALLELUIA *(Matthew 11:29ab)*
Alleluia, alleluia. Take my yoke upon you, says the Lord, and learn from me, for I am meek and humble of heart. *Alleluia, alleluia.*

GOSPEL *(Luke 14:1, 7-14)*
A reading from the holy Gospel according to Luke.
Glory to you, O Lord.

On a sabbath Jesus went to dine at the home of one of the leading Pharisees, and the people there were observing him carefully.

He told a parable to those who had been invited, noticing how they were choosing the places of honor at the table. "When you are invited by someone to a wedding banquet, do not recline at table in the place of honor. A more distinguished guest than you may have been invited by him, and the host who invited both of you may approach you and say, 'Give your place to this man,' and then you would proceed with embarrassment to take the lowest place. Rather, when you are invited, go and take the lowest place so that when the host comes to you he may say, 'My friend, move up to a higher position.' Then you will enjoy the esteem of your companions at the table. For every one who exalts himself will be humbled, but the one who humbles himself will be exalted." Then he said to the host who invited him, "When you hold a lunch or a dinner, **do not invite your friends**✝ or your brothers or your relatives or your wealthy neighbors, in case they may invite you back and you have repayment. Rather, when you hold a banquet, invite the poor, the crippled, the lame, the blind; blessed indeed will you be because of their inability to repay you. For you will be repaid at the resurrection of the righteous."

The Gospel of the Lord. *Praise to you, Lord Jesus Christ.*

PROFESSION OF FAITH *(page 13)*

PRAYER OF THE FAITHFUL

PREPARATION OF GIFTS *(page 16)*

PRAYER OVER THE OFFERINGS
May this sacred offering, O Lord,
confer on us always the blessing of salvation,
that what it celebrates in mystery
it may accomplish in power.
Through Christ our Lord. *Amen.*

PREFACE *(Sundays in Ordinary Time, pages 28–32)*

❖ TAKING A CLOSER LOOK ❖

✛ **Do not invite your friends** The teaching on table fellowship serves as a practical application of the parable of the great supper, which follows it. It speaks both specifically to the exclusivity of the Pharisees and generally to the ethic of reciprocity widely accepted in their world. The maimed, the lame, and the blind were excluded from worship at the Jewish temple and thus would have also been unacceptable dinner guests for the Pharisees. Moreover, none of those mentioned would have been able to repay hospitality in kind. Jesus' challenge to inclusiveness at the Christian eucharistic banquet was a challenge for the early Church (James 2:2-4; Romans 12:16) and remains just as much a challenge today.

COMMUNION ANTIPHON *(Psalm 31 [30]:20)*

How great is the goodness, Lord, that you keep for those who fear you.

Or *(Matthew 5:9–10)*

Blessed are the peacemakers, for they shall be called children of God. Blessed are they who are persecuted for the sake of righteousness, for theirs is the Kingdom of Heaven.

PRAYER AFTER COMMUNION

Renewed by this bread from the heavenly table,
we beseech you, Lord,
that, being the food of charity,
it may confirm our hearts
and stir us to serve you in our neighbor.
Through Christ our Lord. *Amen.*

BLESSING & DISMISSAL *(page 56)* ✢

• RESPONDING TO THE WORD •

Sirach encourages us to be content with our limits and strive to act humbly instead of being arrogant.

➡ *What tends to make me think more of myself and act in a haughty way toward others?*

God no longer appears amidst the fire, thunder, and great signs as on Mt. Sinai.

➡ *What gentle (or not so gentle) signs has God used to get my attention?*

Jesus urges us to break out of our small circle of friends to help those who might be neglected.

➡ *How can I reach out to help the poor, the sick, or the lonely who cannot repay me?*

September 8

SEP
8

Are we up to the challenge?

Following God is not a task for the fainthearted. The first reading and the responsorial psalm are powerful reminders of the greatness of God and the wonder of God's plans. Taking on the larger-than-life task of submitting to God's ways will challenge us. Jesus reminds his followers, and Paul echoes these sentiments from behind bars, that discipleship makes tough demands (such as giving up all your possessions).

Why then should we follow God? Will life not be easier if we follow our own desires or only commit ourselves half-heartedly to Christianity (becoming the proverbial cafeteria Catholic)? The reason most people attempt anything challenging is because of the results. An athlete sacrifices and trains for better performance; a student reads, writes, and reviews consistently to obtain desirable grades. So too, following God will produce greater results than anything else we commit ourselves to.

The result of following God is everlasting life. Our lives are perishable. We return to dust, but God has promised to restore and perfect the life we originally received. Christ came to show us that our earthly lifespan does not have to be all we know. God has prepared something so much better: eternal paradise, for us to enjoy without end.

■ ANDREW HUME

ENTRANCE ANTIPHON *(Psalm 119 [118]:137, 124)*

You are just, O Lord, and your judgment is right; treat your servant in accord with your merciful love.

INTRODUCTORY RITES *(page 10)*

COLLECT

O God, by whom we are redeemed and receive adoption,
look graciously upon your beloved sons and daughters,
that those who believe in Christ
may receive true freedom
and an everlasting inheritance.
Through our Lord Jesus Christ, your Son,
who lives and reigns with you in the unity of the Holy Spirit,
one God, for ever and ever. ***Amen.***

FIRST READING *(Wisdom 9:13–18b)*

Who can know God's counsel,
or who can conceive what the LORD intends?
For the deliberations of mortals are timid,
and unsure are our plans.
For the corruptible body burdens the soul
and the earthen shelter weighs down the mind
that has many concerns.
And scarce do we guess the things on earth,
and what is within our grasp we find with difficulty;
but when things are in heaven, who can search them out?
Or who ever knew your counsel, except you had given wisdom
and sent your holy spirit from on high?
And thus were the paths of those on earth made straight.

The word of the Lord. ***Thanks be to God.***

RESPONSORIAL PSALM *(Psalm 90:3-4, 5-6, 12-13, 14 and 17)*
℟ **In every age, O Lord, you have been our refuge.**

You turn man back to dust,
    saying, "Return, O children of men."
For a thousand years in your sight
    are as yesterday, now that it is past,
    or as a watch of the night. ℟

You make an end of them in their sleep;
    the next morning they are like the changing grass,
Which at dawn springs up anew,
    but by evening wilts and fades. ℟

Teach us to number our days aright,
    that we may gain wisdom of heart.
Return, O LORD! How long?
    Have pity on your servants! ℟

Fill us at daybreak with your kindness,
    that we may shout for joy and gladness all our days.
And may the gracious care of the Lord our God be ours;
    prosper the work of our hands for us!
    Prosper the work of our hands! ℟

SECOND READING *(Philemon 9-10, 12-17)*

I, Paul, an old man, and now also a prisoner for Christ Jesus, urge you on behalf of my child **Onesimus**,✝* whose father I have become in my imprisonment; I am sending him, that is, my own heart, back to you. I should have liked to retain him for myself, so that he might serve me on your behalf in my imprisonment for the gospel, but I did not want to do anything without your consent, so that the good you do might not be forced but voluntary. Perhaps this is why he was away from you for a while, that you might have him back forever, no longer as a slave but more than a slave, a brother, beloved especially to me, but even more so to you, as a man and in the Lord. So if you regard me as a partner, welcome him as you would me.

The word of the Lord. *Thanks be to God.*

ALLELUIA *(Psalm 119:135)*
Alleluia, alleluia. Let your face shine upon your servant; and teach me your laws. *Alleluia, alleluia.*

GOSPEL *(Luke 14:25-33)*
A reading from the holy Gospel according to Luke.
Glory to you, O Lord.

Great crowds were traveling with Jesus, and he turned and addressed them, "If anyone comes to me without hating his father and mother, wife and children, brothers and sisters, and even his own life, he cannot be my disciple. Whoever does not carry his own cross and come after me cannot be my disciple. Which of you wishing to construct a tower does not first sit down and calculate the cost to see if there is enough for its completion? Otherwise, after laying the foundation and finding himself unable to finish the work the onlookers should laugh at him and say, 'This one began to build but did not have the resources to finish.' Or what king marching into battle would not first sit down and decide whether with ten thousand troops he can successfully oppose another king advancing upon him with twenty thousand troops? But if not, while he is still far away, he will send a delegation to ask for peace terms. In the same way, anyone of you who does not renounce all his possessions cannot be my disciple."

The Gospel of the Lord. *Praise to you, Lord Jesus Christ.*

PROFESSION OF FAITH *(page 13)*

PRAYER OF THE FAITHFUL

PREPARATION OF GIFTS *(page 16)*

PRAYER OVER THE OFFERINGS
O God, who give us the gift of true prayer and of peace,
graciously grant that, through this offering,
we may do fitting homage to your divine majesty
and, by partaking of the sacred mystery,
we may be faithfully united in mind and heart.
Through Christ our Lord. *Amen.*

PREFACE *(Sundays in Ordinary Time, pages 28–32)*

❖ TAKING A CLOSER LOOK ❖

✝ **Onesimus** Onesimus was a runaway slave whom Paul converted to Christianity. Paul knew his owner, Philemon, who was also an earlier convert of Paul's in Colossae, in whose home the local congregation now meets. Since the penalties for runaway slaves were severe, Paul writes to Philemon about returning the slave and making himself responsible for all damages due the owner. But playing with the slave's name Onesimus (which means "useful, beneficial"), Paul points out that the slave is now useful to both of them and asks for Philemon's generosity because the slave is now a "beloved brother" of his master as a Christian.

COMMUNION ANTIPHON *(Cf. Psalm 42 [41]:2-3)*

Like the deer that yearns for running streams, so my soul is yearning for you, my God; my soul is thirsting for God, the living God.

Or *(John 8:12)*

I am the light of the world, says the Lord; whoever follows me will not walk in darkness, but will have the light of life.

PRAYER AFTER COMMUNION

Grant that your faithful, O Lord,
whom you nourish and endow with life
through the food of your Word and heavenly Sacrament,
may so benefit from your beloved Son's great gifts
that we may merit an eternal share in his life.
Who lives and reigns for ever and ever. *Amen.*

BLESSING & DISMISSAL *(page 56)* ❖

❖ RESPONDING TO THE WORD ❖

Without God's help, our minds, no matter how sharp, always fall short of understanding God's ways and plans.

➲ *What help do I most need from God today?*

Paul would like to hold on to Onesimus but knows he must send him back to his master.

➲ *What makes me want to hold on tightly to persons I need to let go of?*

Jesus demands that we not let our family or possessions or crosses alter our dedication to him.

➲ *What is my most persistent challenge in trying to follow Jesus more closely?*

September 15

**SEP
15**

How will we answer God's call?

Today's readings remind us of the boundlessness of God's mercy. In our flawed humanity, we continually stray from the path we know leads to eternal life. But God's compassion and forgiveness are much stronger than God's justifiable anger. God never gives up on us.

The first reading speaks of the Israelites turning from God to worship a golden calf, a difficult image to relate to. Yet, we are bombarded daily with calls urging us to acquire more superficial possessions. New cars, bigger homes, clothing, jewels, gadgets—each one is a contemporary "golden calf." How easy it is to succumb to the media's temptations! Yet, God calls us, in the silence of our hearts, to forsake these false gods and return to God. God's tenderness and mercy are always ours for the asking.

Luke's gospel focuses on the pain of loss and the rejoicing that follows its reversal. The most powerful element in this passage is the story of the prodigal son. As we hear it, perhaps we recognize ourselves in the son who abandoned home and family in favor of reckless living. Perhaps we identify with the elder son's discontent and envy when his father warmly welcomes his brother home. Perhaps we relate to both.

Heavenly Father, give us the grace to answer the call to share in your love, mercy, and forgiveness.

▇ **BARBARA D'ARTOIS**

ENTRANCE ANTIPHON *(Cf. Sirach 36:18)*

Give peace, O Lord, to those who wait for you, that your prophets be found true. Hear the prayers of your servant, and of your people Israel.

INTRODUCTORY RITES *(page 10)*

COLLECT

Look upon us, O God,
Creator and ruler of all things,
and, that we may feel the working of your mercy,
grant that we may serve you with all our heart.
Through our Lord Jesus Christ, your Son,
who lives and reigns with you in the unity of the Holy Spirit,
one God, for ever and ever. *Amen.*

FIRST READING *(Exodus 32:7-11, 13-14)*

The LORD said to Moses, "Go down at once to your people, whom you brought out of the land of Egypt, for they have become depraved. They have soon turned aside from the way I pointed out to them, making for themselves a molten calf and worshiping it, sacrificing to it and crying out, 'This is your God, O Israel, who brought you out of the land of Egypt!' I see how stiff-necked this people is," continued the LORD to Moses. "Let me alone, then, that my wrath may blaze up against them to consume them. Then I will make of you a great nation."

But Moses implored the LORD, his God, saying, "Why, O LORD, should your wrath blaze up against your own people, whom you brought out of the land of Egypt with such great power and with so strong a hand? Remember your servants Abraham, Isaac, and Israel, and how you swore to them by your own self, saying, 'I will make your descendants as numerous as the stars in the sky; and all this land that I promised, I will give your descendants as their perpetual heritage.'" So the LORD relented in the punishment he had threatened to inflict on his people.

The word of the Lord. *Thanks be to God.*

RESPONSORIAL PSALM (Psalm 51:3–4, 12–13, 17, 19)
R̸ **I will rise and go to my father.**

Have mercy on me, O God, in your goodness;
   in the greatness of your compassion wipe out my offense.
Thoroughly wash me from my guilt
   and of my sin cleanse me. R̸
A clean heart create for me, O God,
   and a steadfast spirit renew within me.
Cast me not out from your presence,
   and your Holy Spirit take not from me. R̸
O Lord, open my lips,
   and my mouth shall proclaim your praise.
My sacrifice, O God, is a contrite spirit;
   a heart contrite and humbled, O God, you will not spurn. R̸

SECOND READING (1 Timothy 1:12–17)

Beloved: I am grateful to him who has strengthened me, Christ Jesus our Lord, because he considered me trustworthy in appointing me to the ministry. I was once a blasphemer and a persecutor and arrogant, but I have been mercifully treated because I acted out of ignorance in my unbelief. Indeed, the grace of our Lord has been abundant, along with the faith and love that are in Christ Jesus. This saying is trustworthy and deserves full acceptance: Christ Jesus came into the world to save sinners. Of these I am the foremost. But for that reason I was mercifully treated, so that in me, as the foremost, Christ Jesus might display all his patience as an example for those who would come to believe in him for everlasting life. To the king of ages, incorruptible, invisible, the only God, honor and glory forever and ever. Amen.

The word of the Lord. *Thanks be to God.*

ALLELUIA *(2 Corinthians 5:19)*
Alleluia, alleluia. God was reconciling the world to himself in Christ and entrusting to us the message of reconciliation. *Alleluia, alleluia.*

GOSPEL *(Luke 15:1-32 or 15:1-10)*
The shorter version ends at the asterisks.

A reading from the holy Gospel according to Luke.
Glory to you, O Lord.

Tax collectors and sinners✝ were all drawing near to listen to Jesus, but the Pharisees and scribes began to complain, saying, "This man welcomes sinners and eats with them." So to them he addressed this parable. "What man among you having a hundred sheep and losing one of them would not leave the ninety-nine in the desert and go after the lost one until he finds it? And when he does find it, he sets it on his shoulders with great joy and, upon his arrival home, he calls together his friends and neighbors and says to them, 'Rejoice with me because I have found my lost sheep.' I tell you, in just the same way there will be more joy in heaven over one sinner who repents than over ninety-nine righteous people who have no need of repentance.

"Or what woman having ten coins and losing one would not light a lamp and sweep the house, searching carefully until she finds it? And when she does find it, she calls together her friends and neighbors and says to them, 'Rejoice with me because I have found the coin that I lost.' In just the same way, I tell you, there will be rejoicing among the angels of God over one sinner who repents."

* * *

Then he said, "A man had two sons, and the younger son said to his father, 'Father give me the share of your estate that should come to me.' So the father divided the property between them. After a few days, the younger son collected all his belongings and set off to a distant country where he squandered his inheritance on a life of dissipation. When he had freely spent everything, a severe famine struck that country, and he found himself in dire need. So he hired himself out to one of the local citizens who sent him to his farm to tend the swine. And he longed to eat his fill of the pods on which the swine fed, but nobody gave him any. Coming to his senses he thought, 'How many of my father's hired workers have more than enough food to eat, but here am I, dying from hunger. I shall get up and go to my father and I shall say to him, "Father, I have sinned against heaven and against you. I no longer deserve to be called your son; treat me as you would treat one of your hired workers.'" So he got up and went back to his father. While he was still a long way off, his father caught sight of him, and was filled with compassion. He ran to his son, embraced him and kissed him. His son said to him, 'Father, I have sinned against heaven and against you; I no longer deserve to be called your son.' But his father ordered his servants, 'Quickly bring the finest robe and put it on him; put a ring on his finger and sandals on his feet. Take the fattened calf and slaughter it. Then let us celebrate with a feast, because this son of mine was dead, and has come to life again; he was lost, and has been found.' Then the celebration began. Now the older son had been out in the field and, on his way back, as he neared the house, he heard the sound of music and dancing. He called one of the servants and asked what this might mean. The servant said to him,

'Your brother has returned and your father has slaughtered the fattened calf because he has him back safe and sound.' He became angry, and when he refused to enter the house, his father came out and pleaded with him. He said to his father in reply, 'Look, all these years I served you and not once did I disobey your orders; yet you never gave me even a young goat to feast on with my friends. But when your son returns, who swallowed up your property with prostitutes, for him you slaughter the fattened calf.' He said to him, 'My son, you are here with me always; everything I have is yours. But now we must celebrate and rejoice, because your brother was dead and has come to life again; he was lost and has been found.'"

The Gospel of the Lord. *Praise to you, Lord Jesus Christ.*

PROFESSION OF FAITH *(page 13)*

PRAYER OF THE FAITHFUL

PREPARATION OF GIFTS *(page 16)*

PRAYER OVER THE OFFERINGS
Look with favor on our supplications, O Lord,
and in your kindness accept these, your servants' offerings,

• TAKING A CLOSER LOOK •

✝ **Tax collectors and sinners** In Jesus' time, Rome sold the right to collect taxes to the highest bidder, who could charge whatever he wished in order to collect the tax and make a profit. The tax collector, viewed as an extortioner and traitor, was an outcast to his fellow Jews. Sinners were both those who led immoral lives and those whose occupations deliberately transgressed the laws of God—like tax collectors. Jesus turns this thinking around by noting God's unchanging love toward the sinner, for whom the proper response is a conversion of heart.

that what each has offered to the honor of your name
may serve the salvation of all.
Through Christ our Lord. *Amen.*

PREFACE *(Sundays in Ordinary Time, pages 28–32)*

COMMUNION ANTIPHON *(Cf. Psalm 36 [35]:8)*
How precious is your mercy, O God! The children of men seek
shelter in the shadow of your wings.

Or *(Cf. 1 Corinthians 10:16)*
The chalice of blessing that we bless is a communion in the
Blood of Christ; and the bread that we break is a sharing in the
Body of the Lord.

PRAYER AFTER COMMUNION
May the working of this heavenly gift, O Lord, we pray,
take possession of our minds and bodies,
so that its effects, and not our own desires,
may always prevail in us.
Through Christ our Lord. *Amen.*

BLESSING & DISMISSAL *(page 56)* ❖

❖ RESPONDING TO THE WORD ❖

The Israelites worship a golden calf instead of the God they cannot see.	Paul knows that he has been treated mercifully despite his sinfulness.	Jesus searches out those who are lost and need help.
➡ *To what do I give my attention that lures me away from God?*	➡ *How have I shown mercy to others as God did to Paul?*	➡ *How can I be part of finding and helping those who are lost and in need of help today?*

September 22

How do we use God's gifts?

What does it mean to serve God? In today's gospel, the dishonest manager has taken his position for granted. He has been using what belongs to the master to enrich himself and has been caught. Even more than the loss of his stewardship, he fears becoming an outcast. So he for once deals honestly with his neighbors, charging them only what they owe and not extra to line his own pockets. He thus regains his master's favor.

In this story, the master is God and we are the managers of his property. God is the opposite of a self-interested master. God's unfathomable love for us means that God is dedicated to our well-being, showering us with gifts to help us have the ultimate gift: an eternal home with God in heaven. Heaven is not guaranteed; we, like the manager, will have to account for the way we have used God's gifts.

However, we see in the parable that the manager is forgiven the moment he puts his master first, never mind all of the times he ignored him. It is not too late to make sure that we are serving the master we wish to serve. To serve God faithfully with the gifts we have been given means doing our utmost to emulate God's selfless, merciful love.

■ KATE LARSON

ENTRANCE ANTIPHON

I am the salvation of the people, says the Lord.
Should they cry to me in any distress, I will hear
them, and I will be their Lord for ever.

INTRODUCTORY RITES *(page 10)*

COLLECT

O God, who founded all the commands of your sacred Law
upon love of you and of our neighbor,
grant that, by keeping your precepts,
we may merit to attain eternal life.
Through our Lord Jesus Christ, your Son,
who lives and reigns with you in the unity of the Holy Spirit,
one God, for ever and ever. *Amen.*

FIRST READING *(Amos 8:4–7)*

Hear this, you who trample upon the needy
and destroy the poor of the land!
"When will the new moon be over," you ask,
  "that we may sell our grain,
    and the sabbath, that we may display the wheat?
We will diminish the **ephah**,*✝
    add to the **shekel**,✝
    and fix our scales for cheating!
We will buy the lowly for silver,
    and the poor for a pair of sandals;
    even the refuse of the wheat we will sell!"
The LORD has sworn by the pride of Jacob:
    Never will I forget a thing they have done!

The word of the Lord. *Thanks be to God.*

RESPONSORIAL PSALM *(Psalm 113:1-2, 4-6, 7-8)*

R̲ **Praise the Lord who lifts up the poor.** *Or* **Alleluia.**

Praise, you servants of the LORD,
  praise the name of the LORD.
Blessed be the name of the LORD
  both now and forever. R̲
High above all nations is the LORD;
  above the heavens is his glory.
Who is like the LORD, our God, who is enthroned on high
  and looks upon the heavens and the earth below? R̲
He raises up the lowly from the dust;
  from the dunghill he lifts up the poor
to seat them with princes,
  with the princes of his own people. R̲

SECOND READING *(1 Timothy 2:1-8)*

Beloved: First of all, I ask that supplications, prayers, petitions, and thanksgivings be offered for everyone, for kings and for all in authority, that we may lead a quiet and tranquil life in all devotion and dignity. This is good and pleasing to God our savior, who wills everyone to be saved and to come to knowledge of the truth.

  For there is one God.
  There is also one mediator between God and men,
  the man Christ Jesus,
  who gave himself as ransom for all.
This was the testimony at the proper time. For this I was appointed preacher and apostle—I am speaking the truth, I am not lying—, teacher of the Gentiles in faith and truth.

It is my wish, then, that in every place the men should pray, lifting up holy hands, without anger or argument.

The word of the Lord. *Thanks be to God.*

ALLELUIA *(See 2 Corinthians 8:9)*
Alleluia, alleluia. Though our Lord Jesus Christ was rich, he became poor, so that by his poverty you might become rich. *Alleluia, alleluia.*

GOSPEL *(Luke 16:1–13 or 16:10–13)*
The shorter version begins at the asterisks.

A reading from the holy Gospel according to Luke.
Glory to you, O Lord.
Jesus said to his disciples, "A rich man had a steward who was reported to him for squandering his property. He summoned him and said, 'What is this I hear about you? Prepare a full account of your stewardship, because you can no longer be my steward.' The steward said to himself, 'What shall I do, now that my master is taking the position of steward away from me? I am not strong enough to dig and I am ashamed to beg. I know what I shall do so that, when I am removed from the stewardship, they may welcome me into their homes.' He called in his master's debtors one by one. To the first he said, 'How much do you owe my master?' He replied, 'One hundred measures of olive oil.' He said to him, 'Here is your promissory note. Sit down and quickly write one for fifty.' Then to another the steward said, 'And you, how much do you owe?' He replied, 'One hundred kors of wheat.' The steward said to him, 'Here is your promissory note; write one for eighty.' And the master commended that dishonest steward for acting prudently. "For

the children of this world are more prudent in dealing with their own generation than are the children of light. I tell you, make friends for yourselves with dishonest wealth, so that when it fails, you will be welcomed into eternal dwellings."

* * *

(Jesus said to his disciples:) "The person who is trustworthy in very small matters is also trustworthy in great ones; and the person who is dishonest in very small matters is also dishonest in great ones. If, therefore, you are not trustworthy with dishonest wealth, who will trust you with true wealth? If you are not trustworthy with what belongs to another, who will give you what is yours? No servant can serve two masters. He will either hate one and love the other, or be devoted to one and despise the other. You cannot serve both God and mammon."

The Gospel of the Lord. *Praise to you, Lord Jesus Christ.*

PROFESSION OF FAITH *(page 13)*

PRAYER OF THE FAITHFUL

PREPARATION OF GIFTS *(page 16)*

PRAYER OVER THE OFFERINGS

Receive with favor, O Lord, we pray,
the offerings of your people,
that what they profess with devotion and faith
may be theirs through these heavenly mysteries.
Through Christ our Lord. *Amen.*

PREFACE *(Sundays in Ordinary Time, pages 28–33)*

COMMUNION ANTIPHON *(Psalm 119 [118]:4-5)*

You have laid down your precepts to be carefully kept; may my
ways be firm in keeping your statutes.

Or *(John 10:14)*

I am the Good Shepherd, says the Lord; I know my sheep, and
mine know me.

• TAKING A CLOSER LOOK •

✚ **Ephah and shekel** These two words act as a summary of the bartering system that relied on weighing the proper amounts for payment by using balances. The ephah measured the dry capacity for grain or flour (roughly two-thirds of a bushel), and the shekel was the most common basic monetary unit. Driven by their greed, businessmen could use deliberately false or inaccurate weights (for example, made by chiseling out the undersurface or using two similar looking but different weights) to defraud the unsuspecting.

PRAYER AFTER COMMUNION

Graciously raise up, O Lord,
those you renew with this Sacrament,
that we may come to possess your redemption
both in mystery and in the manner of our life.
Through Christ our Lord. *Amen.*

BLESSING & DISMISSAL *(page 56)* ✛

● RESPONDING TO THE WORD ●

Amos is incensed at the greed of the rich who exploit the poor.	Paul encourages us to pray for those in authority.	Jesus knows that honesty and trustworthiness are shown first in little things.
◗ *How can I help to work for or to vote for policies that will help the poor and stop their exploitation?*	◗ *What prayers do I want to pray for both Church and secular leaders?*	◗ *What tempts me to be dishonest or untrustworthy at home or at work?*

September 29

SEP
29

Overcoming temptation

Earthly riches can weaken our ability to see and understand the suffering of others. Today's gospel offers a proud rich man whose spiritual awareness is closed to the needs of the poor man, Lazarus. While the two men should be dependent on each other for help, the rich man has become locked in a life of ease. For all the good he might have done, the rich man's love of money made him morally unresponsive.

In this parable, Jesus makes it clear that we have the spiritual help we need to resist the temptation of pride. There are the words of the prophet Amos warning that wealth tempts people to think only of themselves. More importantly, through the Ten Commandments we are directed to respond righteously to others, especially the poor. Not surprisingly, then, Father Abraham rebukes the rich man with the powerful truth, telling him these spiritual laws and instructions are the firm basis on which to seek salvation.

Fortunately, Jesus offers a parable that shows being merciful and loving can help us overcome temptation. Indeed, reflecting on God's divine love for us is the best place to start. To reduce the suffering of others by our acts of compassion is a fitting response to God's splendid gift.

◾ **ROBERT O'DACRE**

ENTRANCE ANTIPHON *(Deuteronomy 3:31, 29, 30, 43, 42)*

All that you have done to us, O Lord, you have done with true judgment, for we have sinned against you and not obeyed your commandments. But give glory to your name and deal with us according to the bounty of your mercy.

INTRODUCTORY RITES *(page 10)*

COLLECT

O God, who manifest your almighty power
above all by pardoning and showing mercy,
bestow, we pray, your grace abundantly upon us
and make those hastening to attain your promises
heirs to the treasures of heaven.
Through our Lord Jesus Christ, your Son,
who lives and reigns with you in the unity of the Holy Spirit,
one God, for ever and ever. *Amen.*

FIRST READING *(Amos 6:1a, 4-7)*

Thus says the LORD the God of hosts:
   Woe to the complacent in Zion!*
Lying upon beds of ivory,
   stretched comfortably on their couches,
they eat lambs taken from the flock,
   and calves from the stall!
Improvising to the music of the harp,
   like David, they devise their own accompaniment.
They drink wine from bowls
   and anoint themselves with the best oils;
   yet they are not made ill by the collapse of Joseph!

Therefore, now they shall be the first to go into exile,
and their wanton revelry shall be done away with.

The word of the Lord. ***Thanks be to God.***

RESPONSORIAL PSALM *(Psalm 146:7, 8-9, 9-10)*
℟ Praise the Lord, my soul! *Or* **Alleluia.**

Blessed he who keeps faith forever,
secures justice for the oppressed,
gives food to the hungry.
The LORD sets captives free. **℟**
The LORD gives sight to the blind.
The LORD raises up those who were bowed down.
The LORD loves the just;
the LORD protects strangers. **℟**
The fatherless and the widow he sustains,
but the way of the wicked he thwarts.
The LORD shall reign forever;
your God, O Zion,* through all generations. Alleluia. **℟**

SECOND READING *(1 Timothy 6:11-16)*

But you, man of God, pursue righteousness, devotion, faith,
love, patience, and gentleness. Compete well for the faith.
Lay hold of eternal life, to which you were called when you made
the noble confession in the presence of many witnesses. I charge
you before God, who gives life to all things, and before Christ
Jesus, who gave testimony under Pontius Pilate for the noble
confession, to keep the commandment without stain or reproach
until the appearance of our Lord Jesus Christ that the blessed
and only ruler will make manifest at the proper time, the King of
kings and Lord of lords, who alone has immortality, who dwells

in unapproachable light, and whom no human being has seen or can see. To him be honor and eternal power. Amen.

The word of the Lord. *Thanks be to God.*

ALLELUIA *(See 2 Corinthians 8:9)*
Alleluia, alleluia. Though our Lord Jesus Christ was rich, he became poor, so that by his poverty you might become rich. *Alleluia, alleluia.*

GOSPEL *(Luke 16:19-31)*
A reading from the holy Gospel according to Luke.
Glory to you, O Lord.

Jesus said to the Pharisees: "There was a rich man who dressed in purple garments and fine linen and dined sumptuously each day. And lying at his door was a poor man named Lazarus, covered with sores, who would gladly have eaten his fill of the scraps that fell from the rich man's table. Dogs even used to come and lick his sores. When the poor man died, he was carried away by angels to the bosom of Abraham. The rich man also died and was buried, and from the netherworld, where he was in torment, he raised his eyes and saw Abraham far off and Lazarus at his side. And he cried out, 'Father Abraham, have pity on me. Send Lazarus to dip the tip of his finger in water and cool my tongue, for I am suffering torment in these flames.' Abraham replied, 'My child, remember that you received what was good during your lifetime while Lazarus likewise received what was bad; but now he is comforted here, whereas you are tormented. Moreover, between us and you a **great chasm**✢ is established to prevent anyone from crossing who might wish to go from our side to yours or from your side to ours.' He said, 'Then I beg you, father, send him to my father's house, for I have five brothers, so that he may warn them, lest they too come to this place of torment.' But Abraham replied, 'They have Moses and the prophets. Let them listen to them.' He said, 'Oh no, father Abraham, but if someone from the dead goes to them, they will repent.' Then Abraham said, 'If they will not listen to Moses and the prophets, neither will they be persuaded if someone should rise from the dead.'"

The Gospel of the Lord. ***Praise to you, Lord Jesus Christ.***

PROFESSION OF FAITH *(page 13)*

PRAYER OF THE FAITHFUL

PREPARATION OF GIFTS *(page 16)*

PRAYER OVER THE OFFERINGS
Grant us, O merciful God,
that this our offering may find acceptance with you
and that through it the wellspring of all blessing
may be laid open before us.
Through Christ our Lord. *Amen.*

• TAKING A CLOSER LOOK •

✚ **A great chasm** The ancients envisioned the universe to be multi-layered, with three levels of heaven, earth, and the netherworld (under or below the earth). These physical areas are also distinguished by those who dwell in each: God in heaven, mortals on earth, and the dead in the underworld (in Hebrew, *Sheol*). These realms are not only distinct, but separated by such distance that only God (and those whom God sends as messengers like the angels, or Jesus who comes from heaven to earth and then returns at his death) can move from one level to the other.

PREFACE *(Sundays in Ordinary Time, pages 28–32)*

COMMUNION ANTIPHON *(Cf. Psalm 119 [118]:49–50)*
Remember your word to your servant, O Lord, by which you
have given me hope. This is my comfort when I am brought low.

Or *(1 John 3:16)*
By this we came to know the love of God: that Christ laid down
his life for us; so we ought to lay down our lives for one another.

PRAYER AFTER COMMUNION
May this heavenly mystery, O Lord,
restore us in mind and body,
that we may be coheirs in glory with Christ,
to whose suffering we are united
whenever we proclaim his Death.
Who lives and reigns for ever and ever. *Amen.*

BLESSING & DISMISSAL *(page 56)* ✦

✦ RESPONDING TO THE WORD ✦

God condemns the rich whose luxury blinds them to the suffering of others.	Paul reminds Timothy that by his baptism he now must live a godly life.	The rich man never noticed the poor and starving Lazarus right at his gate.
➲ *How can I use my resources to help those who are in need?*	➲ *What helps me to recall my baptismal commitment to live rightly?*	➲ *What can I do to not just notice but actually help the poor and homeless who come into my life?*

October 6

OCT 6

A spirit of power and of love

I am struck by the questions Scripture brings to the forefront. In Habakkuk the prophet laments, "I cry for help but you do not listen!" And in the Gospel of Luke, the apostles implore, "Increase our faith!" I work as a chaplain in two long-term care facilities. I am both humbled and inspired by the persistent and abiding faith of the residents despite or perhaps because of the heavy burdens of illness they carry on a daily basis.

During our discussion groups, faith and matters of faith are topics we explore together. St. Paul's letter to Timothy aptly describes my residents: "For God did not give us a spirit of cowardice but rather of power and love and self-control." My residents are far from timid, their faith not as mere mustard seeds but more like the towering strong branches of mustard plants. Their mantra is "I am so grateful to God for my life."

Our God is merciful, compassionate, and loving. We are called to hone those particular virtues to express our Christian values. I am blessed to have my faith increased by the example of those who suffer. Please pray for residents of long-term care facilities and for their caregivers, for they are true servants of God who care for the forgotten and broken members of the Body of Christ.

■ **MARILYN ELPHICK**

ENTRANCE ANTIPHON

(Cf. Esther 4:17) Within your will, O Lord, all things are established, and there is none that can resist your will. For you have made all things, the heaven and the earth, and all that is held within the circle of heaven; you are the Lord of all.

INTRODUCTORY RITES *(page 10)*

COLLECT

Almighty ever-living God,
who in the abundance of your kindness
surpass the merits and the desires of those who entreat you,
pour out your mercy upon us
to pardon what conscience dreads
and to give what prayer does not dare to ask.
Through our Lord Jesus Christ, your Son,
who lives and reigns with you in the unity of the Holy Spirit,
one God, for ever and ever. *Amen.*

FIRST READING *(Habakkuk 1:2-3; 2:2-4)*

How long, O LORD? I cry for help
but you do not listen!
I cry out to you, "Violence!"
but you do not intervene.
Why do you let me see ruin;
why must I look at misery?
Destruction and violence are before me;
there is strife, and clamorous discord.
Then the LORD answered me and said:
Write down the vision clearly upon the tablets,
so that one can read it readily.
For the vision still has its time,

presses on to fulfillment, and will not disappoint;
if it delays, wait for it,
   it will surely come, it will not be late.
The rash one has no integrity;
   but the just one, because of his faith, shall live.

The word of the Lord. *Thanks be to God.*

RESPONSORIAL PSALM *(Psalm 95:1-2, 6-7, 8-9)*

R⫶ **If today you hear his voice, harden not your hearts.**

Come, let us sing joyfully to the LORD;
   let us acclaim the Rock of our salvation.
Let us come into his presence with thanksgiving;
   let us joyfully sing psalms to him. R⫶
Come, let us bow down in worship;
   let us kneel before the LORD who made us.
For he is our God,
   and we are the people he shepherds, the flock he guides. R⫶
Oh, that today you would hear his voice:
   "Harden not your hearts as at Meribah,*
   as in the day of Massah* in the desert,
where your fathers tempted me;
   they tested me though they had seen my works." R⫶

SECOND READING *(2 Timothy 1:6-8, 13-14)*

Beloved: I remind you, to stir into flame the gift of God that
you have through the **imposition of my hands.**✝ For God
did not give us a spirit of cowardice but rather of power and love
and self-control. So do not be ashamed of your testimony to our
Lord, nor of me, a prisoner for his sake; but bear your share of
hardship for the gospel with the strength that comes from God.

Take as your norm the sound words that you heard from me, in the faith and love that are in Christ Jesus. Guard this rich trust with the help of the Holy Spirit that dwells within us.

The word of the Lord. *Thanks be to God.*

ALLELUIA *(1 Peter 1:25)*
Alleluia, alleluia. The word of the Lord remains for ever. This is the word that has been proclaimed to you. *Alleluia, alleluia.*

GOSPEL *(Luke 17:5-10)*
A reading from the holy Gospel according to Luke.
Glory to you, O Lord.

The apostles said to the Lord, "Increase our faith." The Lord replied, "If you have faith the size of a mustard seed, you would say to this mulberry tree, 'Be uprooted and planted in the sea,' and it would obey you.

"Who among you would say to your servant who has just come in from plowing or tending sheep in the field, 'Come here immediately and take your place at table'? Would he not rather say to him, 'Prepare something for me to eat. Put on your apron and wait on me while I eat and drink. You may eat and drink when I am finished'? Is he grateful to that servant because he did what was commanded? So should it be with you. When you have done all you have been commanded, say, 'We are unprofitable servants; we have done what we were obliged to do.'"

The Gospel of the Lord. *Praise to you, Lord Jesus Christ.*

PROFESSION OF FAITH *(page 13)*

PRAYER OF THE FAITHFUL

PREPARATION OF GIFTS *(page 16)*

PRAYER OVER THE OFFERINGS
Accept, O Lord, we pray,
the sacrifices instituted by your commands
and, through the sacred mysteries,
which we celebrate with dutiful service,
graciously complete the sanctifying work
by which you are pleased to redeem us.
Through Christ our Lord. ***Amen.***

PREFACE *(Sundays in Ordinary Time, pages 28–32)*

• TAKING A CLOSER LOOK •

✚ **Imposition of my hands** The hand (especially the right hand) was a natural symbol for power and strength. Since God's holiness could only be transferred by contact, the imposition or laying on of hands signified the transfer of power, strength, or holiness. It was part of the rituals for sacrifice, for the consecration of priests, and for conferring blessings. Christians use this as a sign of the communication of the Holy Spirit.

COMMUNION ANTIPHON *(Lamentations 3:25)*

The Lord is good to those who hope in him, to the soul that seeks him.

Or *(Cf. 1 Corinthians 10:17)*

Though many, we are one bread, one body, for we all partake of the one Bread and one Chalice.

PRAYER AFTER COMMUNION

Grant us, almighty God,
that we may be refreshed and nourished
by the Sacrament which we have received,
so as to be transformed into what we consume.
Through Christ our Lord. *Amen.*

BLESSING & DISMISSAL *(page 56)* ❖

❖ RESPONDING TO THE WORD ❖

Habakkuk yearns for justice amid the violence and strife of his world.	Paul urges us to stir into flame the gift of God we have received.	Jesus wants us to do more than the minimum that is commanded.
➥ *How can I join with others to help overcome the violence and injustice that permeate our society today?*	➥ *How can I use my gifts from God for greater service to God's people, especially the poor and outcast?*	➥ *What more can I do today to go beyond what is required to help others?*

October 13

OCT
13

God loves us—right here, right now!

A few years ago, my aunt died. My cousin was very upset when he was told the news of her death was online even before he had the opportunity to call people with the sad news. On social media, I often see condolences, birthday wishes, and anniversary wishes. I guess this is good if you are separated by geography and cannot offer these wishes in person, but I would much rather receive a call or a note via "snail mail." To me, it reflects personal care and attention.

In today's readings, Naaman the Syrian and the ten lepers received God's personal attention. Naaman was so grateful that he was willing to offer a great gift in return for God's care. The leper shared the same attitude of thanksgiving as Naaman. Both were outsiders, not Jews; little was expected of them, but both did not take their gift for granted.

Do I realize that God cares for me, not on some computer screen via an impersonal program, but right here, right now? Do I stop to give thanks for God's personal attention in my life? Today, at Eucharist, itself a prayer of thanksgiving and praise, we have the perfect opportunity to say, "Thank you." As we go forth from this celebration, we can continue to express gratitude to God who loves us deeply and personally.

■ **ANTHONY CHEZZI**

ENTRANCE ANTIPHON *(Psalm 130 [129]:3-4)*

If you, O Lord, should mark iniquities, Lord, who could stand?
But with you is found forgiveness, O God of Israel.

INTRODUCTORY RITES *(page 10)*

COLLECT

May your grace, O Lord, we pray,
at all times go before us and follow after
and make us always determined
to carry out good works.
Through our Lord Jesus Christ, your Son,
who lives and reigns with you in the unity of the Holy Spirit,
one God, for ever and ever. *Amen.*

FIRST READING *(2 Kings 5:14-17)*

Naaman went down and plunged into the Jordan seven
times at the word of Elisha, the man of God. His flesh
became again like the flesh of a little child, and he was clean of
his **leprosy.**✝

Naaman returned with his whole retinue to the man of God.
On his arrival he stood before Elisha and said, "Now I know that
there is no God in all the earth, except in Israel. Please accept a
gift from your servant."

Elisha replied, "As the LORD lives whom I serve, I will not
take it;" and despite Naaman's urging, he still refused. Naaman
said: "If you will not accept, please let me, your servant, have
two mule-loads of earth, for I will no longer offer holocaust or
sacrifice to any other god except to the LORD."

The word of the Lord. *Thanks be to God.*

RESPONSORIAL PSALM *(Psalm 98:1, 2–3, 3–4)*

R̸ The Lord has revealed to the nations his saving power.

Sing to the LORD new song,
  for he has done wondrous deeds;
his right hand has won victory for him,
  his holy arm. R̸
The LORD has made his salvation known:
  in the sight of the nations he has revealed his justice.
He has remembered his kindness and his faithfulness
  toward the house of Israel. R̸
All the ends of the earth have seen
  the salvation by our God.
Sing joyfully to the LORD, all you lands:
  break into song; sing praise. R̸

SECOND READING *(2 Timothy 2:8–13)*

Beloved: Remember Jesus Christ, raised from the dead, a descendant of David: such is my gospel, for which I am suffering, even to the point of chains, like a criminal. But the word of God is not chained. Therefore, I bear with everything for the sake of those who are chosen, so that they too may obtain the salvation that is in Christ Jesus, together with eternal glory. This saying is trustworthy:

If we have died with him
  we shall also live with him;
if we persevere
  we shall also reign with him.
But if we deny him
  he will deny us.

If we are unfaithful
    he remains faithful,
    for he cannot deny himself.

The word of the Lord. *Thanks be to God.*

ALLELUIA *(1 Thessalonians 5:18)*
Alleluia, alleluia. In all circumstances, give thanks, for this is
the will of God for you in Christ Jesus. *Alleluia, alleluia.*

GOSPEL *(Luke 17:11–19)*
A reading from the holy Gospel according to Luke.
Glory to you, O Lord.

As Jesus continued his journey to Jerusalem, he traveled
through Samaria* and Galilee. As he was entering a village, ten **lepers**✝ met him. They stood at a distance from him
and raised their voices, saying, "Jesus, Master! Have pity on
us!" And when he saw them, he said, "Go show yourselves to
the priests." As they were going they were cleansed. And one of
them, realizing he had been healed, returned, glorifying God
in a loud voice; and he fell at the feet of Jesus and thanked him.
He was a Samaritan. Jesus said in reply, "Ten were cleansed,
were they not? Where are the other nine? Has none but this
foreigner returned to give thanks to God?" Then he said to
him, "Stand up and go; your faith has saved you."

The Gospel of the Lord. *Praise to you, Lord Jesus Christ.*

PROFESSION OF FAITH *(page 13)*

PRAYER OF THE FAITHFUL

PREPARATION OF GIFTS *(page 16)*

PRAYER OVER THE OFFERINGS
Accept, O Lord, the prayers of your faithful
with the sacrificial offerings,
that, through these acts of devotedness,
we may pass over to the glory of heaven.
Through Christ our Lord. *Amen.*

PREFACE *(Sundays in Ordinary Time, pages 28–32)*

❖ Taking a Closer Look ❖

✝ **Leprosy / lepers** In Scripture, leprosy does not always mean only the illness also known as Hansen's Disease; it also includes a variety of other skin problems, such as fungal infections, eczema, ringworm, or psoriasis. It was the priest's role to decide whether a skin eruption was leprous. If the disease progressed, the person was declared ritually "unclean" and could not participate in community worship. Since ritual impurity jeopardized the pure life and worship of the community, the "unclean" lepers were separated from the community. Obviously such separation also prevented any normal way of making a living and impeded human companionship, other than that of their fellow lepers. Bands of lepers often traveled about together, begging for charity.

COMMUNION ANTIPHON *(Cf. Psalm 34 [33]:11)*

The rich suffer want and go hungry, but those who seek the Lord lack no blessing.

Or *(1 John 3:2)*

When the Lord appears, we shall be like him, for we shall see him as he is.

PRAYER AFTER COMMUNION

We entreat your majesty most humbly, O Lord,
that, as you feed us with the nourishment
which comes from the most holy Body and Blood of your Son,
so you may make us sharers of his divine nature.
Who lives and reigns for ever and ever. *Amen.*

BLESSING & DISMISSAL *(page 56)* #

• RESPONDING TO THE WORD •

The foreigner Naaman tries to find a way to give thanks to God for his healing.

➡ *What can I do today to show my thanks to God?*

Paul claims that God's word is not chained but powerful.

➡ *What can I do to allow God's word to change my actions to become more like those of Jesus?*

Jesus wonders why those healed do not express thanks.

➡ *When have I failed to express my thanks for what God has done for me?*

October 20

OCT 20

The Lord is faithful

In today's gospel, we hear Jesus teach his disciples to be persistent in prayer. Far too often, we are discouraged when a prayer seems to go unanswered. We might question whether it is worth repeating our plea, and feelings of desperation may arise. In today's gospel the parable of the determined widow and the stubborn judge reminds us of the importance of being resolute in our prayer life.

Persistence in prayer is an act of confidence and discipline of the soul that strengthens our relationship with God. It's the subtle understanding and humble acceptance that God's will is perfect and that God's answer will be given at the right time. God's time. Thus, we ought to hope and wait in God. We need that time to comprehend what God is allowing us to experience. Through persistence in prayer, we are encouraged to partake in a communication of love, praise, and trust.

In fact, there is no such thing as an unanswered prayer. There are, perhaps, unexpected answers to our prayers. These answers will always be better than what we could ever expect. After all, we are not pleading with a dishonest judge but with a God who loves utterly.

Keep praying, keep believing, keep hoping: God is already working in your life, in one way or the other. God answers your prayers; the Lord is faithful.

■ **MONICA NINO**

ENTRANCE ANTIPHON *(Cf. Psalm 17 [16]:6, 8)*

To you I call; for you will surely heed me, O God; turn your ear to me; hear my words. Guard me as the apple of your eye; in the shadow of your wings protect me.

INTRODUCTORY RITES *(page 10)*

COLLECT

Almighty ever-living God,
grant that we may always conform our will to yours
and serve your majesty in sincerity of heart.
Through our Lord Jesus Christ, your Son,
who lives and reigns with you in the unity of the Holy Spirit,
one God, for ever and ever. *Amen.*

FIRST READING *(Exodus 17:8–13)*

In those days, Amalek came and waged war against Israel. Moses, therefore, said to Joshua, "Pick out certain men, and tomorrow go out and engage Amalek* in battle. I will be standing on top of the hill with the staff of God in my hand." So Joshua did as Moses told him: he engaged Amalek in battle after Moses had climbed to the top of the hill with Aaron and Hur. As long as Moses kept his hands raised up, Israel had the better of the fight, but when he let his hands rest, Amalek had the better of the fight. Moses' hands, however, grew tired; so they put a rock in place for him to sit on. Meanwhile Aaron and Hur supported his hands, one on one side and one on the other, so that his hands remained steady till sunset. And Joshua mowed down Amalek and his people with the edge of the sword.

The word of the Lord. *Thanks be to God.*

RESPONSORIAL PSALM *(Psalm 121:1-2, 3-4, 5-6, 7-8)*

℟ **Our help is from the Lord, who made heaven and earth.**

I lift up my eyes toward the mountains;
  whence shall help come to me?
My help is from the LORD,
  who made heaven and earth. ℟

May he not suffer your foot to slip;
  may he slumber not who guards you:
indeed he neither slumbers nor sleeps,
  the guardian of Israel. ℟

The LORD is your guardian; the LORD is your shade;
  he is beside you at your right hand.
The sun shall not harm you by day,
  nor the moon by night. ℟

The LORD will guard you from all evil;
  he will guard your life.
The LORD will guard your coming and your going,
  both now and forever. ℟

SECOND READING *(2 Timothy 3:14–4:2)*

Beloved: Remain faithful to what you have learned and believed, because you know from whom you learned it, and that from infancy you have known the sacred Scriptures, which are capable of giving you wisdom for salvation through faith in Christ Jesus. All Scripture is inspired by God and is useful for teaching, for refutation, for correction, and for training in righteousness, so that one who belongs to God may be competent, equipped for every good work.

I charge you in the presence of God and of Christ Jesus, who will judge the living and the dead, and by his appearing and his kingly power: proclaim the word; be persistent whether it is convenient or inconvenient; convince, reprimand, encourage through all patience and teaching.

The word of the Lord. *Thanks be to God.*

ALLELUIA *(Hebrews 4:12)*
Alleluia, alleluia. The word of God is living and effective, discerning reflections and thoughts of the heart. *Alleluia, alleluia.*

GOSPEL *(Luke 18:1–8)*
A reading from the holy Gospel according to Luke.
Glory to you, O Lord.
Jesus told his disciples a **parable**+ about the necessity for them to pray always without becoming weary. He said, "There was a judge in a certain town who neither feared God nor respected any human being. And a widow in that town used to come to him and say, 'Render a just decision for me against my adversary.' For a long time the judge was unwilling, but eventually he thought, 'While it is true that I neither fear God nor respect any human being, because this widow keeps bothering me I shall deliver a just decision for her lest she finally come and strike me.' " The Lord said, "Pay attention to what the dishonest judge says. Will not God then secure the rights of his chosen ones who call out to him day and night? Will he be slow to answer them? I tell you, he will see to it that justice is done for them speedily. But when the Son of Man comes, will he find faith on earth?"

The Gospel of the Lord. *Praise to you, Lord Jesus Christ.*

PROFESSION OF FAITH *(page 13)*

PRAYER OF THE FAITHFUL

PREPARATION OF GIFTS *(page 16)*

PRAYER OVER THE OFFERINGS
Grant us, Lord, we pray,
a sincere respect for your gifts,
that, through the purifying action of your grace,
we may be cleansed by the very mysteries we serve.
Through Christ our Lord. *Amen.*

PREFACE *(Sundays in Ordinary Time, pages 28–32)*

❧ TAKING A CLOSER LOOK ❧

✛ **Parable** A parable (from the Greek, to "throw together" things for comparison or illustration) is a short realistic story intended to encourage reflection by connecting the story to our own life. Since one must be able connect the parable to various aspects of one's life or that of one's family or community, parables are open-ended in their application. Parables were a common teaching device of Jewish rabbis and important to Jesus in his teaching because the only way we have to talk about what is *unfamiliar* to us (God's ruling presence or "kingdom") is in terms of what is *familiar* to us (our everyday life and world). A parable challenges the audience to think about its meaning and change their lives because of what they discover.

COMMUNION ANTIPHON *(Cf. Psalm 33 [32]:18-19)*
Behold, the eyes of the Lord are on those who fear him, who hope in his merciful love, to rescue their souls from death, to keep them alive in famine.

Or *(Mark 10:45)*
The Son of Man has come to give his life as a ransom for many.

PRAYER AFTER COMMUNION
Grant, O Lord, we pray,
that, benefiting from participation in heavenly things,
we may be helped by what you give in this present age
and prepared for the gifts that are eternal.
Through Christ our Lord. *Amen.*

BLESSING & DISMISSAL *(page 56)* ✣

● RESPONDING TO THE WORD ●

Moses needs help to hold up his staff, the sign of God's power, to conquer his enemies.

➲ *To whom do I look for help in overcoming the spiritual difficulties that I face?*

Paul knows that familiarity with the Scriptures equips us for doing good works.

➲ *How has reading and reflecting on Scripture made a difference in my life recently?*

Jesus wants us to be persistent in our prayer.

➲ *For what do I continually ask God for myself? for others?*

October 27

OCT
27

Growing closer to God

Today's readings offer valuable lessons concerning trust and humility, both of which serve as important criteria for Christians in developing healthy prayer practices and a deeper relationship with God.

The first reading from the book of Sirach says God hears and responds to our prayers lovingly. God rewards our loyalty regardless of our journey or identity in life. When we come to the Lord simply and hand our needs and struggles over with complete confidence, we know God will act and answer our prayers.

Yet, as St. Luke reminds us in his account of Jesus' parable of the Pharisee and the tax collector, we must always be grateful for God's gifts, appreciating our blessings but never celebrating them boastfully or excessively. God, in the end, will honor our choice to live a humble life. As evidenced by the tax collector, it is through acknowledging our flaws and asking God for mercy that we experience healing and encouragement.

So as we seek to grow closer to God in our daily living, may we strive to practice greater trust in God's way and humble ourselves before God. In displaying boundless faith in God while living meekly, we open ourselves more fully to being raised in God's unconditional love.

■ **Matt Charbonneau**

ENTRANCE ANTIPHON *(Cf. Psalm 105 [104]:3–4)*

Let the hearts that seek the Lord rejoice; turn to the Lord and
his strength; constantly seek his face.

INTRODUCTORY RITES *(page 10)*

COLLECT

Almighty ever-living God,
increase our faith, hope and charity,
and make us love what you command,
so that we may merit what you promise.
Through our Lord Jesus Christ, your Son,
who lives and reigns with you in the unity of the Holy Spirit,
one God, for ever and ever. *Amen.*

FIRST READING *(Sirach 35:12–14, 16–18)*

The LORD is a God of justice,
    who knows **no favorites**.✝
Though not unduly partial toward the weak,
    yet he hears the cry of the oppressed.
The Lord is not deaf to the wail of the orphan,
    nor to the widow when she pours out her complaint.
The one who serves God willingly is heard;
    his petition reaches the heavens.
The prayer of the lowly pierces the clouds;
    it does not rest till it reaches its goal,
nor will it withdraw till the Most High responds,
    judges justly and affirms the right,
and the Lord will not delay.

The word of the Lord. *Thanks be to God.*

RESPONSORIAL PSALM *(Psalm 34:2-3, 17-18, 19, 23)*
R. **The Lord hears the cry of the poor.**

I will bless the LORD at all times;
  his praise shall be ever in my mouth.
Let my soul glory in the LORD;
  the lowly will hear me and be glad. R.

The LORD confronts the evildoers,
  to destroy remembrance of them from the earth.
When the just cry out, the LORD hears them,
  and from all their distress he rescues them. R.

The LORD is close to the brokenhearted;
  and those who are crushed in spirit he saves.
The LORD redeems the lives of his servants;
  no one incurs guilt who takes refuge in him. R.

SECOND READING *(2 Timothy 4:6-8, 16-18)*

Beloved: I am already being poured out like a libation, and
the time of my departure is at hand. I have competed well;
I have finished the race; I have kept the faith. From now on
the crown of righteousness awaits me, which the Lord, the just
judge, will award to me on that day, and not only to me, but to
all who have longed for his appearance.

At my first defense no one appeared on my behalf, but everyone deserted me. May it not be held against them! But the Lord
stood by me and gave me strength, so that through me the proclamation might be completed and all the Gentiles might hear it.
And I was rescued from the lion's mouth. The Lord will rescue
me from every evil threat and will bring me safe to his heavenly
kingdom. To him be glory forever and ever. Amen.

The word of the Lord. *Thanks be to God.*

ALLELUIA *(2 Corinthians 5:19)*
Alleluia, alleluia. God was reconciling the world to himself in Christ, and entrusting to us the message of salvation. *Alleluia, alleluia.*

GOSPEL *(Luke 18:9-14)*
A reading from the holy Gospel according to Luke.
Glory to you, O Lord.

Jesus addressed this parable to those who were convinced of their own righteousness and despised everyone else. "Two people went up to the temple area to pray; one was a Pharisee and the other was a tax collector. The Pharisee took up his position and spoke this prayer to himself, 'O God, I thank you that I am not like the rest of humanity—greedy, dishonest, adulterous—or even like this tax collector. I fast twice a week, and I pay tithes on my whole income.' But the tax collector stood off at a distance and would not even raise his eyes to heaven but beat his breast and prayed, 'O God, be merciful to me a sinner.' I tell you, the latter went home justified, not the former; for whoever exalts himself will be humbled, and the one who humbles himself will be exalted."

The Gospel of the Lord. *Praise to you, Lord Jesus Christ.*

PROFESSION OF FAITH *(page 13)*

PRAYER OF THE FAITHFUL

PREPARATION OF GIFTS *(page 16)*

PRAYER OVER THE OFFERINGS

Look, we pray, O Lord,
on the offerings we make to your majesty,
that whatever is done by us in your service
may be directed above all to your glory.
Through Christ our Lord. ***Amen.***

PREFACE *(Sundays in Ordinary Time, pages 28–32)*

COMMUNION ANTIPHON *(Cf. Psalm 20 [19]:6)*

We will ring out our joy at your saving help and exult in the
name of our God.

Or *(Ephesians 5:2)*

Christ loved us and gave himself up for us, as a fragrant offering
to God.

● TAKING A CLOSER LOOK ●

✛ **No favorites** In biblical times, the wealthy and powerful
not only wrote the laws but also decided cases; judges, who were
supposed to be impartial, were often susceptible to bribes to decide a case in someone's favor. For the poor—who did not have
the means to influence court decisions—the odds of getting a "just
judge" who would show no favoritism were very slim indeed. Thus
they trusted in their hope that God, who could not be bribed or
controlled, would be the ultimate arbiter of justice.

PRAYER AFTER COMMUNION

May your Sacraments, O Lord, we pray,
perfect in us what lies within them,
that what we now celebrate in signs
we may one day possess in truth.
Through Christ our Lord. *Amen.*

BLESSING & DISMISSAL *(page 56)* ✠

• RESPONDING TO THE WORD •

God hears the cries of the oppressed, and we must help to root out injustice.

➡ *What can I do today to help change little injustices that are found in my household, my workplace, or my neighborhood?*

God rescued Paul though everyone else deserted him.

➡ *Who might be feeling deserted and in need of my help today?*

Jesus describes two ways to approach God in prayer.

➡ *Which of these two approaches is my prayer most like?*

November 1

NOV
1

The saints all share one thing

How many saints do we have? With detailed research we could approximate an answer, but no matter. Today we remember all saints, an innumerable throng!

The 144,000... Twelve (the biblical number signifying completeness) squared—and then multiplied by 1000. Revelation's way of saying "countless!"

Who are they? People of every race and nation and age and status: scholars, beggars, royalty, children, married, single, ordained, and vowed religious.

How do they come to be "saints"? Through the power of the blood of Christ. God's love draws them all!

What do they look like? They may not be recognized as "successes" in our competitive culture. They are powerless, suf-fering, compassionate, hungering for justice, grieving losses and failures, passionate about peacemaking. The saints each have one or more of these characteristics. But one thing they share: they long to see the face of God. That is, they long for life as God desires it for all—and they live to help it happen.

We've known them: parents, colleagues, neighbors, friends, civic leaders, religious ministers, patients, caregivers. We read of them in stories of "unsung heroes." So today, we honor them, by naming some and thinking of those whose names we do not know. We remember them all. We celebrate them all. And, perhaps, we imitate them!

▪ SR. HONORA WERNER, OP

ENTRANCE ANTIPHON

Let us all rejoice in the Lord, as we celebrate the feast day in
honor of all the Saints, at whose festival the Angels rejoice and
praise the Son of God.

INTRODUCTORY RITES *(page 10)*

COLLECT

Almighty ever-living God,
by whose gift we venerate in one celebration
the merits of all the Saints,
bestow on us, we pray,
through the prayers of so many intercessors,
an abundance of the reconciliation with you
for which we earnestly long.
Through our Lord Jesus Christ, your Son,
who lives and reigns with you in the unity of the Holy Spirit,
one God, for ever and ever. *Amen.*

FIRST READING *(Revelation 7:2–4, 9–14)*

I, John, saw another angel come up from the East, holding the
seal of the living God. He cried out in a loud voice to the
four angels who were given power to damage the land and the
sea, "Do not damage the land or the sea or the trees until we put
the seal on the foreheads of the servants of our God." I heard
the number of those who had been marked with the seal, **one
hundred and forty-four thousand** ✝ marked from every tribe of
the children of Israel.

After this I had a vision of a great multitude, which no one
could count, from every nation, race, people, and tongue. They
stood before the throne and before the Lamb, wearing white robes

and holding palm branches in their hands. They cried out in a loud voice:

"Salvation comes from our God, who is seated on the throne,
and from the Lamb."

All the angels stood around the throne and around the elders and the four living creatures. They prostrated themselves before the throne, worshiped God, and exclaimed:

"Amen. Blessing and glory, wisdom and thanksgiving,
honor, power, and might
be to our God forever and ever. Amen."

Then one of the elders spoke up and said to me, "Who are these wearing white robes, and where did they come from?" I said to him, "My lord, you are the one who knows." He said to me, "These are the ones who have survived the time of great distress; they have washed their robes and made them white in the Blood of the Lamb."

The word of the Lord. *Thanks be to God.*

RESPONSORIAL PSALM *(Psalm 24:1bc-2, 3-4ab, 5-6)*

℟ **Lord, this is the people that longs to see your face.**

The LORD's are the earth and its fullness;
the world and those who dwell in it.
For he founded it upon the seas
and established it upon the rivers. ℟

Who can ascend the mountain of the LORD?
or who may stand in his holy place?
One whose hands are sinless, whose heart is clean,
who desires not what is vain. ℟

He shall receive a blessing from the LORD,
a reward from God his savior.

Such is the race that seeks him,
that seeks the face of the God of Jacob.
℞ **Lord, this is the people that longs to see your face.**

SECOND READING *(1 John 3:1-3)*

Beloved: See what love the Father has bestowed on us that
we may be called the children of God. Yet so we are. The
reason the world does not know us is that it did not know him.
Beloved, we are God's children now; what we shall be has not
yet been revealed. We do know that when it is revealed we shall
be like him, for we shall see him as he is. Everyone who has this
hope based on him makes himself pure, as he is pure.

The word of the Lord. *Thanks be to God.*

ALLELUIA *(Matthew 11:28)*

Alleluia, alleluia. Come to me, all you who labor and are burdened, and I will give you rest, says the Lord. *Alleluia, alleluia.*

GOSPEL *(Matthew 5:1-12a)*

A reading from the holy Gospel according to Matthew.
Glory to you, O Lord.

When Jesus saw the crowds, he went up the mountain,
and after he had sat down, his disciples came to him. He
began to teach them, saying:
"Blessed are the poor in spirit,
for theirs is the Kingdom of heaven.
Blessed are they who mourn,
for they will be comforted.
Blessed are the meek,
for they will inherit the land.
Blessed are they who hunger and thirst for righteousness,

for they will be satisfied.
Blessed are the merciful,
for they will be shown mercy.
Blessed are the clean of heart,
for they will see God.
Blessed are the peacemakers,
for they will be called children of God.
Blessed are they who are persecuted for the sake of righteousness,
for theirs is the Kingdom of heaven.
Blessed are you when they insult you and persecute you and
utter every kind of evil against you falsely because of me. Rejoice
and be glad, for your reward will be great in heaven."

The Gospel of the Lord. *Praise to you, Lord Jesus Christ.*

PROFESSION OF FAITH *(page 13)*

PRAYER OF THE FAITHFUL

PREPARATION OF GIFTS *(page 16)*

PRAYER OVER THE OFFERINGS
May these offerings we bring in honor of all the Saints
be pleasing to you, O Lord,
and grant that, just as we believe the Saints
to be already assured of immortality,
so we may experience their concern for our salvation.
Through Christ our Lord. *Amen.*

PREFACE: THE GLORY OF JERUSALEM, OUR MOTHER
It is truly right and just, our duty and our salvation,
always and everywhere to give you thanks,
Lord, holy Father, almighty and eternal God.

For today by your gift we celebrate the festival of your city,
the heavenly Jerusalem, our mother,
where the great array of our brothers and sisters
already gives you eternal praise.

Towards her, we eagerly hasten as pilgrims advancing by faith,
rejoicing in the glory bestowed upon those exalted members
  of the Church
through whom you give us, in our frailty, both strength
  and good example.

And so, we glorify you with the multitude of Saints and Angels,
as with one voice of praise we acclaim:
Holy, Holy, Holy Lord God of hosts... *(page 35)*

● TAKING A CLOSER LOOK ●

✝ **One hundred and forty-four thousand** Although some
Christian groups have taken this number as the actual count of those
saved, it is evident both from the general way large numbers are
used in the Bible and from the text that follows that this is a symbolic
number. For people without sophisticated mathematics, large numbers are almost always symbolic, the way we say "million" or "zil-
lion" for emphasis. In everyday life, counting to 144,000 of anything
would be a major chore. The number means that an incredibly large
number of Jews are saved. But this is not all the saved because there
is an additional "great multitude" of non-Jews. This is John's way of
saying that the number of those saved is innumerable.

COMMUNION ANTIPHON *(Matthew 5:8–10)*

Blessed are the clean of heart, for they shall see God. Blessed
are the peacemakers, for they shall be called children of God.
Blessed are they who are persecuted for the sake of righteousness, for theirs is the Kingdom of Heaven.

PRAYER AFTER COMMUNION

As we adore you, O God, who alone are holy
and wonderful in all your Saints,
we implore your grace,
so that, coming to perfect holiness in the fullness of your love,
we may pass from this pilgrim table
to the banquet of our heavenly homeland.
Through Christ our Lord. *Amen.*

SOLEMN BLESSING: ALL SAINTS *(Optional, page 63)*

BLESSING & DISMISSAL *(page 56)* ✣

● RESPONDING TO THE WORD ●

John sees the
heavenly worship
offered by all the
angels and saints.

⬦ *How might I
deepen my spirit of
worship at Mass?*

Like children who
imitate their parents,
we grow spiritually
by imitating God.

⬦ *What characteris-
tics of God do I most
want to imitate?*

Jesus' beatitudes
reveal the ideal at-
titudes that ought
to be adopted by
his disciples.

⬦ *Which beatitude
would I most like
to make my own
today? Why?*

November 3

Welcome Jesus with a humble heart

The Lord, with loving care and concern, constantly seeks out the lost. Jesus always searches for anyone who may have gone astray, rich or poor. He wishes to offer everyone the opportunity to repent and start again.

In today's gospel, Jesus reached out to Zacchaeus, a wealthy tax collector who had climbed a tree to catch a glimpse of him. The Lord pronounced his name as an old friend would and spoke to him with tenderness. Jesus looked beyond his faults and errors and saw into his heart, just as he sees into ours.

On that day, Jesus entered Zacchaeus' home and his life. The mercy and love he showed Zacchaeus touched and transformed the tax collector. Zacchaeus was no longer absorbed with money but now saw the suffering of his neighbor. He responded generously to Jesus' call by resolving to change his ways, making restitution to those he had defrauded and sharing his possessions with the poor.

Jesus invites us to receive him as Zacchaeus did—joyfully. No matter how far we may have fallen, Jesus always offers us God's generous mercy and unconditional love. He looks beyond our mistakes and calls each of us by name. We too can be like Zacchaeus. Respond to Jesus' call without hesitation and welcome him with a humble, open heart.

◼ **NADA MAZZEI**

ENTRANCE ANTIPHON *(Cf. Psalm 38 [37]:22-23)*

Forsake me not, O Lord, my God; be not far from me! Make haste and come to my help, O Lord, my strong salvation!

INTRODUCTORY RITES *(page 10)*

COLLECT

Almighty and merciful God,
by whose gift your faithful offer you
right and praiseworthy service,
grant, we pray,
that we may hasten without stumbling
to receive the things you have promised.
Through our Lord Jesus Christ, your Son,
who lives and reigns with you in the unity of the Holy Spirit,
one God, for ever and ever. ***Amen.***

FIRST READING *(Wisdom 11:22–12:2)*

Before the LORD the whole universe is as a grain from a balance

> or a drop of morning dew come down upon the earth.

But you have mercy on all, because you can do all things;

> and you overlook people's sins that they may repent.

For you love all things that are

> and loathe nothing that you have made;
> for what you hated, you would not have fashioned.

And how could a thing remain, unless you willed it;

> or be preserved, had it not been called forth by you?

But you spare all things, because they are yours,

> O LORD and lover of souls,
> for your imperishable spirit is in all things!

Therefore you rebuke offenders little by little,
    warn them and remind them of the sins they are
        committing,
    that they may abandon their wickedness and believe in you,
        O Lord!

The word of the Lord. *Thanks be to God.*

RESPONSORIAL PSALM *(Psalm 145:1-2, 8-9, 10-11, 13-14)*
℞ **I will praise your name for ever, my king and my God.**

I will extol you, O my God and King,
    and I will bless your name forever and ever.
Every day will I bless you,
    and I will praise your name forever and ever. ℞

The Lord is **gracious and merciful,**☩
    slow to anger and of great kindness.
The Lord is good to all
    and compassionate toward all his works. ℞

Let all your works give you thanks, O Lord,
    and let your faithful ones bless you.
Let them discourse of the glory of your kingdom
    and speak of your might. ℞

The Lord is faithful in all his words
    and holy in all his works.
The Lord lifts up all who are falling
    and raises up all who are bowed down. ℞

SECOND READING *(2 Thessalonians 1:11–2:2)*

Brothers and sisters: We always pray for you, that our God may make you worthy of his calling and powerfully bring to fulfillment every good purpose and every effort of faith, that the name of our Lord Jesus may be glorified in you, and you in him, in accord with the grace of our God and Lord Jesus Christ.

We ask you, brothers and sisters, with regard to the coming of our Lord Jesus Christ and our assembling with him, not to be shaken out of your minds suddenly, or to be alarmed either by a "spirit," or by an oral statement, or by a letter allegedly from us to the effect that the day of the Lord is at hand.

The word of the Lord. *Thanks be to God.*

ALLELUIA *(John 3:16)*
Alleluia, alleluia. God so loved the world that he gave his only Son, so that everyone who believes in him might have eternal life. *Alleluia, alleluia.*

GOSPEL *(Luke 19:1–10)*
A reading from the holy Gospel according to Luke.
Glory to you, O Lord.

At that time, Jesus came to Jericho* and intended to pass through the town. Now a man there named Zacchaeus,* who was a chief tax collector and also a wealthy man, was seeking to see who Jesus was; but he could not see him because of the crowd, for he was short in stature. So he ran ahead and climbed a sycamore tree in order to see Jesus, who was about to pass that way. When he reached the place, Jesus looked up and said, "Zacchaeus, come down quickly, for today I must stay at your house." And he came down quickly and received him with joy. When they all saw this, they began to grumble, saying, "He has gone to stay at the house of a sinner." But Zacchaeus stood there and said to the Lord, "Behold, half of my possessions, Lord, I shall give to the poor, and if I have extorted anything from anyone I shall repay it four times over." And Jesus said to him, "Today salvation has come to this house because this man too is a descendant of Abraham. For the Son of Man has come to seek and to save what was lost."

The Gospel of the Lord. *Praise to you, Lord Jesus Christ.*

PROFESSION OF FAITH *(page 13)*

PRAYER OF THE FAITHFUL

PREPARATION OF GIFTS *(page 16)*

PRAYER OVER THE OFFERINGS
May these sacrificial offerings, O Lord,
become for you a pure oblation,
and for us a holy outpouring of your mercy.
Through Christ our Lord. *Amen.*

PREFACE *(Sundays in Ordinary Time, pages 28–32)*

• TAKING A CLOSER LOOK •

✝ **Gracious and merciful** In the Old Testament, "gracious" and "merciful" are characteristics of God's special covenant love (Hebrew, *hesed*) that binds God to us. God's attitude of love or attachment to the covenant community includes aspects of loyalty, dependability, trustworthiness, and an eagerness to help when situations turn bad. Like a father or patron of a family, God is an especially generous benefactor who lavishes gifts (Greek: *charis*, Latin: *gratia*) on them. These are not distributed because of the recipients' merits, but strictly out of God's favor or mercy. Mercy is not simply the response felt toward those who are suffering; it is also God's fierce desire to be with us and save us.

COMMUNION ANTIPHON *(Cf. Psalm 16 [15]:11)*
You will show me the path of life, the fullness of joy in your presence, O Lord.

Or *(John 6:58)*
Just as the living Father sent me and I have life because of the Father, so whoever feeds on me shall have life because of me, says the Lord.

PRAYER AFTER COMMUNION
May the working of your power, O Lord,
increase in us, we pray,
so that, renewed by these heavenly Sacraments,
we may be prepared by your gift
for receiving what they promise.
Through Christ our Lord. *Amen.*

BLESSING & DISMISSAL *(page 56)* ✠

✦ RESPONDING TO THE WORD ✦

God loves us and corrects us "little by little."

➡ *How has God been correcting me so that my actions show more love toward others?*

Paul prays that we be worthy of our call and bring our good works to fulfillment.

➡ *What good works am I being called to do to make Christ more known by others?*

Zacchaeus' attitudes toward the poor are completely turned around.

➡ *How can I be more conscious of the poor and the conditions that allow the poor to be oppressed?*

November 10

The life of the resurrection

Through his exchange with the Sadducees, Jesus gives a glimpse into the life of the resurrection. What can we know about it? What should we expect? How should we prepare? What will happen to our relationships through the resurrection?

In his answer, Jesus escapes the boundaries of anything his audience had ever heard. He describes the resurrection as a call to a bigger life. To live in God is more than a mortal existence: it is an active participation in God's salvation for the world. This resurrection, understood as life in God, is sustained by a renewed relationship to God, ourselves and others.

That is why our hope is in the God who renews the world. A hope not just in something that may not be or in something that has long since past, but a hope rooted in a relationship that continues to transform us every day.

When we view the past, present, and future in light of the resurrection, we are in solidarity with those who have gone before, those who journey with us now and those who are yet to come. It is the "bigger picture" and a shared mission with the saints to help transform the world by the love of God that transforms our own hearts. Even now, in God "we live and move and have our being" (Acts 17:28).

■ KELLY BOURKE

ENTRANCE ANTIPHON *(Cf. Psalm 88 [87]:3)*

Let my prayer come into your presence. Incline
your ear to my cry for help, O Lord.

INTRODUCTORY RITES *(page 10)*

COLLECT

Almighty and merciful God,
graciously keep from us all adversity,
so that, unhindered in mind and body alike,
we may pursue in freedom of heart
the things that are yours.
Through our Lord Jesus Christ, your Son,
who lives and reigns with you in the unity of the Holy Spirit,
one God, for ever and ever. *Amen.*

FIRST READING *(2 Maccabees 7:1-2, 9-14)*

It happened that seven brothers with their mother were arrest-
ed and tortured with whips and scourges by the king, to force
them to eat pork in violation of God's law. One of the brothers,
speaking for the others, said: "What do you expect to achieve
by questioning us? We are ready to die rather than transgress the
laws of our ancestors."

At the point of death he said: "You accursed fiend, you are depriving us of this present life, but the King of the world will raise
us up to live again forever. It is for his laws that we are dying."

After him the third suffered their cruel sport. He put out his
tongue at once when told to do so, and bravely held out his hands,
as he spoke these noble words: "It was from Heaven that I received
these; for the sake of his laws I disdain them; from him I hope to receive them again." Even the king and his attendants marveled at the
young man's courage, because he regarded his sufferings as nothing.

After he had died, they tortured and maltreated the fourth brother in the same way. When he was near death, he said, "It is my choice to die at the hands of men with the hope God gives of being raised up by him; but for you, there will be no resurrection to life."

The word of the Lord. *Thanks be to God.*

RESPONSORIAL PSALM *(Psalm 17:1, 5-6, 8, 15)*

℞ **Lord, when your glory appears, my joy will be full.**

Hear, O LORD, a just suit;
    attend to my outcry;
    hearken to my prayer from lips without deceit. ℞
My steps have been steadfast in your paths,
    my feet have not faltered.
I call upon you, for you will answer me, O God;
    incline your ear to me; hear my word. ℞
Keep me as the apple of your eye,
    hide me in the shadow of your wings.
But I in justice shall behold your face;
    on waking I shall be content in your presence. ℞

SECOND READING *(2 Thessalonians 2:16–3:5)*

Brothers and sisters: May our Lord Jesus Christ himself and God our Father, who has loved us and given us everlasting encouragement and good hope through his grace, encourage your hearts and strengthen them in every good deed and word.

Finally, brothers and sisters, pray for us, so that the word of the Lord may speed forward and be glorified, as it did among you, and that we may be delivered from perverse and wicked people, for not all have faith. But the Lord is faithful; he will strengthen you and guard you from the evil one. We are confident of you in the Lord that what we instruct you, you are doing and will continue to do. May the Lord direct your hearts to the love of God and to the endurance of Christ.

The word of the Lord. *Thanks be to God.*

ALLELUIA *(Revelation 1:5a, 6b)*
Alleluia, alleluia. Jesus Christ is the firstborn of the dead; to him be glory and power, forever and ever. *Alleluia, alleluia.*

GOSPEL *(Luke 20:27–38)*
For the shorter version, omit the indented part in brackets.

A reading from the holy Gospel according to Luke.
Glory to you, O Lord.

Some **Sadducees,**† those who deny that there is a resurrection, came forward

[and put this question to Jesus, saying, "Teacher, Moses wrote for us, *If someone's brother dies leaving a wife but no child, his brother must take the wife and raise up descendants for his brother.* Now there were seven brothers; the first married a woman but died childless. Then the second and the third married her, and likewise all the seven died childless. Finally the woman also died. Now at the resurrection whose wife will that woman be? For all seven had been married to her."]

Jesus said to them, "The children of this age marry and remarry; but those who are deemed worthy to attain to the coming age and to the resurrection of the dead neither marry nor are given in marriage. They can no longer die, for they are like angels; and they are the children of God because they are the ones who will rise. That the dead will rise even Moses made known in the passage about the bush, when he called out 'Lord,' the God of Abraham, the God of Isaac, and the God of Jacob; and he is not God of the dead, but of the living, for to him all are alive."

The Gospel of the Lord. *Praise to you, Lord Jesus Christ.*

PROFESSION OF FAITH *(page 13)*

PRAYER OF THE FAITHFUL

PREPARATION OF GIFTS *(page 16)*

PRAYER OVER THE OFFERINGS
Look with favor, we pray, O Lord,
upon the sacrificial gifts offered here,
that, celebrating in mystery the Passion of your Son,
we may honor it with loving devotion.
Through Christ our Lord. *Amen.*

PREFACE *(Sundays in Ordinary Time, pages 28–32)*

• TAKING A CLOSER LOOK •

✛ **Sadducees** The Sadducees were a small religious group within Judaism. Drawn from the priestly and higher social classes, many Sadducees were on the Sanhedrin (the chief judicial council). Conservative in both politics and religion, the Sadducees accepted as Scripture only the written Law and rejected the Pharisees' adoption of the unwritten traditions. They urged peaceful collaboration with the Romans because of their concern for the temple as the religious and financial center for Judaism and so were often accused of undesirable compromises in order to retain their power. The Sadducees disappeared as a group in 70 AD when Jerusalem was sacked by the Romans and the temple destroyed.

COMMUNION ANTIPHON *(Cf. Psalm 23 [22]:1–2)*

The Lord is my shepherd; there is nothing I shall want. Fresh and green are the pastures where he gives me repose, near restful waters he leads me.

Or *(Cf. Luke 24:35)*

The disciples recognized the Lord Jesus in the breaking of bread.

PRAYER AFTER COMMUNION

Nourished by this sacred gift, O Lord,
we give you thanks and beseech your mercy,
that, by the pouring forth of your Spirit,
the grace of integrity may endure
in those your heavenly power has entered.
Through Christ our Lord. *Amen.*

BLESSING & DISMISSAL *(page 56)* ✤

◆ RESPONDING TO THE WORD ◆

The martyrs die hoping they will be raised to new life.	Paul knows that God gives us strength in times of temptation.	Jesus affirms that God takes special care of us even beyond our death.
➦ *What most encourages my hope for new life after death?*	➦ *What strength has God given me recently to resist my temptations?*	➦ *How have I experienced "the God of the living" taking special care of me?*

November 17

A sign of joy and hope

Images of strife and the temple being destroyed are terrifying but familiar. The images in today's readings remind us that we live in an in-between time. In the second reading, St. Paul calls us to live our waiting with commitment by turning away from idleness and by imitating the kingdom for which we wait, a kingdom the psalmist says is just, equitable, and joyful. Jesus encourages us to trust God more fully, for God will give us words and wisdom so we may witness to his love.

In 2016, at the end of the Jubilee Year of Mercy, Pope Francis named the Thirty-Third Sunday in Ordinary Time the World Day of the Poor. The Pope entreats the faithful to reach out in solidarity to those most in need. This calls us to live our waiting with commitment, stepping out of certainties and comforts, and entering vulnerability.

As we approach Advent, we ask for the grace to be fully present with love and compassion to the suffering of our time. By doing so, we prepare our hearts to receive God's love born as an infant messiah. Our lives lived in faithful witness to the kingdom that is to come become a sign of joy and hope for today.

■ **MICHAEL AND VANESSA NICHOLAS-SCHMIDT**

ENTRANCE ANTIPHON *(Jeremiah 29:11, 12, 14)*

The Lord said: I think thoughts of peace and not of affliction. You will call upon me, and I will answer you, and I will lead back your captives from every place.

INTRODUCTORY RITES *(page 10)*

COLLECT

Grant us, we pray, O Lord our God,
the constant gladness of being devoted to you,
for it is full and lasting happiness
to serve with constancy
the author of all that is good.
Through our Lord Jesus Christ, your Son,
who lives and reigns with you in the unity of the Holy Spirit,
one God, for ever and ever. *Amen.*

FIRST READING *(Malachi 3:19-20a)*

Lo, the day is coming, blazing like an oven,
when all the proud and all evildoers will be stubble,
and the day that is coming will set them on fire,
leaving them neither root nor branch,
says the LORD of hosts.
But for you who fear my name, there will arise
the sun of justice with its healing rays.

The word of the Lord. *Thanks be to God.*

RESPONSORIAL PSALM *(Psalm 98:5-6, 7-8, 9)*

℞ **The Lord comes to rule the earth with justice.**

Sing praise to the LORD with the harp,
 with the harp and melodious song.
With trumpets and the sound of the horn
 sing joyfully before the King, the LORD. ℞

Let the sea and what fills it resound,
 the world and those who dwell in it;
let the rivers clap their hands,
 the mountains shout with them for joy. ℞

Before the LORD, for he comes,
 for he comes to rule the earth,
He will rule the world with justice
 and the peoples with equity. ℞

SECOND READING *(2 Thessalonians 3:7-12)*

Brothers and sisters: You know how one must imitate us. For we did not act in a disorderly way among you, nor did we eat food received free from anyone. On the contrary, in toil and drudgery, night and day we worked, so as not to burden any of you. Not that we do not have the right. Rather, we wanted to present ourselves as a model for you, so that you might imitate us. In fact, when we were with you, we instructed you that if anyone was **unwilling to work,** ✝ neither should that one eat. We hear that some are conducting themselves among you in a disorderly way, by not keeping busy but minding the business of others. Such people we instruct and urge in the Lord Jesus Christ to work quietly and to eat their own food.

The word of the Lord. *Thanks be to God.*

ALLELUIA *(Luke 21:28)*
Alleluia, alleluia. Stand erect and raise your heads because your redemption is at hand. *Alleluia, alleluia.*

GOSPEL *(Luke 21:5-19)*
A reading from the holy Gospel according to Luke.
Glory to you, O Lord.

While some people were speaking about how the temple was adorned with costly stones and votive offerings, Jesus said, "All that you see here—the days will come when there will not be left a stone upon another stone that will not be thrown down."

Then they asked him, "Teacher, when will this happen? And what sign will there be when all these things are about to happen?" He answered, "See that you not be deceived, for many will come in my name, saying, 'I am he,' and 'The time has come.' Do not follow them! When you hear of wars and insurrections, do not be terrified; for such things must happen first, but it will not immediately be the end." Then he said to them, "Nation will rise against nation, and kingdom against kingdom. There will be powerful earthquakes, famines, and plagues from place to place; and awesome sights and mighty signs will come from the sky.

"Before all this happens, however, they will seize and persecute you, they will hand you over to the synagogues and to prisons, and they will have you led before kings and governors because of my name. It will lead to your giving testimony. Remember, you are not to prepare your defense beforehand, for I myself shall give you a wisdom in speaking that all your adversaries will be powerless to resist or refute. You will even be handed over by parents, brothers, relatives, and friends, and they will put some of you to death. You will be hated by all because of my name, but not a hair on your head will be destroyed. By your perseverance you will secure your lives."

The Gospel of the Lord. ***Praise to you, Lord Jesus Christ.***

PROFESSION OF FAITH *(page 13)*

PRAYER OF THE FAITHFUL

PREPARATION OF GIFTS *(page 16)*

PRAYER OVER THE OFFERINGS
Grant, O Lord, we pray,
that what we offer in the sight of your majesty
may obtain for us the grace of being devoted to you
and gain us the prize of everlasting happiness.
Through Christ our Lord. ***Amen.***

PREFACE *(Sundays in Ordinary Time, pages 28–32)*

◆ TAKING A CLOSER LOOK ◆

✦ **Unwilling to work** The problem of idleness in the Thessalonian community may have been a reaction to the expectation of an imminent end to human affairs or a consequence of the belief that "the day of the Lord is already here" (2:2). The context would seem to indicate that such idleness was a misunderstanding of mutual support in a community largely composed of the poor. Paul reminds the community both of the tradition he taught them and of his own example. The idle, whom Paul describes in a wordplay as "busybodies" instead of "busy," are told to earn their own living, while the community is encouraged to persevere in doing good.

COMMUNION ANTIPHON *(Psalm 73 [72]:28)*

To be near God is my happiness, to place my hope in God the Lord.

Or *(Mark 11:23-24)*

Amen, I say to you: Whatever you ask in prayer, believe that you will receive, and it shall be given to you, says the Lord.

PRAYER AFTER COMMUNION

We have partaken of the gifts of this sacred mystery,
humbly imploring, O Lord,
that what your Son commanded us to do
in memory of him
may bring us growth in charity.
Through Christ our Lord. *Amen.*

BLESSING & DISMISSAL *(page 56)* ✤

❖ RESPONDING TO THE WORD ❖

Malachi foresees the day when God comes in justice to judge the world.	Paul urges us to imitate his hard work and not burden others.	Jesus promises that amid trials and difficulties he will give us wisdom in speaking our witness to him.
➡ *How have I already experienced God's presence making me more sensitive to my participation in injustice?*	➡ *What can I do to take some of the burden from others by sharing more in the work of my parish or faith community?*	➡ *When have I been given just the right words to offer some needed help to others?*

November 24

Jesus shows us how to lead

Early in his papacy, Pope Francis used a striking image to describe the kind of leadership priests should exercise in their faith communities. He urged them to be shepherds marked by "the smell of the sheep." A similar image appears in today's first reading, where God names King David as the shepherd of "my people Israel." The reading from Colossians describes the supreme authority of Christ over all things. Yet throughout his earthly ministry Jesus modeled servant leadership, which we could also call "shepherd leadership."

The daily news often shows a different style of leadership, characterized by arrogance, greed, hunger for power, and a disregard for the common good. The kind of leadership suggested in today's readings, by contrast, is marked by service, humility, and compassion. As the taunting onlookers in the gospel scene mock the kingship of Jesus, we get a glimpse into the heart of true leadership. In the interaction between the crucified Jesus and the "good thief," we see an example of a humble petitioner—"Jesus, remember me"—receiving not judgment but forgiveness: "Today you will be with me in Paradise."

Today we seek the grace to practice and to encourage, through our prayers and our actions, the kind of shepherd leadership modeled by Jesus.

■ KRYSTYNA HIGGINS

ENTRANCE ANTIPHON *(Revelation 5:12; 1:6)*

How worthy is the Lamb who was slain, to receive
power and divinity, and wisdom and strength and
honor. To him belong glory and power for ever
and ever.

INTRODUCTORY RITES *(page 10)*

COLLECT

Almighty ever-living God,
whose will is to restore all things
in your beloved Son, the King of the universe,
grant, we pray,
that the whole creation, set free from slavery,
may render your majesty service
and ceaselessly proclaim your praise.
Through our Lord Jesus Christ, your Son,
who lives and reigns with you in the unity of the Holy Spirit,
one God, for ever and ever. *Amen.*

FIRST READING *(2 Samuel 5:1-3)*

In those days, all the tribes of Israel came to David in Hebron
and said: "Here we are, your bone and your flesh. In days past,
when Saul was our king, it was you who led the Israelites out and
brought them back. And the LORD said to you, 'You shall shepherd my people Israel and shall be commander of Israel.'" When
all the elders of Israel came to David in Hebron, King David
made an agreement with them there before the LORD, and they
anointed him king of Israel.

The word of the Lord. *Thanks be to God.*

RESPONSORIAL PSALM *(Psalm 122:1-2, 3-4, 4-5)*

℟ Let us go rejoicing to the house of the Lord.

I rejoiced because they said to me,
    "We will go up to the house of the Lord."
And now we have set foot
    within your gates, O Jerusalem. ℟
Jerusalem, built as a city
    with compact unity.
To it the tribes go up,
    the tribes of the Lord. ℟
According to the decree for Israel,
    to give thanks to the name of the Lord.
In it are set up judgment seats,
    seats for the house of David. ℟

SECOND READING *(Colossians 1:12-20)*

Brothers and sisters: Let us give thanks to the Father, who has made you fit to share in the inheritance of the holy ones in light. He delivered us from the power of darkness and transferred us to the kingdom of his beloved Son, in whom we have redemption, the forgiveness of sins.

    He is the image of the invisible God,
        the firstborn of all creation.
For in him were created all things in heaven and on earth,
        the visible and the invisible,
            whether thrones or dominions or principalities or powers;
        all things were created through him and for him.
He is before all things,
        and in him all things hold together.

He is the head of the body, the church.
He is the beginning, the firstborn from the dead,
    that in all things he himself might be preeminent.
For in him all the fullness was pleased to dwell,
    and through him to reconcile all things for him,
    making peace by the blood of his cross
    through him, whether those on earth or those in heaven.

The word of the Lord. *Thanks be to God.*

ALLELUIA *(Mark 11:9, 10)*
Alleluia, alleluia. Blessed is he who comes in the name of the
Lord! Blessed is the kingdom of our father David that is to
come! *Alleluia, alleluia.*

GOSPEL *(Luke 23:35–43)*
A reading from the holy Gospel according to Luke.
Glory to you, O Lord.

The rulers sneered at Jesus and said, "He saved others, let him
save himself if he is the chosen one, the Christ of God." Even
the soldiers jeered at him. As they approached to offer him wine they
called out, "If you are King of the Jews, save yourself." Above him
there was an inscription that read, "This is the King of the Jews."

Now one of the criminals hanging there reviled Jesus, saying,
"Are you not the Christ? Save yourself and us." The other, however, rebuking him, said in reply, "Have you no fear of God, for
you are subject to the same condemnation? And indeed, we have
been condemned justly, for the sentence we received corresponds
to our crimes, but this man has done nothing criminal." Then he
said, "Jesus, remember me when you come into your kingdom."

He replied to him, "Amen, I say to you, today **you will be with me in Paradise."**✠

The Gospel of the Lord. *Praise to you, Lord Jesus Christ.*

PROFESSION OF FAITH *(page 13)*

PRAYER OF THE FAITHFUL

PREPARATION OF GIFTS *(page 16)*

PRAYER OVER THE OFFERINGS
As we offer you, O Lord, the sacrifice
by which the human race is reconciled to you,
we humbly pray
that your Son himself may bestow on all nations
the gifts of unity and peace.
Through Christ our Lord. *Amen.*

PREFACE: CHRIST, KING OF THE UNIVERSE
It is truly right and just, our duty and our salvation,
always and everywhere to give you thanks,
Lord, holy Father, almighty and eternal God.

For you anointed your Only Begotten Son,
our Lord Jesus Christ, with the oil of gladness
as eternal Priest and King of all creation,
so that, by offering himself on the altar of the Cross
as a spotless sacrifice to bring us peace,
he might accomplish the mysteries of human redemption
and, making all created things subject to his rule,
he might present to the immensity of your majesty
an eternal and universal kingdom,

a kingdom of truth and life,
a kingdom of holiness and grace,
a kingdom of justice, love and peace.

And so, with Angels and Archangels,
with Thrones and Dominions,
and with all the hosts and Powers of heaven,
we sing the hymn of your glory,
as without end we acclaim:
Holy, Holy, Holy Lord God of hosts... (page 35)

COMMUNION ANTIPHON (Psalm 29 [28]:10-11)
The Lord sits as King for ever. The Lord will bless his people
with peace.

• TAKING A CLOSER LOOK •

✛ **You will be with me in Paradise** One common Jewish view of life after death imagined a series of "heavens" or stages for the ascent of the dead to dwell with God. Paradise (from a Persian word for the enclosed park or garden of a royal palace) is an imaginative description of the "third heaven" (see 2 Corinthians 12:2), which may have been imagined as the "final heaven" where God dwells or as an intermediate stopover after which one ascends to the final heaven to dwell with God. Jesus' words to the thief are found only in Luke and reaffirm Luke's portrait of Jesus as the Son of Man: full of compassion, love, patience, and forgiveness. To be with Christ in paradise is the promise for those who acknowledge Jesus' kingship.

PRAYER AFTER COMMUNION

Having received the food of immortality,
we ask, O Lord,
that, glorying in obedience
to the commands of Christ, the King of the universe,
we may live with him eternally in his heavenly Kingdom.
Who lives and reigns for ever and ever. *Amen.*

BLESSING & DISMISSAL *(page 56)* ✣

• RESPONDING TO THE WORD •

David is God's choice for leading God's people.	God has brought us into Christ's kingdom community.	Jesus' kingly role is not for himself but to help others.
➡ *How can I help to lead others to God?*	➡ *How can I thank God for this wonderful gift?*	➡ *How can I imitate Jesus by thinking and acting for others instead of for myself?*

Praying
and Living
the Eucharist

Praying with the Scriptures

The Bible's message is that God desires to be with us in our world for a relationship. God invites us into a relationship that will not end with death but will go on forever. Building and nurturing this relationship is what living with Christ is all about.

Each week our Sunday Scripture readings help us to deepen our relationship with Jesus. Through Scripture, we learn who God is and who we are. We also discover ways to grow in our relationship with God and with others. By reading, reflecting, and discussing the meaning of these readings, we find keys to imitating Jesus' example, making his vision and values our own and discovering what a relationship with God demands.

A EUCHARISTIC FORMAT: PATTERN FOR OUR SPIRITUALITY

In our Eucharist and also in our preparation for the Eucharist, we imitate Jesus' actions at the Last Supper—*take, bless, break, share*. Jesus' command to *do this in his memory* characterizes not just our worship but our very lives and mission as Christians.

Participating in the eucharistic liturgy and living eucharistic lives is our way of thanking Jesus and of celebrating and nurturing his continual presence with us, not only in church but in all the moments and situations of our daily lives. Through our deepening experience of Christ in word and sacrament, we announce and celebrate the good news of God's presence among us.

The elements of the simple eucharistic format—*take, bless, break, share*—provide a pattern that can assist us in our goal of praying and living the Eucharist.

■ **TAKE** To "take" is to accept the reality of the moment, to open ourselves to God's presence and God's gifts as they present themselves to us. We take a few moments of quiet to become centered, prayerful, and attentive to God's presence.

■ **BLESS** To "bless" is to acknowledge God's role in something—as in the biblical acclamation, *Bless the Lord, O my soul!* When we think of God's creation, how can we not give thanks and praise? The word "eucharist" actually comes from the Greek *eucharistia* ("thanksgiving").

■ **BREAK** To "break" the bread of our lives is to be willing to break through to the deeper meaning of our experience. To do that, we explore Sacred Scripture, we think about the ways that God is speaking to us in the events of our lives, we reflect on the words of Jesus, we listen to the wisdom of the Church's teachings—we open ourselves to the voice of God as it whispers to us in our daily experiences. And we discover God's love and forgiveness in the midst of our own brokenness.

■ **SHARE** Christian spirituality is not a narrowly focused "God and me" affair. Christians discover that "I" is never alone; "I" is always an "I *in Christ*." And as one realizes his or her identity as a member of Christ's body, one discovers that the true "I" is really a "we."

We have been called into communion with God and with one another. Our own experience of Jesus leads us to ministry, to share the gifts that God has given us, and to bring the fruits of our prayer to others and to our world.

SAMPLE FORMAT FOR PERSONAL REFLECTION

» TAKE Find a quiet spot where you can read, reflect, and pray. If you wish to record your thoughts and experiences, have your prayer journal handy. Take a few moments of quiet to become prayerful and centered.

» BLESS Begin your reflection time with a prayer. You may wish to use a spontaneous prayer, the Collect for the coming Sunday, or one from *A Treasury of Prayers* (page 597).

» BREAK
- *Read:* Read the Scripture readings from the coming Sunday. Pause in silence to be attentive to God's message for you today.
- *Reflect:* Read the Sunday reflection found at the start of the coming Sunday.
- *Respond:* To explore the meaning of the readings, consider first the questions in the *Responding to the Word* at the end of each Sunday. If you wish to explore the readings further, choose one or more of the *Basic Questions for Exploring Scripture* (page 583).

After reflecting on the questions and writing down your answers in your prayer journal, if you wish, take some time to be quiet and attentive to Christ's presence with you—where he wants to dwell right now.

» SHARE Close with a spontaneous prayer, one chosen from the Mass for the coming Sunday, or one from *A Treasury of Prayers* (page 597).

Now you are better prepared to share the good news with others in the coming week!

Basic Questions for Exploring Scripture

There are several basic questions and some follow-up questions that we can use to explore any biblical reading. (Note that not all of these questions are equally answered in every passage.)

What does this text tell me about God? about Jesus? about the Holy Spirit?

• Does this confirm what I already know? • Is there something new here that I had not noticed before? • What does God want me to know or do?

What does God/Jesus/the Holy Spirit do in relation to us and our world?

• How is the divine presence and power revealed? • Why does God come to us? • What is required of us to do or not do?

What does this text tell me about myself?

• How am I like the person(s) in Scripture? • How would I respond if this happened to me? • How would I be changed if I did what the text says? • What challenged me to live out my faith more fully?
• What surprised me the most about this passage? • What puzzled me the most? • What made me most comfortable? Why?
• What made me most uncomfortable? Why?

What do I learn about the community that God desires?

• What does this text tell me about how to love God? • What does this text tell me about how to love others? • What guidelines for better community living does the passage offer?

The Practice of Lectio Divina

Lectio divina ("sacred reading") is a contemplative way of reading Sacred Scripture that has been part of the Christian tradition since the third century.

We may find it helpful to think of it as involving three "moments" or stages: reading, meditating, and praying.

READING

This *first moment* consists in our reading a short Scripture passage slowly, attentively, repeatedly—and aloud whenever possible. We may wish to choose the gospel reading for the coming Sunday and read it from the previous Monday all through the week.

Paying close attention to the story, and especially to the words themselves, we let ourselves *enjoy* the story and even grow to *love* the story and the very words in which it is told. When a word or phrase catches our attention, we may jot it down or simply stay with it for awhile to savor its message, allowing its fullness to penetrate our being.

MEDITATION

Reading leads us naturally to the *second moment*: meditation. Having settled on one section, phrase, or even a single word, we let its meaning unfold in our hearts.

Our meditation can take place as we sit in quiet prayer or as we perform the simple activities of our day. It may last an hour, a day, or over the course of a week.

During meditation, we may find ourselves focusing on the present: what does this text have to say about what is happening in my life or in the world around me now? Something in the text may jog a memory of an experience from our own lives. Or we may find that, when we return to our daily activities, some event or situation will unexpectedly bring us back to the text. In either case, the Holy Spirit may be trying to open up a dialogue with us!

PRAYER

Prayer, the *third moment*, also occurs naturally. This is not an intellectual exercise, but a dialogue with God. We respond authentically and spontaneously—as we would in a conversation with a close friend.

Our prayer may take four different forms:

- *Thanksgiving:* When the text reminds us of blessings and good things we have known, we praise and thank God.
- *Repentance:* When we become aware of wrong we have done or good we have failed to do, we humbly ask for forgiveness.
- *Petition:* When the text reminds us of our own needs or of the needs of others, we ask God for guidance and assistance.
- *Contemplation:* By grace, we may be led to a deeper moment of prayer in which we are no longer thanking or repenting or asking, but simply joyfully resting in God's presence, trustfully leaving ourselves in God's hands. This is called contemplative prayer.

I would like to recall and recommend the ancient tradition of
lectio divina: *the diligent reading of Sacred Scripture accompanied by prayer brings about that intimate dialogue in which the person reading hears God who is speaking, and in praying, responds to God with trusting openness of heart. If it is effectively promoted, this practice will bring to the Church—*
I am convinced of it—a new spiritual springtime."

➥ POPE BENEDICT XVI

The Liturgical Calendar:
UNFOLDING THE MYSTERY OF CHRIST

One way the Church tells the story of God's saving activity is by its calendar. "Within the cycle of a year, she unfolds the whole mystery of Christ. Recalling thus the mysteries of redemption, the Church opens to the faithful the riches of her Lord's powers and mercies, so that they are in some way made present at all times, and the faithful are enabled to lay hold of them and become filled with saving grace" (Vatican II, *Constitution on the Sacred Liturgy*, #102). During this yearly cycle, we remember our story and deepen our understanding of its meaning for us.

The Church year is anchored by two segments: **Advent–Christmas–Epiphany** and **Lent–Holy Week–Easter**. **Pentecost** and the **Sundays in Ordinary Time** fill out the rest of the year. The overall pattern highlights the transitions from darkness to light to manifestation, and from promise to fulfillment to proclamation.

ADVENT, CHRISTMAS, AND EPIPHANY

Advent, the time of preparation for Christmas, begins on the fourth Sunday before Christmas. As December's darkness and short days permeate our lives, the Church proclaims that Christ comes as the light of the world. Christmas celebrates the mystery of God's incarnation—God-with-us as one of us in human flesh.

Christmas is followed by the Epiphany, celebrating the visit of the magi who traveled from afar to worship the babe in Bethlehem. They represent all the nations of the world searching for their savior. The revelation of God's light and the fulfillment of God's promise in Jesus lead to the proclamation of this good news. In the season after Epiphany, we share the news that God's love is available for every person, for all of creation!

LENT, HOLY WEEK, AND EASTER

The Church's greatest feast and most important rites were celebrated on Easter—the time of initiation, when new members would be baptized and emerge into a new life of fellowship. Today, the seasons of Lent and Easter retain this baptismal focus. Vatican II has renewed the ancient practice of initiation in its Rite of Christian Initiation for Adults (RCIA).

The forty days (excluding Sundays) of Lent recall Jesus' forty days in the wilderness prior to his public ministry. Lent is a time of inwardness, of spiritual discipline, and of growth. During Lent we seek out the shadows in our souls, inviting Christ's light to illumine them.

Lent concludes with Holy Week when we recall the last events of Jesus' life, beginning with his entry into Jerusalem (Passion or Palm Sunday). Then the most sacred Three Days (the Triduum) recall Jesus' Last Supper (Holy Thursday), his crucifixion and death (Good Friday), and his resurrection (Easter Vigil and Easter Day). Then, for fifty days, we bask in the joy of the resurrection and the promise of new life with God forever.

PENTECOST AND ORDINARY TIME

Witnesses are needed to guide others to discover the transforming presence of God. At Pentecost, the Holy Spirit descends on the disciples, uniting them as a community and giving them new tongues to proclaim the good news of God's triumph over death to the ends of the earth.

After Pentecost, we continue with Ordinary Time. It is "ordinary" not because it is common but because the Sundays are counted (they are "in order"). Each Sunday we follow Jesus and have the opportunity to move ever more deeply into sharing in his life, death, and resurrection.

As we attune ourselves to the rhythms of the Church's liturgical year, the mysteries of the Lord's life are made present, and our lives are sanctified by our participation.

Understanding the Lectionary

Since its beginning, the Church has gathered faithfully every Sunday to listen carefully to God's word. The Lectionary for Mass is the selection of the most important Bible readings for use at Mass. Through them the Church remembers and renews its relationship with God.

THE LECTIONARY'S ARRANGEMENT

The lectionary is not a chronological approach to reading the Bible, nor is it a book-by-book approach. Each week the gospel readings are closely linked to the seasons of the Church's life cycle, its liturgical calendar. In the first half of the Church year, we follow the major events of the life of Jesus, including his birth, death, resurrection, and the birth of the Church, and in the second half we study Jesus' actions and teachings.

In addition, the lectionary provides an opportunity to remember great persons in Church history on saints' days and to celebrate special events in the life of a parish, such as confirmation. Throughout the year, Scriptures have been chosen for their appropriateness for the occasions on which they are read.

THE EVOLUTION OF THE CURRENT LECTIONARY

From the time of the Council of Trent (1545-63), when the liturgy was fixed in the form that was familiar to all Catholics before Vatican II, the selection of lectionary readings consisted simply of a one-year cycle that included two Sunday readings, one from a New Testament letter or epistle and another from one of the gospels. The gospel readings were taken mostly from Matthew and Luke, with very few from Mark or John. The Old Testament was read only on Epiphany and during Holy Week.

The liturgical renewal of Vatican Council II (1962-65) directed that the "treasures of Scripture" be made more available so that the faithful would be fed on this richer fare. This momentous change reversed the previous limitation of Scripture by adding an additional reading that, for the first time in centuries, opened the riches of the Old Testament to the weekly Christian gathering (and the Acts of the Apostles during the Easter Season).

The new lectionary includes the following features:

- **Three-year Cycle of Readings:** The Sunday lectionary covers the most significant parts of the Old and New Testaments every three years. The three years, designated A, B, and C, always begin on the First Sunday of Advent. Each of the cycles focuses on one of the synoptic gospels. In Year A, Matthew is read; Year B, Mark; Year C, Luke. The Gospel of John is used during all three years on certain feast days, during Holy Week, and during the Easter season. Since the Gospel of Mark is so brief, the sixth chapter of John's gospel (on the Bread of Life) is read for five weeks of Year B.

- **Four Readings Every Sunday:** Each Sunday, four Scripture passages are assigned to be read: the first reading from the Old Testament (except during the Easter season), chosen to coincide thematically with the gospel; a responsorial psalm relating to the first reading or to the liturgical season; the second reading from the letters or other New Testament writings; and finally the gospel reading.

- **The selected readings are about:**
  - **Christ,** so as to unfold the mystery of Christ's person and teachings over the cycle of the year (see Vatican II, *Constitution on the Sacred Liturgy* [CSL], #102)
  - **Salvation history,** in order to show the place of Christ in God's plan of salvation, thus connecting God's work with Israel (Old Testament) to God's work in Christ (New Testament) (CSL, #5)
  - **"The guiding principles of the Christian life"** (CSL, #52), to help people understand the Christian message and live it more fully in their everyday lives.

This Year's Scriptures:
THE GOSPEL OF LUKE

In the three-year lectionary cycle, the Sunday gospel readings for this year (liturgical Year C), are taken primarily from the Gospel of Luke. Each of the gospels proclaims that the good news of our salvation (our right relationship with God) is best understood by attending closely to the life of Jesus of Nazareth. The gospel writers' strategy was to invite readers to identify with Jesus and the disciples in the story and follow Jesus as they did.

HOW LUKE'S GOSPEL CAME ABOUT

In the mid-eighties of the first century, Luke adapted Mark's gospel to the needs of his primarily Gentile community, which was probably located in Antioch, the center of the Christian missionary effort to include the Gentiles. Luke tells the story of our salvation in two volumes, his gospel and the Acts of the Apostles. Luke wanted to show that what happened to Jesus was foreshadowed in the Old Testament and continued after Jesus' death in the lives of the Christian disciples.

LUKE'S PORTRAIT OF JESUS THE PROPHET

Luke characterizes Jesus as a prophet "mighty in word and deed" (24:19; see also 4:24, 7:16, 7:39) whose job description (4:16-30, 7:22-23) is taken from the prophet Isaiah. As a spokesperson for God, his prophetic message is an invitation to see the world from God's perspective rather than from a human viewpoint.

Luke focuses on Jesus' healing-saving activity. Born "a Savior" (2:11), he comes "to seek and to save what is lost" (19:10). Since in

Greek the same word means both to save and to heal, Luke stresses that our bodily and spiritual health are interconnected. When Jesus tells those he cures, "Go, your faith has saved you," this could also be translated "your faith has healed you" (7:50, 8:48, 17:19, 18:42).

JESUS, THE HEALING PROPHET

Jesus' ministry of healing brings God's salvation, and so breaks across all our humanly created boundaries. Like a magnet, Jesus draws the poor, the outcasts, the sick, women, and foreigners to himself for healing. His powerful parables about the lost coin, the lost son, and the lost sheep (15:1-32) challenge us to reach out beyond our narrow and comfortable borders to also seek and save the lost.

JESUS, THE PROPHET OF JUSTICE

Luke also emphasizes that Jesus takes up the prophetic cause for social justice. At the start of his ministry, Jesus associates his work with that of the spirit-filled prophet Isaiah (4:16-30). During his ministry, Jesus will reach out to the poor, the blind, the downtrodden, prisoners, and those who need to experience God's reversal of the human value system.

In the beatitudes and woes (6:20-26), Jesus describes God's values and God's ways. Quite unexpectedly, God's blessing is not bestowed on the rich but on the poor, the hungry, the sorrowing, the hated, the persecuted, and the rejected.

CONCERN FOR THE POOR

Luke's special concern for the poor is revealed in the many sayings and stories of Jesus that deal with the issues of rich and poor.

When borrowing from Mark, Luke usually intensifies Mark's emphasis on the rich and poor. He also introduces many new passages that mention the poor, stories that are not found in the other gospels—Mary's Magnificat (1:39-54), Jesus' sermon at Nazareth (4:16-30), the good Samaritan who uses his wealth to help another (10:29-37), the great supper (14:16-24), the rich fool (12:16-21), the rich man and Lazarus (16:19-26), and Zacchaeus (19:1-10), who represents the right response of a wealthy person to Jesus' presence and preaching.

JESUS, THE SUFFERING PROPHET

Jesus' advocacy for justice inevitably led to a confrontation with the Jewish and Roman authorities, who conspired to bring about his murder. Luke understands this suffering as an essential part of the prophet's role (13:33-34). In his version of Christ's passion, Luke portrays Jesus as an innocent martyr. Pilate (23:4, 14, 22), Herod (23:15), and the Roman centurion at the foot of the cross (23:47) all declare Jesus innocent. Jesus dies as he lived—forgiving his persecutors and saving a repentant thief.

MARY, LUKE'S MODEL DISCIPLE

For Luke, Mary stands out as a true model of genuine discipleship. Like the prophets of old, she responds wholeheartedly to God's call. Her "Let it be" starts God's work both in her body and in her life to bring forth Jesus (1:26-38). She keeps all these things in her heart and ponders them (2:19). During Jesus' ministry, she "hears the word and acts on it" (8:21). After the Resurrection she is found praying in the community of disciples as they await the Pentecostal empowerment of the Holy Spirit for their mission (Acts 1:14).

Luke highlights the way of discipleship more clearly in the Acts of the Apostles. The risen Christ reveals to the disciples that the kingdom will come through their Spirit-filled witness to the ends of the earth (1:8). They will witness with their words and with their lives. As Paul demonstrates, being a Christian demands fearless witness and a shattering of the borders between Jew and Gentile to build a new community in Christ.

CHRISTIAN DISCIPLESHIP: FOLLOWING JESUS ON THE JOURNEY TO GOD

More than any other gospel writer, Luke structures his gospel life of Jesus according to the familiar pattern of a journey. We often use this journey pattern to chart our experience of changes both in space—going *from* a starting point *through* a transition *to* a new place—and in time—*from* the past *through* the present and *to* the future.

This familiar "from-through-to" pattern of a journey describes Jesus' gospel life. He comes *from* God to become human in Mary's womb. He moves back toward God *through* a life of service dedicated to establishing God's kingdom community in Galilee. He confronts opposition and is killed in Jerusalem. He is rewarded by God with new life and finally returns *to* God to continue the relationship begun here on earth. He invites each of us to follow by imitating this journey with him.

The journey of Christ is the pattern that each Christian must follow. His journey is our journey, too.

Liturgical and Devotional Prayer:
WHAT'S THE DIFFERENCE?

There are real differences between liturgical and devotional prayer, but they are linked; we need both, and both have the same goal: to help us grow in our life as Catholic disciples of our Lord. But just what are the major differences between these types of prayer? Here are a few central elements:

Liturgical prayer—officially, the celebration of the seven sacraments and the Liturgy of the Hours—is always primary. These celebrations are primary because these are the privileged ways we enter into Christ's paschal mystery (his life, death, and resurrection that bring life to the world) and learn to live this mystery in our own lives. While we are meant to pray these prayers in a deeply personal way, they are also always intended to link us to the whole Church at prayer. They belong to everybody, which is why the Church insists that individuals may not change them. Liturgical prayer *shapes us* into being ever more perfect members of the Body of Christ.

Devotional prayers, in the words of Vatican II's *Constitution on the Sacred Liturgy*, "should be so drawn up that they harmonize with the liturgical seasons, accord with the sacred liturgy, are in some fashion derived from it, and lead people to it, since the liturgy by its very nature far surpasses any of them" (#13). Devotions are meant to be prayed in a deeply personal way, and may or may not have a communal dimension. *We shape* these prayers to meet our personal prayer needs and encounter God in our daily lives, which in turn helps make us ready for full, conscious, and active participation in the liturgy. There are no required forms of devotional prayer—individuals are free to create or adopt and pray them as meets their needs, within the guidelines set by the Church.

What kind of guidelines? Along with the quote from the *Constitution on the Sacred Liturgy* given above, the Church advises, for example, that these devotions not be overly sentimental. They should not lead one into superstition or be based solely on legendary tales. They should not be added to the liturgy or preferred to liturgical prayer. People are free to pray them or not. They should help us relate emotionally—with the heart and not just the intellect— to the central mysteries of our faith. They should increase our yearning for liturgical prayer and help us pray the Mass deeply and reverently. And their ultimate aim should be the same as that of the liturgy: to say with St. Paul, "I live now, not I, but Christ lives in me" (Galatians 2:20).

Mass and Eucharistic Adoration provide an example of the difference between liturgical and devotional prayer. The Mass is the weekly or daily way we join ourselves to the dying and rising of the Lord. We gather through, with, and in Christ to offer thanks and praise to the Father and to be transformed by the Holy Spirit into the body and blood of Christ in our world—and to eat and drink of Christ's body and blood that we are, and are becoming.

Eucharistic Adoration (in the form of prayer before the tabernacle), on the other hand, is a wonderful way to pause in our busy lives, to step into the presence of God, and to marvel at the great mystery of love celebrated in the Eucharist, to thank God for it, and to pray about what it means to share in Christ's Body and Blood and be his disciples in the world around us.

Of the two, the Mass is always primary, because it is the action of our entering into the paschal mystery. Adoration is meant to strengthen our desire to participate in the Mass and to pray it more deeply, with our heart, mind, and soul. Because Adoration is derived from the eucharistic liturgy and meant to lead us back to the eucharistic liturgy, it has the same goal as the liturgy: to praise and thank God and to help us lead more Christ-like lives in all that we do.

*Prayer is the source and origin of every
upward journey toward God. Let us each,
then, turn to prayer and say to our Lord
God: "Lead me, O Lord, on your path,
that I may walk in your truth."*

❧ St. Bonaventure

A Treasury
of Prayers

PRAYERS FROM THE BIBLE

The Lord's Prayer: found in Matthew 6:9-13 and in Luke 11:2-4, it is also used in our eucharistic liturgy (page 53)

Song of Moses: from Exodus 15 (page 318)

Paul's Prayers: from Ephesians 1 (page 75) and 2 Thessalonians 2-3 (page 562)

Canticle of Zechariah (Benedictus): *Luke 1:68-79*
Blessed be the Lord, the God of Israel;
   he has come to his people and set them free.
He has raised up for us a mighty savior,
   born of the house of his servant David.
Through his prophets he promised of old
   that he would save us from our enemies,
   from the hands of all who hate us.
He promised to show mercy to our fathers
   and to remember his holy covenant.
This was the oath he swore
   to our father Abraham: to set us free from the hands of our enemies,
   free to worship him without fear,
   holy and righteous in his sight all the days of our life.
You, my child, shall be called the prophet of the Most High,
   for you will go before the Lord to prepare his way,
   to give his people knowledge of salvation
   by the forgiveness of their sins.
In the tender compassion of our God
   the dawn from on high shall break upon us,

to shine on those who dwell in darkness and the shadow of death,
and to guide our feet into the way of peace.

Canticle of Mary (Magnificat): *Luke 1:46-55*

My soul proclaims the greatness of the Lord,
    my spirit rejoices in God my Savior
    for he has looked with favor upon his lowly servant.
From this day all generations will call me blessed:
    the Almighty has done great things for me,
    and holy is his Name.
He has mercy on those who fear him in every generation.
He has shown the strength of his arm,
    and has scattered the proud in their conceit.
He has cast down the mighty from their thrones,
    and has lifted up the lowly.
He has filled the hungry with good things,
    and the rich he has sent away empty.
He has come to the help of his servant Israel
    for he has remembered his promise of mercy,
    the promise he made to our fathers,
    to Abraham and his children for ever.

The Song of Simeon: *Luke 2:29-32*

Lord, now let your servant go in peace;
    your word has been fulfilled:
my own eyes have seen the salvation
    which you have prepared in the sight of every people:
a light to reveal you to the nations
    and the glory of your people Israel.

Paul's Blessing: *Ephesians 3:16-21*
May you be strengthened with power
through God's Spirit in your inner self.
May Christ dwell in your hearts through faith;
so that you, rooted and grounded in love, may have
strength to comprehend with all the holy ones
what is the breadth and length and height and depth,
and to know the love of Christ
that surpasses knowledge, so that you may be filled
with all the fullness of God.
Now to God, who by the power at work within us is able
to accomplish far more than all we ask or imagine,
be glory in the church and in Christ Jesus
to all generations, forever and ever. Amen.

PRAYERS FROM THE CHRISTIAN TRADITION

Glory be to the Father
Glory be to the Father,
    and to the Son,
    and to the Holy Spirit.
As it was in the beginning, is now,
    and ever shall be, world without end. Amen.

The Hail Mary
Hail Mary, full of grace, the Lord is with thee.
Blessed art thou among women
and blessed is the fruit of thy womb, Jesus.

Holy Mary, Mother of God, pray for us sinners,
now and at the hour of our death. Amen.

Hail, Holy Queen (Salve Regina)

Hail, holy Queen, mother of mercy,
our life, our sweetness and our hope.
To you do we cry, poor banished children of Eve;
to you do we send up our sighs,
mourning and weeping in this valley of tears.
Turn then, most gracious advocate,
your eyes of mercy toward us,
and after this, our exile, show unto us
the blessed fruit of your womb, Jesus.
O clement, O loving, O sweet Virgin Mary.

Anima Christi

Soul of Christ, be my sanctification;
Body of Christ, be my salvation;
Blood of Christ, fill all my veins;
Water of Christ's side, wash out my stains;
Passion of Christ, my comfort be;
O good Jesu, listen to me;
In Thy wounds I fain would hide;
Ne'er to be parted from Thy side;
Guard me, should the foe assail me;
Call me when my life shall fail me;
Bid me come to Thee above,
With Thy saints to sing Thy love,
World without end. Amen.
(Translation by Bl. John Henry Cardinal Newman)

The Memorare

Remember, most gracious Virgin Mary,
that never was it known that anyone
who fled to your protection, implored your help,
and sought your intercession, was left unaided.
Inspired with this confidence, I fly to you,
O Virgin of virgins, my mother.
To you do I come; before you I stand,
sinful and sorrowful.
Mother of the Word Incarnate,
despise not my petitions
but in your mercy hear and answer me. Amen.

The Angelus

The angel of the Lord declared unto Mary,
    and she conceived of the Holy Spirit. *Hail Mary...*
Behold, the handmaid of the Lord;
    be it done to me according to your word. *Hail Mary...*
And the word was made flesh,
    and dwelt among us. *Hail Mary...*

Pray for us, O holy Mother of God;
    that we may be made worthy of the promises of Christ.

Pour forth, we beseech you, O Lord,
your grace into our hearts
that we, to whom the incarnation of your Son
was made known by the message of an angel,
may by his passion and cross
be brought to the glory of his resurrection.
We ask this through the same Christ, our Lord. Amen.

Act of Contrition

My God, I am sorry for my sins with all my heart.
In choosing to do wrong and failing to do good,
I have sinned against you
whom I should love above all things.
I firmly intend, with your help,
to do penance,
to sin no more,
and to avoid whatever leads me to sin.
Our Savior Jesus Christ suffered and died for us.
In his name, my God, have mercy. Amen.

Regina Caeli (Queen of Heaven)

O Queen of heaven, rejoice, alleluia!
　For he whom you chose to bear, alleluia!
Is risen as he said, alleluia!
　Pray for us to God, alleluia!
Rejoice and be glad, O Virgin Mary, alleluia!
　For the Lord is truly risen, alleluia!

O God, by the resurrection of your Son, our Lord,
You were pleased to make glad the whole world;
grant, we beseech you, that through
the intercession of the Virgin Mary, his mother,
we may attain the joys of everlasting life,
through the same Christ our Lord. Amen.

THE ROSARY

Like the prayer beads that are used in many religious traditions, the rosary keeps our hands moving while our minds and hearts are meditating on the mysteries of Jesus' life, death, and resurrection. While using the rosary, we focus on twenty events or mysteries in the life and death of Jesus and reflect on how we share with Mary in the saving work of Christ today. Reading a related passage from the Bible helps to deepen meditation on a particular mystery. The Scripture citations given here are not exhaustive. Many other biblical texts are also be suitable for your prayerful reflection.

To pray the rosary:

- Begin the rosary at the crucifix, making the Sign of the Cross and praying the **Apostles' Creed**
- At the first large bead say the **Our Father**, then for the three beads pray the **Hail Mary** for each of the gifts of faith, hope, and love, then **Glory be to the Father.**
- For each mystery, begin with the **Our Father** (the single bead), then recite the **Hail Mary** ten times, and end with **Glory be to the Father**

The Five Joyful Mysteries
The Annunciation (Luke 1:26-38)
The Visitation (Luke 1:39-56)
The Nativity (Luke 2:1-20)
The Presentation (Luke 2:22-38)
The Finding in the Temple (Luke 2:41-52)

The Five Mysteries of Light
The Baptism in the Jordan (Matthew 3:13-17)
The Wedding at Cana (John 2:1-12)
The Proclamation of the Kingdom (Mark 1:14-15)
The Transfiguration (Luke 9:28-36)
The First Eucharist (Matthew 26:26-29)

The Five Sorrowful Mysteries
The Agony in the Garden (Matthew 26:36-56)
The Scourging at the Pillar (Matthew 27:20-26)
The Crowning with Thorns (Matthew 27:27-30)
The Carrying of the Cross (Matthew 27:31-33)
The Crucifixion (Matthew 27:34-60)

The Five Glorious Mysteries
The Resurrection (John 20:1-18)
The Ascension (Acts 1:9-11)
The Descent of the Holy Spirit (John 20:19-23)
The Assumption of Mary (John 11:26)
The Crowning of Mary (Philippians 2:1-11)

PRAYERS FROM THE SAINTS

May the angel of peace watch over us

May God the Father, who made us, bless us.
May God the Son send his healing among us.
May God the Holy Spirit move within us
and give us eyes to see with, ears to hear with,
and hands that your work might be done.
May we walk and preach the word of God to all.
May the angel of peace watch over us
and lead us at last by God's grace to the kingdom. Amen.

● St. Dominic (1170-1221)

O Love

O Love Almighty, in your love confirm me.
O Love most wise, give me wisdom in the love of you.
O Love most valuable, grant that I may live only for you.
O Love most faithful, in all my tribulations comfort me.
O Love always with me, work all my works in me.
O Love victorious, grant that I may persevere in you. Amen.

● St. Gertrude the great (1256-1302)

To be like Jesus

O God, make us more like Jesus.
Help us to bear difficulty, pain, disappointment, sorrow,
knowing that in your perfect working and design
you can use such bitter experiences to shape our characters
and make us more like our Lord.
We look with hope for that day when we shall be wholly like Christ,
because we shall see him as he is. Amen.

● St. Ignatius of Antioch (35-108)

Lord, make me an instrument of your peace
Lord, make me an instrument of your peace.
Where there is hatred, let me sow love;
where there is injury, pardon;
where there is doubt, faith;
where there is despair, hope;
where there is darkness, light;
and where there is sadness, joy.
Divine Master, grant that I may not so much seek
to be consoled as to console,
to be understood as to understand,
to be loved as to love.
For it is in giving that we receive,
in pardoning that we are pardoned,
and in dying that we are born to eternal life. Amen.
● INSPIRED BY ST. FRANCIS OF ASSISI (1181/82-1226)

May we serve others
Make us worthy, Lord, to serve others throughout the world
who live and die in poverty and hunger.
Give them, through our hands, this day their daily bread.
And by our understanding love, give peace and joy. Amen.
● ST. TERESA OF CALCUTTA (1910-1997)

Help me to seek you
Grant me, O Lord my God, a mind to know you, a heart to seek you,
wisdom to find you, conduct pleasing to you,
faithful perseverance in waiting for you,
and a hope of finally embracing you. Amen.
● ST. THOMAS AQUINAS (1225-1274)

Thankful is the life I live

Christ, O Creator, hear my cry,
I am all yours, your call I hear,
My Savior, Love, yours am I,
My heart to yours be ever near.
Whether in life or death's last hour,
If sickness, pain, or health you give,
Or shame or honor, weakness, power,
Thankful is the life I live. Amen.

● St. Teresa of Ávila (1515-1582)

Day by day

Thanks be to you, my Lord Jesus Christ,
for all the benefits that you have won for us,
for all the pains and insults that you have borne for us.
O most merciful Redeemer, Friend, and Brother,
may we know you more clearly, love you more dearly,
and follow you more nearly, day by day. Amen.

● St. Richard de Wyche, Bishop of Chichester (1197-1253)

O Heart of Love

O my God, fill my soul with holy joy,
courage and strength to serve you.
Enkindle your love in me and then walk with me
along the next stretch of road before me.
I do not see very far ahead, but when I have arrived
where the horizon now closes down,
a new prospect will open before me,
and I shall meet it with peace. Amen.

● St. Teresa Benedicta of the Cross [Edith Stein] (1891-1942)

MORNING PRAYERS

I give you this day

My God, I give you this day.
I offer you, now, all of the good that I shall do,
and I promise to accept, for love of you,
all of the difficulty that I shall meet.
Help me to conduct myself during this day
in a way that pleases you. Amen.

- St. Francis de Sales (1567-1622)

To please you always

I pray you, most gentle Jesus, by your precious blood,
deliver me from all evils, past, present, and to come.
Give me a lively faith, a firm hope, and perfect charity,
so that I may love you with all my heart,
and all my soul, and all my strength.
Make me firm and steadfast in good works,
and grant me perseverance in your service
so that I may be able to please you always. Amen.

- St. Clare of Assisi (1194-1253)

Help us to follow your will

O Father, the first rule of our Savior's life was to do your will.
Let his will of the present moment
be the first rule of our daily life and work,
with no other desire
but for its most full and complete accomplishment.
Help us to follow it faithfully,
so that in doing what you wish we will be pleasing to you. Amen.

- St. Elizabeth Ann Seton (1774-1821)

EVENING PRAYERS

O Lord, draw near

We bring before you, O Lord,
the troubles and perils of people and nations,
the sighing of prisoners and captives, the sorrows of the bereaved,
the necessities of strangers, the helplessness of the weak,
the despondency of the weary, the failing powers of the aged.
O Lord, draw near to each, for the sake of Jesus Christ our Lord. Amen.

● St. Anselm of Canterbury (1033-1109)

May your will be my will

O God, fortify me with the grace of your Holy Spirit
and give your peace to my soul
that I may be free from all
needless anxiety, solicitude, and worry.
Help me to desire always that which is
pleasing and acceptable to you
so that your will may be my will. Amen.

● St. Frances Xavier Cabrini (1850-1917)

An evening prayer

Lord, our God, we are in the shadow of your wings.
Protect us and bear us up.
You will care for us as if we were little children, even to our old age.
When you are our strength, we are strong;
but when we are our own strength, we are weak.
Our good always lives in your presence,
and we suffer when we turn our faces away from you.
We now return to you, O Lord,
that we may never turn away again. Amen.

● St. Augustine of Hippo (354-430)

RECEIVING COMMUNION OUTSIDE MASS

In the celebration of the Eucharist we recognize the presence of Christ in the priest, in the word proclaimed, in the prayer and song of the assembly, and above all in the consecrated elements. Our eucharistic communion with Christ and one another is the living sign of our belonging to Jesus' kingdom community. So from its beginning, the Christian community has always made provision for those who are unable to be present to celebrate this eucharistic communion with Christ. The communion ritual outside of Mass mirrors the same four parts that give the Mass its structure: an introductory rite, a liturgy of the word, a liturgy of the Eucharist, and a concluding rite. You may wish to begin with the following prayers of preparation:

For the extraordinary minister of Holy Communion

O loving God, may your healing and nurturing presence be clearly evident in my whole being today: in my speaking and listening, in my attitude of compassion and understanding. Help me to communicate to those who are homebound the love and care of Christ and of our Christian community from whom I am sent. Let all that is in my mind, all that comes from my lips and from within my heart, reflect the greatness of your love. Amen.

For the communicant

This prayer may be said by the communicant, a family or household member, or the minister.

O loving and faithful God, you invite us to share in the eucharistic food, a sign of your commitment to be with us each day of our life's journey. Despite our personal limitations, you love us completely and nourish us with your divine life. Give us the strength we need to meet whatever challenges that we are now experiencing. Amen.

INTRODUCTORY RITE

May the blessing of God, the love of Christ,
the power of the Holy Spirit,
and the good wishes of our parish community be with you.
And with your spirit.

Use the Collect from any Sunday or from Holy Thursday (page 273).

LITURGY OF THE WORD

Jesus' words offer comfort in our time of need
and invite us to continue to be like Jesus
even in the difficult times of our lives.

*Read aloud one of the Sunday Scripture readings from this missal or a
reading from the suggestions below. After some time for quiet reflection,
pray the Responsorial Psalm together and/or share one or two thoughts
about the reading.*

*The following readings from this missal are also especially appropriate
for a communion service.*

Holy Thursday: Mass of the Lord's Supper, page 273
Feast of the Most Holy Body and Blood of Christ, page 417
How to pray (Luke 11:1-13), page 455
The body of Christ (1 Corinthians 12:12-30), page 150
Love is... (1 Corinthians 12:31–13:13), page 156
A spirit of wisdom (Ephesians 1:17-23), page 388
Holy, Holy, Holy (Isaiah 6:1-2a, 3-8), page 162
Peter's love (John 21:1-19), page 363
Come to me (Isaiah 55:1-11), page 322

RECEPTION OF THE EUCHARIST

The Lord's Prayer
Hearing God's word has drawn us together, and now we deepen our communion by sharing the body of Christ. To prepare ourselves for his coming, let us pray as he taught us: *Our Father...*

Invitation to communion
This bread that we share is the body of Christ,
the sign of his endless love and the gift of himself
so that we may live with God now and forever.
Take and eat this bread with confidence that Jesus' presence in it
will nourish you, heal and strengthen you, and transform you from within.

As the bread is given, the minister says:
The Body of Christ. *Amen.*

CONCLUDING RITE

After communion, allow time for quiet reflection to attend to Jesus' presence. You may wish to say a prayer such as the Anima Christi (page 601) or Psalm 23 (page 231).

Prayer after communion
Pray this prayer after communion or one from a Sunday:
Gracious God, you have nourished us with the bread that makes us one in Christ. Fill us with your Spirit, make us one in peace and love, and help us to bring your salvation and joy to those we meet today. We ask this through Christ our Lord. *Amen.*

Conclude by sharing a sign of peace with one another.

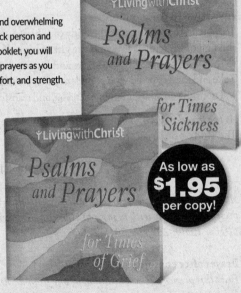

Pronunciation Guide for Biblical Words

*Many biblical personal and place names are familiar to us and so offer little problem with their pronunciation. The following lists only unfamiliar names that might be difficult to pronounce. Words marked with an asterisk (*) in the readings are found in this pronunciation guide. The **bold syllable** indicates the accent for the word.*

Abel-meholah
  (**ay**-buhl-mee-**hoh**-luh)

Amalek (**am**-uh-lek)

Aramean (ahr-ah-**mee**-ahn)

Arimathea (ahr-uh-muh-**thee**-uh)

Attalia (ah-**tal**-ee-ah)

Barabbas (buh-**rab**-uhs)

Bethany (**beth**-uh-nee)

Bethphage (beth-**fuh**-dzhee)

Caiaphas (**kahy**-uh-fuhs)

Capernaum (kuh-**pur**-ney-uhm)

Cappadocia (kap-uha-**doh**-shuh)

Caesar (**see**-zer)

Cephas (**see**-fahs)

Chaldeans (kal-**dee**-uhns)

cherubim (**cher**-uh-bim)

Cilicia (si-**lish**-uh)

Cyrenian (sahy-**ree**-nee-uhn)

Didymus (**did**-ee-muhs)

Ebed-melech (**ee**-bed-**mee**-lehk)

Elamites (**ee**-luh-mahyts)

Ephah (**ef**-ah)

Ephrathah (**ef**-rah-thah)

Horeb (**hohr**-eb)

Iconium (ahy-**koh**-nee-uhm)

Ituraea (ih-**tu**-ree-ah)

Javan (**dzhay**-ven)

Jericho (**jer**-i-koh)

Levite (**lee**-vahyt)

Lysanias (lai-**say**-nee-uhs)

Lystra (**lihs**-tra)

Massah (**mah**-suh)

Medes (**meeds**)

Meribah (**mehr**-ih-bah)

Mesopotamia
  (mes-uh-puh-**tey**-mee-uh)

mitre (**mahy**-ter)

Midian (**mid**-ee-uhn)

Mosoch (**mah**-sahk)

myrrh (**mur**)

Onesimus (o-**neh**-sih-muhs)

Pamphylia (pam-**fil**-ee-uh)

Parthians (**pahr**-thee-uhns)

Phrygia (**frij**-ee-uh)

Pisidia (pih-**sid**-ee-uh)

Qoheleth (ko-**hehl**-ehth)

Quirinius (kwih-**rihn**-ee-uhs)

Sanhedrin (san-**hee**-drin)

Samaria (suh-**mair**-ee-uh)

Seba (**see**-buh)

Shaphat (**shay**-fat)

Sheba (**shee**-buh)

Sidon (**sahyd**-n)

Sychar (**sahy**-kar)

Tarshish (**tahr**-shish)

tetrarch (**te**-trahrk)

Trachonitis (trak-o-**nai**-tihs)

Tubal (**tyoo**-b'l)

Uzziah (uh-**zahy**-uh)

Zacchaeus (za-**kee**-uhs)

Zarephath (**zar**-eh-fath)

Zechariah (zek-uh-**rahy**-uh)

Zion (**zahy**-uhn)